THE MUGHAL NOBILITY UNDER AURANGZEB

THE MUGHAL [illegible]
AUR[illegible]

Revised Edition

M. ATHAR ALI

OXFORD
UNIVERSITY PRESS

OXFORD
UNIVERSITY PRESS

A Library Building, Jai Singh Road, New Delhi 110 001

versity Press is a department of the University of Oxford. It furthers the
sity's objective of excellence in research, scholarship, and education
by publishing worldwide in

Oxford New York

Athens Auckland Bangkok Bogota Buenos Aires Cape Town
Chennai Dar es Salaam Delhi Florence Hong Kong Istanbul Karachi
Kolkata Kuala Lumpur Madrid Melbourne Mexico City Mumbai
Nairobi Paris São Paolo Shanghai Singapore Taipei Tokyo Toronto Warsaw

with associated companies in Berlin Ibadan

Published in India
By Oxford University Press, New Delhi

First edition published by
the Department of History,
Aligarh Muslim University, 1966

This revised edition published by Oxford University Press 1997
Oxford India Paperbacks 2001

ISBN 019 5655990

Printed in India at Sai Printo Pack Pvt. Ltd., New Delhi 110 020
and published by Manzar Khan, Oxford University Press
YMCA Library Building, Jai Singh Road, New Delhi 110 001

To
The Memory of
My Father
SAIYID SALAMAT ALI

PREFACE

THIS book is based on a Ph.D. thesis submitted with the same title to the Aligarh Muslim University in 1961. It has been prepared under the Research Scheme of the Department of History, which made it possible for me to pursue my research for a number of years.

I am grateful to Mr. Badr-ud-Din Tyabji, the then Vice Chancellor of the University, for having taken the trouble of reading this book in typescript and making suggestions in regard to its presentation.

I also take this opportunity to thank my teachers and colleagues to whom I am deeply indebted.

I must express my deep sense of gratitude to my supervisor, Dr. Satish Chandra, who was always very generous to me, both with his time and attention. Professor Mohammad Habib has given me guidance on a large number of points; and only those who have benefited from his stimulating discourses can really appreciate the broad understanding of the basic problems that one can gain from him. I have also obtained constant inspiration from Professor S. A. Rashid's sympathetic interest in my work. Professor S. Nurul Hasan has always been very helpful to me, and I have the greatest pleasure in thanking him for all he has done to make the writing of this book possible. I have also been helped in various ways by my esteemed friend and colleague, Dr. Irfan Habib.

I am greatly obliged to Maharaj Kumar Raghubir Singh, M. P., for his kind permission to use his magnificent library of manuscripts at Sitamau. I am also grateful to the staff of the Maulana Azad Library and to Mrs. Saeeda Ansari of the Library of the Department of History, for their helpful cooperation.

I should like to thank my colleagues, Messrs Iqtidar Alam Khan, Ahsan Jan Qaisar, Refaqat Ali Khan, Ahsan Raza Khan and Satish Kumar, and Miss Aziza Hasan for their help in correcting the typescript and checking the proofs and in other matters.

Finally, I must acknowledge my deep gratitude to my wife, Feroza Khatoon, for her cooperation and indulgence in the face of the strain and stress which the writing of this book involved.

January 1966 M. ATHAR ALI

ABBREVIATIONS

The abbreviations have been generally used in the tables and the Appendix only.

Al.	*Alamgir Nama* by Muhammad Kazim.
M. A.	*Ma'asir-i Alamgiri.*
A. M. T.	*Arkan-i Ma'asir-i Taimuriya.*
T. M.	*Tarikh-i Muhammadi.*
T. U.	*Tazkarat-ul Umara.*
Akh.	*Akhbarat-i Darbar-i Mu'alla.*
B. S.	*Basatin-us Salatin.*
S. D. A.	*Selected Documents of Aurangzeb's Reign.*
Farhat.	*Farhat-al Nazirin.*
Adab.	*Adab-i Alamgiri.*
Ruq.	*Ruqa'at-i Alamgir.*
Z. A.	*Zawabit-i Alamgiri.*
Hatim Khan.	*Alamgir Nama.*
Kamwar.	*Tazkarat-us Salatin-i Chaghta.*
Isar Das.	*Futuhat-i Alamgiri.*
Mamuri.	*"Tarikh-i Aurangzeb".*
M. U.	*Ma'asir-ul Umara.*

PREFACE TO THE NEW EDITION

The present work was originally published in 1966 under the Research and Publication Programme in Medieval Indian History at the Department of History, Aligarh Muslim University, a programme instituted in 1953 through special funding by the Government of India. It was part of an effort to enlarge and, wherever necessary, modify our knowledge of Medieval India by extensive and critical exploration of published and archival source-material, especially in Persian. There was much interest evoked in the data and conclusions presented in my book, at least to judge from the reviews that appeared and the fact that the publishers brought out a reprint edition, the first one being soon exhausted. Thereafter it has remained out of print for some twenty years or more.

During this period I continued to remain involved with the subject, mainly collecting information on the ranks (*mansabs*) and offices of the Mughal nobility. The result of my research for the period before Aurangzeb was embodied in the *Apparatus of Empire*, Volume I, published in 1985 by the Oxford University Press. Since then I have been collecting information for the reign of Aurangzeb: the material here is so extensive that only now I am able to foresee a completion of the computer-set tables. Ideally, I should have incorporated much of this data and other information in the text of the present book; but this was not possible, given the circumstance that the text is to be photo-printed from the previous edition. It was, therefore, found desirable to restrict the interference with the old text to what were essentially proof-corrections; and to present part of the new information (especially from *Apparatus of Empire, I*) and my reactions to some notable contributions in related fields, in a special introduction to this edition.

For my research, especially since I retired in 1989 from the post of Professor at the Aligarh Muslim University I am beholden to a generous National Fellowship from the Indian Council of Historical Research. Professor Irfan Habib as Coordinator, Centre of Advanced Study in History, Aligarh Muslim University, gave me the necessary facilities to work at the Centre all these years. With his sudden removal from that position in May 1996, the facilities given to me were also simultaneously withdrawn: the link between this and what was happening at Delhi at the time (the fleeting formation of an anti-secular government) could be the subject of fruitful historical research in future.

I should like to take this occasion to thank especially those friends who during these last few months have helped me to continue with my work, Professor Shireen Moosvi, Mr S. Ali Nadeem Rezavi, and Mr Ishrat Alam, and — optimistic as ever — Professor Irfan Habib.

An author always likes to see his book in print — even an old one in a new garb. Needless to say, therefore, that I am especially beholden to the Oxford University Press and its energetic Director of academic publications, Mr Rukun Advani for bringing out this edition of *The Mughal Nobility under Aurangzeb.*

Aligarh
November 1996

M. ATHAR ALI

CONTENTS

INTRODUCTION TO NEW EDITION

When this book was written, originally as a doctoral thesis, in the early 1960s, the object was to test a number of hypotheses which held the field at that time. Jadunath Sarkar in his magisterial work, *A History of Aurangzib* (in which Sarkar turned from a sympathetic biographer in volume one to a trenchant critic in the subsequent volumes), saw Aurangzeb's religious bias, and an increasing lack of balance in its pursuit, generate a 'Hindu Reaction', whose baneful consequences his own undoubted ability and strong will could not stem.[1] S.R. Sharma, in his *Religious Policy of the Mughal Emperors*, underlined the same argument, furnishing substantiation from quantitative data which suggested a decline of the Hindu component in the Mughal nobility.[2] Faruki in his *Aurangzeb and His Times* answered Sarkar, essentially transferring the blame from Aurangzeb to the *shariat*.[3] On the other hand, historians like I.H. Qureshi accepted the Sarkar–Sharma hypothesis of a decline in the position of the Hindu nobility, and acclaimed this as an achievement rather than a lapse on the part of Aurangzeb. With this controversy dominating the academic space, it seemed best for me to go to the evidence with an open mind and make a detailed survey of the Mughal nobility and trace the changes in its composition (based on the *mansabs*, or numerical ranks held), making for the purpose as comprehensive a scrutiny of contemporary evidence as possible. The scrutiny was partly qualitative, partly quantitative. The evidence I assembled did not in any sense exonerate Aurangzeb, but I think it did set different limits within which the Emperor's personal preferences and decisions had impact; and it suggested a number of other factors, besides the one of religious bias, that seemed to lie behind changes in the composition and conduct of the nobility.

Other sets of questions to which I was obviously responding were formulated by Satish Chandra (*Introduction to Parties and Politics at the Mughal Court, 1707–40*, Aligarh, 1959) and Irfan Habib (*Agrarian System of Mughal India, 1556–1707*, Bombay, 1963). Continuing in the tradition of Ibn Hasan and Saran, they argued that the Mughal Empire was a centralised and fairly systematised polity; but, going further, Satish Chandra implicitly, and Irfan Habib explicitly, identified another class sharing in political dominance, which, in contrast to the nobility, was

[1] Jadu Nath Sarkar, *A History of Aurangzib*, 5 vols, Calcutta, 1912–30.

[2] S.R. Sharma, *The Religious Policy of the Mughal Emperors*, Oxford, 1940; 2nd edn, Bombay, 1962.

[3] M. Faruki, *Aurangzeb and His Times*, Bombay, 1935.

totally segmented and localised, namely that of the *zamindars.* Irfan Habib argued that the relationship between the two classes was one of adjustment and contradiction, and that the vicissitudes of this relationship explained much of internal Mughal history. With these arguments before me, it became necessary to explore the extent of *zamindar* penetration of the Mughal nobility and test the thesis of increasing exploitation and the postulation of an agrarian crisis. This I found to be an area where qualitative evidence overshadowed the quantitative; and if my own preferences went against Bernier's picture of a nobility driven by its members' instability of fortune to reckless self-defeating exploitation of the peasantry, it was a preference that was stated necessarily with much caution and circumspection.

Since the first edition of my book came out in 1966, some thirty years have passed; and during these years much has been written on Mughal history, and some new questions have been asked. Were I to sit down to write my book now, my text would doubtless be different from that printed in 1966: I would clearly have been obliged to find space for considering views published since that time, and also invoke the aid of much new evidence unearthed.

One currently popular enterprise is to cut to size the pre-modern Indian state, especially in its imperial incarnations. The theory of the 'segmentary' state, with its rituals and symbols, originating in social anthropology and with particular reference to Africa south of the Sahara, was applied to early medieval South India by Burton Stein, out to challenge the view of the Chola Empire as a centralised entity.[4] G. Fussman and Romila Thapar have applied it to the Mauryan Empire;[5] and inevitably, with Perlin and Wink in the van, the Mughal Empire has come under scrutiny from those who intuitively feel that a powerful state could not have existed in India before the English *sahibs* arrived.

Parallel to the above, C.A. Bayly put forward the captivating hypothesis that the decline of the Mughal Empire was a positive phenomenon, since it released the innovative enterprise of local or regional 'corporate groups'. Such groups won the collaboration of the English East India Company, so that the early British rule was really a continuation, and not a supplanting, of the preceding Indian regimes. Chetan Singh has pushed back the existence of such regional elites already within seventeenth-century Mughal Empire, and Muzaffar Alam has endorsed the Bayly thesis in seeing positive features in both the seventeenth-century Empire and its shrinking successor states of the next century.

[4] Burton Stein, *Peasant State and Society in Medieval South India*, Delhi, 1980.

[5] Fussman, 'Central and Provincial Administration in Ancient India: The Problem of the Mauryan Empire', *Indian Historical Review*, vol. XIV, nos, 1–2, 1987–88; R. Thapar, *The Mauryas Revisited*, Centre for Studies in Social Sciences, Calcutta, 1984, pp. 1–23.

On the very impressionistic foundations on which this theory rests, I have written elsewhere; and I take the liberty of referring the reader to two of my papers, one of which deals with the question of regional affinities of the Mughal nobility, that could well have been included as an appendix to the present edition, while the other takes up the issue of the 'personality' of the eighteenth century.[6] I would endorse J.F. Richards's sagacious statement that 'the reality' of 'Mughal centralized power' is one matter; whether 'this was good or bad' is quite a different one.[7]

On the issue of centralisation I have not seriously felt that a change in the position adopted in my book is called for. Rather, on both the *mansab* and *jagir* systems, detailed studies have reinforced the basic view, even when calling for certain modifications in the picture I had presented in the first edition.

On the numbers and composition of the *mansabdars* constituting the class whose higher ranks formed the Mughal nobility (*umara*), I have been collecting further material in connection with my project of presenting a comprehensive chronological list of all imperial awards of ranks, appointments, titles and *jagirs* in the Mughal Empire gathered from the sources and archives. Volume One of this work has appeared as *Apparatus of Empire*, Oxford University Press, Delhi, 1985. This volume set out the list for the period 1574–1658; and in the introduction I presented numerical data, based on the details assembled, which may now be compared with similar data that appeared in the first edition of my book.

The argument that there had been a tendency to expand the numbers of *mansabs* and *mansabdars* (1st ed., p. 9), is supported by the new figures given in the *Apparatus*, pp. xiii–xvi. The total *mansabs* of those holding 1,000 *zat* increased from 163,000 (*zat*) in 1595–96 to 629,500 *zat* and 499,450 *sawar* in 1657, on the eve of Aurangzeb's accession (p. xiv). In his first two years (A.H. 1037 and 1038), Shahjahan granted net enhancements of 48,900 *zat* and 45,650 *sawar* (p. xiv), figures that are slightly divergent from those in the 1st ed., p. 10 (43,500 *zat* and 44,420 *sawar*), but bear out the fact that in his first two years, Aurangzeb was obliged to grant more *mansabs* (89,000 *zat*, 54,000 *sawar*) than his predecessor. For decades (based on lunar years) one can present the picture as follows:

[6] M. Athar Ali, 'The Mughal Polity . . . A Critique of "Revisionist" Approaches,' *Modern Asian Studies*, vol. 27, University of Cambridge, 1993; 'Recent Theories of the Indian Eighteenth Century', *Indian Historical Review*, vol. XIII, Delhi, 1986.

[7] John F. Richards, *New Cambridge History of India*, I, 5, *The Mughal Empire*, Cambridge, 1993, p. xv.

NET PROMOTIONS

		Zat	Sawar
Shahjahan	1st decade	100	90,385
	2nd decade	-5,050	130,215
	3rd decade	97,100	68,470
Aurangzeb	1st decade	73,700	103,950[8]

These figures show that despite some effort to restrain enhancement of ranks, Aurangzeb's awards of *mansabs* over the whole first decade in the net were considerable, though largely in line with Shahjahan's rather generous awards in his third decade. The inherent tendency in Mughal administration to enhance *mansab* ranks, with consequent possible pressure on resources, is thus manifest.

On the ethnic composition of the nobility under Aurangzeb I am not aware of any substantive questioning of the data presented in the first edition. Certain figures for the earlier period given in that edition should, however, be modified or reinforced on the basis of the more comprehensive survey of the sources in the *Apparatus*. My revised finding is that in Shahjahan's 30th regnal year (1656–57), there were 53 Turanis of 1,000 and above, as against 67 in 1658–78; and 75 Iranis in 1656–57, as against 136 in 1658–78. Thus, the advance in the position of the Iranis in the first phase of Aurangzeb's reign, in relation to the Turanis, when compared with the position in Shahjahan's time is especially marked. The Afghans too made some gains. At 16 among 248 nobles of 1,000 and above, they comprised a fraction above 6 per cent during the period 1656–57; during 1658–78 the corresponding figure was 43 out of 486, or a little under 10 per cent. The Indian Muslims' share remained practically stable: 27, or nearly 11 per cent in 1656–57; they were, at 65, some 13.4 per cent during the period 1658–79. The Rajputs constituted at 46 nearly 18.5 per cent of nobles of 1,000 *zat* and above in 1656–57, a share higher than 14.6 per cent for the period 1658–78; the decline in Rajput influence, despite the high ranks of Jai Singh and Jaswant Singh, was thus perceptible even in the first phase of Aurangzeb's reign. As against this, the Marathas, at 7, a little over 2.5 per cent in 1656–57, accounted for 5 per cent in the period 1658–78. The Hindus, as a whole, numbered 56, i.e. 22.4 per cent in 1656–57, and 21.6 per cent during the period 1658–78, so that the overall change in their strength was insignificant.

If the foreigners and their descendants (Iranis and Turanis) are to be juxtaposed to the rest, the foreigners comprised over 51.5 per cent of the nobles of 1,000 *zat* and above in 1656–57 and practically the same

[8] Figures for the first decade of Aurangzeb's reign calculated from the table 'Net total ranks granted' on p. 10 of the first edition.

percentage (51.6 per cent) during the period 1658–78. Here too, except for a greater enhancement of the Iranis' share at the expense of the Turanis, the situation remained unchanged between the last years of Shahjahan's and the first two decades of Aurangzeb's reign.[9]

If still more detailed research has not so far indicated the necessity of any significant revision in the view taken in the first edition of this book on the changes in the ethnic composition of the Mughal nobility under Aurangzeb, one item that was practically passed over in silence at that time does now need some comment. This was the social anthropology of the 'ethnic' groups that I have established, largely following the classification and nomenclature of my sources. I had assumed a complete lack of mobility among the groups. While it would be superfluous to say that, given the well-known caste and religious taboos, an integration of Irani and Rajput elements through intermarriages could simply not occur, there would still be room for the possibility that the Iranis and Turanis intermarried. For this it would be desirable to analyse marriages and reconstruct family trees. Irfan Habib, carrying out a comprehensive study of material on Nur Jahan's family, including that relating to 'marriages of members of Nur Jahan's family with those of other families', noted that 'with the single exception of the royal house, all these other families (with which marriages were contracted) are found to be of Persian origin'.[10] There is little reason to believe that Nur Jahan's family was exceptional among the Iranis. Yet, although the strong probability is that intermarriages among the main Muslim groups were rather rare, it would be fruitful to work out genealogies and patterns of marriage alliances of some of the higher noble families to determine the degree of mutual isolation of these groups during the seventeenth century. Too little work has been done on these lines so far.

When the first edition of this book came out, modern analytical work on the *mansab* system mainly consisted of a book by Abdul Aziz and an important article by W.H. Moreland.[11] Since the publication of the first edition of this book, Shireen Moosvi has gone very thoroughly into the evolution of the *mansab* system under Akbar;[12] and Irfan Habib has subjected the period between Akbar and Aurangzeb to two intensive surveys.[13]

[9] The new information collected for 1656–57 is analysed in *Apparatus*, p. xx.

[10] *Medieval India—A Miscellany*, K.A. Nizami (ed.), I, Bombay, 1969, p. 80. See genealogical charts, pp. 82–5. The family had known marital alliances with seven Iranian families.

[11] Abdul Aziz, *The Mansabdari System and the Mughal Army*, Lahore, 1945; W.H. Moreland, 'Rank (*mansab*) in the Mogul State Service', *Journal of Royal Asiatic Society (JRAS)*, 1936, pp. 641–65.

[12] Shireen Moosvi, 'Evolution of the *Mansab* System Under Akbar Until 1596–97', *JRAS*, 1981, pp. 173–85.

[13] Irfan Habib, 'The *Mansab* System, 1595–1637', *Proceedings of the Indian History Congress*, 29th Session, 1967, I, pp. 221–42; and 'Mansab Salary Scales under Jahangir and Shah Jahan', *Islamic Culture*, vol. LIX, no. 2, 1985, pp. 203–27.

I am happy to find that these researches have not substantially modified the description of the *mansab* system I had offered on the basis mainly of the evidence from the reigns of Shahjahan and Aurangzeb. Rather, their attempt has been to show how the system developed into the kind I had portrayed from the time of its establishment under Akbar. Moosvi has demonstrated how the *sawar* rank originated out of the advance payments (*barawurdi*) for part of the maintenance of troops required by the *mansab*-number under Akbar. Irfan Habib has been mainly concerned with changes in the *mansab* pay and military obligations under Jahangir and Shah Jahan. What occasions surprise is that while new administrative measures and conventions heavily altered the profile of the *mansab* system within fifty years of the writing of the *A'in-i Akbari*, there was so little change in it after 1645. Aurangzeb during his entire reign of nearly fifty years made no significant change in the system, down to scales of pay, obligations according to *sawar* ranks and month-ratio, composition of military contingents, etc.

Such lack of concern for reform in the organisation of what was the 'steel frame' of the Mughal Empire during Aurangzeb's entire reign is hard to explain, even when full recognition is extended to Aurangzeb's anxiety to maintain a tried and tested system exactly as he had found it. Yet there were factors that made such rigid adherence to the inherited system difficult. One was the tendency to increase the number of *mansabdars* forced on the Mughal emperor by political exigencies. How these numbers increased during the seventeenth century was brought out in the first edition (pp. 7–11). Some new data given in the *Apparatus*, such as the number of *zat* rank holders of 500 *zat* and above at five different points, reinforces the view that the increase was inexorable.

1595	*1621*	*1637–38*	*1647–48*	*1656–57*
123	242	419	443	518

Of these, all the figures appear to be reliable except that for 1621, which could be an undercount.[14] Clearly, the tendency towards rank inflation is obvious. The question is whether it continued under Aurangzeb. As was admitted in the first edition of this work, no official lists of the kind are available for the period of Aurangzeb. The numerical data based on the lists of *mansab* holders of 1,000 *zat* and above which I myself constructed, respectively for the periods 1658–78 (pp. 175–215) and 1679–1707 (pp. 216–71), must be regarded as incomplete; while relevant for examining relative shares of different ethnic groups, they are obviously deficient for the purposes of comparison with the earlier

[14] *Apparatus of Empire*, p. xx.

complete tables in absolute terms. I am at the moment engaged in compiling the massive data on all rank-awards in appointments from the historical works and documents of Aurangzeb's reign, and I hope from that work this deficiency will be partly rectified, enabling us to speak with greater confidence in our absolute figures as well. But at the moment, I am not able to present the figures that will hopefully emerge in *Apparatus*, II, though the work is in an advanced stage.

The total figures of 575 holders of 1,000 *zat* and above for the period 1679–1707, which is an undercount, do suggest a notable increase in the *mansabs* over the earlier period, 1658–78, where the corresponding figure is 486, though undoubtedly the earlier period is shorter. But one must set the increase in aggregate pay-claims against the additional revenue resources of the territories annexed during the period in the Deccan. With appropriate manipulation of *jamadami* (assessed revenue) and assignment of month-ratios to individual nobles for setting their military obligations, the basic schedules and rules could have continued without much modification. In other words, rather surprisingly, the increase in numbers of ranks was not anywhere near the scale witnessed between 1595 and 1656–57, an increase of 4.2 times (ranks of 500 *zat* and above), and totally out of proportion with the actual addition of territory within that period. One can only hold that Aurangzeb did his best to hold back the pressures for higher *mansabs* with greater vigour than his predecessors were able to do. He could, therefore, in large measure, avoid the formal pay-deflation by which his predecessors had countered the rank-inflation. The consequential changes in the required size of military contingents could also be avoided.

It is less easy to see how the *mansab* rules could be made to accommodate the changing needs of military organisation. They were originally made when mounted archers were the mainstay of the Mughal army. Irvine indeed noted that the matchlock 'up to the middle of the 18th century was looked on with less favour than the bow and arrow which still held their ground'.[15] Even so it cannot be imagined that all musketeers were in the direct employ of the Emperor and that no noble was expected to maintain them as part of his obligatory military contingent. It is not yet clear how the musketeers were adjusted against the bow-bearing cavalry in the prescribed rules. It seems, indeed, that the rules contemplated an army mainly of cavalry, where the breeds of horses and the rider's skill with the bow were the main considerations. In 1666, observers like Bernier thought that the advantage still lay with such troops: 'It cannot be denied that the cavalry of this country manoeuvre

[15] William Irvine, *The Army of the Indian Mughals: Its Organisation and Administration*, reprint, Delhi, 1962, p. 103. Irvine seems himself to fall with this opinion and calls the matchlock 'a combrous and probably ineffective weapon . . . left mainly for the infantry' (p. 91).

with much ease, and discharge their arrows with astonishing quickness, a horseman shooting six times, before a musketeer can fire twice.'[16]

In 1695 Careri, speaking of the army of 'the Great Mogul', says, 'most of the soldiers have bows and arrows',[17] while Manucci (*c.* 1700) notes that 'the Mahomedan great men pride themselves much upon their good shooting with bow and arrow', practising the art 'many times a day'.[18]

While it may be conceded that by mid-seventeenth century mounted archers could still prevail against infantry carrying heavy, cumbersome muskets, it is unlikely that by 1700 this remained the case. As Iqtidar Alam Khan has pointed out, the diffusion of the manufacture and use of muskets was causing anxiety to the Mughal administration in the time of Aurangzeb.[19] If so, the very rigidity of the *mansab* regulations worked against the formation of a kind of army (preferably, a directly paid standing army, and not one raised through contract farms, as was the Mughal army),[20] in which the arms of musketeers and artillery were given their due. In such circumstances two things could happen: The Mughal army could become increasingly obsolete; and, with this obsolescence, the entire structure of *dagh-tas'hiha* (verification) could lose its relevance. This is an aspect which, I am afraid, I entirely overlooked in the first edition. I hasten to pinpoint it now, because it seems to me that the purely military factors in the decline of the Mughal Empire need to be given adequate attention.

On the features of the *jagir* system under Aurangzeb as described by me in Chapter III of this book, no major disagreement has appeared in published work. It is true that Muzaffar Alam has casually contested the finding, based on extensive material cited in my text (pp. 78–9, 92–4), that *jagir* transfers not only continued till the end of Aurangzeb's reign, but, if anything, tended to become more frequent. He tells us, on the other hand, that such transfer, encountering resistance from nobles 'was left unimplemented in a number of cases in the 17th century'.[21] Since he does not provide reference to a single such case, or to any contemporary statement of such failure to implement *jagir* transfer orders during the period before 1707, one is at a loss to understand the basis for so confident an assertion.

More substantive is J.F. Richards's questioning of my thesis of a 'crisis in the *jagirdari* system' in the last years of Aurangzeb. It is worth noting

16 *Bernier's Travels*, A. Constable (tr.), V.A. Smith (ed.), London, 1916, p. 48.

17 S.N. Sen, *Indian Travels of Thevenot and Careri*, Delhi, 1949, p. 242.

18 Niccolav Manucci, *Storia do Mogor*, tr. W. Irvine, London, 1907–8, I, p. 140.

19 Iqtidar Alam Khan, 'Socio-Political Implications of the Dissemination of Handguns in Mughal India' (Mohammad Habib Memorial Vol., forthcoming).

20 Cf. W.H. Moreland, 'Rank (*Mansab*) in the Mughal State Service', *JRAS*, 1936, pp. 641–65.

21 Muzaffar Alam, *The Crisis of Empire in Mughal North India: Awadh and Punjab, 1707–48*, Delhi, 1986, p. 5.

that he at least originally confined his doubts to the situation in the annexed kingdom of Golkunda, becoming the province of Haiderabad upon annexation (1687).[22] Such are the attractions of a new faith, that Muzaffar Alam, without any further evidence, supposes the theory of *jagir* crisis to have been refuted ('demolished') by Richards for the whole of the Deccan.[23] It is, however, important to realise that Richards's doubts were based entirely on one document, which gives only the specifications of the area held in *khalisa* and *paibaqi* (lands temporarily held by the Treasury prior to assignment in *jagir*) and does not mention *jagirs* at all, if one goes by Richards's own tabular analysis of it.[24] It is apparently a paper compiled immediately upon conquest. Since the Qutb-Shahi Kingdom had a system of revenue farms (*ijara*) rather than *jagir* assignments,[25] it would be natural to expect that the Mughal government would first have a statement of fiscal resources compiled, with *paibaqi* possibly representing the pool out of which *jagirs* would be assigned to nobles posted there; and *khalisa* would, for the moment, be a very large area, pending decision as to what would in due course be retained out of it. The exceptional nature of the situation and untypicality of the document (no *jagirs*, only *khalisa* and *paibaqi*) is borne upon us, when we compare it with another statement, giving the breakdown of the assignments of the Karnatak portion (19 *sarkars*) of the *suba* of Haiderabad in A.H. 1117/1706. All figures are in rupees and annas, representing the fixed assessment (*jama'i muqarrari*). Its information may be tabulated as follows:

A. *Khalisa sharifa*		990,679.14
Includes territory in control of polygars	138,427.13	
Peshkash (Tribute)	23,000.00	
	161,427.13	
B. (With) *Jagirdars*		6,080,125.10
(Includes) *Qiladars*	1,177,688.70	
Daud Khan	557,651.12	
Bahadur Khan	176,538.40	
Abdun Nabi	143,444.12	

[22] Richards, *Mughal Administration in Golkunda*, Oxford, 1975, pp. 158, 308–9.

[23] Alam, *Crisis of Empire*, p. 7. Incidentally, none of the proponents of the *jagir* crisis have argued that it was confined only to the Deccan, 'a deficit area' (!)

[24] J.F. Richards, *Mughal Administration in Golconda*, pp. 160–1. Read 'Khalisa Sharifa' for 'Khalisa Sharif' in the heading of col. 1.

[25] Cf. W.H. Moreland, *Relations of Golconda*, London, 1931.

Sa'adullah Khan	15,591.70	
Roshan Beg Khan	8,346.00	
Troops (*ahsham*)	1,994,173.30	
Service staff	6,816.5 ½	
Miscellaneous	2,013,875.7 ½	
C. *Inam*, etc.		28,223.4 ½
Includes *inam*	25,610.4 ½	
Cash-grants	2,613.0	
D. Temporary levies (*sih-bandi*) accompanying *Amirul Umara*, etc. (*Jama'* assigned to levy under each officer separately stated)		5,249,305.0
E. *Paibaqi*		3,291,863.5 ¼
Area under polygars	2,629,216.4	
Balance	662,647.1 ½	
Total[26]		15,640,202.8

While there are presumably some misreadings or misprints in the published document, the totals being not exactly consistent with the detailed figures in some cases, still the thrust of the contents is obvious. The *khalisa sharifa* accounts for barely 6 per cent of the *jama'*. The *paibaqi* amounted to 20 per cent of the *jama'*, but of this the bulk was really in the hands of Polygars, so that only a small balance of a little above 4 per cent of the *jama* remained effectively available for assignment in *jagir* for revenue- extracting purposes. If the entire phenomenon of the *jagir* crisis is to be judged on the basis of just a single document or a pair, one may argue that here, by 1706, we have good testimony for the intense pressure for *jagirs*, which contemporaries were speaking of. But clearly, the question is not one to be settled by stray documents; and I am not convinced that contemporary 'qualitative' depictions of the phenomenon must necessarily be disbelieved.

While re-reading my Chapter IV, I would continue to argue (as on pp. 98–9) that there could be a connection between Shahjahan's death (1666), signifying the removal of a possible replacement, and the rather meagre results in the net of Aurangzeb's feverishly active military policy pursued until then, on the one hand, and the purposeful enforcement of a policy of religious discrimination which began thereafter, on the other. But perhaps my original text is far too confident in making it

26 The document is published in *Selected Documents of Aurangzeb's Reign*, Yusuf Husain Khan (ed.), Haiderabad, 1959, pp. 233–5.

appear that Aurangzeb's turn towards an active religious policy could thus be 'rationally' explained. This I may say was not even my intention. I did not intend to exclude Aurangzeb's own strong grounding in orthodox Islam. His attitude before 1666 was already different from that of Shahjahan, as manifested in his withdrawal of a number of cash and land grants to Hindus during the early years of his reign.[27] Shahjahan's death and the lack of military success can only be seen as circumstances which drew Aurangzeb more towards the strengthening of a policy already embryonically present.

Had my book in its 1966 garb been published today, I am sure some reviewer would have expressed his astonishment that on so crucial a theme as revenue-farming (*ijara*), I should have devoted barely one and a half pages (pp. 83–4), and that too in connection with the administration of *jagirs*. With C.A. Bayly's *Rulers, Townsmen and Bazars*, published in 1983, 'revenue-farming' has indeed aggressively moved to the centrestage of Mughal and late-Mughal history as a leading institution of 'warrior entrepreneur(ship)', a channel serving equally well for ensuring smoother cash flows and better local collaboration.[28] What in the seventeenth and eighteenth centuries was regarded as an evil feature, contributing to overtaxation and 'rack-renting', has come to be regarded, post-Bayly, as an innovative institution of great vigour. Thus Muzaffar Alam, deprecating the earlier view of the institution, champions the cause of the Sayyid brothers' protege Ratan Chand, a major practitioner of revenue-farming, in the reign of Farrukh Siyar (1713–19).[29] The key-stone to the whole arch of the new doctrine has now been doubtless laid by the identification of revenue-farming with a 'portfolio capitalism' by Subrahmaniam and C.A. Bayly.[30]

I regret I am unable to share in the euphoria over the discovery of new virtues in the old virus of farming. Revenue-farming existed at all levels of Mughal administration in the seventeenth century; but, so long as the empire functioned as a centralised apparatus, it was kept under control. In December 1702–January 1703, Prince A'zam, Governor of

[27] See Bernier, p. 341. The formal general order, however, came later, in 1672–73 (*Mirat-i Ahmadi*, I, p. 288).

[28] Bayly, *Rulers, Townsmen and Bazars: North Indian Society in the Age of British Expansion, 1770–1870*, pp. 164–70.

[29] *The Crisis of Empire in Mughal North India*, Delhi, 1986, pp. 39–42. On p. 318, Alam takes *ijara* to be one of the main indicators of the 18th century endeavour to make use of possibilities of growth within existing social structures. On p. 42 he invents a term, *baqqaliat* (translated by him as shopkeeping), not found in his source (Khafi Khan, II, 902 or anywhere else). The translation too is wrong: *baqqal* was the Indo-Persian term for a *banya*, not green-grocer or shopkeeper.

[30] 'Portfolio Capitalists and the Political Economy of Early Modern India', *Indian Economic and Social History Review*, vol. XXV, no. 4, 1988, pp. 401–24.

Gujarat, considered the farming out of the *sarkar* of Sorath (or/and its *faujdari*). He had two offers: Muhammad Beg Khan, offering to maintain the entire local levies (*sih-bandis*) and pay Rs 3 lakhs, guaranteed by a reliable banker (*sahukar*); and Safdar Khan Babi offering Rs 2½ lakhs, presumably on the same conditions. But the prince rejected both bids for the express reason that he could not assign duties in his own establishment (*sarkar-i 'ali*) to imperial officers (*banda-ha-i padshahi*).[31] Here, then, high-titled nobles were seeking to take on farm revenue of a large area: no local entrepreneurship was even remotely involved. At the other end, again in Gujarat, we are introduced to 'the Prince of Revenue-farmers, the chief of merchants, khwaja X', who was seeking the farm of a single village, the evidence coming from a collection of documents, compiled in *c.* 1648.[32] Here, then, we have the case of, perhaps, a true 'portfolio [proto-]capitalist'.

However varied the class of revenue-farmers, the general administrative doctrine was against the institution because of its inevitable oppressiveness. In 1634, praising a *jagirdar*, the author of *Mazhar-i Shahjahani* says that the *jagirdar* rejected the offer of local headmen (*arbab*) and others for taking the revenue-farm of a *pargana* at Rs one lakh, where the regular realisation was only Rs 20,000, because he knew that 'in the practice of *ijara* lies the ruin of the country'.[33] But then he did not have the acumen of some modern historians.

In my book I had expressed some reserve towards Irfan Habib's then recent thesis of the 'agrarian crisis' in Aurangzeb's reign, the cause of which, following Bernier, was laid at the door of the *jagir*-transfer system, and the consequent over-exploitation of the peasantry.[34] I had thought that the imperial checks upon the *jagirdars*' exactions and internal administration could not be regarded as entirely ineffective.[35] My doubts have been borne out by Shireen Moosvi's detailed study of the statistical evidence, which has strongly suggested that the 'crisis' of the 1660s was a passing phase, and conditions subsequently improved in Northern India.[36] Such an agricultural revival could hardly have been possible if there had been a continuously climbing curve of pauperisation due to excessive pressure from the Mughal nobility. One should rather ascribe the long-drawn-out scarcity of the 1660s more to abnormal failures of the monsoon than to the fault of any human agency.

[31] Royal Asiatic Society (London) MS, *Akhbarat*, A 193, 197.

[32] Blochet Suppl. Pers. 482, f. 12a.

[33] Yusuf Mirak, *Mazhar-i Shahjahani*, ed. Sayyid Husamuddin Rashidi, Hyderabad (Sind), 1962, pp. 52–3.

[34] Irfan Habib, *Agrarian System of Mughal India*, Bombay, 1963, pp. 317–51.

[35] My reservations appear on p. 92 of the first edition of my *Mughal Nobility*. Similar doubts are now recorded by J.F. Richards in *Mughal Empire*, Cambridge, 1993, pp. 291–2.

[36] Shireen Moosvi in *Studies in History*, 1 (i), New Series, 1985, pp. 45–55.

The whole question of the decline of the Mughal Empire has been recently clouded by the debate on the nature of that Empire. As we have noticed earlier, taking cues from Burton Stein's *Peasant State and Society*, Frank Perlin[37] and Andre Wink[38] have tried to build up a picture of the pre-colonial state, which basically starts by discounting the information we have for the Empire from sources within it. Characteristically, they tend to dismiss much of the evidence from Mughal historians and documents (largely in Persian) as merely normative, or formalistic, given to 'semantic idiom'.[39] Such an attitude—it is so easy to put the words 'Empire' and its 'decline' within inverted commas and claim victory!—would, of course, make a study like the present one an illusory exercise. But there are hardly any recognised methods of historical research by which such a vast amount of record, largely mutually consistent in areas beyond the alleged 'semantic idiom', can be ignored for the purpose of any worthwhile consideration of the inner structure of the Empire and its role in society and economy. Part of the trouble, perhaps, is that much of the criticism of the Mughal material has come from those who are not at home with it. The argument they adopt would practically rule out the entire official and semi-official records of any government as admissible evidence for political or institutional history. It seems to me that while Persian documentation of the Mughal Empire must be subjected, piece by piece, to such criticism as is to be applied to all historical evidence, it cannot be condemned as a class. The picture of the Mughal Empire that it offers, as of a centralised system, with due depiction also of factors and circumstances opposed to such centralisation, is a fairly credible one. It will be seen that in the present book too both sides of the picture are given emphasis, though my evidence comes overwhelmingly from the large store of Persian documentation. Whether this is a more reasonable way of reconstructing history than the one of proceeding from Perlin's theory of *watan* or Wink's of *fitna* as the cornerstone of Indian polity, I leave to the reader to judge.

[37] Frank Perlin, 'State Formation Reconsidered', *Modern Asian Studies*, 19.3 (1985), pp. 415–80.

[38] Andre Wink, *Land and Sovereignty in India*, Cambridge, 1986.

[39] Wink, op. cit., p. 6.

INTRODUCTION

It is an oft-repeated dictum that in Indian historical writing the ruled have been largely ignored. Yet it is equally true that the rulers too have not received adequate attention. There exist, of course, many impressive biographies of Indian monarchs and histories of royal dynasties. But kings, however despotic they might have been, and however grandiose their pretensions, after all represented only a part—even though an essential part—of the ruling class. The remaining members of the ruling class, who appear usually, but not invariably, as nobles or officers of the kings, also deserve close attention. Yet it need hardly be argued that the composition, traditions, predilections, etc., of this class, or of the various strata that might comprise it, are of at least as much importance as the characters and policies of individual monarchs.

This book, as its title shows, does not pretend to cover the medieval period, or the whole of the Mughal times, but concerns itself only with the nobility of the last Indian Empire under the last of its great Emperors. In so far as it is an excursion into a largely uncharted field, it is, perhaps, best that it should aim at surveying only a small part of the vast field. For various reasons the subject confined within these limitations may still be considered not unimportant. The Mughal Empire began to disintegrate under Aurangzeb's own eyes and the processs of dissolution became only more marked and rapid under his successors. In other words at a time when the West was forging ahead in every field of life, Indian society was not only static, nor even stagnant, but, politically at least, degenerating and even receding from the levels it had previously reached. In what ways is this political decline, of such momentous consequence for the later course of Indian history, to be explained? Obviously such an explanation, to be plausible, cannot be provided on the basis of speculation or *a priori* assumptions or by simple appeal to the usual text-book formulae (e.g. personal degeneration of the kings, luxurious life at the court, inefficiency of administration), which are of doubtful value precisely because they can be applied with equal ease to every dynasty or empire. A detailed study of all the elements of the structure of the Mughal Empire can perhaps better supply the groundwork for such an explanation. Among these elements, the Mughal ruling class occupies a noteworthy place; and a detailed analysis of its nature and role would seem to be desirable. The principal object of this study of the Mughal nobility, attempted with particular reference to the reign of Aurangzeb (1658-1707), is, therefore, to describe the institutions and traditions that defined its organisation and policies, and the stresses and the strains to which it was subjected or to which it itself gave rise.

In order to prevent any misunderstanding it should be made clear that the use of the term 'nobility' in the title does not in any way anticipate the conclusions reached in this book about the actual nature and position of the Mughal ruling class. It is far from the intention of the author to assume that the Mughal ruling class was comparable in nature to either the nobles of the Roman Empire or the feudal nobility of Europe. The term 'nobility', despite these dangers of misinterpretation, remains convenient, because it generally denotes the class of persons who were officers of the king and at the same time formed the superior class in the political order and in this book has been used strictly in this sense. This word has also a further advantage in that it is the conventional English equivalent to the Arabic-Persian term *Umara* (plural of *amir*), which in the Mughal times was applied to all officers holding the *mansabs* (ranks) of 1,000 and above, i.e. to all the higher strata of the official class. It should be added that this book does not pretend to comprehend within its scope all *mansabdars*, or holders of ranks who formed the bulk of the official class, but only the *mansabdars* of such ranks and status as could reasonably be counted in the ranks of the ruling class, on the basis of their power and income. For this reason, it has been considered useful for the purposes of this study to adopt the rank of 1,000 *zat* as setting the dividing line, at least in the time of Aurangzeb, between those who were mere officials, and those who, in addition, could also claim to have a voice in the government of the empire.

The size and composition of the Mughal nobility have been subjected to a certain amount of discussion, but it has unfortunately not been comprehensive, nor, in some cases, free from inaccuracies. In particular, the questions needing elucidation concern the number of nobles at various times; the rate at which the number increased, and the effects this increase had on the income of the nobility and its internal cohesion. As to internal cohesion, we have to study the groups and the races, which formed the Mughal nobility, considering specially the question of the position of foreigners (and descendants of foreigners) and the Indians, and, similarly, the position of the followers of the two main religious communities, the Muslims and Hindus. In answering these questions, specially the two last-mentioned, present-day sentiment, no less than present-day prejudice, would be a bad counsellor. An attempt is, therefore, made in this book to answer these questions only on the basis of statements of, and facts given by contemporaries, and on that of biographical information collected from all our various sources in respect of all the nobles holding the *mansabs* of 1,000 and above in the time of Aurangzeb. This information, when statistically presented, reveals many interesting facts which otherwise would not strike a student of the subject. It should, however, be borne in mind that statistical presentation has its own pitfalls. Not only should the information on which it is based be comprehensive, but various qualifications are always necessary whenever such information is reduced to a simplified form for purposes of comparison. Obviously, statistical presentation in such a subject as this can hardly ever be refined enough to be taken as offering the last word in historical evidence, yet its importance as a check on generalisations found in our sources or in modern writers, as well as its value for suggesting further avenues of enquiry, can hardly be denied.

The Mughal nobility, as is well known was organised within the framework of the *mansabdari* system. A number of the essential features of the *mansab* system have been illumined by modern research. We know that each officer was assigned a pair of numbers, designated *zat* and *sawar*, which gave his place in the official hierarchy. It has been shown further (by Moreland and Abdul Aziz, in particular) that the *zat* rank indicated the personal status of the officer, and also, through sanctioned schedules, his personal pay; and the *sawar* rank determined the military contingent he was to maintain, and indicated the payment to be made to him for maintaining this contingent. But beyond this, much has remained obscure. An important object of this study has been to eliminate as far as possible these obscurities in order to gain a clear view of how the *mansabdari* system really functioned under Aurangzeb. It is feared that this will lead the reader into the realm of tedious detail and complexity. But this cannot be avoided since the points discussed relating to the income, and the obligations of the nobility are not of incidental, but central importance to our subject as a whole.

The Mughal nobles obtained their salary either in cash or through assignment of the revenues of various territories, known as *jagirs*. We are indebted to Moreland for a clear exposition of the basic features of the system of these assignment. But the problems which the *jagirdars* (holders of *jagirs*) faced in the work of revenue collection and government, specially in the 17th century, stand in need of detailed treatment. At the same time the ways in which the Emperor sought to restrain the authority of the *jagirdars*—and the extent to which he succeeded in it—have to be carefully studied. We have to see in particular whether the system under Aurangzeb was the same, in all essential features, as under his predecessors, or whether there were changes in it, or, again, whether it was showing any signs of stress and strain. Bernier's famous statement that the system of transfer of *jagirs* was leading to great oppression and ruining the peasantry, has been supported strenuously by some recent writers, and certainly needs to be examined in the light of all the evidence from Aurangzeb's reign.

The existence of the class of *zamindars*, whether chiefs or holders of superior rights over land or its produce, was an important factor in the political society of the time. The relations between this class and the Mughal nobility need to be investigated. The place occupied by elements of *zamindari* origin in the Mughal ruling class and the attitude of the latter towards the class of *zamindars* as a whole are interesting questions that need elucidation. For the time of Aurangzeb, when revolts against the Empire, led by *zamindars*, seem to have become widespread, answers to these questions assume great importance.

The reign of Aurangzeb extended for nearly fifty years. In the course of his reign, the Emperor formulated policies on various political problems which deeply affected the nobility. The Emperor's attitude towards various sections of the nobility was, of course, of signal importance. Interest, not unnaturally, has centred on Aurangzeb's policy towards the Rajputs which has been linked with his religious policy. An effort has been made in this book to trace the development of this policy, to distinguish its phases, and to put it into a proper perspective.

The Deccan loomed very large in Mughal politics under Aurangzeb; and the attitude of different nobles towards the policy pursued in the Deccan is of great interest. With the Deccan involvement of the last twenty-five years of Aurangzeb, when the Emperor personally undertook to annex practically the whole of the peninsula, fresh difficulties as well as opportunities appeared for the nobility. A study of these could help us to understand how the process of disintegration within the nobility had begun even under Aurangzeb himself.

Finally, there is need for the study of the way of life of the nobles, and their role in administration and economic life. Admittedly here we run the risk of undue generalisation from individual cases. An attempt has been made to retain balance by examining contemporary statements critically while not rejecting the evidence for anything ascribed to the nobles simply because in our eyes today it seems extremely unethical or immoral. Answers to two questions, in particular, should be attempted : How should we evaluate the Mughal nobles as upholders of efficient government ? And how far did the nobility, by its expenditure, investment or its conduct, contribute to, or retard, economic growth?

The source-material for our study is fortunately very extensive. It is true that except for the first ten years of Aurangzeb's reign, we lack the official Persian chronicles which provide us with such a wealth of information about the reigns of Akbar and Shahjahan. But Aurangzeb's reign is far richer in the primary sources : administrative manuals, official records, *Akhbarat* (court news-letters), other documents, letters, etc. It is covered also by important unofficial histories and biographical dictionaries. Few of these Persian sources have been published, and most of the material is available only in manuscript. Sir Jadu Nath Sarkar in his monumental *History of Aurangzeb—Mainly based on Persian Sources* was able to show what a wealth of information could be extracted from these documents. Since his time many additional records have become accessible, and works of historical interest discovered. On the basis of this evidence, it is now possible to have information on almost all aspects of the political history of the period.

The Persian evidence is supplemented by the accounts left by European travellers, the commercial records and private papers of the English and the other European merchants. Most of the important English accounts have been published; and accounts of many European travellers are available in English translations. A large number of English commercial and private documents too have been published; though in proportion to their bulk, such documents usually have little to offer that is of relevance to our subject. There is a recent tendency to belittle the importance of the European evidence. It is true, of course, that while using the accounts of foreign travellers we should distinguish between what they wrote on the basis of hearsay and on that of first-hand knowledge, between scandal and fact. But we should be grateful to these foreign writers for the descriptions they provide of things which Indian writers thought too well-known or too trivial or too discreditable to notice. Certainly, we should be nearer the truth only if we are able to combine, and check and collate, information derived from both the indigenous Persian sources and the European sources.

CHAPTER I

NUMERICAL STRENGTH AND COMPOSITION OF THE NOBILITY

NUMBER OF THE MANSABDARS

THE *mansabdars* formed the ruling group in the Mughal Empire. Almost the whole nobility, the bureaucracy as well as the military hierarchy, held *mansabs*. Consequently, the numerical strength of the *mansabdars* and their composition during the different periods materially influenced not only politics and administration, but also the economy of the empire. It is, therefore, necessary to examine the size of this group and its composition in order to understand the position of the nobility under Aurangzeb. In this connection, emphasis has been laid on the *mansabdars* of 1,000 and above, since only these were entitled to be called *amirs* (nobles).

There are only two contemporary statements available giving details about the total number of *mansabdars*. The first statement is made by Abdul Hamid Lahori, who says that in the 20th year of Shahjahan's reign there were 8,000 *mansabdars* and 7,000 *ahadis* and mounted artillerymen (i.e. troopers directly in the pay of the Emperor).[1] During Aurangzeb's reign—probably some time before 1690—we get the figure of 14,449 for the *mansabdars*, *ahadis* (*du-aspa-sih-aspa*), gunners and attendants.[2] This total conforms to that of Lahori, but the figure for the *mansabdars* is not separately stated. This deficiency is partly made up, however, by classifying the Emperor's servants as *mansabdaran-i-naqdi* (receiving cash salaries) who were 7,457 and *jagirdars* who were 6,992.[3] Since it is almost certain that the *ahadis*, etc. were all paid in cash, while only a small portion of the *mansabdars* were on the cash list, it may be deduced from these figures that the number of *mansabdars* proper (excluding the *ahadis*, etc.) did not exceed 8,000. If this assumption is correct, it would mean that there was no increase in the total number of *mansabdars* between the 20th regnal year of Shahjahan and the year to which the figures of the *Zawabit* relate. But since the latter year is not clearly specified, we should not attach too much importance to this

[1] *Badshah Nama* II, p. 715.

[2] *Zawabit-i Alamgiri*, f. 15a.

[3] *Zawabit-i Alamgiri*, f. 15a; *Mumalik-i Mahrusa-i Alamgiri*, f. 137b. S. R. Sharma is thus not correct in supposing that the figure of 14,449 in the *Zawabit-i Alamgiri* is for *mansabdars* only. (*Religious Policy of Mughal Emperors*, p. 132).

comparison. It is quite possible that its statistics were derived from an earlier period of Aurangzeb's reign.

From the inconclusive nature of this comparison, we have to pass on to other data. The most prominent among these are the lists of *mansabdars* of 200 *zat* and above in the *Ain* and 500 *zat* and above in the *Badshah Namas* of Lahori and Waris.[1] The list of the *Ain* includes all *mansabdars* of Akbar's time, i.e. all those who had received a *mansab* of 200 or above up till the 40th regnal year, when the *Ain* was written. Lahori gives us two lists, one for the first decade and the other for the second decade of Shahjahan's reign; Waris's list relates to the third decade. In these three lists, the names of *mansabdars* are given according to ranks held by them in the years specified, but those who had died or were dismissed in the preceding decades are also listed, according to the ranks held by them last. Finally, Muhammad Salih gives us a list of all the *mansabdars* of Shahjahan's reign, according to the highest rank reached by them. Salih's list is apparently based on the lists of Lahori and Waris; but he also took into account the new appointments and promotions made in the last three (lunar) years of Shahjahan's reign.[2]

Unfortunately, there are no official lists of this kind for Aurangzeb's reign. This gap can only be filled by collecting information about individual *mansabdars* and their ranks from the surviving historical materials. Two lists embodying the information collected by me and relating to the periods, 1658-78 and 1679-1707 are given in an appendix. All nobles holding *mansabs* of 1,000 *zat* or above have been entered in each list according to the highest ranks reached by them within either period. A number of names are, therefore, common to both lists. I have attempted to make the lists as complete as possible by drawing not only upon histories and biographical dictionaries, but also upon the *Akhbarat*, collections of letters and other records. For the highest class of nobles, who held the rank of 5,000 *zat* and above, the lists are likely to be complete. For the lower two classes, i.e., *mansabdars* from 1,000 to 2,700, the list for 1658-78 is likely to be more complete than that for 1679-1707. This is chiefly owing to the fact that for the first ten years of the reign the official history of Muhammad Kazim, the *Alamgir Nama*, which gives details of almost all promotions to ranks of 1,000 *zat* and above, is available. Thereafter, we have no comparable account and it is likely that the lower ranks have not been mentioned by our authorities. Thus, though the list of 1679-1707 may require little addition as far as the number of *mansabdars* of 3,000 (*zat*) to 4,500 is concerned, the number of *mansabdars* of 1,000 (*zat*) to 2,700 is probably much below the actual number.

The nature of these lists cannot be directly compared with the lists of Lahori and Waris, which relate to shorter periods of time. They

[1] *Ain*, Vol. I, 160-65; *Badshah Nama*, I, pp. 292-328; Vol. II, 717-52.

[2] *Amal-i Salih*, III, pp. 448-89.

are more like the lists of the *Ain* and Salih. A comparati... *mansabdars* from the *Ain* and Salih and the two lists prepared by ... given below:

	Ain	*Salih*	1658-78	1679–1707
Mansabdars excluding sons and grandsons of the Emperor	40 *years of Akbar's reign*	30 *solar years of Shahjahan's reign*	(21 *years*)	(29 *years*)
5,000 and above	29	49	51	79
3,000 to 4,500	30	88	90	133
1,000 to 2,700	74	300	345	363
TOTAL	133	437	486	575

It is obvious that there was a great increase in the number of *mansabdars* of all grades between the 40th year of Akbar and the 30th year of Shahjahan.[1] We are here, however, more concerned with the difference between Salih's list and the two lists of Aurangzeb's *mansabdars*.

It will be noticed that there were as many as 51 *mansabdars* of 5,000 *zat* and above during the first twenty (solar) years of Aurangzeb's reign, while in Shahjahan's entire reign of 30 years there were only 49 such *mansabdars*. The number of *mansabdars* of the two other classes, i.e. *mansabdars* of 3,000 to 4,500 and 1,000 to 2,700 is larger for the first twenty years of Aurangzeb's reign, though in neither case is the difference substantial.[2] This increase was probably due to the new appointments and promotions, which Aurangzeb made during and immediately after the War of Succession in order to consolidate his position. Shahjahan on coming to the throne was much better placed, and granted fewer increments in ranks, as may be seen from the following figures :

[1] The increase would be equally marked, if one were to be more precise and compare the numbers of *mansabdars* of above 1,000 *zat* alive in the 40th year of Akbar (based on the *Ain's* list) and in the 10th year of Shahjahan (based on Lahori). In the former year there were 34 such *mansabdars*, in the latter, 191—an increase of some 5·5 times.

[2] See the lists of Aurangzeb's *mansabdars* at the end of the book.

ADDITIONAL RANKS GRANTED
(Figures show total of net increase in the *zat* and *sawar* ranks)

	First two regnal years of Shahjahan	*First two regnal years of Aurangzeb*
Zat	43,500	89,000
Sawar (*du-aspa-sih-aspa* counted as double)	44,420	54,000[1]

However, it seems that Aurangzeb tried to check the grant of promotions in the succeeding eight regnal years as is clearly indicated by the following table based on the *Alamgir Nama* :

NET TOTAL RANKS GRANTED

	Regnal Years								
	1-2	3	4	5	6	7	8	9	10
Zat	89,000	17,700	−10,900	5,000	−7,200	1,100	−10,500	−20,500	10,000
Sawar	54,000	16,450	− 7,550	5,230	8,700	17,550	2,400	1,400	5,770

It was, perhaps, as a result of this restriction on the promotions granted each year that the period as a whole shows no great increase in the number of *mansabdars* over that of Shahjahan. On the other hand, the statistics concerning *mansabdars*, *ahadis* etc. given in the *Zawabit-i Alamgiri* probably relate to one of the closing years of the period 1658-78.

The next period (1679-1707) shows a considerable increase in the total number of *mansabdars*. This period exceeds the previous period by eight years, but the increase of *mansabdars* cannot be accounted for on that ground alone. While the *mansabdars* of 5,000 and above in all the 33 years of Shahjahan's reign numbered 49, as compared to 47 in the first twenty years of his reign,[2] the difference here is between 51 for the first 21 years of Aurangzeb's reign and 79 for the last twenty-nine years, showing an increase of 56 per cent. The number of *mansabdars* of 3,000 to 4,500 also increases from 90 to 133, an increase of 48 per cent. In the third category—holders of *mansabs* of 1,000 to 2,700—there is a

[1] The figures for Shahjahan's first two regnal years are based on the promotions and appointments recorded by Qazwini and Lahori, and for Aurangzeb's first two years on those recorded by Kazim in the *Alamgir Nama*.

[2] This has been arrived at by adding together Lahori's two lists, but eliminating the number of names common to both.

slight increase from 345 to 363, but this is probably owing to the fact that all the *mansabdars* of this grade have not been referred to by our authorities.

It seems clear from what has been said above that the real increase in the number of *mansabdars*, especially of the higher grades, took place in the later years of Aurangzeb's reign after he had started operations for the annexation of the entire Deccan and an ever-extending war had to be waged against the Marathas. There was considerable recruitment during this period of Deccani and Maratha nobles, many of whom were given big promotions, sometimes as reward for good service but mostly as bribe for desertion. The number of *mansabdars* became so large that there were complaints that no *jagirs* were left for being granted to them.[1] The crisis became so acute that the Emperor and his ministers repeatedly contemplated the stoppage of all fresh recruitment,[2] but the force of circumstances prevented them from giving effect to this decision.

Composition of the Nobility

The Mughal nobility was theoretically the creation of the Emperor. It was he alone who could confer, increase, diminish or resume, the *mansab* of any of his subjects. It would be wrong, however, to suppose that the Mughal nobility was open to all who could fulfil certain criteria of merit and competence to the satisfaction of the Emperor. The *mansabdars* were not only public servants, but also the richest class in the Empire and a closed aristocracy and entrance into this class was not easily available to ordinary subjects, whatever their merits.

Khanazads

The most important factor which was taken into account when nobles were appointed was heredity. The *Khanazads*, or sons and descendants of *mansabdars*,[3] had the best claim of all. This may be seen from the fact that out of a total of 486 *mansabdars* holding ranks of 1,000 and above during the years, 1658-78, 213 were either sons or close blood-relations (excluding those merely connected by marriages) of other *mansabdars*. During the period of 1679-1707, such *mansabdars* numbered 272 out of 575. Further details are given in the table below:

[1] Khafi Khan, II, pp. 396-97; Mamuri, ff. 156b-157a; *Dastur-al Amal-i Agahi*, f. 36; *Raqaim-i Karaim*, f. 28b.

[2] Khafi Khan, II, pp. 411-12.

[3] For the definition of *Khanazad*, see *Bahar-i Ajam*, s.v. The term *Khanazads*, though meaning 'the offspring of slaves' or slave-officers was applied to all *mansabdars*, who were the relations or descendants of *mansabdars*.

'A' 1658-78

Mansabdars	*Total*	*Khanazads*	*Percentage*
5,000 *zat* and above	51	25	49
3,000 to 4,500	90	61	68
1,000 to 2,700	345	127	37
	486	213	44

'B' 1679-1707

Mansabdars	*Total*	*Khanazads*	*Percentage*
5.000 *zat* and above	79	24	30
3,000 to 4,500	133	70	53
1,000 to 2,700	363[1]	178	49
	575	272	47

It would seem from these figures that the *Khanazads* constituted a little less than half of the nobility during both periods. But the increase in the proportion of their number during the period, 1679–1707, is probably illusory, and it may be noted that in the highest class (5,000 and above), where our information about the total number of *mansabdars* is more complete, their proportion had fallen from 25 out of 51 to 24 out of 79. The proportion rises as we come to the lower ranks, but our lists for the lower ranks are not so complete. Also our authorities are more inclined to take notice of *mansabdars*, who were descended from prominent nobles, than of other *mansabdars* of the same rank, who did not belong to distinguished families. A contemporary writer, in fact, laments in a long passage that during this period the *Khanazads* were being pushed aside by a flood of new appointees, principally, the Deccanis.[2]

Zamindars

On the whole, it may be said that although a large portion of the nobility was recruited on the basis of hereditary claims, a slightly larger portion consisted of persons who did not belong to families of those already holding *mansabs*. Such persons came from a variety of classes. A number of them were persons who already had both distinction and power in the land. To this group belonged the *zamindars* or chiefs within the empire. The inclusion of *zamindars* among the officers of the state was no innovation of the Mughals,[3] but it is true that Akbar gave it a very great importance by granting *mansabs* to a large number of *zamindars*

[1] See Tables 3(*a*) and 3(*b*) at the end of the chapter.

[2] Mamuri, ff. 156b—157a; Khafi Khan, II, pp. 396-7.

[3] See references to *rais* under Balban in Barani, *Tarikh-i Firuz Shahi* ed. Professor S.A. Rashid, Aligarh, Vol. I, pp. 62, 102, 125, 163.

and their relations. Their ancestral domains were left to them, being treated as their *watan-jagirs*, but as government officers ordinary *jagirs* were assigned to them in all parts of the Empire.[1] During the first part of Aurangzeb's reign (1658-78), there were no fewer than 68 officers who were also *zamindars* out of a total of 486 higher officers. Among the 575 *mansabdars* during the years 1679-1707, 81 were *zamindars* also. But out of these, 29 *zamindars* in the earlier period, and the same number in the later period, were new entrants whose predecessors had not held *mansabs*. The following table[2] provides further details :

'A' 1658-78

	Total Mansabdars	*Total zamindars*	*Zamindars whose fathers or blood relations were already mansabdars*	*Other Zamindars*
5,000 *zat* and above	51	7	5	2
3,000 *zat* to 4,500	90	11	10	1
1,000 *zat* to 2,700	345	50	24	26
	486	68	39	29

'B' 1679-1707

	Total Mansabdars	*Total zamindars*	*Zamindars whose fathers or blood relations were already mansabdars*	*Other Zamindars*
5,000 *zat* and above	79	15	6	9
3,000 *zat* to 4,500	133	20	13	7
1,000 *zat* to 2,700	363	46	33	13
	575	81	52	29

Nobles coming from other States

Then there were nobles and high officers of other states, who were given a place in the Mughal nobility on account of their experience, status and influence or of the contingents they commanded and the territories they controlled. A notable example of this was the conferment of a rank upon Husain Pasha, the Ottoman governor of Basra, immediately upon his arrival in India. For the Persian, Chaghtai and Uzbek nobility, India had traditionally been an El Dorado where fortunes could be rapidly made. In the Deccan, military necessity required that the largest number of nobles and officers of the independent states, both in times of peace and war, be won over to the Mughal side.

[1] See Chapters II and III.

[2] Based on the appendix at the end of the book.

They had to be granted *mansabs* high enough to induce them to betray their own states. Mir Jumla presents a classic example of this type; but almost all Deccani *mansabdars*, whether Bijapuris, Haiderabadis or Marathas, belonged to this category.[1]

A very small portion of the Mughal nobility was recruited from those who had no claims to high birth but were pure administrators or accountants. Such were the members of the accountant castes, Khatris, Kayasths, etc. Usually they received low ranks when appointed officers or clerks in the financial departments.[2] But a few of them rose to higher ranks. Under Akbar there had been Raja Todar Mal. Raja Raghunath, the *diwan* in the early years of Aurangzeb, rose to the high rank of 3,000/700 after a purely financial career. In our lists of Aurangzeb's nobles, this class is included among 'other Hindus', i.e. Hindus other than Rajputs and Marathas. In the period 1658-78, there were 7 'other Hindus' enjoying ranks of 1,000 *zat* and above out of a total of 486 *mansabdars*. In the period 1679-1707, the number rose to 13 out of 575.

Finally, *mansabdari* ranks were also awarded to scholars, religious divines, men of letters, etc. Abul Fazl in the time of Akbar and Sa'adullah Khan and Danishmand Khan during the reign of Shahjahan owed their high ranks to their talent as men of letters. Fazil Khan, Aurangzeb's minister in the early years of his reign, who held the rank of 5,000/2,500, was also a scholar and a physician whose name, before he received his title from Shahjahan, was Hakim Alaul-Mulk Tuni. Among Aurangzeb's own recruits to the services from this class were Munshi Qabil Khan (1,000/70) and Inayatullah Khan Kashmiri (2,000/250). A few theologians and religious scholars were also awarded *mansabs*.[3]

Racial and Religious Groups

The Mughal nobility, after its first phase of development during the

[1]See Tables 4(*a*) and 4(*b*) at the end of the chapter.

Mirza Raja Jai Singh won over Mulla Ahmad Naitha, the leading noble of Bijapur and on the recommendation of the Raja, Mulla Ahmad was given the rank of 6,000/6,000 (*Alamgir Nama*, 919-920; *Futuhat-i Alamgiri*, ff. 103b, 116b, 117b, 165b; *Akhbarat*, 8th R.Y.). For the practice of inciting the commanders and military generals of the enemy to desert their master as followed in the Deccan, see Manucci, IV, pp. 239-40. Even when the Deccan states were finally annexed, their nobles were given a place within the Mughal nobility. See *Zawabit-i Alamgiri*, ff. 163a-163b; *Ma'asir-i Alamgiri*, 184, 254; Khafi Khan, II, 304, 373, 370; *Mamuri*, 187a; *Akhbarat*, 7th Ziqada, 44th R.Y.

[2]Gopinath, when appointed *Pesh-dast* (chief clerk) of the *diwani* of the Deccan in 1644, received the rank of 1,000/20, the same as enjoyed by his predecessor (*Selected Documents of Shahjahan's Reign*, 64). Similarly Bhimsen, the author of *Nuskha-i-Dilkusha*, was a Kayasth Saksena by caste. His father had the *mansab* of 150/10 in the early years of Aurangzeb (Dilkusha, f. 21a). Bhimsen himself became a *mansabdar* for sometime before joining service under Raq Dalpat Bundela.

[3]For example Shaikh Abdul Qawi reached 5,000/400; Mulla Iwaz Wajih, 1,000/200.

reigns of Babur and Humayun and the early years of Akbar, came to consist of certain well-recognised racial groups. There were the Turanis (Central Asians), Iranis (Persians), Afghans, Shaikhzadas (Indian Muslims, consisting of a number of sub-groups), and the Rajputs. Later on, in the 17th century, with the advance of Mughal power in the Deccan, there was an influx of the Deccanis, i.e. Bijapuris, Haiderabadis and Marathas. A very interesting description of the composite nature of the Mughal nobility is given by Chandrabhan Brahman, who wrote during the last years of Shahjajhan's reign.

"From different races, Arabs, Persians, Turks, Tajiks, Kurds, Lars Tatars, Russians, Abyssinians, Circassians, etc. and from the country of Rum (Turkey), Egypt, Syria, Iraq, Arabia, Persia, Gilan, Mazandran, Khurasan, Sistan, Trans-Oxiana, Khwarazm, the Qipchaq Steppes, Turkistan, Gharjistan, Kurdistan, various classes and groups of persons from every race and people have sought asylum in the Imperial Court, and various groups of Indians, men possessed of knowledge and skill as well as men of the sword, viz. Bukhari and Bhakkari Saiyids of correct lineage, Shaikhzadas of noble ancestry, tribes (*ulusat*) of the Afghans such as Lodis, Rohilas, Khwaishgi, Yusufzai, etc. and clans of Rajputs, (styled) *rana*, *raja*, *rao* and *rayan*, such as Rathors, Sisodias, Kachhwahas, Haras, Gaurs, Chauhans, Jhalas, Chandravats, Jadauns, Tonwars, Baghelas, Bais, Badgujar, Panwars, Bhadurias, Solankis, Bundelas, Sekhawats and all other people of India, such as the races of Ghakkars, Langahs, Khokars, Baluch and other races, men of the pen and men of the sword, holding the positions of 7,000 to 1,000 and 1,000 to 100, and 100 to *ahadi*, and *zamindars* of the deserts and mountains, from the country of Karnatik, Bengal, Assam, Udaipur, Srinagar, Kamaun Bandhu, Tibet, and Kishtwar, etc. in the Empire, whole classes and groups of them, have obtained the privilege of kissing the threshold of the Imperial Court."[1]

These various elements were incorporated into the Mughal service largely as a result of historical circumstances, but partly (specially the Rajputs) as a result of planned imperial Policy. Akbar's policy seems to have been to integrate all these elements into a single imperial service. He often assigned officers belonging to various groups to serve under one superior officer. At the same time, the distinct or separate character of each group was respected. The imperial government regulated the proportion of men belonging to his own race or clan which a *mansabdar* could recruit.[2]

There was, therefore, diversity in unity; and the diversity was capable of producing tensions. Mirza Hakim had pinned his hopes on these tensions in 1581. He expected that the Iranis and Turanis in Akbar's forces would go over to his side, while the Rajputs and Afghans would

[1]*Guldasta*, Aligarh; Sir Sulaiman Collection 666/44, ff. 4b-5a.
[2]*Kkulasat-us Siyaq*, f. 54b.

be slaughtered and the other Indians would be captured.[1] Akbar's policy of *Sulh-i Kul* was partly motivated by a desire to employ elements of diverse religious beliefs—Sunnis (Turanis and most of the Shaikhzadas), Shias (including many Iranis) and Hindus (Rajputs)—and to prevent sectarian differences among them from interfering with their loyalty to the throne.[2] In the early years of Jahangir it was felt, at least by Mirza Aziz Koka, that the Emperor was hostile to the Chaghtais (Turanis) and Rajputs, while he was showing undue favours to the Khurasanis (Iranis) and Shaikhzadas.[3] But there seems to be no convincing evidence for this.[4]

It is clear, however, that there existed a certain amount of jealousy among the various sections of the nobility. Aurangzeb's nobility must have inherited both this tradition of internal rivalry and distrust as well as the dominant spirit of unity engendered by a common loyalty to the throne. In the following pages an attempt has been made to study how each of these elements fared under Aurangzeb. We will endeavour to find out how far the Emperor followed a consciously planned policy towards the various sections of the nobility and how the changes in the strength of each of them reacted upon the solidarity and cohesion of the nobility and the Empire as a whole.

The Foreign Nobility

Commenting on the list of *mansabdars* in the *Ain*, Moreland says that just under 70 per cent of the nobles whose origin is known were foreigners belonging "to families which had either come to India with Humayun or had arrived at the Court after the accession of Akbar."[5] This high proportion of *mansabdars* belonging to families from foreign lands continued under Akbar's successors. Thus, Bernier described the nobility during the early years of Aurangzeb's reign as "a medley of Uzbecs, Persians, Arabs and Turks, or descendants from these people". He adds elsewhere that the "*omaras* mostly consist of adventurers from different nations who entice one another to the Court".[6] We cannot really consider descendants of immigrants who had come from abroad a couple of generations back and had lost all contact with their own country as 'foreigners' in any real sense of the word.[7] But even if we regard them

[1] *Akbar Nama*, III, 366. The Mirza's advisers did not know, adds Abul Fazl, the extent of loyalty which the Turanis and Iranis felt for Akbar, nor how brave the Rajputs and other Indians were.

[2] Cf. *Dabistan-i Mazahib*, ed. Nazar Ashraf, Calcutta, pp. 431-32.

[3] *Arzdasht-i Muzaffar*, ff. 19a-19b; Cf. Hawkins, *Early Travels*, 106-7.

[4] See Rifaqat Ali Khan's paper, 'Jahangir and the Rajputs', *Proceedings of Indian History Congress*, Aligarh Session, 1960, pp. 223-25, for an examination of this evidence.

[5] *India at the Death of Akbar*, pp. 69-70.

[6] Bernier, 209, 212.

[7] For a discussion of this point, see Satish Chandra, *Parties and Politics at the Mughal Court*, pp. XXIX ff.

as 'foreigners', Bernier's statement would only be partly true for Aurangzeb's early years. This is brought out by the charts based on the lists of nobles of Aurangzeb's reign. It thus appears that in 1658-78 out of a total of 417 *mansabdars* of 1,000 *zat* and above, whose origin can be determined, 202 or slightly less than half, were foreigners; and of these 55 are known to have been born outside India. In 1679-1707, out of 482 *mansabdars* of 1,000 and above whose origin can be determined, 197 were foreigners, of whom 46 were born outside India.[1] It is clear from these figures that there had been a distinct decline in the number of nobles directly coming from foreign countries since the time of Akbar, and in the course of Aurangzeb's long reign, direct recruitment of foreigners declined even more sharply, as is apparent from the proportionately lower number of foreign-born nobles in the second period as compared to the first. The decline is still more remarkable if only the highest ranks are considered. In 1658-78, out of 51 *mansabdars* of 5,000 and above, no less than 32 were foreigners, of whom 15 were born outside India, while the origin of 2 cannot be determined. In 1679-1707 out of 66 *mansabdars* of 5,000 and above, whose origin can be determined, only 20 were foreigners, of whom just 6 were born outside India.[2]

It is possible to point out various reasons for this decline. The Uzbek and Safavid Kingdoms were no longer as powerful as they had been before and consequently the same number of nobles of administrative experience and status no longer came to India from those lands for recruitment to the Mughal nobility. Moreover, Aurangzeb's attention was concentrated for the most part of his reign on the Deccan and he never aspired to follow a forward or militaristic policy in the North-West like his father or great grand-father. He was, therefore, not likely to go out of his way to offer exceptional inducements to Turani and Irani nobles to desert their masters for Mughal service.

On the other hand, there is no evidence that Aurangzeb ever consciously set out to 'Indianise' the nobility. Such 'Indianisation' as occurred was purely the result of historical circumstances, and not of a deliberate policy. Indeed, there is some evidence to show that a distinction was maintained even in the time of Aurangzeb between the foreign and local elements in the nobility. It appears to have been assumed that the Turanis and Iranis should command a higher status than those belonging to clans that had their homes in India. Thus a great Rajput noble himself, Mirza Raja Jai Singh, is found expressing surprise that instead of his

[1] See Tables 1(*a*) and 1(*b*) at the end of the chapter. The number of nobles of 1,000 and above whose country of origin cannot be determined are 69 in the list of 1658-1678 and 93 in that of 1679-1707, i.e. respectively 14.4 per cent and 16 per cent of the total. They are all Muslims. Thus, while calculating the relative strength of individual Muslim groups, it may be permissible to deduct their number from the total in order to state the percentage, it should be counted in the total when the purpose is to find the relative strength of Muslims or Hindus as a whole, or of individual Hindu groups.

[2] See Tables 1(*a*) and 1(*b*) at the end of the chapter.

own nominees for the posts of fort-commandants in the Deccan, who from their names seem to have been Turanis and Iranis, Aurangzeb should have preferred to appoint to these posts men "belonging to the races of Indian-born (Hindūstān-zād) Sayyids and Mughals and Shaikhzadas (Indian Muslims) and Rajputs".[1] This prejudice seems to have found reflection in the practice, reported by Bernier, of Mughal officers marrying women from Kashmir, so that their "children may be whiter than the Indians and pass for genuine Mogols".[2] However, the very paucity of indications of such prejudice suggests that to postulate the existence of any deep-rooted jealousy or struggle between the 'foreigners' and 'Indians' merely on the grounds of their place of birth would be hazardous.

The Turanis and Iranis

The so-called foreigners consisted largely of the Turanis and Iranis. Turani was a term applied to any person coming from Central Asia, where the Turkish languages were spoken. In spite of the fact that it is not possible to explain the tussle between the officers of Aurangzeb entirely in terms of a conflict between the Iranis and the Turanis, it cannot be denied that Irani and Turani group-consciousness did exist and was at times used for factional ends. It is, therefore, necessary to examine the proportion of the Iranis and Turanis in the higher official grades. Since the ruling family was of Turani origin, one might expect that the Turanis would be the dominant section of the foreign nobility but this was not so. Bernier noted that "the Court itself does not now consist as originally, of real Mogols"; and the lists of Aurangzeb's nobles bear him out completely. In 1658-78, there were 67 Turani *mansabdars* of 1,000 and above out of 486, while in 1679-1707, they numbered only 72 out of 575.[3] That is to say, only 13·7 per cent of the nobles in the first period and 12·5 per cent in the second were Turanis. The decline in the Turanis' position probably took place much before Aurangzeb's reign. We have already seen that Jahangir was charged with hostility towards the Turanis. It may be noted that the decline of the Uzbek Kingdom started much earlier than the decline of the Safavids. Moreover, the Turanis, especially the Badakhshis, were generally regarded as uncultured and boorish in India.[4] An officer of Aurangzeb's court who went so far to say in the imperial presence that the word of a Turani could not be trusted, only earned a mild reproof asking him to remember that his Emperor was also a Turani.[5]

[1]Munshi Bhag Chand, *Jami-al Insha*, Br. M.Or.1702, f.67a.
[2]Bernier, p. 404.
[3]See Tables 2(*a*) and 2(*b*) at the end of the chapter.
[4]*Mirat-al Istilah*, f. 78a.
[5]Mamuri, f. 179b; Khafi Khan, II, 378-79.

Iranis

The *Iranis*, also called Khurasanis and Iraqis, comprised the Persian speaking peoples from Herat up to Baghdad i.e. the inhabitants of the whole of the present-day Persia and the Persian-speaking parts of Afghanistan and Iraq. Aziz Koka's letter, referred to earlier, shows that there existed from earlier generations cosnsiderable jealousy between the Turanis and Iranis. The fact that the Turanis were generally Sunnis and most Iranis were Shias[1] sometimes lent a religious colour to the controversy. The Iranis were supposed to be far more cultured, and won special favour under both Jahangir and Shahjahan. It has been suggested that in the War of Succession Aurangzeb rallied the Sunnis against the Shias,[2] but there is really no basis for this assertion. Out of 124 nobles of 1,000 and above, who are known to have supported Aurangzeb up to the battle of Samugarh, 27 were Iranis, 4 of them holding rank of 5,000 *zat* and above. As against this, 23 out of 87 of Dara Shukoh's supporters were Iranis.[3] After all, Mir Jumla and Shaista Khan, the leading Irani nobles, were Aurangzeb's partisans. Similarly, there does not seem to be much weight in Bernier's statement that Prince Shuja was supported by the Persians.[4] Only one of his ten known supporters, holding rank of 1,000 *zat* and above, was an Irani.[5]

Thus Aurangzeb's victory did not affect the position of the Iranis in any way. Bernier says that the 'greater part' of his foreign nobility consisted of Persians,[6] and Tavernier says that the Persians occupied 'the highest posts' in the Mughal Empire.[7] This statement can be proved by statistics. Out of 486 *mansabdars* in 1658-78, 136 were Iranis, quite dwarfing the Turanis, who numbered 67. In 1679-1707, their number still remained high—126 out of a total of 575. On the top rung of the ladder, 23 Iranis held the rank of 5,000 and above in 1658-78 and 14 in 1679-1707, while the number of Turanis was 9 and 6 respectively.

The Iranis maintained their position partly because of the influx of Iranis serving in the Deccan Kingdoms. Here the Iranis had long been dominant;[8] and Mir Jumla provides an example of an Irani noble entering Mughal service through the Deccan. Aurangzeb is also said to have entertained great confidence in officers from Khawaf, a province of Persia, who became recipients of considerable favours during his reign.[9]

[1]On most Irani nobles being Shias, see Badauni, II, pp. 326-7.

[2]See I.A. Ghori in *Journal of Pakistan Historical Society*, Vol. VIII, part II, pp. 97-119.

[3]See Tables in Chapter IV. [4]Bernier, 8, 26.

[5]See Table in Chapter IV. [6]Bernier, 3. [7]Tavernier, II, 138. [8]Tavernier, II, 138

[9]Cf. Khafi Khan II, p. 72, who says in an interesting passage : "Owing to Shaikh Mir's sacrificing his life in the service of the Emperor, the Emperor — a (great) patron of *Khanazads* — began to bestow great favour on all men of Khawaf. So much so that during Aurangzeb's reign, the people of Khawaf, which is the least-regarded of all parts of Khurasan, came into prominence and obtained promotions, never seen in the histories of previous rulers. In fact, although the people of Khawaf are in appearance rough and rude as compared to the other people of Khurasan, most of them are efficient and upright in the discharge of their duties. In justifying loyalty to their salt they can be counted among the steadfast ones (in the Empire)."

Nor was the position of the Persians affected by the Sunni orthodoxy of the Emperor. He once refused to make an appointment to the office of *bakhshi* which was suggested to him on the ground that the existing incumbent was a Shia.[1]

The Afghans

The Afghans had a chequered history within the Mughal nobility. They cannot properly be regarded as foreign immigrants because their homelands lay within the Mughal Empire. During the time of the Delhi Sultans, the Afghans had been looked upon with contempt as robbers and plunderers.[2] However, by the time of Firoz Shah, some of the Afghans had acquired prominence as nobles. With the establishment of the Lodi Kingdom, they came to constitute the governing class, and the influx of the Afghans from 'Roh' to Hindustan proper reached its height. When their Kingdom was overthrown by Babur, some of them made their peace with the conqueror. The short-lived Sur Empire, followed by the Mughal restoration, made the Afghan chiefs suspects in the eyes of the Mughals, and Akbar seems to have kept most of them at arm's length.[3] Jahangir, however, began to encourage the Afghans, as is evidenced particularly by the position accorded by him to Khan-i Jahan Lodi.[4] Under Shahjahan, after Khan-i Jahan Lodi's rebellion, the Afghans apparently suffered a set-back and, we are told, that Shahjahan placed no trust in the Afghans.[5]

Aurangzeb as a prince seems to have made an attempt to win over the Afghans. In a letter he expresses surprise that his proposal for promoting an Afghan officer was turned down by the Emperor simply because of his race.[6] Still more revealing is the fact that out of the 124 nobles of 1,000 *zat* and above, who supported Aurangzeb up to the battle of Samugarh, 23 were Afghans, while there was only one Afghan among 87 nobles of this status on the side of Dara Shukoh.[7]

According to Abul Fazl Mamuri, Aurangzeb in the early years of his reign exercised great care to see that the Afghans did not get undue promotions.[8] In our lists of *mansabdars* of 1,000 and above during 1658-78, we find 43 Afghan officers out of a total of 486. In the second period, 1679-1707, the Afghans numbered 34 out of a total of 575. But this decline is probably due to the incompleteness of our lists for the

[1] *Ahkam*, 39.

[2] See Isami, *Futuh-us Salatin*, ed. Mehdi Hasan, p. 244.

[3] *Dilkusha*, f. 84b.

[4] For further elucidation of this point, see Dr. A. Rahim's article, 'Jahangir's Policy towards the Afghans', *Journal of Pakistan Historical Society*, 1959, Vol. VII, Part III, pp. 205-20.

[5] *Dilkusha*, ff. 84b, 173b; *Durr-al Ulum*, f.15a. The *jagir* of an Afghan officer Bahadur Khan, who had rendered distinguished service in Balkh and Badakhshan, was resumed by Shahjahan on the charge of negligence of duty. (*Amal-i Salih*, III, p. 23.)

[6] *Adab-i Alamgiri*, f. 143. [7] See Tables in Chapter IV. [8] Mamuri, f. 156b.

lower ranking *mansabdars*. Thus, while there were only three Afghans holding the rank of 5,000 and above in 1658-78, there were no less than ten in the same category in the period 1679-1707. Aurangzeb's later years, therefore, showed a considerable increase in the number of the Afghan nobility. But it appears that this was mainly owing to the recruitment of a large number of Afghans formerly serving in the Bijapur Kingdom.

Contemporary observers write of the Afghan nobility with an obvious feeling of aversion. The Afghans came from a tribal society and even when they were appointed Mughal officers, they still remained tribal leaders and employed men from their own tribes and clans. Manucci points out that they wore aristocratic dress only for the court. When they returned, they put away the dress for the simple costumes of their race.[1] Bhimsen has even graver objections to the Afghans: The Afghans were spread all over India and were everywhere a cause of turbulence and disorder. Their power increased after Aurangzeb's departure for the Deccan, and many of them, who were not admitted to the imperial service, raised private armies which put into the shade the contingents of many imperial officers.[2] The growth in the number of Afghan nobles weakened the internal cohesion of the nobility, and, in turn, reacted unfavourably on the fortunes of the Empire, particularly when the dominating personality of Aurangzeb was removed from the scene and still new weaknesses crept into the central government.

Indian Muslims

The Indian Muslims, popularly known as *Shaikhzadas*, belonged largely to certain important clans, like the Saiyids of Barha and the Kambus. There were 65 Indian Muslims out of a total of 486 *mansabdars* of 1,000 and above in 1658-78, i.e. 13·4 per cent; in 1679-1707 they were 69 out of 575 or 12 per cent. In 1658-78, there were 4 Indian Muslims enjoying the rank of 5,000 and above; in 1679-1707, there were 10.[3]

It seems that behind this slight relative decline in the strength of the Indian Muslims lay the eclipse of certain old elements, offset by the entry of new sections. The Saiyids of Barha and the Kambus, who had held leading positions since the time of Akbar, were no longer equally prominent during the later years of Aurangzeb. The Saiyids of Barha, who traditionally formed the vanguard of the Mughal armies and were very proud of their martial qualities,[4] were distrusted by Aurangzeb.[5] This was probably because the Barha Saiyids had been loyal supporters of Dara Shukoh. Among the new groups that were brought in, the most

[1] Manucci, II, p. 453. [2] *Dilkusha*, ff. 173b-174a.
[3] See Tables 2(*a*) and 2(*b*) at the end of the chapter.
[4] *Tuzuk-i Jahangiri*, p. 366. [5] *Ahkam*, 32, 8.

prominent were the native Deccanis (i.e. excluding those Deccanis, who were Irani, Turani or Afghan, but including the Abyssinians of the Western Coast). "The Kashmiris were also promoted in larger numbers. We are told that in the early years of Aurangzeb's reign, the Kashmiris, specially the Chaks, seldom got any *mansab*."[1] But during the later years of the reign, their number increased.

RAJPUTS

Aurangzeb's policy towards the Rajputs has been considerably clouded by controversy. This is not surprising as it is—or has been supposed to be—closely connected with his religious policy, and the latter has aroused passionate debate for a long time. For the sake of clarity of discussion, however, it is desirable to examine the position of the Rajputs in the nobility without taking for granted its association with the religious policy of Aurangzeb.

Shahjahan was a devout Muslim king, who adopted a number of measures to show his orthodoxy. Yet his reign saw a very great increase in the number of Rajput *mansabdars*, as is shown by the lists given in Lahori and Waris.[2] Aurangzeb, too, was a devout Muslim; and he was censured at Shahjahan's court for harbouring hostility towards the Rajputs.[3] But this was apparently a passing phase, and in the years immediately preceding the War of Succession, Aurangzeb seems to have made an earnest attempt to win over the leading Rajput chiefs to his side. His *nishans* issued to Rana Raj Singh of Mewar have survived.[4] In these he promised the Rana to restore all the territories annexed from Mewar in 1654 as a punishment for the refortification of Chitor by the Rana. In one *nishan* he makes a promise in ringing tones that he would follow the religious policy of his ancestors declaring that "a King who practices intolerance towards the religion of another, is a rebel against God".[5] Qanungo has shown at length how Mirza Raja Jai Singh had become a secret supporter of Aurangzeb, and played a key role in the overthrow of Dara Shukoh.[6] It is true that among Aurangzeb's 124 supporters

[1]Mamuri, f. 156b-To be a Kashmiri was one of the disqualifications cited by Aurangzeb in a letter to prince Muazzam. (*Raqaim-i Karaim*, f. 15a-b.)

[2]This point was first made out by S.R. Sharma, *Religious Policy of the Mughal Emperors*', pp. 98-101, where the actual numbers are given.

[3]*Adab-i Alamgiri*, ff. 24a, 25a; *Ruq'at-i Alamgir*, pp. 113, 115. It is interesting that this was in connection with a protest lodged by Aurangzeb at Shahjahan's rejection of his suggestion for granting promotion to Rao Karan.

[4]*Vir Vinod*, II, pp. 423-24, 426-27; *Adab-i Alamgiri*, ff. 325a, 326a.

[5]*Ibid.*, pp. 419-20 *note*. This *nishan* has been translated by me in my paper, 'The Religious Issue in the War of Succession, 1658-59', read before the Aligarh Session of the Indian History Congress, 1960. Reprinted in Medieval India Quarterly, vol. V, PP. 80-87,

[6]*Dara Shukoh*, passim, but especially, pp. 175-78.

of 1,000 and above before the battle of Samugarh, there were only 9 Rajputs, while Dara Shukoh could count 22 Rajputs among his 87 known supporters of the same rank.[1] But this is mainly because in this enumeration Jai Singh and the Kachwahas have been excluded from the ranks of Aurangzeb's supporters since they were then in the army of Sulaiman Shukoh which was marching against Shuja. Moreover, Dara Shukoh's list shows so many Rajputs because these Rajputs were then at the Court and had no alternative but to support Dara. In actual fact, there was little personal loyalty for Dara among the Rajputs. As prince Akbar later wrote to Aurangzeb, Dara Shukoh was "in reality prejudiced against and hostile to the race" of Rajputs: "If he had made friends with them from the first, he would not have fared as he did."[2]

During the early years of his reign, Aurangzeb seems to have treated the Rajputs with a certain amount of consideration, and in some respects their position actually improved over what it had been in Shahjahan's time. There had been no Rajput officer throughout the reign of Shahjahan holding the rank of 7,000. Now Mirza Raja Jai Singh and Jaswant Singh—the latter, in spite of his role at the battles of Dharmat and Khajwah—were promoted to 7,000/7,000. Ever since Man Singh's recall from Bengal in 1606, no Rajput noble had been entrusted with an important province (apart from Jaswant Singh's appointment to Malwa late in 1658). Now in 1665 Jai Singh was made the Viceroy of the Deccan, not in the role of an adviser to a prince, but in his own right. This was amongst the highest and most important charges in the Mughal empire, with which normally only princes were entrusted. Jaswant Singh, too, was twice appointed Governor of Gujrat (1659-61 and 1670-72). Bernier who was at Agra till 1665, could therefore note that "the Great Mogal, though a Mohomedan, and as such an enemy to the Gentiles (Hindus), always keeps in his service a large retinue of Rajas, treating them with the same consideration as his other Omrahs, and appointing them to important commands in his armies".[3]

An interesting method of studying Aurangzeb's policy towards the Rajputs during the first decade of his reign is suggested by the information concerning *mansab* promotions and reductions (including *mansabs* lapsing with the death, retirement and dismissal of the incumbents) in the official chronicle, the *Alamgir Nama* of Muhammad Kazim. The Table on the next page puts this information in a statistical form.

This table shows that the statement that the position of the Rajputs improved during the early years of Aurangzeb's reign has to be qualified. In Salih's list of *mansabdars* of Shahjahan's reign we find that out of 437

[1]See Tables in chapter IV.

[2]Royal Asiatic Society, London, MS. 173; printed in Abdul Ghani, *Karnama-i Rajputan*, p. 132.

[3]Bernier, 40.

	Net Increase or Decrease in mansabs (excluding those of the Imperial Princes)			
	I-II *Yrs.*	III-VI *Yrs.*	VII-X *Yrs.*	I-X *Yrs.*
Zat				
Total	89,000	4,600	−10,000	83,600
Rajputs	12,600	1,000	− 1,600	12,000
%	14.16	21.74	16.00 (of the reduction)	14.35
Sawar				
Total	54,000	5,430	27,320	86,750
Rajputs	11,900	1,350	− 2,500	10,750
%	22.04	24.86	− 9.15	12.40

nobles holding the rank of 1,000 *zat* and above, 82 (or 18·7 per cent.) were Rajputs. While the nobles of 1,000 *zat* and above in all held a total of 10,07,000 *zat*, the Rajputs accounted for 178,500 or 17·7 per cent of this total. The figure of 14·35 per cent of net *zat* ranks granted during the whole of the first decade shows that on the whole the old proportion was not being maintained. It also seems that while during the first six years of the decade, the Rajputs were granted relatively higher ranks (specially as far as the *sawar* ranks are concerned), during the last four years, their position declined appreciably. The *sawar* ranks held by them were reduced in absolute terms while there was a considerable *net* increase in the *mansabs* granted to nobles in general.

There may, therefore, be much truth in Mamuri's statement that in the period before his departure for the Deccan, Aurangzeb had been exercising restraint in promoting the Rajputs.[1] The above table suggests that this restraint might well have become a deliberate imperial policy even before the end of the first decade of the reign.

This new imperial outlook was reflected in Aurangzeb's handling of the question of succession to the Marwar throne upon the death of Jaswant Singh in December, 1678. A detailed discussion of the whole issue of succession and the factors that led to the Rajput rebellion of 1680-81 is not relevant for our purpose here.[2] Aurangzeb evidently wished to assert the central authority; he converted even Jodhpur into *Khalisa* (or Crown Territory), immediately upon the death of Jaswant Singh, despite protests by Jaswant Singh's chief Queen and officers. However, there is no evidence that this was meant to be the prelude to a scheme

[1] Mamuri, f. 156 b.

[2] For a discussion regarding the Rajput question, and the attitude of the nobility towards it, see Chapter IV.

for destroying all Rajput Kingdoms.[1] The fact that Jaswant Singh had left no son at his death gave Aurangzeb an excuse for bringing parts of Marwar under direct Mughal administration in order to provide *jagirs* for the Raja's officers. But with the posthumous birth of two sons to the queens of Jaswant Singh, a new situation arose; and Aurangzeb sought to salvage something of his old plan by nominating Inder Singh to the *gaddi*. It seems that Aurangzeb wished to remain, as far as was possible, within the bounds of custom and precedent. After all, the Mughal Emperors had not hesitated to grant *tikas* in violation of the Rajput customary law of succession.[2] At the same time Aurangzeb made peace on rather liberal terms with Mewar in 1681, despite two years of bitter fighting in which most of the state had been over-run.[3] The 1680-81 rebellion had only involved the Rathors and Sisodias. The other clans not only remained aloof, but served under the Mughals. The *Waqa-i Ajmer* gives frequent reports of Rajput officers joining the Mughal army with their contingents. The rebellion, therefore, did not initiate any great decline in the fortunes of the Rajput nobility. Though in the period, 1679-1707, we find only 73 Rajput officers out of a total 575—a mere 12·6 per cent,[4] compared to the proportionate number of the Rajputs in 1658-78, which was 14.6 per cent—this may be held to mark a decline. It should, however, be remembered that this was a decline generally suffered by the non-Deccani elements. If we take non-Deccani nobles alone, the number of Rajputs amounted to 16·6 per cent of the total during the period, 1658-78; while during the period, 1679-1707, the Rajputs numbered 17·6 per cent. This latter was the period of the Deccan wars in which Rajput contingents rendered gallant service. Indeed, prince Azam's wife could call upon the Haras to offer their lives in defence of her camp from the Marathas by exclaiming that "the honour of the Chaghtais is one with the honour of the Rajputs".[5]

These statistics do not lend support to the view that there was a special discrimination against the Rajputs after 1678. S.R. Sharma has tried to show that Aurangzeb as a rule granted smaller ranks to new Rajput chiefs than those of their predecessors, even though these ranks were held against hereditary lands or *watan-jagirs*.[6] However, there is no evidence that Aurangzeb annexed any part of the Rajput states at the time of new successions. What Aurangzeb could have done was to

[1] Cf. Sarkar, *History of Aurangzeb*, Vol. III, p. 367.

[2] Eg. *Tuzuk-i Jahangiri*, p. 106; *Adab-i Alamgiri*, f. 26a; *Ruq'at-i Alamgir*, p. 120.

[3] By this peace (made with Rana Jai Singh), the entire territory of Mewar was restored to the Rana with the exception of those *parganas* which had been annexed to the Empire in 1654, but returned in 1659. The Rana was granted the same rank as his father, 5,000/5,000.

[4] See Table 2 (*b*) at the end of the chapter.

[5] Sarkar, History of *Aurangzeb*, Vol. IV, p. 302, (Sarkar quotes the *Akhbarat* without giving the year and the date, but the present writer has not found this reference anywhere in the *Akhbarat*).

[6] *Religious Policy of the Mughal Emperors*, p. 134.

have restricted such rank promotions as would have entitled the Rajput chiefs to claim imperial *jagirs* in addition to their *watan-jagirs*. A Rajput chief generally held imperial *jagirs* outside his *watan;* so that when he died, only part of his *jagir* and, therefore *mansab*, would go to his heir, and not the whole. As Rana Amar Singh wrote in a letter to Asafuddaula (A.D.1708): "The previous Emperors, keeping in view (the paucity of) the resources of Rajputana, have been pleased to assign to the ancestors of the present chiefs, *parganas* and *in'am* lands besides their *watan jagirs*, in return for which they have always rendered excellent service."[1] It will also be a mistake to suppose that the Rajputs were deliberately humiliated in Aurangzeb's later years. True, such tokens of honour as the putting of *tika* on the forehead of their Rajas by the Emperor himself or the chief *wazir* were withdrawn.[2] But the Rajputs were certainly given a higher status than the rest of their co-religionists, and all Rajputs who were in imperial service, were exempted from the *jizya*.[3]

On the other hand, it will also be a mistake to suppose that Aurangzeb followed a policy towards the Rajputs entirely in the same spirit as Akbar. We have already noted that Aurangzeb began to exercise a certain restraint in the appointments and promotions of the Rajputs before the end of the first decade of the reign. During the last thirty years of his reign, the Emperor's attitude is clarified by the treatment of some distinguished Rajput officers. Ram Singh Hara, Dalpat Rao Bundela and Jai Singh Sawai were three Rajput officers who served in the Deccan with their full contingents.[4] Yet, Dalpat only held the rank of 3,000/3,000, Ram Singh Hara of 3,000/1,500 (200 x 2-3h)and Raja Jai Sing of 2,000/2,000. When Jai Singh was appointed by prince Bidar Bakht to serve as his deputy in Malwa in 1705, Aurangzeb forbade his sitting on a *masnad* and made it clear that a Rajput could not ordinarily be appointed a Governor or even a *faujdar*.[5]

DECCANIS

The word Deccani means a 'southerner', and the Mughals applied this name to all those nobles belonging to the Deccan kingdoms, who took service with them. An official document of Aurangzeb's 11th regnal year states that all nobles, whether of Indian or foreign origin, who had taken service with either Bijapur or Golkunda before joining Mughal service, were to be considered Deccanis.[6] Though many of the Marathas, who were by birth Deccanis *par excellence*, were technically

[1] *Vir Vinod*, 111, 777-78.
[2] *Ma'asir-i Alamgiri*, p. 176.
[3] Isar Das, f. 74a-b.
[4] *Dilkusha*, f. 140a-141a.
[5] Inayatullah's *Ahkam-i Alamgiri*, f. 62b.
[6] *Selected Documents of Aurangzeb's Reign*, p. 64,

excluded by this order, they were generally counted among Deccanis by contemporary writers, and may be so designated.

In our general tables regarding the composition of Aurangzeb's nobility, no separate column has been provided for Deccanis — those among them who were Iranis being grouped under Iranis, Afghans under Afghans, Turanis under Turanis, and the rest either under other Muslims or Indian Muslims. Only the Marathas are listed separately. These tables, therefore, offer no index to the position of the Deccanis in the nobility. The figures for Deccanis i.e. all nobles covered by the official definition of Deccani, *plus* the Marathas, holding the *zat* ranks of 1,000 and above in the two periods of 1658-78 and 1679-1707 are set out in the following table:

	1658–78			1679–1707		
	Total	*Deccanis*	*Percentage of the Deccanis to the total*	*Total*	*Deccanis*	*Percentage of the Deccanis to the total*
5,000 and above	51	10	19.6	79	48	60.8
3,000 to 4,500	90	13	14.4	133	34	25.5
1,000 to 2,700	345	35	10.1	363	78	21.5
Total	486	58	11.8	575	160	27.8

It appears clearly from this table that the Deccanis did not form a very large proportion of Aurangzeb's nobility in the first period. Not only were they few in numbers, but they were also regarded as a subordinate class of nobles. Their high *mansabs* did not reflect their real income or power. As Abul Fazl Mamuri tells us: "Although in order to win them over the Emperor (Aurangzeb) granted them high *mansabs*, yet they were put on a three or four months scale of pay and a fourth part of their total pay claim (*talab*) was deducted according to the regulations for pay in the Deccan. He (Aurangzeb) also exercised caution in granting them *jagirs*."[1] One reason for this, no doubt, was that, thanks to the desolation of the Deccan peasantry, revenue collection in the Mughal Deccan was only 1/3 or 1/4 of the *jama*[2] towards the end of Shahjahan's reign. There is no evidence to suggest that the situation had improved greatly in Aurangzeb's reign. For this reason the *jagirs* in the Deccan, which were most often awarded to Deccanis, were on the lowest 'month-scales'. The practice of deducting a fourth part of the Deccani's pay-claim had already become an established rule under Shahjahan,[3] and

[1] Mamuri, f. 156b; *Dilkusha*, f. 31b.

[2] *Adab-i Alamgiri*, ff. 25b. 33a-33b, 35b, 36b, 43a.

[3] *Selected Documents of Shahjahan's Reign*, pp. 1-27, 13 and passim.

an official order of Aurangzeb's 11th regnal year also firmly reiterates it. All those who had been in the service of the Deccan states had to suffer this deduction. "Only if a person has come direct from Persia, and it is proved that he has not taken service with these (Kingdoms of Bijapur and Haiderabad), they are not to deduct a fourth (from his pay claim)."[1]

The picture, however, changed in the second period when Aurangzeb went to the Deccan in 1681, and embarked on a policy which ultimately led to the annexation of the whole Deccan. During this period, there was a large-scale recruitment of Deccani nobles into Mughal Service — Bijapuris, Haiderabadis and Marathas were either induced to surrender their fortresses and districts, or were admitted to service when Bijapur and Golkunda were finally conquered. Even the condition of providing sureties was waived for Deccani recruits.[2] As Aurangzeb was even then unable to secure a military decision against the Marathas, the policy of bribing the Deccanis had to be continued until it played havoc with the historic composition as well as status of the Mughal nobility.

If we keep in view the territories added to the Empire as a result of Aurangzeb's annexations in the Deccan, the influx of the Deccanis does not at first sight seem disproportionate. The *jamadami* (assessed revenue figures by which *jagirs* were assigned in lieu of pay) of the provinces of the Deccan about 1667 was 32.1 per cent of the total *jama* of the Empire,[3] while the number of Deccani nobles of 1,000 *zat* and above during the period, 1658-78, was no more than 11.8 per cent. After the annexation of Bijapur and Golkunda, the *jamadami* of the Deccan rose to 43.5 per cent of the total *jama* of the Empire in 1687-91,[4] while the number of Deccanis amounted to 27.9 per cent of the nobles of 1,000 and above during the whole period, 1679-1707. Yet at the same time these figures show a certain imbalance. While the share of the Deccan in the *jamadami* of the Empire between 1667 and 1691 increased only by 35.5 per cent the proportion of the Deccani nobles between 1658-78 and 1679-1707 rose by 136.5 per cent. Though at first the Deccanis were assigned *jagirs* in the Deccan only, yet since the presence of non-Deccanis in large numbers in the Deccan was essential from a military point of view, the Deccan could not provide for all of them, and *jagirs* had eventually to be assigned to the Deccanis in other parts of the Empire as well.

Abul Fazl Mamuri, in a passage which has escaped the notice of Khafi Khan, gives expression to the feeling of resentment among the older

[1] *Selected Documents of Aurangzeb's Reign*, p. 64.

[2] *Ibid.*, p. 182. The Deccanis exempted were those holding up to 1,000 *zat* ranks.

[3] *Mirat-al Alam*, ff. 214b-215; *Jama* of the Empire : 9,24,17,16,082 *dams*; Deccan provinces, 2,96,70,00,000 *dams*.

[4] *Zawabit-i Alamgiri*, ff. 3a-5b; *Jama* of the Empire : 13,80,23,56,000 *dams*; Deccan provinces : 6,00,22,22,140 *dams*.

nobility—the *Khanazads*—at the influx of the 'Upstart' Deccanis in the later years of Aurangzeb. "At last, things reached such a state that the whole country was assigned to the new recruits from the Deccan and their agents, through bribery, obtained the choicest (*jagirs*) yielding the highest revenue for the Deccanis, and it was plain for all to see that the ranks and numbers of the new and unknown *mansabdars* went on increasing while the *mansabs* of the old *mansabdars* went on declining".[1]

All the Deccanis, however, did not fare equally well. Those who got *jagirs* in the Deccan were hardly in an enviable position. As early as 1677 the Deccanis had been exempted from paying the charges of *khurak-i filan-i halqa* (feeding the elephants of the imperial stables) because "of their distressed circumstances and the low income of their *jagirs*".[2] With the rise of Maratha power, the expanding circle of Maratha depredations and finally the famine of 1702-4, their condition worsened. Bhimsen, in the last year of Aurangzeb's reign, after describing the ravages that the Deccan was undergoing, remarks that many *mansabdars* of the country (i.e. the Deccan) not finding it possible to realise anything from their *jagirs* were actually deserting to the Marathas.[3]

MARATHAS

EVER since Malik Ambar utilised the Maratha chiefs and their followers (*bargis*) on a large-scale, the Mughals had begun to realise the value of the Marathas in the Deccan wars. Maratha turn-coats played a leading part in the great defeat which Malik Ambar suffered in 1616 at the hands of Shahnawaz Khan. A new phase in Maratha recruitment began in the early years of Shahjahan's reign when the Emperor himself proceeded to the Deccan with the object of extinguishing the Ahmadnagar Kingdom. The rise of Maratha power, which was manifested in the establishment of an independent Maratha state in the Deccan by Shivaji, created a new situation. The growing importance of the Marathas in the affairs of the Deccan was reflected in a steady expansion of the Maratha element within the Mughal official class, which sought to meet the new challenge not only by military measures but also by a simultaneous attempt to absorb some sections of the Marathas in the Mughal nobility. The table on the next page shows the rapid growth in the numbers and position of the Marathas in the nobility.

Thus, Aurangzeb by force of circumstances had to open the gates wide to admit the Marathas in his service with succeeding years. He had failed to win over Shivaji with a grant of 5,000/5,000, and the Maratha leader had fled from his court. Now, in his last years, Shivaji's grandson, Shahu, enjoyed the rank of 7,000/7,000 and so was counted

[1] Mamuri, ff. 156b-157a.

[2] *Selected Documents of Aurangzeb's Reign*, 115.

[3] *Dilkusha*, f. 140a.

	Shahjahan	1658–78	1679–1707
5,000 and above	3	3	16
3,000 to 4,500	6	6	18
1,000 to 2,700	4	18	62
	13	27	96
Total number of Marathas as per cent of total *mansabdars*	2.9	5.5	16.7

among the highest nobles of the Empire—if only in a titular sense.

The attempt to win over Maratha chiefs by grant of *mansabs* ultimately proved a failure. As some Maratha chiefs were won over, others took their place in building new fortresses or ravaging Mughal districts. Perhaps the most important reason for this was that Maratha society was not organised on the lines of the Rajput clans, where the submission of the chief led to the submission of the entire clan. Among the Marathas so long as plunder and opposition offered any prospects, leaders of military bands or petty *zamindars* could always grow into rebel chieftains. The result was that the Maratha nobility under Aurangzeb was always unstable in its allegiance, with the chiefs coming over to the Mughals and then frequently deserting them. The Maratha nobility, therefore, never won any real position of influence within the Mughal governing class corresponding in any way to that of the Rajputs. Their presence was not indicative of a constructive expansion of the Mughal Empire, but was a symptom of its decline and decay.

Hindus

The Rajputs and the Marathas together formed the overwhelming majority of the Hindu nobility of Aurangzeb. It has been suggested that not only the Rajputs, but the Hindu nobility as a whole, suffered a set-back under Aurangzeb. S.R. Sharma has drawn up a list of 160 Hindu *mansabdars* of 1,000 *zat* and above under Aurangzeb.[1] He believes on the basis of this list that the number of Hindu nobles remained the same as under Shahjahan, while the total number of *mansabdars* doubled.[2] Neither of the assumptions involved in this statement can be accepted. We have shown that the idea of a two-fold increase in the nobility under Aurangzeb is based on a misreading of the *Zawabit-i Alamgiri*, the total figures for *mansabdars*, *ahadis*, artillerymen, etc. being taken as applying to nobles alone.[3] At the same time, Sharma's total of Hindu *mansabdars*

[1] *Religious Policy of the Mughal Emperors*, 178-80.
[2] *Ibid.*, 131.
[3] *Ibid.*, 131-132.

under Aurangzeb is based on incomplete data and cannot serve as a basis for a definite conclusion.[1] In the lists appended to this book, the names of all *mansabdars* of 1,000 and above, whether Hindu or Muslim, noticed in the sources have been given. Although these lists again might be incomplete, they may perhaps be considered reliable as to the proportion between Hindu and Muslim nobles, the margin of error being the same on both sides. In the table below, the figures of Hindu nobles have been set side by side with the number of *mansabdars*, serving in 1595, based on the *Ain*, and Salih's list of *mansabdars* of Shahjahan's reign.

	Akbar 1595		*Shahjahan* 1628-58		*Aurangzeb* 1658-78		*Aurangzeb* 1679-1707	
	Total	*Hindus*	*Total*	*Hindus*	*Total*	*Hindus*	*Total*	*Hindus*
5,000 and above	7	1	49	12	51	10	79	26
3,000 to 4,500	10	1	88	22	90	18	133	36
1,000 to 2,700	17	6	300	64	345	77	363	120
500 to 900	64	14						
Total	98	22	437	98	486	105	575	182

For better appreciation of the position of the Hindu nobles, their number may also be stated as a percentage of the total:

	Akbar 1595	*Shahjahan* 1628-58	*Aurangzeb* 1658-78	*Aurangzeb* 1679-1707
5,000 and above	14.3	24.5	19.6	32.9
3,000 to 4,500	10.0	25.0	20.0	27.1
1,000 to 2,700	35.3	21.3	22.3	33.1[2]
500 to 900	21.8			
Total	22.5	22.4	21.6	31.6

[1]S.R. Sharma says in his text (p. 131) that he had found names of 148 Hindu *mansabdars* of 1,000 and above under Aurangzeb, but in his appendix he gives the names of 160. My own lists contain the names of 251 Hindu *mansabdars* of the same category. My lists have been compiled independently and do not give 14 out of the 160 names listed in Sharma's appendix. Of these Pratap shown by Sharma as holder of 5,000 *zat*, was really only an agent of Shambha, who held this rank. (*Dilkusha*, f. 35a-b; *Selected Documents of Aurangzeb's Reign*, p.66). I have grave doubts about some of the others out of these 14 as well, such as Santaji Jadaun (5,000 *zat*) and Raja Jai Singh of Toda (5,000 *zat*). (Raj Singh, *faujdar* of Toda in 1700, only held the rank of 400/300, *Akhbarat*, 18 Shaban, 43 R.Y.)

[2] See Tables 2(*a*) and 2(*b*) at the end of the chapter.

It will be noticed that in the first part of Aurangzeb's reign, the position of Hindu nobles declined slightly, but in the last twenty-nine years it improved appreciably with the result that during this time there were more Hindus in service proportionately than under Shahjahan or, indeed, at any former period.

These tables, would, therefore, provide a fine lawyer's answer to any charge that Aurangzeb discriminated against Hindu *mansabdars.* Yet the matter is not really so simple. The number of Hindus in the period is inflated because of the influx of the Marathas, who began to outnumber the Rajputs in the nobility. They were not recruited to the service on account of a policy of religious tolerance, but had practically forced their way in. Before Aurangzeb's fatal involvement in the Deccan had compelled him to begin admitting Marathas wholesale in order to secure their submission, he had in fact tried to reduce the number of Hindu nobles. This is clear from the figures for 1658-78. As we have seen, the number of the Rajputs began to decline towards the end of this period, and continued to go down in the next. However, not much can be built either way exclusively on these figures, and the fact remains that despite Aurangzeb's avowed policy of religious discrimination, the Hindus continued to form a large section of his nobility.

From the foregoing account it should be clear that a marked expansion of the nobility did not take place till Aurangzeb embarked on the policy of annexing the entire Deccan. As a result of fresh recruitment made during this period, the internal composition of the nobility changed in some material respects. The Deccanis, including the Marathas, came to form a high proportion of the nobility, particularly in the higher ranks. There was a corresponding decline in the position of some of the older elements, such as the Rajputs, Saiyids of Barha, and others. The Turanis and Iranis also lost a little of their previous eminence. The Afghans improved their positions owing to the influx of the Afghan officers who had been previously in the service of Bijapur.

Abul Fazl Mamuri summed up the changes by saying that the *Khanazads* — i.e. nobles belonging to families previously connected with imperial service — were the chief losers. There may be some element of exaggeration in his statement, but our evidence largely bears him out. The new recruits were not admitted primarily on account of their ability and talent but because they already held power in the Deccan and could only be won over by being offered high ranks. Recruitment from the aristocratic families of Central Asia and Persia also continued, but on a much smaller scale. There was very little opportunity for the non-aristocratic educated classes. There may have been a few promotions of scholars like Bakhtawar Khan and Inayatullah Khan, but their number was limited. There was, however, room for adventurers, who first organised their troops and established themselves as chiefs or rulers in areas outside the control of the Empire and then sought to enter imperial service. Many Maratha chiefs offer an excellent illustration of this curious procedure. But in their normal recruitment, the Mughals had no adequate machinery to admit anyone on the basis of talent: family and clan were too often the deciding factors.

TABLE 1 (*a*)

THE PROPORTION OF INDIANS, FOREIGNERS AND DESCENDANTS OF FOREIGNERS AMONGST THE MANSABDARS OF AURANGZEB
1658—1678

Indians	*Foreigners and Descendants of Foreigners*				*Group not known*	*Grand Total*	*Remarks*
	Born in India	*Born outside India*	*Birth Place not known*	*Total number of the foreigners and their descendants*			
Mansabdars of 5,000 and above							
17	14	15	3	32	2	51	Out of 2 *mansabdars* whose group is not known, one was born in India and about the other it is not known whether he was born in India or not.
Mansabdars of 3,000 to 4,500							
38	34	10	4	48	4	90	Out of 4 *mansabdars* whose group is not known, 2 were born in India and about the remaining 2, it is not known whether they were born in India or outside India.
Mansabdars of 1,000 to 2,700							
160	69	30	23	122	63	345	Out of 63 *mansabdars* whose group is not known, 4 were born in India and about the rest it is not known whether they were born in India or not.
215	117	55	30	202	69	486	

TABLE 1 (*b*)

THE PROPORTION OF INDIANS, FOREIGNERS AND DESCENDANTS OF FOREIGNERS AMONGST THE MANSABDARS OF AURANGZEB

1679—1707

Indians	*Foreigners and Descendants of Foreigners*				*Group not known*	*Grand Total*	*Remarks*
	Born in India	*Born outside India*	*Birth place not known*	*Total of the foreigners and their descendants*			
Mansabdars of 5,000 and above							
46	14	6		20	13	79	Out of the 13 *mansabdars* whose group is not known, 3 were born in India and about the remaining ten, it is not known whether they were born in India or outside India.
Mansabdars of 3,000 to 4,500							
58	46	15	1	62	13	133	Out of the 13 *mansabdars* whose group is not known, 4 were born in India and about the remaining 9, it is not known whether they were born in India or outside India.
Mansabdars of 1,000 to 2,700							
181	82	25	8	115	67	363	Out of 67 *mansabdars* whose group is not known, 10 were born in India and about the remaining 57 we cannot say whether they were born in India or outside India.
285	142	46	9	197	93	575	

TABLE 2 (*a*)

RACIAL AND RELIGIOUS COMPOSITION OF AURANGZEB'S NOBILITY
1658 – 1678

Iranis	Turanis	Afghans	Indian Muslims	Other Muslims	Total Muslims	Rajputs	Marathas	Other Hindus	Total Hindus	Grand Total
Mansabdars of 5,000 and above										
23	9	3	4	2	41	6	3	1	10	51
Mansabdars of 3,000 to 4,500										
32	16	9	10	5	72	11	6	1	18	90
Mansabdars of 1,000 to 2,700										
81	42	31	51	63	268	54	18	5	77	345
136	67	43	65	70	381	71	27	7	105	486

TABLE 2(*b*)

RACIAL AND RELIGIOUS COMPOSITION OF AURANGZEB'S NOBILITY
1679 – 1707

Iranis	Turanis	Afghans	Indian Muslims	Other Muslims	Total Muslims	Rajputs	Marathas	Other Hindus	Total Hindus	Grand Total
Mansabdars of 5,000 and above										
14	6	10	10	13	53	5	16	5	26	79
Mansabdars of 3,000 to 4,500										
40	22	4	18	13	97	15	18	3	36	133
Mansabdars of 1,000 to 2,700										
72	44	20	41	66	243	53	62	5	120	363
126	72	34	69	92	393	73	96	13	182	575

TABLE 3(*a*)

KHANAZADS AND ZAMINDARS
1658 – 1678

Descendants of Mansabdars Khanazads	*Not descended from Mansabdars*	*Zamindars*		*Total Zamindars*	*Grand Total*
		Those whose blood relations were in service	*Those who them-selves entered the service*		
Mansabdars of 5,000 and above					
20	24	5	2	7	51
Mansabdars of 3,000 to 4,500					
51	28	10	1	11	90
Mansabdars of 1,000 to 2,700					
103	192	24	26	50	345
174	244	39	29	68	486

TABLE 3(*b*)

KHANAZADS AND ZAMINDARS
1679 – 1707

Descendants of Mansabdars (Khanazads)	*Not descended from Mansabdars*	*Zamindars*		*Total Zamindars*	*Grand Total*
		Those whose blood relations were in service	*Those who them-selves entered the service*		
Mansabdars of 5,000 and above					
18	46	6	9	15	79
Mansabdars of 3,000 to 4,500					
57	56	13	7	20	133
Mansabdars of 1,000 to 2,700					
145	172	33	13	46	363
220	274	52	29	81	575

TABLE 4(*a*)

DECCANIS
1658 – 1678

	Total No. of mansabdars	*Deccanis and South Indians*
Mansabdars of 5,000 and above	51	10
Mansabdars of 3,000 to 4,500	90	13
Mansabdars of 1,000 to 2,700	345	35
	486	58

TABLE 4(*b*)

DECCANIS
1679 – 1707

	Total No. of mansabdars	*Deccanis and South Indians*
Mansabdars of 5,000 and above	79	48
Mansabdars of 3,000 to 4,500	133	34
Mansabdars of 1,000 to 2,700	363	78
	575	160

CHAPTER II

ORGANISATION OF THE NOBILITY — MANSAB, PAY, CONDITIONS OF SERVICE

Evolution of the Mansab System

The term *mansab* (office, position, rank) indicated under the Mughals the position of its holder (*mansabdar*) in the official hierarchy. A *mansab* by itself did not constitute any office; but apart from determining the status of its holder, it also fixed his pay while it laid upon him the obligation of maintaining a definite number of troopers with horses and equipment.

Long before the period of the Indian Mughals, the organisation of the cavalry in large Turkish armies was modelled on the decimal system. Under the Delhi Sultans, the ideal system laid down was that ten horsemen (*sawars*) should be put under one *sar-i khail;* ten *sar-i khails* under one *sipah-salar;* ten *sipah-salars* under one *amir;* ten *amirs* under one *malik;* 10 *maliks* under one *khan;* and at least ten *khans* under the King. Thus a *sar-i khail* would command ten men, a *sipah-salar* 100, an *amir*, 1,000, a *malik*, 10,000, a *khan*, 100,000.[1] This, of course, is a suppositious calculation only, and there is also an error in Barani's account. An Arab account of the 14th century tells us that in the Indian army "the *khan* has under him 10,000 riders, the *malik* 1,000, the *amir* 100, the *sipah-salar* less than that," so that the size of contingents of the officers of the three highest ranks is reduced to one-tenth.[2] In the army of the Chengizi Mongols, from whom the Indian Mughals claimed descent, the smallest unit was that of ten horsemen, ten officers of such units being under 'a commander of 100', 'ten commanders of 100' being under 'a commander of 1,000' and ten 'commanders of 1,000' under one commander of 10,000.[3] A unit of 10,000 was generally called a *tuman*. The basic principle in this system seems to be that the lower officers are direct subordinates of the higher and their contingents form part of the latter's. Thus, if the *khan* in the Delhi Sultanate was supposed to have 10 000

[1] Barani, *Ta'rikh-i Firuz Shahi*, ed. Prof. S. A. Rashid, I, p. 167 (Bib. Ind. Ed., p. 145). Advice of Bughra Khan to Kai-Qubad. Bughra Khan wanted 10 *khans* in the empire, but according to Barani's calculation this would mean an army of one million—a preposterous figure.

[2] Shahabuddin al-Umari, *Masalik-al Absar fi Mamalik-al Amsar*, tr. Spies, Rashid and Haq, p. 28 ; also al-Qalqashandi, *Subh-al A'sha*, extracts translated by Dr Otto Spies as *An Arab Account of the 14th Century*, p. 67.

[3] H.H. Howorth, *History of the Mongols*, Part I, pp. 108-9.

horsemen, these were identical with the contingents of the 10 *maliks* serving under him, and so on.

It has been suggested that the origins of the *mansab* system lay in this 'decimal' system of organisation of armies.[1] There may be some truth in this, but it is important to remember that the *mansabdari* system as instituted by Akbar was different in certain vital respects from the earlier system; and it was both more complex and more manageable.

In the Mughal *mansab* system all *mansabdars* owed direct subordination to the King, whether they commanded 10 *sawars* or 5,000. The distinction between the *Umara* (the higher *mansabdars*) and the rest was purely conventional, and did not affect the system of military organisation. Thus a *mansabdar* of 5,000 did not make up his contingent by having under him 5 *mansabdars* of 1,000 *sawars;* his rank represented his own contingent exclusively. He might have his own subordinate officers to look after various units of his contingent; but such officers could not be *mansabdars*, unless they had their own contingents separate from that of their superior.[2]

Secondly, the Mughal *mansab* was dual, represented by two numbers, one designated *zat* ('personal') and the other *sawar* ('cavalry'). From the closing years of Akbar's reign, the number of the *zat* itself became a fictitious number, the chief use of which, besides indicating the salary according to the pay scale in force, was to place the holder in his appropriate position in the official hierarchy.[3] The *sawar* rank, on the other hand, determined the number of horsemen and horses the *mansabdar* was required to maintain. It may, therefore, be styled the cavalry or military rank. We first meet it in the garb of a second rank in the later years of Akbar.

Now, the germs of the two ranks were present even in the earlier periods, whenever we see a clear deviation from the ideal. Thus Barani quotes Balban as declaring that if a *malik* does not have a full contingent of 10,000, he does not deserve this title.[4] Yet the same historian tells us that *malik* Baq Baq, the Governor of Badaun, had 4,000 troopers (*chakar*); and he makes this statement in a context which suggests that Baq Baq had an exceptionally large contingent.[5] Thus while nominally Baq Baq was a commander of 10,000, he maintained but 4,000 troopers. Moreland has also shown how in the time of the early Mughals, officers with high

[1] See for example, Abdul Aziz, *The Mansabdari System and the Mughal Army*, pp. 16-25.

[2] This might happen when a senior member of a family was given a high *mansab*, and his relations, who were grouped with him, lesser *mansabs*. The total of *mansabs* of the relatives frequently exceeded that of the senior member, so that it is obvious that they were essentially separate ranks, requiring the maintenance of separate contingents.

[3] Moreland, *JRAS*, 1936 p. 647; Abdul Aziz, *The Mansabdari System and the Mughal Army*, p. 93.

[4] Barani, *op. cit.*

[5] Barani, *Tarikh-i Firuz Shahi*, ed. Prof. S.A. Rashid, I, p. 48.

titles seldom maintained contingents corresponding to their titles, and he has suggested that Akbar's dual ranks were designed to meet this situation.[1] The nominal rank was confined to the *zat* rank, so as to determine the hierarchical position of the various nobles. But to see that there was a proper check on maintenance of contingents according to the salary or income granted to each noble, a *sawar* rank was instituted which was always either equal to or less than the *zat* rank.[2]

While the basic elements of Akbar's *mansabdari* system were retained in the 17th century, certain new features also appeared. Thus under Jahangir, we first hear of the *du-aspa sih-aspa* rank; under Shahjahan we have new scales of pay, 'month-ratios' and new regulations prescribing the sizes of contingents under various *sawar* ranks. On these and other features, such as conditional (*mashrut*) ranks, which might have existed under Akbar as well, our information becomes very extensive under Aurangzeb. In the following pages we shall first treat of the ranks, the method and scales of pay, and, then, the military obligations imposed upon the *mansabdars*.

ZAT AND SAWAR RANKS

In the time of Akbar, as we have already remarked, the *sawar* rank was normally either equal to or lower than the *zat* rank. This, broadly speaking, continued to be the position under his successors. Abdul Aziz has cited five instances where the *sawar* rank was higher than the *zat* rank, but he is of the opinion that these are errors of transcription.[3] During the second half of Aurangzeb's reign, however, there were quite a large number of *mansabdars*, whose *sawar* rank was higher than their *zat* rank.[4] In some instances, it is true, the *sawar* rank was conditional (*mashrut*); and in the Jaipur *Akhbarat* we find a larger number of instances

[1] "Rank (*mansab*) in the Mughal State Service"; *JRAS*, 1936, pp. 641-65. For the introduction of the *mansab* under Akbar, see A. J. Qaisar, *Proc. Ind. Hist. Cong.* Delhi session 1961, pp. 155-56.

[2] Abul Fazl says, "For this cause (to help him) did His Majesty establish the ranks (*mansab*) of *mansabdars* from the *dahbashi* (Commander of ten) to *dahhazari* (Commander of ten thousand) limiting however all commands above five thousand to his august sons...The monthly grants to the *mansabdars* vary according to their contingents (*sawars*). An officer whose contingent (*sawar*) comes up to his *mansab* is put in the first class of his rank. If his contingent (*sawar*) is one half and upwards (of the *mansab*) he is put in the second class, the third class contains those contingents which are still less." *Ain-i Akbari*, Vol. I, pp. 123-24. Tr. Blochmann, ed. Phillot, p. 248. *Akbar Nama* puts this classification under the year 1003 A. H. (A.D. 1595)

This principle for sub-classification of each *zat* rank is also given in the *Khulasat-us Siyaq* f. 48b; and *Mirat-al Istilah*, 15a-15b.

According to the author of *Mirat-al Istilah*, a *mansabdar* who held a rank below 500 was not given the *sawar* rank. (f. 15b). But there are innumerable instances of the *sawar* rank being granted to persons holding *zat* ranks below 500 throughout the 17th century.

[3] Abdul Aziz. '*The Mansabdari System and the Mughal Army*', p. 3.

[4] See Appendix 'A' at the end of the chapter.

where the ordinary rank *plus* the conditional *sawar* rank was higher than the *zat* rank.[1] But there are also many instances where the *sawar* rank was not wholly or partly conditional, and yet was higher than the *zat* rank.[2] The fact that the *sawar* rank rose above the *zat* rank in a fairly large number of cases, particularly during the later years of Aurangzeb's reign, may have been partly due to the scarcity of able and experienced officers,[3] which led the emperor to assign larger contingents to persons on whose efficiency he could rely; considerations of economy may also have induced the Emperor to raise the forces maintained by the nobles without increasing their *zat* rank in proportion. But whatever may have been the causes of allowing the *sawar* rank to exceed the *zat* rank, the practice was apparently limited. Also it did not usually apply to the higher ranks of the *mansabdars*. It was not a basic or deliberate reform, the device being employed only where expediency dictated it.

Conditional Rank ('mashrut')

Conditional (*mashrut*) ranks were usually added to the previous *zat* and *sawar* ranks. According to the author of the *Mirat-al Istilah*, the unconditional *sawar mansab* was given along with the *zat* rank, and the 'conditional' *mansab* was given in view of the services required of a particular officer at a particular post. For example, if a *mansabdar* was appointed as *faujdar* of a particular area, and it was felt that for the satisfactory discharge of his duties an additional 100 *sawar* rank was required by him, then the *mansab* of the *faujdar* was conditionally increased so as to enable him to employ 100 *sawars*, and a *jagir* to provide the salary of this rank was also given to him. When he was transferred from the post, the conditional *mansab* was normally cancelled and the additional *jagir* resumed.[4] Sometimes the whole or a part of a conditional *mansab*

[1] Rawat Mal Jhala, was appointed as *qal'adar* and *faujdar* of Beni Shah Dark alias Prakash Garh and was given the conditional promotion of 200 *sawars*, so ultimately his rank became 700/900 (*Akhbarat*, 4th Moharram, 45th R.Y.). Kartalab Khan, *diwan* of Bengal and *faujdar* of Makhsusabad, was also appointed *faujdar* of Bardwan and Medni Pur and was given the conditional promotion of 500 *sawars*, so ultimately he had the rank of 900/1,000 (26th Safar, 45th R.Y.) Shuja'at Khan, the *subedar* of Gujrat, was also appointed *faujdar* of Jodhpur and was given the conditional promotion of 4,000 *sawars*, so ultimately his rank became 5,000/8,000 (Mirat-i Ahmadi, Vol. I, p. 317).

[2] It may be argued that where the *sawar* rank was higher than the *zat* rank, it was either *mashrut*, or included *du-aspa sih-aspa* (2×3h) rank. Thus, 1,000/1,200 might mean 1,000/1,000 (200×2-3h). However, this argument cannot be accepted without definite proof. The *Akhbarat* generally mention the number of *du aspa sih aspa* separately in describing the rank of a *mansabdar*.

[3] Thus in the *Raqaim-i Karaim* Aurangzeb regrets that efficient persons were not available, f. 6a; *Dilkusha*, f. 139a; *Kalmat-i Taiyabat*, f. 21a, 83a, 97b, 135b, 135b; *Waqa-i Ajmer*, p. 645.

[4] *Mirat-al Istilah*, f. 14b. Muzaffar, son of Sher Babi, was given a conditional rank of 400/400 for the duration of his appointment to the *faujdari* of Pargana Katri etc. (*Mirat-i Ahmadi* Vol. I, pp. 289-90). Conditional *mansab* of Rad Andaz Khan was cancelled when he was

was made unconditional, but this was considered a promotion and usually given as a mark of favour.[1]

THE DU-ASPA SIH-ASPA RANK

As has been mentioned above, the reign of Jahangir saw an important innovation in the *mansabdari* system, viz. the introduction of the *du-aspa sih-aspa* rank. In the 10th year of Jahangir's reign, when Mahabat Khan was appointed to serve in the Deccan, as a mark of special distinction 1,700 *sawars* out of his rank were made *du-aspa sih-aspa*.[2] This is the earliest instance mentioned of the *du-aspa sih-aspa* rank being granted to any noble. While there are only a few recorded cases of *du-aspa sih-aspa* rank being granted during the reign of Jahangir, they came to be granted quite frequently during Shahjahan's reign. This can be seen from the following table of *mansabdars* of the rank of 1,000 *zat* and above holding such ranks :

	Total	*Holders of du-aspa sih-aspa ranks*
10th year of the Reign[3]	191	12
20th year of the Reign[4]	219	23
30th year of the Reign[5]	253	25

In Aurangzeb's reign, the number of the recipients of this rank increased further. During the first twenty years of his reign there were not

---

transferred from the *faujdari* of Lonar etc. (*Akhbarat*, 23rd Safar, 36th R.Y. of Aurangzeb). Conditional *mansab* of Shaikh Anwar was cancelled when he was transferred from the *qal'adari* and *faujdari* of Ram Nagar (2nd Shaban, 37 R.Y.). Conditional promotion of Shuja 'at Khan was cancelled, (*Mirat-i Ahmadi*,, Vol. I, p. 317). Conditional promotion of Muhammad Beg was cancelled (*Akhbarat*, 8th Zilhij, 43 R.Y.). Conditional promotion of Aurang Khan was cancelled when he was transferred from the *faujdari* of Dhawar (18th Rajab, 46 R.Y.). Conditional *mansab* of Wali Dad Khan was cancelled when he was transferred from the *qal 'adari* of Dev Durk (13th Rabi, II, 38 R.Y.).

[1] The conditional *sawars* of Himmat Yar, the *faujdar* of Silhat were made unconditional (*Akhbarat*, 16th Zilhij, 38 R.Y.). 300 *sawars* out of the conditional *mansab* of Muhammad Salih were made unconditional, when he was appointed as *faujdar* of Fatehpur Sikri (28th Zilhij, 45 R.Y.). Rawat Mal Jhala was appointed *qal 'adar* and *faujdar* of Parnala and had the *mansab* of 700/700, out of which 300/200 were unconditional and the rest were conditional (4th Moharram, 45th R.Y.). 200 conditional *sawars* out of the rank of Khuda Band Khan were made unconditional (11th Ramzan, 45th R.Y.).

[2] *Tuzuk*, p. 147. (But Mahabat Khan failed to discharge his duties properly. So the additional grant of *du-aspa sih-aspa* was withdrawn and the additional salary attached to it was cancelled, p. 190). However, in the 19th R.Y. of Jahangir, Mahabat Khan was given the *mansab* of 7,000/7,000 (2-3h) (*Tuzuk*, Mirza Hadis' continuation, p. 391). Asaf Khan was given the rank of 7.000/7,000 (2-3h) towards the end of Jahangir's reign; *Badshah Nama*, Vol. I, p. 113.

[3] Lahori, *Badshah Nama*, vol. I, pp. 292-312.

[4] Lahori, *Badshah Nama*, Vol. II, pp. 717-37.

[5] Waris, *Badshah Nama*, Or. 1675, ff. 200a—214a.

less than 68 *mansabdars* who held the *du-aspa sih-aspa* rank out of a total number of 486 *mansabdars* of 1,000 *zat* and above. In the remaining part of Aurangzeb's reign, 70 out of 575 *mansabdars* of 1,000 *zat* and above are recorded as holding this rank.[1]

The *du-aspa sih-aspa* rank was theoretically regarded as a part of the *sawar* rank. The usual official formula for stating the rank, is, for example, "4,000 *zat* 4,000 *sawar* all (*hama*) *du-aspa sih-aspa*" which would mean 4,000/4,000+4,000; or 4,000 *zat*, 4,000 *sawar*, of which 1,000 *du-aspa sih-aspa*, i.e. 4,000/4,000+1,000. It could therefore, never exceed the *sawar* rank. If any portion of the *sawar* rank became *du-aspa sih-aspa*, the rest of the rank was termed *barawurdi*. That is, if out of 4,000 *sawars*, 1,000 were *du-aspa sih-aspa*, the remaining 3,000 were *barawurdi*.[2] For the latter portion the noble was paid at the same rate as for the ordinary rank and his obligations were also on the same scale, while for the *du-aspa sih-aspa*, his pay and obligations both were doubled. In other words, from the point of view of pay and military obligations, the rank of 4,000 *sawar*, of whom 1,000 were *du-aspa sih-aspa*, really meant 5,000 *sawars* (i.e. 3,000 ordinary+1,000 2−3h=3,000 ordinary +1, 000 × 2 ordinary =5,000 ordinary). From this it may be deduced that when the emperor wanted to favour a man or desired that he should maintain a larger contingent without raising his *zat* rank (which had usually to be higher than the *sawar*), he did so by granting a *du-aspa sih-aspa* rank.[3]

Pay For The Ranks

The nobility of the Mughals depended practically for all its income on the pay it received from the State, whether in the form of cash or *jagirs*. The pay each noble received was determined by the *mansab* or rank he held. Sometimes, nobles were assigned additional pay as *inam*,[4] but this payment could be regarded as being only supplementary to the amount paid against *mansabs*. A *mansab*, as we have already noticed, was always dual, *zat* and *sawar*. The *sawar* rank itself came to be supplemented in the case of some by an additional rank of the same genus, known as *du-aspa sih-aspa*. Each of these ranks separately entitled its holder to make a claim, known as *talab*, for definite amounts of pay, which was laid down by the established scales.[5]

[1] Based on information set out in the Appendix at the end of the book.

[2] For the use of the term *barawurdi*, see *Selected Documents of Shahjahan's Reign*, pp. 138, 141, 159, 160, 208; Lahori, ii, p. 507; *Ilm-i Navisindgi*, f. 146a; *Selected Documents of Aurangzeb's Reign*, pp. 5, 6, 10, 47, 102, 103, 111, 121, ff. Cf. Moreland, *JRAS*, 1936, pp. 662-64.

[3] Cf. *Mirat-al Istilah*, f. 15b.

[4] Cf. the case of Mirza Raja Jai Singh, *Alamgir Nama*, p. 618.

[5] The subject has been clearly discussed so far by Moreland *JRAS*, 1963, pp. 661-65. Moreland's study was based mainly on some Jaipur records. A number of documents printed in the *Selected Documents of Shahjahan's Reign*, specially, pp. 64, 73, 79-84, 109-113, 150-52, 175-177,

Before examining the broad principles on which these pay scales were formulated, we should bear in mind the fact that the *zat* rank was basically personal while the *sawar* rank (and the supplementary *du-aspa sih-aspa* rank) fixed the contingents to be maintained by the nobles. It follows, therefore, that while the pay for the first rank was chiefly meant to provide the recipient the wherewithal to maintain himself and his family, and the cost of his personal establishment, payments on the second and third items were meant to meet the expenses of his contingents. Thus, in making out the pay certificates, the pay on the former account was termed *Khasah* (personal) and the latter *tabinan* (contingent or followers).[1] The sanctioned schedules of pay for the different ranks from the time of Akbar onwards are available, and these can also be supplemented by numerous references to the calculation of the pay of individual nobles.[2] In accordance with the purpose for which the salary was paid, the scales for each category of ranks display certain features which may be noted.

(*i*) The salary for the *zat* rank is stated separately for each rank, since the pay fixed for one number of *zat* rank usually bore no arithmetical proportion to another *zat* rank. The salary did not rise proportionately as one proceeded to higher ranks. Secondly, below the rank of 5,000 the pay for *zat* rank was fixed differently for three categories: first, when the *sawar* rank was equal to, or not less than half the *zat* rank; second, when the *sawar* rank was half the *zat* rank; and third, when it was less than half. The pay for the first grade was higher than that for the second, and higher for the second than for the third.

(*ii*) The salary for the *sawar* rank is not given separately for each rank, but the rate is invariably stated per unit of the *sawar* rank. To calculate the pay due on any *sawar* rank, one has to multiply this amount by the number of the rank. This method of calculation becomes understandable when we remember that what we are considering here are the 'contract rates' for maintaining the required contingents. The amount paid on an average to ten horsemen would be ten times that paid to one, and, therefore, the pay for higher ranks had to increase in exact arithmetical proportion.

(*iii*) The *du-aspa sih-aspa* rank was regarded as part of the *sawar* rank[3] with this peculiarity that the obligation for the number covered by this

fully bear out the description given by Moreland of the method of calculating the pay due and the significance of the term *talab*.

[1] See *Selected Documents of Shahjahan's Reign*, pp. 109-12, 176.

[2] *Ain*, I, pp. 124-31. The *Farhang-i Kardani*, ff. 43-49, reproduces the scales issued in the 9th year of Shahjahan's reign by Afzal Khan; the *Selected Documents*, pp. 79-84, contain a schedule issued in the 14th year by Islam Khan, and *Dastur-al Amal-i Alamgiri*, ff. 121-23, a schedule issued by Sadullah Khan in the same reign. To Aurangzeb's reign belong pay schedules contained in the *Zawabit-i Alamgiri*, ff. 42b-45b, *Halat-i Mumalik-i Mahrusa-i Alamgiri*, ff. 149b-51b. The scales are set out in tabular form in appendix 'B' at the end of this chapter.

[3] We have 5,000 *zat*, 4,000 *sawar* all of which (*hama*) *du-aspa sih-aspa*.

rank was double the obligation for the ordinary rank.[1] The pay for it had, therefore, to be double that of the ordinary rank. For example, if the rank of a *mansabdar* was 3,000 *sawar* of which 1,000 were *du-aspa sih-aspa*, and 8,000 *dams* was the rate per unit of *sawar* rank, the pay would be calculated as follows:

3,000 *sawar* rank of which 1,000 are *du-aspa sih-aspa.* Therefore, there are 2,000 *barawurdi* (ordinary) *sawars* whose pay would be 2,000 × 8,000 = 16,000,000 *dams*. And 1,000 *du-aspa sih-aspa* whose pay would be 1,000 × 8,000 × 2 = 16,000,000 *dams*. Total 32,000,000 *dams*.[2]

The salary for the *sawar* rank would thus always be substantially higher than the pay for the *zat* rank of the same number, for the simple reason that while the former was meant to provide funds for the maintenance of the troops, the latter was the personal salary of the noble.

While in the *Ain* the salaries are given in terms of rupees, the later scales state them in terms of *dams*.[3] The *jama* or the figure at which each *pargana* was assessed for purposes of assignment (*jagir*) in lieu of pay, was worked out in terms of *dams* from the time of Akbar onwards and it must have appeared best to state the pay schedules in the same unit of money (the *dam*) as the *jagir* assessments.

Moreland has shown how the pay for both the *zat* and *sawar* ranks was gradually reduced between the time of Akbar and Shahjahan.[4] There is considerable evidence in various documents and manuals of the period, which were not available to Moreland but which corroborate his conclusions. It is, therefore, not necessary for us to go into this matter in detail. The scales fixed by Shahjahan are available to us in no less than three

[1] Cf. Lahori, *Badshah Nama*, II, p. 507.

[2] The statement that the *du-aspa sih-aspa* rank was paid at double the rate of *barawurdi* or at 16,000 *dams* per unit of the rank, is made in *Dastur-al Amal-iIlm-i Navisindgi*, Add. 6599. f. 146a. Moreland, (*JRAS*, 1936, p. 662) refers to a *farman* in the Jaipur Records where a calculation is made on this basis. One can similarly deduce this from cases wherever the total salary of *mansabdars* holding *du-aspa sih-aspa* rank is mentioned, e.g. Lahori, *Badshah Nama*, II, 258, 321, 715; Salih, III, p. 246. It may be noticed that the *du-aspa sih-aspa* rank was supposed to carry pay at double the ordinary rate simply because the number of the rank was deducted from the *sawar* rank. Otherwise the result would be the same if one were to regard it as an additional rank paid at the same rate. That is, in our hypothetical case, if we were to add the *du-aspa sih-aspa* rank to the *sawar* rank and multiply the number so obtained, viz. 4,000 by the flat rate of 8,000 *dams*, the total would be the same—32,000,000 *dams*. Thus in Salih, III, p. 112, the conversion of 1,000 *sawar* into *du-aspa sih-aspa* in the case of Jai Singh is shown to result in an addition of 8,000,000 *dams* (1,000 × 8,000) to his total pay.

[3] Cf. Manucci, II, pp. 374-5. "When the King fixes or gives orders about the allowance of a *mansabdar* or an *omara*, he does not talk of rupee but of *dams*, which is a money of account of which they make forty go to the rupee." In a country with a bimetallic currency, the value of the coins of the two metals would be constantly changing; so for official purposes the currency was made monometallic based on the silver rupee. Whatever its value in copper currency at any time, the silver rupee was considered to be equal to forty *dams*. This *dam* (*dam-i tankhwahi*) was, of course, a non-existent copper coin. The real copper coins circulated for what they were worth.

[4] *JRAS*, 1936, pp. 641-65.

authorities,[1] while schedules giving similar scales belonging to the time of Aurangzeb are still more numerous.[2] It appears from a study of the *Dastur-al Amals* of Aurangzeb's reign that the scales fixed by Shahjahan were continued by Aurangzeb without any alterations whatsoever. The detailed figures of pay for the *zat* ranks are the same, while for the *sawar* ranks payment continued to be made at the rate of 8,000 *dams* per unit. A comparative table showing the figures for various *zat* ranks in schedules belonging to the two reigns is given in an appendix at the end of the chapter.

MONTH-SCALES

A feature which appeared first in the reign of Shahjahan, but soon became all-pervasive, was the institution of month-scales or ratios. This seems to have arisen out of the difference between the official assessment of *jagir* (*jama*) and the actual revenue collection (*hasil*).[3]

Thus when a man obtained a *jagir* whose *jama* equalled his annual salary-claim (*talab*) on paper, he might in actual fact find it yielding him only one-half or one-fourth of his claim. In such cases the *jagir* might be known respectively as *shashmaha* (six monthly) or *sih maha* (three monthly).[4] Where the *jama* greatly exceeded the actual realisation, the *jagir* would be very low in the month-scale. In the later years of Shahjahan the actual *hasil* of the Mughal Deccan amounted to about one quarter of the *jama* (i.e. equal to three months only).[5] The *jagirs* of most *mansabdars* in the Deccan were accordingly not more than four-monthly and often even less.[6] Conditions seem to have been better in Northern India. In the later years of Shahjahan and in the reign of Aurangzeb, we hear of complaints that a transfer from Northern India to the Deccan entailed a *jagir* on a lower month-scale.[7]

The month system was applied also to cash salaries. Naturally a person having a five month *jagir* could not be paid a full '12-monthly' salary whenever he was made a *naqdi*. Shahjahan, in a *farman* issued in the 27th R.Y., declares that cash salaries (*tankhwah-i naqdi*) were never to be fixed above 'eight-monthly' or below '4-monthly' rates. An exception was made only in the case of the two highest nobles of the

[1] & [2] See appendix 'B'.

[3] See the chapter on '*jagirdari*'.

[4] See Irfan Habib, *The Agrarian System of Mughal India*, 264-5 and *n*. When Lahori, II, 507, lists the military obligations of nobles according to month ratios, he speaks of their *jagirs* being 12- monthly or 11- monthly and so on.

[5] *Adab-i Alamgiri*, ff. 25b, 18b-19a; 24b; *Selected Documents of Aurangzeb's Reign*, p. 115.

[6] *Adab-i Alamgiri*, f. 25b; *Ruq'at-i Alamgir*, 116-17. Elsewhere it is said that the *jagirs* of most of the *mansabdars* in the Deccan were either 4- monthly or less. (*Adab*, f. 33a-b); *Ruq'at-i Alamgir*, 129.

[7] *Adab-i Alamgiri*, ff. 35b, 36b, 40a-40b, 43a; *Ruq'at-i Alamgir*, 88, 136-37; *Selected Documents of Aurangzeb's Reign*, p. 84.

empire, besides princes of royal blood, who received their pay on a '10-monthly' scale.[1]

In the case of the *hasil* realised from his *jagir* by an assignee, the proportion it bore to the *jama* would, of course, only roughly correspond with the exact proportion of the month-scale. A *jagirdar* would seldom recover just exactly 5/12 or 7/12 of his paper salary. In cash payments, however, the month-proportion would be exactly followed. Certain manuals contain a table showing the amount to be paid to a *mansabdar* receiving cash salary under each month-ratio in rupees and annas (the actual currency), if his annual paper salary was one lac *dams*.[2]

12-months	*11-months*	*10-months*	*9-months*
Rs. 2,500	Rs. 2291/10½	Rs. 2,083/5¼	Rs. 1875
8-months	*7-months*	*6-months*	*5-months*
Rs. 1,666/10½	Rs. 1,458/5¼	Rs. 1,250	Rs. 1,041/10½
4-months	*3-months*	*2-months*	*1-month*
Rs. 833/5¼	Rs. 625	Rs. 416/10½	Rs. 208/5¼

In the *Zawabit-i Alamgiri* similar tables are given also for cases where the salary was 100 *dams*, 1,000 *dams* and 10,000 *dams*. In all these tables the exact arithmetical proportions have been followed. The *Khulasat-us Siyaq* gives the annual pay for each month-ratio sanctioned for various *zat* ranks.

It is explicitly stated in one manual that the tables given above apply only to pay due on *zat* ranks of the *naqdis*. For their *sawar* rank (*tabinan*) payment was made for various month-rates according to an altogether different scale. This scale is given under the heading '*tabinan*' and reads as follows :[3]

12-months	*11-months*	*10-months*	*9-months*
Per head (*fi-nafar*) per month Rs.40/-	Per head per month Rs. 37/8	Per head per month Rs. 35/-	Per head per month Rs. 32/8

[1] *Mirat-i Ahmadi*, I, 228. In his 21st R.Y. Aurangzeb ordered that the *naqdis* should no longer be paid on a '8-monthly or 7-monthly' basis; only the '6- months' scale was sanctioned. (*Ma'asir-i Alamgiri*, p. 160).

[2] *Zawabit-i Alamgiri*, ff. 41b-45b; *Halat-i Mumalik-i Mahrusa-i Alamgiri*, ff. 149a-151b; *Farhang-i Kardani*, ff. 43-49; Bodl. O.390 f. 40a (reference given by Dr Irfan Habib). Cf. also *Khulasat-us Siyaq*, ff. 49b-50a. There are some discrepancies in the figures in these manuals, but they appear to have arisen entirely out of errors of transcription.

[3] Bodl. 0.390 f. 42a-43a. The table in *Farhang-i Kardani*, f. 24a-b, reproduces a table identical with this down to six-months. Then it reads as follows: 5-months Rs. 20/13; 4-months Rs. 16/10; 3-months Rs. 12/7-1/2. It does not go any further; *Zawabit-i Alamgiri*, ff. 45b-46b; *Mumalik-i Mahrusa-i Alamgiri*, ff. 151b-152a.

8-months	*7-months*	*6-months*	*5-months*
Per head per month Rs. 30/-	Per head per month Rs. 27/8	Per head per month Rs. 25/-	Per head per month Rs. 22/8
4-months	*3-months*	*2-months*	*1-month*
Per head per month Rs. 20/-	Per head per month Rs. 17/8	Per head per month Rs. 15/-	Per head per month Rs. 12/8

The significance of this table can be understood only when we refer to the *farman* issued by Shahjahan in his 27th year. This order declares : "Whereas it has been represented to the Court that the nobles (*umara'*) and *mansabdars*, who receive cash instead of *jagirs* are paid for each horse branded (*asp daghi*) after deducting the difference for the seven *rasad* horses of *jagirdars*, rupees thirty in case of '8-months', '7-months' and '6-months'; and in five-months and four-months rupees twenty-six, it has been decreed that it is not reasonable to pay Rs.30/– for '8-months', or fall below '4-months', we have determined that from the beginning of the solar month of Mihr to the end of Isfandarmuz of this year, the branding according to the established Rule of One-fifth (i.e. whereby cavalry to the fifth of the number of the *sawar* rank had to be maintained) should be followed, paying per horse, Rs.30/- for '8-months', Rs.27/8 for '7-months', Rs.25/- for '6-months', Rs.22/8 for '5-months' and Rs.20/- for '4-months,."[1] This may be read along with a letter of Aurangzeb written in the 29th year of Shahjahan which quotes an imperial order to the effect that the pay for '3-months' and '2-months' for which Rs.17/8 and Rs.15/- have respectively been sanctioned (elsewhere) has been fixed (in the case of the Deccan) from the beginning of the month of Mihr, Kharif Yunt Il, at Rs.20/- per head per month, i.e. at the same rate as for '4-months'.[2]

From this evidence, the following points are established. First, those receiving cash salaries were not paid in the year for their *sawar* rank a sum equal to the number of the *sawar* rank multiplied by 8,000 *dams* as was done in case of those who were assigned *jagirs*. On the other hand, the method was, first, to determine the contingent which the *mansabdar* was required to maintain according to his *sawar* rank. In case of *naqdis* this was fixed under 'the Rule of One-fifth'. Then the number of *sawars* so fixed was multiplied by the rate of rupees forty per month being paid under the '12-monthly' scale. For those placed in the lower month-scales, the rate per *sawar* was reduced, but not in

[1] *Mirat-i Ahmadi*, I, pp. 227-28.

[2] *Adab-i Alamgiri*, ff. 33a-33b, *Ruq'at-i Alamgir*, p. 129.

the same proportion as that of the respective number of the months to twelve. It is these rates which have been reproduced in the table above and form the subject of Shahjahan's *farman*.

The details of men and horses required of *mansabdars* under the "Rule of the One-fifth" are available to us in the *Badshah Nama* and *Khulasat-us Siyaq*.[1] By working from these and using the table above, we can arrive at the pay due to the *naqdi* of any *sawar* rank on any month-scale. The second column in the table below shows the pay of *naqdi* holders of 100 *sawar* arrived at by this means. In the third column is given the pay calculated from rates established previous to Shahjahan's 27th year (7-4 month) and those continued in the Deccan subsequently (3-2 months). The fourth shows the pay calculated on the basis of the rate of 8,000 *dams* per unit of *sawar* rank, the figures for each month representing exact arithmetical proportions.

I	II	III	IV
12-months	Rs. 21,120		Rs. 20,000 (=8,00,000 *dams*)
11	18,000		18,333
10	15,120		16,666
9	12,480		15,000
8	10,440	Rs. 10,440	13,333
7	8,250	9,000	11,666
6	6,600	7,920	10,000
5	5,400	6,240	8,333
4	3,840	4,992	6,666
3	2,520	2,880	5,000
2	1,440	1,920	3,333
1	600	—	1,666

A curious feature revealed by this table is that the pay was higher per horse for the *naqdis* placed in higher month-scales than for those in the lower. The situation for the lower categories was better before Shahjahan's order of the 27th year as indicated by figures in column III. One can also understand why Aurangzeb as Viceroy of the Deccan should have so strongly urged the modification of this order, and be so grateful when Shahjahan made an exemption in the case of the Deccan for those placed in the 2 and 3 months-scales.[2] Aurangzeb as Emperor appears, however, to have forgotten his own pleas as Viceroy, and as the table we have reproduced proves, continued the new scale established by Shahjahan. The pay schedule from 12 to 7 months, however, came to be merely of academic interest, since Aurangzeb decided, in his 21st year, to lower Shahjahan's maximum allowance of 8-months to 6-months for all *naqdis*.[3]

[1] See the section on Military Obligation of *mansabdars*, infra p. 47.
[2] *Adab-i Alamgiri*, 33a-33b; *Ruq'at-i Alamgir*, p. 129.
[3] *Ma'asir-i Alamgiri*, p. 160.

Deductions from Pay

As against the sanctioned claim (*muqarrara talab*) there used to be a number of deductions. The largest was made in the case of 'Dakhinis', i.e. Bijapuri, Haiderabadi and Maratha officers, who took service with the Mughals. Their total salary due on both their ranks was first calculated and then a fourth part of it was deducted, *jagirs* or cash-pay being assigned for the remainder only. This deduction was known as '*waza-i dam-i chauthai*' or '*Deduction of one-fourth in Dams*'. This deduction was already established in the time of Shahjahan and was continued by Aurangzeb.[1]

The *chauthai* was a deduction applying only to a particular section of the nobility. There was, however, a charge not perhaps of the same magnitude, but still quite substantial, which applied to all nobles unless specifically exempted. This comprised a number of items, grouped together collectively under *khurak-i dawwab* ('fodder for beasts'). Originally it seems to have been merely an obligation to maintain certain number of elephants, horses, camels and carts belonging to the Emperor. The number was regulated according to the *zat* rank of the officer. In the *Ain*, a full scale of the numbers to be maintained is set out under each rank.[2] Though the term *khurak-i dawwab* is not to be found in Abul Fazl, it is obvious that he refers to the same obligations. In an manual of Aurangzeb's reign we find a reference to this term as meaning fodder for animals, which are put in the charge of the nobles.[3] The number of animals (horses and elephants) fed by officers of each rank is actually specified.[4]

From entrusting animals to the nobles the next step was to keep the animals in the imperial stables and to demand that the nobles pay for feeding them there.[5] Thus in the tables referred to above, besides the number of animals, the standard cost for feeding each is also specified. By the time of Shahjahan it had apparently become the practice to deduct the cost of the *khurak* or *rasad-i khurak* from the *talab* or salary demand of the noble.[6] In Aurangzeb's reign, however, we find that the practice was

[1] For this deduction, see *Zawabit-i Alamgiri*, f. 43b., in *Selected Documents of Aurangzeb's Reign*, pp. 63-64, an imperial decision of the 11th year is set out to the effect that the *chauthai* was to be deducted from the pay of all those who had served under Bijapur and Haiderabad (Golkunda) governments, even if they had originally come from Persia. See also Abul Fazl Mamuri, f. 156b where he speaks of the deduction of a fourth part from the pay of the Deccanis, i.e. all those people who were the servants of Shambha and the Bijapuris and Haiderabadis, who joined imperial service. For the deduction of *chauthai* in the reign of Shahjahan, see *Selected Documents of Shahjahan's Reign*, pp. 2, 18; *Adab-i Alamgiri*, f. 25b.

[2] *Ain*, I, pp. 124-131; cf. Abdul Aziz, *The Mansabdari System and the Mughal Army*, pp. 50-57.

[3] Bodl. Fraser 86, f. 75b.

[4] *Ilm-i Navisindgi*, f. 146a-147a.

[5] Cf. Manucci, II, 372-73.

[6] *Selected Documents of Shahjahan's Reign*, p. 1; *Ilm-i Navisindgi*, f. 147a.

of assigning the *jagirs* for the full salary and then demanding the *khurak* in kind or cash; *sazavals* or imperial messengers used to be sent to exact it from the *jagirdars*.[1] This seems to have been greatly resented by the nobles. In the 46th R.Y. of Aurangzeb's reign, the Emperor consented to abolish the system in respect of the *khurak* for elephants. Now this charge was to be again converted into *dams*, and *jagirs* with equivalent *jama* were to be taken away from the *jagirdars*, freeing them from the obligation of obtaining supplies or paying in cash for the animals.[2] In the next reign the measure was extended to cover the whole of the *khurak-i dawwab* to the great relief of all the *mansabdars*.[3]

The *khurak-i dawwab* was not imposed under the rules on any officer drawing 14 lacs of *dams* or less, nor on those who had no *sawar* ranks or held ranks below 400 *zat* or 200 *sawar*.[4] Apart from this, individual officers could sometimes be exempted by the emperor from this obligation.[5]

There was another deduction technically known as *irmas*. This, according to Badauni, was another name for *talab-i ijnas* (or demand for supplies).[6] Ilahadad Faizi in his dictionary states that *ijnas* was a term used in Akbar's Government for all that was given to the troops apart from cash and their salary, and he follows Badauni in identifying it with *irmas*.[7] Apparently this payment-in-kind was valued and deducted from the salary.[8] From what Abul Fazl says in the *Ain*, it would appear that this was a deduction against which the emperor presented horses to the nobles.[9] In a salary statement of Shahjahan's reign, this deduction is coupled with *rasad-i khurak* and *chauthai*, the two other important deductions.[10]

From the salaries paid in cash to *naqdis*, there were a number of deductions such as the *du-dami* (i.e. 2 *dams* in the rupee) amounting to 5 per cent.[11]

In addition to these deductions, there were fines or *jurmana*. These were imposed for various reasons, but mostly for deficiencies in the contin-

[1] Letters of Ali Quli Khan, *Matin-al Insha*, Bodl. MS. ff. 71a-72a, 74a-74b. When in the 37th year, a noble prayed for exemption from the charge, Aurangzeb ordered apparently as a concession that 'the *dam* (of the *khurak*) be deducted from his *jagir*'. (*Akhbarat*, 3rd Rabi I, 37th R.Y.).

[2] *Akhbarat*, 3 Rabi I, 46 R.Y.

[3] Khafi Khan, II, 602-03.

[4] *Ilm-i Navisindgi*, ff. 146a-147a; Fraser 86, ff. 75b-76a.

[5] *Ma'asir-i 'Alamgiri*, p. 86; *Akhbarat*, 15th Safar, 36 R.Y.; 28 Ziqada, 28 Rabi I, R.Y. 38; 13 Rabi II, 39 R.Y.; 2nd Safar 43 R.Y.; 27 Rabi II, 46 R.Y.

[6] *Badauni*, II p. 202.

[7] *Madar-ul Afazil*, ed. Dr Muhammad Baqar, Lahore, A. H. 1334, p. 55. (where *irmas* has, however, been misread as Aznas).

[8] Cf. Bernier, pp. 215-6, who refers to *ijnas* as "Agenas"

[9] *Ain*, Vol. I, pp. 132.

[10] *Selected Documents of Shahjahan's Reign*, 1-2.

[11] *Selected Documents of Shahjahan's Reign*, 26, 27, 64, 70; *Zawabit-i Alamgiri*, p. 37b; *Selected Documents of Aurangzeb's Reign*, pp. 241-42.

gents required from the nobles. If more than a fourth of the cavalrymen were entered as '*fauti*' (dead) or *firari* (fled), that is, if more than 1/4 of the persons were new recruits since the last muster, the noble had to pay a fine of 4 *muhars* for each *sawar* so presented. For any deficiency in horses, a fine of 2 *muhars* per horse was charged.[1]

The emperor sometimes used to order advances to be made to *mansabdars*, especially while on expeditions. This was known as *masaidat*. In the Balkh and Badakhshan campaigns, for example, sums of money amounting to as much as 1/4th of their pay was advanced to the *naqdis*.[2] Besides cash advances, horses and equipment were also lent as part of *masaidat*.[3] All this was converted into a cash claim against the officer concerned and was known as *mutaliba* (treasury claim). So an English factor writing in A.D. 1656 defined *mutaliba* as "moneys lent out of the king's cussena (*khazana*) to umharaes (*Umara*) when they are employed in any war to be repaid out of their jaggeeris (*jagirs*").[4]

But the *mutaliba* probably also included items other than *masaidat*, such as *jurmana* or fines. In any case, officers often owed large amounts to the Treasury. When Ali Mardan Khan died, the *mutaliba* against him amounted to no less than 50 lakhs of rupees.[5] The official chronicler of Aurangzeb praises him for having remitted the *mutaliba* contracted by the forefathers and ancestors of his officers. As for *mutaliba* due from the father, it was to be remitted if the son was a *mansabdar* of 4,000 or less. From others the *mutaliba* was claimed if they had inherited a large amount from their father; it was to be partly remitted if they had inherited a small amount and completely remitted in case they had inherited nothing.[6] Although the *mutaliba* was thus apparently allowed to accumulate, it was normally exacted by the resumption of a *jagir* of equivalent revenue.[7] Sa'adullah Khan, the famous minister of Shahjahan, was suspected of having favoured the nobles by allowing the *mutaliba* against them to accumulate without calling them to account.[8]

During the earlier period whenever the *muhasiba* (settlement of accounts) took place, the *mutaliba* usually exceeded the *talab* or unsatisfied claims of the officers. But in the later years of Aurangzeb's reign conditions changed; officers did not get *jagirs* for long periods and so their claims went on accumulating. Now that the balance was often in the favour of the nobles, the policy of the administration changed and the officers usually found it very difficult to obtain a settlement or *muhasiba*

[1] Fraser, 86, f. 13a-13b; *Zawabit-i Alamgiri*, 40a.
[2] Lahori, *Badshah Nama*, II, 507.
[3] *Akhbarat*, 6th Ramzan, 49 R.Y.; 18th Ziqada, 38th R.Y.
[4] *English Factories*, 1655-60, p. 67.
[5] *Amal-i Salih*, III, 248. [6] *Alamgir Nama*, p. 1083.
[7] Cf. *Dilkusha*, f. 139a, where the complaint is made that *jagirs* are resumed on account of *mutaliba, masa'idat, jurmana*, etc.
[8] *English Factories*, 1655-60, pp. 66-67.

from the finance department. "And if through great endeavour, winning a patron and employing an ardent and capable agent (*vakil*) and after running about for seven or eight months and spending a large amount" Mamuri tells us, "an officer succeeded in proving his claim (*talab*), he would only be able to get a fourth of the money from the treasury after the greatest effort. In the end, gradually, all order disappeared."[1]

To sum up, Moreland has conclusively proved that the salaries payable to *sawars* were gradually reduced from the time of Akbar to the time of Shahjahan and Aurangzeb. This reduction did not, however, have much direct bearing on the income of the nobles themselves owing to the reduction in their military obligations. The introduction of the month-scales in the time of Shahjahan, on the other hand, had a direct bearing on the pay scales of the nobles, since it not only involved a reduction in the salary payable for the employment of *sawars*, but also the personal salary payable to the nobles under the head of *zat*. The contention that the month-scale was applied only to the *sawar*[2] rank is shown to be untenable by the evidence cited above. Since it had become usual in the time of Aurangzeb to assign *jagirs* on a scale not higher than a six-month scale, the reduction in salaries was fairly considerable. This was counterbalanced to some extent by a drastic scaling down of the obligations of the nobles for the maintenance of *sawars* and horses, as will be explained later. In addition, considerable deductions were made under a number of heads from the time of Shahjahan onwards. It would, therefore, appear that the net income of the nobles in the time of Shahjahan and Aurangzeb definitely declined, though it is difficult to form a precise idea of the extent of the decline.

Military Obligation of Mansabdars

As we have noticed, the system of double ranks (*zat* and *sawar*) made its appearance during the second half of Akbar's reign. The motive probably was to compel every *mansabdar* to actually maintain the number of horses and cavalrymen expected of him for the imperial service. But dishonesty among the nobles was found to be so widespread that a mere paper edict could not remove it. Therefore to check all evasions of military obligations, Akbar introduced *dagh* (branding) for the horses and *chehra* (descriptive rolls) for the men.[3]

[1] Mamuri, f. 182b; Khafi Khan, II, 396-7; *Dastur-al Amal Agahi*, f. 53; *Raqaim-i Karaim*, f. 8b. See also *Waqa-i Niamat Khan Ali*, p. 16.

[2] Abdul Aziz, *The Mansabdari System and the Mughal Army*, p. 69.

[3] *Ain*, Vol. I, p. 135; (Tr.) pp. 266-67: "The servants (*mansabdars*) of His Majesty have their horses every year newly marked, and thus maintain the efficiency of the army, as by their endeavours unprincipled people learn to choose the path of honesty. If a *mansabdar* delays bringing his men to the muster, one tenth of his *jagir* (*iqta*) is withheld. Formerly, when the mark was repeated, they put the number on the muster of the horse, marking, for example, a

It seems from the account given by Abul Fazl that during the reign of Akbar a *mansabdar* was expected to bring for muster the number of men indicated by his *sawar* rank and was penalised in case of any default. An interesting point to consider is whether the number which the *mansabdars* were required to bring as equal to their *sawar* ranks, was that of horsemen or horses. We know that according to the rule prescribed by Akbar, each contingent had to have horses double the number of horsemen. Thus, a man holding 100 *sawar* rank was required to maintain either 100 men and 200 horses or 50 men and 100 horses.[1] Since in Shahjahan's time under the "Rule of One-third", he would have had to bring 33 men and sixty-six horses, and the gap between 100 and 33 is substantial, it seems probable that in Akbar's time no more than 50 men and 100 horses were required for 100 *sawar* rank. But this is largely a matter of conjecture.[2]

It appears that in the time of Jahangir the check over the contingents maintained by the *mansabdars* slackened. But for this again there is no postitive proof.[3] When Shahjahan came to the throne, he apparently reorganised the whole *mansabdari* system on a new basis. Akbar's rules and regulations were enforced with some modifications, while he also gave formal status to the actual position with regard to the contingents maintained by the nobles. The main features of the *mansabdari* system, especially with reference to *dagh*, are clear from a passage in the *Badshah Nama* of Lahori. The author says that it was the law of the empire that those *mansabdars*, who had *jagirs* in any of the provinces of Hindustan and were posted in the same province in which their *jagirs* lay, were to bring to the muster horsemen equal in number of one-third of their *sawar* rank. But if posted outside the province of their *jagirs*, they were only obliged to one-fourth, and if in Balkh and Badakhshan, one-fifth.[4]

---

horse with a '2' when it was mustered the second time and so on, but now as each class of soldiers had a particular mark, the mark is only repeated at the subsequent musters. In case of *ahadis*, the former custom was retained; some *bitikchis*, and near servants of His Majesty who have no leisure to look after *jagirs*, receive their monthly salaries in cash and muster their horses every eighteen months. Grandees, whose *jagirs* are very remote, do not bring their horses to the muster before twelve years have elapsed, but when six years have elapsed since the last muster, one-tenth of their income is retrenched. And if a *mansabdar* has been promoted to a higher *mansab* and three years have elapsed since he last presented his horses at a muster, he receives a *zat* (personal) increase of salary but draws the allowances for the increased number of his men (only) after the first muster. His old and new men then get their assignments. If at the renewal of the mark at subsequent musters, any soldier brings a superior horse in exchange of his old one, he is taken before his Majesty, who inspects and accepts it."

[1] *Ain-i Akbari*. Vol. I, pp. 123-24.

[2] Evidence of a sort in favour of our suggestion comes from a letter of Abul Fazl, preserved in a collection of a doubtful genuineness. This letter, shows that a *mansabdar* of 100 *sawar* had to bring at the maximum 50 horsemen. (*Ruqat-i Abul Fazl*, p. 45, Newal Kishore Ed.)

[3] For a discussion, see Moreland, *JRAS*, 1936, pp. 641-65.

[4] Lahori, *Badshah Nama*, II, pp. 505-7.

The last rule was applied later on to all those posted in the Kabul province.[1] It seems that the *naqdis* or *mansabdars* paid in cash were required to muster their contingents according to the rule of One-fifth. This is clearly stated in a *farman* (or rather, *dastur-al amal*) issued in the 27th year of Shahjahan.[2] We also get a confirmation of these new rules from the *Khulasat-us Siyaq* which was written in the later years of Aurangzeb.[3]

With regard to the holders of the *du-aspa sih-aspa* ranks, Lahori makes it clear that the obligations required under the *du-aspa sih-aspa* rank were exactly double that under ordinary (*barawurdi*) *sawar* rank. Thus whereas under the 1/5th Rule, a 5,000 *sawar* rank on a 12 month-scale would require 1,000 men and 2,200 horses, a *sawar* rank of 5,000 all *du-aspa sih-aspa* would require 2,000 men and 4,400 horses.[4]

Lahori specifies the actual numbers of men and horses—that is, the number of *sih-aspas*, *du-aspas* and *yak-aspas* or three-horse, two-horse and one-horse troopers—which had to be mustered under the Rule of One-fifth on each month-scale against a *mansab* of 5,000 *sawar*. His statements are reproduced below in a tabular form for the sake of convenience.

Months	*Sih-aspa (men with 3 horses each)*	*Du-aspa (men with 2 horses each)*	*Yak-aspa (men with one horse each)*	*Total*	
				Men	*Horses*
12	300	600	100	1,000	2,200
11	250	500	250	1,000	2,000
10	–	800	200	1,000	1,800
9	–	600	400	1,000	1,600
8	–	450	550	1,000	1,450
7	–	250	750	1,000	1,250
6	–	100	900	1,000	1,100
5	–	–	1,000	1,000	1,000[5]

In the table the number of horses is comparatively less in each lower step in the month-scale. The proportion of horses given against each month-ratio should not be assumed to be on the same scale as prescribed for the One-third and One-fourth Rules, so that Abdul Aziz is clearly in error when he compiles a table showing men and horses required under the latter rules, by merely adapting the figures given by Lahori

[1] *Mirat-i Ahmadi*, I, 228 (Shahjahan's *farman*, 27th R.Y.). But see *Waqa-i Ajmer*, where a Rajput officer serving in Kabul was required to muster men under the rule of 1/4th. In the 25th R.Y. of Shahjahan, Jai Singh was summoned to court to be sent with prince Aurangzeb on the Qandahar expedition. Jai Singh was asked to bring his contingent according to the 1/4th rule, and if that was not feasible, then according to 1/5th rule (*Jaipur Documents* No. 79 p. 145).

[2] *Mirat-i Ahmadi*, Vol. I, p. 228.

[3] *Khulasat-us Siyaq*, f. 54 a.

[4] Lahori, *Badshah Nama*, II, pp. 506-7.

[5] Ibid.

for the One-fifth Rule.[1] In fact we have the information about the requirements under the 'One-third Rule' in the *Khulasat-us Siyaq*. The *Khulasat-us Siyaq* also proves that the rates of remounts given in *Badshah Nama* were not only enforced for the North-Western Campaigns of Shahjahan, but came to be fixed permanently for all cases where the *mansabdars* served under the 'One-fifth Rule'. This means that the system established by Shahjahan continued under Aurangzeb. The tables from the *Khulasat-us Siyaq* are reproduced below; these tables assume that the obligations are for a holder of 100 *sawar* rank. To compare these figures with those in the table of *Badshah Nama*, we have to multiply each of the figures here by 50.

A: "RULE OF ONE-FIFTH FOR NAQDIS FOR 100 SAWAR RANK"

Months	*Sih-aspa*	*Du-aspa*	*Yak-aspa*	*Men*	*Horses*
12	6	12	2	20	44
11	5	10	5	20	40
10	–	15	5	20	35
9	–	12	8	20	32
8	–	11	9	20	31
7	–	5	15	20	25
6	–	2	18	20	22
5	–	–	20	20	20
4	–	–	16	16	16
3	–	–	12	12	12
2	–	–	8	8	8
1	–	–	4	4	4

B : "MANSABDARS WHO ARE POSTED (IN A PROVINCE) AND HAVE JAGIRS IN THE SAME PROVINCE, MUSTER UNDER THE ONE-THIRD RULE".

Months	*Du-aspa*	*Yak-aspa*	*Men*	*Horses*
12	22	12	34	56
11	17	17	34	51
10	12	22	34	46
9	8	26	34	42
8	3	31	34	37
7	1	33	34	35
6	–	34	34	34
5	–	24	24	24
4	–	18	18	18
3	–	14	14	14
2	–	11	11	11
1	–	9	9	9[2]

[1] Cf. Noman A. Siddiqi in *Proc. Ind. Hist. Cong.*, Delhi Session, 1961, pp. 157-162.

[2] *Khulasat-us Siyaq*, ff. 54a-54b. Cf. *Waqa-i Ajmer*, p. 339 (1/3rd Rule applied for serving in the same province). One-fourth and One-fifth Rule applied for branding (*Mirat-i Ahmadi*, Vol.

It is interesting to note that except in a few details the table for the One-fifth Rule in the *Khulasat-us Siyaq* is on the same scale as in Lahori. Only it goes down to one month whereas the latter closes with the fifth-month scale.[1] However, it should not be concluded from this that *jagirs* on a one-month scale or two-month scale were granted in the time of Aurangzeb. No instance has yet come to light where a *jagir* below a 3-month scale was granted.

Many of the detailed regulations prescribed for branding and checking the contingents of the *mansabdars* have come down to us, notably in the *Zawabit-i Alamgiri* and *Khulasat-us Siyaq*.[2] The *naqdi mansabdars* (drawing their salary in cash) were required to obtain a renewal certificate (*tashiha*) twice a year from the branding officials. If a *mansabdar* failed to obtain the renewal certificate within six months, an extension of two months was to be given to him. If he failed even then to obtain the renewal certificate, all his salary exceeding eight months was to be withheld.[3]

As for *mansabdars* who were partly paid in cash and partly in *jagir*, if more than half of their salary was paid in *jagir*, they were expected to obtain the branding certificate according to the rules for *jagirdars* — that is, they were to present their horses for branding annually and in case of delay a six months' extension was given to them. In case of further delay their salary was withheld or adjusted according to the rules for *jagirdars*. If the *mansabdar* was paid more than half of his salary in cash, the rules prescribed for *naqdis* were applied to him. If half of the salary of the *mansabdar* was paid in cash and half in *jagir*, he was allowed an extension in case of delay according to the *naqdi* rules.[4]

It appears however from the *Waqa-i Ajmer* that an order was issued in Aurangzeb's 23rd year requiring all *naqdis* to present their contingents for branding every three months and all *jagirdars* every six months.[5]

A *farman* of Shahjahan preserved in the *Mirat-i Ahmadi* (A.D. 1652) lays down the rules whereby fractions of horses required under branding were to be completed or ignored. Thus in case of a *sawar* rank of five, one horseman was to be regarded sufficient for branding purposes under the One-fourth Rule (the extra fraction of 1/4th 'horseman' being disregarded). In case of a *sawar* rank of ten, the required contingent

I, pp. 227-29); One-fourth Rule applied for checking the contingent of Aqil Khan, (*Akhbarat*, 15th Shaban, 10th R.Y.) *Malumat-ul Afaq*, pp. 196-97.

[1] The variations of scale in men and horses are as follows per hundred *sawar* rank :

	Lahori		*Kkulasat-us Siyaq*	
Months	Men	Horses	Men	Horses
10	20	36	20	35
8	20	29	20	31

In both cases the figures given in *Khulasat-us Siyaq* seem merely to have arisen out of errors of transcription.

[2] For the duties of *darogha-i tashih*, see *Hidayat-al Qawaid*, ff. 36a-37a.

[3] *Zawabit-i Alamgiri*, ff. 38a-40b.

[4] *Zawabit-Alamgiri*, ff. 38a-40b.

[5] *Waqa-i Ajmer*, p. 639.

under the One-fourth Rule was 2½ horsemen, the officer had the option of bringing either three or two horses. If he brought three *sawars* to the brand, the supply of provision to the extent of half-a-*sawar* was to be added to his salary, and if he brought two *sawars* the supply of provision to the extent of one-half of a *sawar* was to be deducted. In case of a rank of 15 *sawars* he was required to bring only four horses for branding. The *zamindars* were to bring *sawars* to the number of half of their *sawar* rank for branding. The quality of the horses to be brought to the muster was also carefully regulated. According to the *farman* cited above, *tazi* horses were not to be branded in any province except in the Deccan, Ahmadabad, Bengal and Orissa.[1]

However, according to the *Khulasat-us Siyaq*, *mansabdars* drawing their salaries in cash were to bring only Turki horses for branding, and *jagirdars* had to make up 2/3rd of the required number with Turki and Yabu horses and 1/3 with Tazi.[2]

Branding was also enforced to check the animal corps required under the *zat* rank.[3] Branding was not enforced in the case of *mansabdars* of 5,000 *zat* or above, but all *mansabdars* below this rank had to submit to it.[4] In the 25th R. Y., we find Aurangzeb issuing an order that all the *mansabdars* serving in the Deccan up to the *zat* rank of 5,000 should bring their horses (required against the *zat* rank) for branding.[5]

A serious view was always taken of cases where the *mansabdars* failed to maintain the required contingent. Thus, on one occasion, it was reported to Aurangzeb that a hundered gunners were appointed under Sa'adat Khan but at the time of checking only sixty-five were present and thirty-five came afterwards. The Emperor ordered that attendance certificate be refused.[6] The *mansabdar* whose contingents fell below the required number was punished by demotion or fines, and his *jagir* was often reduced.[7]

On the other hand, in special circumstances, the Emperor might reduce the quota of *sawars* which a *mansabdar* was required to maintain. Thus in the 38th R.Y., Aurangzeb reduced the contingent

[1] *Mirat-i Ahmadi*, Vol. I, pp. 228-29; Cf. ibid, p. 173.

[2] *Kkulasat-us Siyaq*, f. 54b.

[3] *Ain*, Vol. I, p.135. *Khulasat-us Siyaq*, f. 54b.

[5] *Akhbarat*, 21st Shawwal, 25th R.Y.

[6] *Waqa-i Ajmer*, p. 537. On another occasion the Court was informed that the sons of Raja Rai Singh did not maintain more than one hundred *sawars* and at the time of branding borrowed the *sawars* of Harnath Kachwaha. It was also recommended by the officer concerned that the Raja be directed to explain why he was not maintaining the requisite contingent (*Ibid.*, p. 542).

[7] *Mirat-i Ahmadi*, Vol. I, pp. 265-66; *Selected Documents of Shahjahan's Reign*, pp. 165-72. It is further stated that out of the total grant of the sum of 320,000 *dams*, sixty eight thousand, eight hundred *dams* should be withheld, until the grant holder's horses had gone through the processes of branding.

The salary was paid on producing the *Sanad* of brand, etc. *Waqa-i Ajmer*, p. 529.

of Hamid Khan from 1/4th to 1/5th.[1] In 1685 when Firoz Jang Bahadur was ordered to set out with provisions and a large force to reinforce Prince Azam at Bijapur, the Emperor exempted the *mansabdars* of 100 to 400 stationed at the court from the brand under the 1/3rd Rules, to enable royal officials to purchase their horses for replenishing the Cavalry of the Prince.[2] Sometimes the emperor exempted a *mansabdar* who was given a conditional promotion, from *dagh* (branding) to the extent of his conditional promotion only.[3] In some cases, the Emperor exempted the *mansabdar* from *dagh* for a limited period. Thus, in the 38th R.Y., Aurangzeb exempted Baqi Khan *Kotwal* and *Faujdar* of Shahjahanabad from *dagh*.[4] In the 8th R.Y. of Aurangzeb, when Mir Aziz wanted to go to Haj, he was exempted from *dagh* till his return.[5]

Recruitment and Promotion

In theory all *mansabdars* were appointed directly by the emperor, and, as far as possible, candidates for enrolment as *mansabdars* were required to appear personally before him. The imperial eye was considered to be sharp and penetrating enough to discern the merits and demerits of every man. Abul Fazl says, "His Majesty sees through some men at the first glance, and confers upon them high rank".[6] The *Bakhshi* was responsible for presenting all candidates—Iranis, Turanis, Rumis, Ferangis, Hindis and Kashmiris—who came for service before the emperor.[7]

However, another method of recruitment was that the leading nobles of the empire, particularly governors of provinces and leaders of military expeditions, recommended persons for appointment to the emperor. Their recommendations were generally accepted and *mansabs* were given to the persons they recommended.[8] Sometimes, the emperor ordered

[1] *Akhbarat*, 25th Ziqada, 38th R.Y.

[2] *Ma'asir-i Alamgiri*, p. 264-65; *Dilkusha*, 90b.

[3] *Akhbarat*, 23rd Safar, 36th R.Y., 2nd Safar 43rd R.Y. 29th Moharram 38th R.Y.; 300 *sawars* out of the conditional *mansab* of Khuda Banda Khan were exempted from branding (11th Ramzan, 45th R.Y.).

[4] *Akhbarat*, 28th Rabi I, 38th R.Y.

[5] *Akhbarat*, 7th Jamada II, 8th R.Y.

[6] *Ain*, Vol. I, p. 248(Tr.), 124 (Text), Chandra Bhan Brahman's *Guldasta*, f. 8a. Pratab Singh and others, five persons, the sons of Sunder Das Sisodia, were presented to emperor Aurangzeb for the award of *mansabs* and they were awarded suitable *mansabs*. (*Akhbarat*, 8th Zilhij, 20th R.Y.). Man Singh and others, the sons of Raja Rai Singh were presented to emperor Aurangzeb for the award of the *mansabs*. All of them were granted suitable *mansabs*. (3rd Shaban, 24th R.Y.). Islam Khan, *hakim* of Basra, visited Aurangzeb in the 11th R.Y. and was awarded a *mansab* of 5,000/5,000, Cf. Khafi Khan, Vol. II, p. 234. Mamuri, f. 144a.

[7] *Ain*, Vol. I, p. 108. For the duties and functions of the *bakhshi* see *Hidayat-al Qawaid*, f. 11b-12a.

[8] For example: Mulla Ahmad Naitha was given the rank of 6,000/6,000 on the recommendation of Jai Singh (*Alamgir Nama*, pp. 919-20); Murtaza Khan, son of Kakur Khan, was given the *mansab* of 400/100 on the recommendation of Zulfiqar Khan Bahadur (*Akhbarat*, 9th

persons recommended by nobles for the award of a petty *mansab* to be presented at a review and after that the *mansab* was awarded.[1] Princes of the royal family also recommended persons to the Emperor for appointment and their recommendations were accepted in most cases.[2]

Once a recommendation was submitted to the Emperor and approved by him, an elaborate procedure was followed for preparing the appointment order. The royal approval was sent to the *diwan*, the *bakhshi* and the *sahib-i taujih* (military accountant) for inspection. It was presented to the Emperor once more after it had passed through these imperial officers, and after the Emperor had approved a second time, the formal appointment order (*farman*) was drawn up, requiring the seals of various officers, specially the *diwan* and *bakhshi*, before it was issued under the seal of the *wazir*.[3]

Every candidate for a *mansab* had to provide a surety (*zamin*) and this rule was very rigorously enforced. Manucci says, "All soldiers, high and low, generals and captains, are forced to give surety and without it they cannot obtain employment. The practice is so common and so general that even the princes find it necessary to conform to the custom".[4] It appears that professional bankers or money-lenders of standing were accepted as sureties by the administration.[5] Persons standing as surety were held responsible for the behaviour of the *mansabdar* and undertook to meet any claims of the government against the *mansabdar* concerned, if the latter failed to meet them.[6] Sureties were, therefore, difficult to obtain and were apparently bought. Thus it was regarded as a great

---

Ziqada, 39th R.Y.); Sardar Singh Hara was given the *mansab* of 500/200 on the recommendation of Ruhullah Khan (2nd Shawwal, 25th R.Y.); Dankat Rao, the *Zamindar* of Alwar Kunda was given the *mansab* of 500/200 on the recommendation of Rustam Dil Khan (1st Moharram, 45th R.Y.); Raj Singh was appointed *faujdar* of Toda on the recommendation of Saiyed Abdullah Khan, the *nazim* of Ajmer, and was given the *mansab* of 400/300 (18th Shaban, 43rd R.Y.); Saiyid Shah was given the rank of 5,000/2,000 on the recommendation of prince Bidar Bakht (24th Shawwal, 45th R.Y.). Donbri Rao was given the rank of 1,500/1,000 on the recommendation of Tarbiyat Khan (*Ma'asir-i Arkan-i Taimuria*, f. 131a).

[1] Bahramand Khan recommended some of his servants to emperor Aurangzeb for the award of *mansabs*. The Emperor ordered the candidates to be presented for review (*Akhbarat*, 21st Rabi I, 44th R.Y.).

[2] Jagat Singh and others were recruited in the imperial service on the recommendation of Prince Shah Alam (*Akhbarat*, 8th Shaban, 24th R.Y.); Prince Azam recommended some persons for the grant of suitable *mansabs* and his recommendation was accepted (*Akhbarat*, 13 Ramzan, 13th R.Y.). Aurangzeb recommended to Shahjahan a number of persons for the grant of *mansabs*. (*Adab-i Alamgiri*, ff. 108a-109a.)

[3] The details of procedure are described in Ibn Hasan, *The Central Structure of the Mughal Empire*, p. 93 ff. see also *Ain*, I, p. 136 and *Zawabit-i Alamgiri*, ff. 17, 30b.

[4] Manucci, Vol. II, p. 377.

[5] Lendesiana, No. 353, Folios unmarked; "The surety of Bheku Sahu for one lakh of Rupees in favour of Saval Singh Khattri who was given the charge of *pargana* of Bidhnur was accepted through a *hasbul hukm* from the Mughal Court" A.D. (1689-90).

[6] See the undertaking of a *zamin* in *Farhang-i Kardani*, f.20a *Zawabit-i Alamgiri*, ff. 19b, 25a, 32b.

concession to the Deccanis when Aurangzeb exempted them from this obligation.[1]

The procedure for the grant of promotions to *mansabdars* was similar to the procedure for the grant of the initial *mansab*. The recommendation (or *tajwiz*) for promotion was usually made by princes, commanders or governors, under whom the *mansabdar* happened to be serving.[2] It was the general custom for the Emperor to award promotion in *mansabs* on the occasion of the festivities,[3] at the beginning of the regnal year, and on his birthday celebrations.[4] But promotions were also granted on other occasions, such as the beginning or the end of a military expedition.[5]

Promotions were awarded for various reasons. Gallantry in military service and merit occupied a high place;[6] at the other end of the scale were promotions granted on receipt of a handsome present or *peshkash* from a noble.[7] Promotion was also generally, though not invariably, given when an officer was found to be really deserving a higher post. In any case, we often find the ranks of the *mansabdars* being increased simultaneously with their appointments to higher posts. A list of such promotions, where the increase granted was in the basic personal rank (and not *mashrut*, i.e. to be relinquished when the *mansabdar* was transferred from that post), is given below. However, there are cases of appointments to higher posts without a corresponding increase in the *mansab*. An increase in the *mansab* was usually proportionate to the *mansab* already held, the grant of an increase larger than the original rank being quite exceptional. Normally, a promotion by an additional *mansab* of more than 50 per cent of the original was not granted, as a

[1] '*Selected Documents of Aurangzeb's Reign*', p. 182.

[2] *Akhbarat*, 29th Rabi II, 8th R.Y. (Qutbuddin Khan, Raghunath Singh and Inayat Khan were promoted to higher ranks).

[3] *Ma'asir-i 'Alamgiri*, passim. [4] *Alamgir Nama*.

[5] In 1665 Prince Muhammad Muazzam, along with Maharaja Jaswant Singh, was deputed to safeguard the Mughal frontier against the Shah of Persia. The nobles who were appointed with the Prince were promoted and awarded *khilats* and titles etc. *Alamgir Nama*, pp. 976–77. In 1661 when some *zamindars* of Jammu rebelled, all officers who were sent to punish them were promoted, pp. 757-58. After the conquest of Bijapur, all the *mansabdars* from the rank of 20 up to 7,000, who had been conducting military operations against Bijapur, were promoted (*Futuhat-i Alamgiri*, f. 105b). The names of all the nobles, who were promoted after the conquest of Bijapur, are given, and their original *mansabs* and promotions are separately indicated; *Zawabit-i Alamgiri*, ff. 159b-63a. When Hyderabad was conquered, all *mansabdars* who were participating in the siege were promoted, ff. 163b-65a. In 1666 when the Afghan leaders submitted, Aurangzeb promoted all nobles who were conducting the war against the Afghans (*Alamgir Nama*, pp. 1056-57). After the conquest of Purandhar, when Shivaji surrendered, all nobles serving with Raja Jai Singh in this expedition were promoted (*Alamgir Nama*, 907-908). After the conquest of Khulna, at the recommendation of Fateh Ullah Khan, Aurangzeb promoted all *mansabdars* of the brotherhood of the Khan (Khafi Khan, Vol. II, p. 494).

[6] *Dilkusha*, f. 97a-b, 115a and passim; *Adab-i Alamgiri*, ff. 21b-22b, 25a.

[7] See Chapter V, Section 'The Conduct of Nobles in Administration'.

Name	Post	Previous Rank (if known)	Promotion	Source
1. Shah Nawaz Khan	*subedar* of Gujrat	5,000/5,000	1,000/1,0002-3h	*Alamgir Nama*, p. 210.
2. Fidai Khan	*faujdar* of Oudh and Gorakhpur	4,000/2,000	1,500 *sawars*	*Adab-i Alamgiri*, f. 260a
3. Amir Khan	*subedar* of Kabul	4,000/4,000	1,000/1,000 (2-3h)	*Alamgir Nama*, p. 661.
4. Shahamat Khan	*faujdar* of Ghaznin	3,000/1,000	1,000 *sawars*	*Adab-i Alamgiri*, f. 286b.
5. Arab Khan	*faujdar* of Bahraich	3,000/700	800 *sawars*	*Adab-i Alamgiri*, f. 279b.
6. Muhammad Beg	*faujdar* of Miyan Doab	1,000/600	500/100	*Adab-i Alamgiri*, f. 241.
7. Kamgar Khan	*faujdar* of Sikandarpur	1,000/400	500/300	*Adab-i Alamgiri*, f. 280a
8. Mahmud	*faujdar* of one of the *mahals*.	1,000/200	800 *sawars*	*Mirat-al Alam*, ff. 160a-160b.
9. Tarbiyat Khan	*faujdar* of Orissa promoted to the rank of 4,000/3,000 (500×3-2h)			*Mirat-al Alam*, f. 208a.
10. Ikram Khan	*faujdar* in the vicinity of Akbarabad.		1,000 *sawars*	*Adab-i Alamgiri*, f. 280b
11. Zabardast Khan	*faujdar* of Hoshangabad promoted to the rank of 1,000/1,000 (2-3h)			*Mirat-al Alam* f. 160a-160b.

glance at the promotions set out in our authorities will make clear. Thus, the author of *Ma'asir-al Umara* expresses surprise at the sudden promotion by Aurangzeb of Khan-i Jahan Bahadur Zafar Jang from 700 *zat* to 5,000.[1] All *mansabs* above 7,000/7,000 (2–3h) were reserved for princes of the Imperial family.[2]

[1] *Ma'asir-ul Umara*, I, 813.

[2] When Jai Singh had reached this rank, he could be rewarded further only by way of *inam*, but not by further increase in rank (*Alamgir Nama*, p. 618); *Alamgir Nama* of Hatim Khan, ff. 109a, 124a; *Mirat-al Alam*, f. 160a; *Mirat-i Jahan Numa* f. 268a. The only noble who ever passed this barrier was Asaf Khan, who was awarded the rank 9,000/9,000 (2-3h) by Shahjahan. But Shahjahan decided that this was an exceptional case and no other noble was to be promoted beyond 7,000/7,000 (Lahori, *Badshah Nama*, II, p. 25).

Escheat

No discussion of the pay and conditions of service of the nobles can be complete without considering how far they enjoyed security of the wealth accumulated by them during their tenure of service and could pass it on to their heirs. Cases of punishment for specific crimes or faults apart, the Mughal nobles generally seem to have enjoyed such security during their life-time. But it is a matter of controversy whether the wealth of a noble could safely pass on to his legal heirs. There is some evidence that the king claimed a right to the property of all his deceased officers.

The claim of the king over the possessions and riches accumulated by his officers dates from an early period in the history of monarchy among the Musalmans. The introduction of slavery provided the Abbasid Caliphs a legal pretext (i.e. in terms of the *shariat*) for claiming the property of their officers. The property acquired by a slave, under Muslim law, always belonged to his master in the life-time as well as after the death of the slave, while the property of a free man went to his sons or blood relations.[1] The Sultans of Delhi too used to have a large number of slave officers. Even a Sultan so anxious to maintain conformity with Muslim law as Firuz Tughlaq justified the confiscation of the property of an officer of his on the ground that he had been his manumitted slave.[2]

The Indian Mughals seem to have followed the Delhi Sultans in not having any real slave-officers of status and yet in making claims upon their 'free' officers that could only be made under Muslim law upon slaves. This royal claim to succession is not elaborated in the *Ain-i Akbari*, but is noticed by a series of European travellers from the time of Akbar onwards.[3] Among the earliest is, perhaps, that found in Hawkins, where we are told that "the custom of this Mughal Emperor is to take possession of his nobles treasure when they die, and to bestow on their children what he pleaseth, but commonly he dealeth well with them and

[1] See Levy, *Social Structure of Islam*, Cambridge, 1957, p. 78. The appointment of slaves (generally of Turkish birth) gave the Abbasids and other rulers, who preferred to base their government on slave-officers, a *shariat* or legal right which they would not have had over a bureaucracy recruited from free-born citizens. The *shariat* places the slave, whatever his status, under three restrictions : he cannot marry without the permission of his master; when he dies his master, is his sole heir; lastly, all his children, in their turn, are the slaves of his master. This extra-ordinary authority which the *shariat* gives to the master over his slaves is probably the cause of those slave bureaucracies, which we find recurring in Islamic history.

[2] Afif, *Tarikh-i Firuz Shahi*, p. 445. The officer was Bashir Imad-ul Mulk, who left behind 12 crores of *tankas*; of this amount, 9 crores were escheated to the crown and the remaining 3 crores were distributed among Imadul-Mulk's sons, sons-in-law, wives, adopted sons and slaves. But legally the Sultan had no power to inherit a manumitted slave, and Firuz's action must be regarded as an "act of state".

[3] Bernier; 211-12; Manucci II, p. 417; Careri, p. 241; Pelsaert, Tr. Moreland, *Jahangir's India*, pp. 54.-56.

unto the eldest son he hath a very great respect, who in time receiveth the full title of his father".[1]

Now, what is clearly stated here and in other European accounts is that the Emperor first actually took possession of the entire wealth of the noble, and then disposed of it as he chose, taking some part of it for himself and leaving the rest to the heirs of the nobles in portions determined by himself. That this was not a figment of the imagination of the foreigners shown by the actual instances from the period of Akbar and Shahjahan.

When Munim Khan died in 1575, all his wealth and property was escheated to the crown, the term used for it being *zabt*. It is true that he had died without heirs (he had one son living whom he had disowned) and so the state could be his only heir.[2] However, when Abul Fazl, who had many sons, was murdered, his entire moveable property was presented before Akbar and it is recorded that as a mark of favour to his family the Emperor refused to confiscate it.[3] The action taken by Shahjahan with regard to Ali Mardan Khan's property upon his death in 1657, offers, perhaps, the best illustration of the actual position before the accession of Aurangzeb.

The whole property of the deceased, amounting in cash and goods, to one crore of rupees, was seized (*baqaid-i zabt dar amad*). From bountiful generosity, the Emperor bestowed thirty lacs on Ibrahim Khan, and twenty lacs on the remaining three sons and ten daughters, while fifty lacs were appropriated to the imperial treasury against the *mutaliba*.[4]

What is of particular interest, here, is that the imperial right did not remain confined to realising the *mutaliba*, i.e. the amount borrowed by the deceased noble from the imperial treasury, but extended to the disposal of his entire inheritance in complete disregard of the Muslim law of inheritance. The law gave equal shares to all brothers and the sisters are given half the brother's share; yet in this case one son (not the eldest) got 30 lacs, while three sons and ten daughters had to rest content with twenty lacs.[5] In the case of a Hindu noble, Raja Bithaldas, Shahjahan asserted his right to deal with the inheritance with a similar disregard of Hindu law. Out of ten lacs left by the Raja, 6 lacs were bestowed on the eldest son, while the other three sons got 3 lacs, 60 thousand and 40 thousand respectively.[6]

[1] Purchas, III, p. 34. [2] Bayazid, 349; Badauni, II, 217-18.

[3] *Waqiat-i Asad Beg*, Br. M. Or. 1996, f. 6.

[4] *Amal-i Salih*, III, 246-8; *Tuhfa-i Shahjahani*, f. 27b.

[5] When Islam Khan died, it was expressly laid down that only the *mutaliba* and the presents he had received from the *zamindars* of the Deccan were to be appropriated to the imperial treasury. The remainder of his property was bestowed upon his heirs, who were ordered to distribute it among themselves according to the *shariat* (Waris, 16-17). An exception, perhaps, that proves the rule.

[6] Waris, f. 154.

In effect, therefore, the Emperor did not confiscate the entire property of a noble; he only took his *mutaliba* and if he chose, something more. But theoretically, he was the sole heir and when he passed on the inheritance to the members of the deceased noble's family, he could follow his own will in its distribution. The *Qazis* were not entitled to interfere.

To Aurangzeb is attributed a radical revision of this system by two contemporary historians. They denounce the old iniquitous practice of sequestering the property of nobles, who had no dues to pay to the imperial treasury and declare that Aurangzeb waived all claims to the property of his nobles beyond claiming the *mutaliba*.[1]

Fortunately, the text of the order which Aurangzeb issued on the subject has survived in the great collection of documents preserved in the *Mirat-i Ahmadi*.

In this *farman* issued in 1666 Aurangzeb instructed all the provincial *diwans* that when a servant of the state died leaving no legal heir behind him and without any state dues against him, his property should be deposited in the *bait-ul mal*. If he owed something to the state, the state dues should be realised and then the rest of the property deposited in the *bait-ul mal*. If he had heirs and also owed something to the state, they should attach his property within three days of his death. If the property exceeded the amount of his debt to the state, they were to take the amount of the debt only and deliver the rest to his heirs, after the latter had legally established their right. If the state-claims exceeded the property of the deceased, the whole of the property was to be confiscated. If the deceased noble owed nothing to the state, his whole property was to be handed over to his legal heirs and the state officials were asked not to interfere with it.[2] This order was reinforced by another in 1691, which called upon the officers not to attach the property of nobles whose heirs were in government service, because the latter could be asked to pay the *mutaliba* contracted by the deceased.[3]

A number of instances can be cited to show that Aurangzeb's orders were followed and the claim over the property of the *mansabdars* was limited to the *mutaliba*.

In 8th regnal year, on Rahmat Khan's death, it was ordered that the state dues alone were to be recovered from his property and the rest handed over to his heirs.[4] In 1099 A.H. (A. D. 1687) Shaikh Mohiuddin, the *sadar* and the *amin* of *jiziya* of the province of Gujarat, died.

[1] *Ma'asir-i Alamgiri*, p. 531; *Mirat-al Alam*, f. 211b.

[2] *Mirat-i Ahmadi*, Vol. I, pp. 135, 267 and 319.

[3] *Mirat-i Ahmadi*, Vol. I. pp. 326.

[4] *Akhbarat*, 9th Jamada II, 8th R.Y. : Order issued on the petition of Abdur Rahim Khan son-in-law of Rahmat Khan. In 1662 Ali Yar Beg died; only the *mutaliba* (state-dues) were recovered from the deceased noble's property and the rest was handed over to his heirs (*Selected Waqa-i of the Deccan*, No. 14, p. 50).

His son, Shaikh Ikramuddin, stood surety for the payment of the state-dues, and so the property of the deceased was not confiscated.[1] In the 44th R.Y. of Aurangzeb (A.D. 1700) when Sher Afgan Khan died, his property was passed on to his legal heirs.[2] In 1113 A.H. (A.D. 1701) when Shuja'at Khan, the *subedar* of Gujarat died, the Emperor permitted his heirs to succeed to his property, which was not confiscated. Only the elephants and horses, etc., belonging to the Khan were taken and sent to the court.[3] In A.D. 1702, Fazil Khan, the *Naib-i Mir Saman* submitted before the Emperor that a deceased officer, Lutfullah Khan, owed one lakh and seventy thousand rupees to the state, and his heirs had been permitted to succeed to his legacy. The Emperor ordered the horses and elephants of the Khan to be confiscated, but the rest of his property was left to his heirs.[4]

It is, however, not possible to take these examples as a sufficient proof that Aurangzeb basically modified the older practice of escheat. Bernier's statements on this point may be disregarded because they refer to the period before the date of Aurangzeb's first order (A.D. 1666) and, therefore, relate to the system in force before his reform. Yet Manucci, who wrote at the close of Aurangzeb's reign, says flatly :

"He (Aurangzeb) seizes everything left by his generals, officers and other officials at their death, *in spite of his having declared that he makes no claims on the goods of defunct persons*. Nevertheless, under the pretext that they are his officers and in debt to the crown, he lays hold of everything. If they have widows, he gives them a trifle every year and some land to furnish a subsistence."[5]

The italicised words show that Manucci was aware of Aurangzeb's order of 1666 and 1691 and, perhaps, of the acclamation of the author of these orders by his courtiers. He says that these orders were in fact often violated and that the Emperor continued to enforce his claims on the property of his officers, which he had publicly renounced.

That Manucci is not entirely wrong is supported by a number of actual cases, where the right of escheat was in fact claimed.

In A.D. 1694 Mukhtar Khan, the *nazim* of the Gujarat *suba* died, and Muhammad Tahir, the *diwan* of the province of Gujarat along with other

[1] *Mirat-i Ahmadi*, Vol. I, p. 319. The property of late Rashid Khan was given to his son, Muhammd Husain, and he was asked to pay the state-dues which his father owed (*Akhbarat*, 10th Rabi I, 45th R.Y.). In 1676 Islam Khan Rumi died fighting against the Bijapuris. His possessions amounting to three lakhs of rupees and twenty thousand *asharfis*, which had been confiscated in Ujjain and Sholapur, were restored to his sons and they were directed to pay the state-dues which their father owed (*Ma'asir-ul Umara*, Vol. I, pp. 246-47).

[2] *Akhbarat*, 5th Zilhij, 44th R.Y.

[3] *Mirat-i Ahmadi*, Vol. I, p. 345. The property of late Ikhlas Khan was handed over to his sons, only the horses and elephants etc. were confiscated for the State, (*Akhbarat*, 19th Rajab, 43rd R.Y.).

[4] *Akhbarat*, 7th *Shaban*, 46th R.Y.

[5] Manucci II, p. 417, Cf. H.H. Das, *Norris Embassy to Aurangzeb*, 146.

officials confiscated all the property left by him.[1] In A.D. 1682 Muhammad Amin Khan died, and Muhammad Latif, the *diwan* and the officers of the province of Gujarat, confiscated the whole of his moveable and immoveable property, including his animals.[2] After the death of Amir Khan, the *subedar* of Kabul, Aurangzeb directed Asad Khan to write to the *diwan* of Lahore, to attach his property with great care and diligence so that nothing may escape their hands. He was also asked to get information from other sources and to take possession of everything found at any place belonging to Amir Khan.[3] In A.D. 1678 Jaswant Singh died and Aurangzeb ordered his entire treasure and wealth to be confiscated.[4] However, in the case of Jaswant Singh it is known that he had large state-dues against him.[5] We can thus enumerate the cases where property of dead nobles was seized on behalf of the Crown and make a long list, but it is not quite clear in all these cases whether the seizure was only to recover the *mutaliba* or to enforce the right of escheat.[6]

On the basis of this evidence, we may refuse to join the panegyrists of Aurangzeb in regarding him as a reformer, who liberated the nobility from the yoke of the escheat system. We have seen that the 'yoke' was really a light one even before Aurangzeb. It amounted in practice to only : (*a*) that the state-dues should be the first claim on the estate of a deceased officer and (*b*) that in disposing of the rest of his property, the king, and not the *shariat*, should have the decisive voice. The orders of 1666 and 1691 confirmed the first of these two rights, but theoretically abandoned the second. Yet in practice, as we have seen, Aurangzeb enforced this right whenever he chose. The two orders he issued were self-denying ordinances, which he might, or might not, enforce in particular cases.

[1] *Mirat-i Ahmadi*, Vol. I, pp. 510-11.

[2] *Mirat-i Ahmadi*, Vol. I, p.302. For full details of the property of Mohammed Amin Khan deceased which was confiscated for the state, see *Ma'asir-i Alamgiri*, p. 226.

[3] *Raqaim-i Karaim*, f. 14a. About two lakhs of rupees, some *asharfis* and jewels belonging to the late Amir Khan, were concealed by his sons but later on the property was discovered and escheated. *Akhbarat*, 25th Rabi I, 44th R.Y., *Kalamat-i Taiyabat*, f. 24b; H.H. Das, *Norris Embassy to Aurangzeb*, p. 285.

[4] *Waqa-i Ajmer*, pp. 77, 81, 83 and 84; *Ma'asir-i Alamgiri*, p. 173.

[5] *Mirat-i Ahmadi*, Vol. I, p. 277. Dilir Khan had state-dues against him, so at his death Aurangzeb ordered that his property should be escheated. (*Dilkusha*, f. 83b.).

[6] Abdul Nabi, the *faujdar* of Mathura, was killed during a fight by a musket ball, and his entire property was confiscated for the state. (Kamwar, *Tazkara-i Salatin-i Chaghta*, f. 280b; *Ma'asir-i Alamgiri*, p. 83). The property of Bakhshi-al Mulk Mukhlis Khan was confiscated after his death. (*Akhbarat*, 4th Shaban, 44th R.Y. of Aurangzeb). The property of Arshad Khan was confiscated for the state after his death (*Akhbarat*, 10th Rabi I, 45th R.Y.). Muhammad Jafar was deputed to attach the property of Qasim Khan deceased (19th Jamada II, 39th R.Y.). The entire property of Shaista Khan deceased was escheated to the crown. (*Ma'asir-ul Umara*, Vol. II, p. 705). In the 38th R.Y. of Aurangzeb, Khan-i Jahan Bahadur Zafar Jang Kokaltash died, the entire property of the deceased Khan was escheated for the state (Dilkusha, f. 118b.).

On a more general view, taking the Mughal 'system of escheat' as a whole, it is difficult to agree with some European travellers and modern writers[1] in considering it the source of all evils. Bernier, for example, denounced it as 'a barbarous' custom. He declared that it made it impossible for families to retain their status and wealth : "The king being the heir of all their possessions, no family can long maintain its distinction, but after the Umrah's death, is soon extinguished, and the sons or at least the grandsons, reduced generally to beggary..."[2] Moreland suggests that the escheat system created great insecurity for the nobles and was the reason why the nobles spent huge amounts on luxuries and did not save and invest.[3]

These statements assume that the Emperor in practice exercised his rights over his nobles' property and confiscated it entirely or the larger part of it. This is far from the truth. All the nobles were not spendthrifts; many of them saved and accumulated large amounts. Pelsaert, indeed, was surprised that despite the escheat system the nobles continued to amass wealth, and was led to believe that wealth was loved for its sake alone.[4] In fact every noble felt confident that his wealth, after meeting the *mutaliba*, would remain with his heirs, although one son (generally the eldest but possibly another son who was his or the king's favourite) would get more than the others. This was why they amassed wealth and accumulated riches. The escheat system had, therefore, a more theoretical and legal than economic significance.

[1] Sarkar, *Mughal Administration*, 3rd ed. 1935, pp. 175-76.

[2] Bernier, 211-12; See also Careri, p. 241.

[3] *India At the Death of Akbar*, pp. 262-63.

[4] Pelsaert. Tr. Moreland, *Jahangir's India*, pp. 54-56.

Appendix A

MANSABDARS WHOSE SAWAR RANK EXCEEDED THE *ZAT* RANK

Name	*Rank*	*Source*
1. Faujdar of Gorakhpur (Name not given)	3,000/4,000	*Akhbarat*, 28th Moharram, 43 R.Y.
2. Kishore Singh Hara	2,500/3,000	,, 28th Jamada, 38 R.Y.
3. Khwaja Muhammad Arif Mujahid Khan	2,500/2,800	,, 16th Rabi II, 39 R.Y. Kamwar, f. 273a.
4. Rao Dalpat	2,500/2,700	*Dilkusha*, f. 136a.
5. Hadi Khan	2,000/2,400	*Akhbarat*, 13th Ramzan, 13 R.Y.
6. Ram Chand	2,000/3,000	*Ma'asir-i-Alamgiri*, 423
7. Qabad Khan	2,000/2,500	*Alamgir Nama*, p. 120.
8. Sardar Khan	2,000/2,500	,, ,, p. 629.
9. Sher Afgan	1,500/1,700	*Ma'asir-i-Alamgiri*, p. 381.
10. Alah Dad Khan	1,500/2,000	*Akhbarat*, 15th Jamada II, 46 R.Y.
11. Dilir S/o Bahadur Rohela	1,000/1,200 (500x2-3h)	*Alamgir Nama*, p. 661.
12. Mohtasham Khan	1,000/1,200 (1,000x2-3h)	*Akhbarat*, 15th Jamada II, 46 R. Y. ,, 16th Rajab, 24 R. Y.
13. Kakur Khan	1,000/1,200	,, 8th Ziqada, 39 R.Y.
14. Saiyid Hasan Ali Khan	1,000/1,200	,, 28th Ziqada, 43 R.Y.
15. Iftikhar Khan	1,000/1,500	,, 26th Rajab, 45 R.Y.
16. Kr. Bijai Singh	1,000/2,000	,, 9th Ramzan, 44 R. Y.
17. Mamur Khan	1,000/1,200	,, 4th Ziqada, 46 R. Y.
18. Rahman Dad Khan	1,000/1,500	,, 15th Jamada II, 46 R.Y.
19. Samandar Khan	1,000/1,200	,, 1st Moharram, 45 R.Y.
20. Abdul Samad Khan	1,000/1,100 (300x2-3h)	,, 7th Ziqada, 38 R.Y.
21. Muhammad Murad Khan	900/1,000	,, 10th Rabi I, 45 R.Y.
22. Bahram	1,000/1,700	*Alamgir Nama*, p. 1039
23. Kartalab Khan	900/1,000	*Akhbarat*, 26th Safar, 45 R. Y.
24. Najaf Quli	800/1,000	,, 5th Moharram, 45 R. Y.
25. Fateh Jalauri	700/1,400	,, 15th Shaban, 24 R. Y.
26. Aurang Khan	700/900 (400x2-3h)	,, 28th Ramzan, 46 R. Y.
27. Hafiz Khan	700/900	,, 29th Safar, 46 R. Y.
28. Khwaja Khuda Yar Khan	700/1,000	,, 14th Rabi II, 44 R. Y.
29. Agha Quli Khan	700/800	,, 9th Ziqada, 40 R. Y.
30. Rawat Mal Jhala	700/900	*Akhbarat*, 4th Moharram, 45 R.Y.

Name	Rank	Source
31. Mir Mubarakullah	700/1,000	*Ma'asir-ul-Umara'*, I, 204-5.
32. Muhammad Kamyab	600/620	*Akhbarat*, 8th Zilhij, 43 R.Y.
33. Shukrullah Khan	500/1,700	„ 13th Ramzan, 47 R.Y. *Ma'asir-i-Alamgiri*, pp. 303-4.
34. Abul	500/600	*Akhbarat*, 11th Zilhij, 38 R.Y.
35. Himmat Yar	500/900	„ 16th Zilhij, 38 R.Y.
36. Khan Chand Bundela	500/650	„ 1st Rabi II, 38 R.Y.
37. Muhammad Salih	500/700	„ 28th Zilhij, 45 R.Y.
38. Khidmat Talab Khan Shah Beg	500/640	„ 2nd Moharram, 45 R.Y.
39. Asfandiyar	500/700	„ 27th Safar, 45 R.Y.
40. Mir Muhammad Latif	500/600	„ 9th Ramzan, 44 R.Y.
41. Wali Dad	500/650	„ 19th Moharram, 45 R.Y.
42. Saiyid Mudassir	500/600	„ 11th Shaban, 43 R.Y.
43. Niyaz Khan	500/800	*Ma'asir-i-Alamgiri*, p. 474.
44. Faujdar Khan	500/700	*Akhbarat*, 2nd Shaban, 37 R.Y.
45. Tilok Singh	400/450	„ 13th Rabi II, 38 R.Y.
46. Muhammad Rafi	400/650	„ 4th Jamada I, 38 R.Y.
47. Dilawar Khan S/o Alah Dad Khan	400/500	„ 19th Ziqada, 38 R.Y.
48. Shakir Khan	400/1,000 (200x2-3h)	„ 13th Ramzan, 47 R.Y.
49. Qasim Khan	400/700 (250x2-3h)	„ 6th Rajab, 46 R. Y.
50. Muhammad Qasim S/o Sher Khan	400/450	„ 13th Rajab, 43 R.Y.
51. Muhammad Sharif	400/560	„ 16th Moharram, 38 R.Y.
52. Keshaw Das	300/500	„ 5th Ziqada, 38 R.Y.
53. Mir Muhammad Sanji	300/700	„ 29th Rabi II, 38 R.Y.
54. Dilawar Khan	300/700	„ 1st Ramzan, 46 R.Y.
55. Saf Shikan Khan	300/500 (400x2-3h)	„ 29th Safar, 46 R.Y.
56. Ram Chand S/o Dalpat Bundela	300/500	„ 3rd Moharram, 45 R.Y.
57. Azam S/o Himmat	300/420	„ 28th Safar, 43 R. Y.
58. Muhammad Sardar S/o Dindar	100/400 (200x2-3h)	„ 19th Zilhij, 43 R.Y.
59. Bhim Singh	300/400	„ 5th Rajab, 39 R. Y.
60. Gharib Das	300/500	„ 21st Jamada II, 39 R.Y.
61. Muhammad Murad	300/450	„ 3rd Jamada II, 38 R.Y.
62. Nur Khan	300/450	„ 1st Moharram, 38 R.Y.

APPENDIX B

TABLE SHOWING THE PAY FOR *ZAT* RANK
(7,000 *Zat*)

Source	*Page or Folio Reference*	*Class I*
Ain-i Akbari Vol. I	p. 124	Rs. 45,000 (Per month) 21,600,000 *dams* (annual)
Farhang-i Kardani	ff. 43-49	14,000,000 *dams* (annual)
Selected Documents of Shahjahan's Reign	p. 80	14,000,000 *dams* (annual)
Dastur-ul ʻAmal-i ʻAlamgiri	f. 125a.	14,000,000 *dams* (annual)
Zawabit-i ʻAlamgiri	ff. 42b-45b.	14,000,000 *dams* (annual)
Mumalik-i-Mahrusa-i Alamgiri	f. 149b.	14,000,000 *dams* (annual)
Khulasat-us siyaq	ff. 48b-49a	14,000,000 *dams* (annual)
Malumat-ul Afaq	pp. 195-96	14,000,000 *dams* (annual)

TABLE SHOWING THE PAY FOR *ZAT* RANK
(5,000 *Zat*)

Source	*Page or Folio Reference*	*Class I*	*Class II*	*Class III*
Ain-i Akbari Vol. I	p. 124	Rs.30,000 (Per month) 14,400,000 *dams* (annual)	Rs.29,000 (Per month) 13,920,000 *dams* (annual)	Rs.28,000 (Per month) 13,440,000 *dams* (annual)
Farhang-i Kardani	ff. 43-49	10,000,000 *dams* (annual)	9,700,000 *dams* (annual)	9,400,000 *dams* (annual)
Selected Documents of Shahjahan's Reign	p. 80	10,000,000 *dams* (annual)	9,700,000 *dams* (annual) 9,800,000 [1]*dams* (annual)	9,400,000 *dams* (annual) 9,600,000 [1]*dams* (annual)
Dastur-ul ʻAmal-i ʻAlamgiri	f. 125a-125b	10,000,000 *dams* (annual)	9,700,000 *dams* (annual)	9,400,000 *dams* (annual)
Zawabit-i ʻAlamgiri	ff. 42b-45b	(9,400,000)[2]*dams* (annual)	9,700,000 *dams* (annual)	9,400,000 *dams* (annual)
Halat-i-Mumalik-i-Mahrusa i Alamgiri	f. 149b	10,000,000 *dams* (annual)	9,700,000 *dams* (annual)	9,400,000 *dams* (annual)
Khulasat-us Siyaq	ff. 48b-49a	10,000,000 *dams* (annual)	9,700,000 *dams* (annual)	9,400,000 *dams* (annual)
Malumat-ul Afaq	pp. 195-96	10,000,000 *dams* (annual)	9,700,000 *dams* (annual)	9,400,000 *dams* (annual)

[1] According to the previous scales in force.

[2] The figure within brackets seems to be a mistake of transcription.

TABLE SHOWING THE PAY FOR *ZAT* RANK
(4,000 *Zat*)

Source	*Page or Folio Reference*	*Class I*	*Class II*	*Class III*
Ain-i Akbari Vol. I	p. 125	Rs.22,000 (Per month) 10,560,000 *dams* (annual)	Rs.21,800 (Per month) 10,464,000 *dams* (annual)	Rs.21,600 (Per month) 10,368,000 *dams* (annual)
Farhang-i Kardani	ff. 43-49	8,000,000 *dams* (annual)	7,700,000 *dams* (annual)	7,400,000 *dams* (annual)
Selected Documents of Shahjahan's Reign	p. 80	8,000,000 *dams* (annual)	7,700,000 *dams* (annual) 7,800,000[1]	7,400,000 *dams* (annual) 7,600,000[1]
Dastur-Ul'Amal-i Alamgiri	ff. 125a-125b	8,000,000 *dams* (annual)	7,700,000 *dams* (annual)	7,400,000 *dams* (annual)
Zawabit-i 'Alamgiri	ff. 42b-45b.	8,000,000 *dams* (annual)	7,700,000 *dams* (annual)	7,400,000 *dams* (annual)
Mumalik Mahrusa-i 'Alamgiri	f. 150a	8,000,000 *dams* (annual)	7,700,000 *dams* (annual)	7,400,000 *dams* (annual)
Khulasat-us Siyaq	ff. 48b-49a.	8,000,000 *dams* (annual)	7,700,000 *dams* (annual)	7,400,000 *dams* (annual)
Malumat-ul Afaq	pp. 195-196	8,000,000 *dams* (annual)	7,700,000 *dams* (annual)	7,400,000 *dams* (annual)

[1] "According to the previous scales in force."

TABLE SHOWING THE PAY FOR *ZAT* RANK
(3,000 *Zat*)

Source	*Page or Folio Reference*	*Class I*	*Class II*	*Class III*
Ain-i Akbari Vol. I	p. 126	Rs. 17,000 (Per month) 8,160,000 *dams* (annual)	Rs. 16,800 (Per month) 8,064,000 *dams* (annual)	Rs. 16,700 (Per month) 8,016,000 *dams* (annual)
Farhang-i Kardani	ff. 43-49	6,000,000 *dams* (annual)	5,700,000 *dams* (annual)	5,400,000 *dams* (annual)[1]
Selected Documents of Shahjahan's Reign	p. 81	6,000,000[1] *dams* (annual)	5,700,000 *dams* (annual)[1] 5,800,000 (According to the former Dastur-ul-Amal).	5,600,000 *dams* (annual)
Dastur-ul Amal-i Alamgiri	ff. 125a-b.	6,000,000 *dams* (annual)	5,700,000 *dams* (annual)	5,400,000 *dams* (annual)
Zawabit-i Alamgiri	ff. 42b-45b	6,000,000 *dams* (annual)	5,700,000 *dams* (annual)	5,400,000 *dams* (annual)
Mumalik Mahrusa i Alamgiri	f. 150a	6,000,000 *dams* (annual)	5,700,000 *dams* (annual)	5,400,000 *dams* (annual)[1]
Khulasat-us Siyaq	ff. 48b-49a.	6,000,000 *dams* (annual)	5,700,000 *dams* (annual)	5,400,000 *dams* (annual)[1]

[1] "According to the previous scales in force."

TABLE SHOWING THE PAY FOR *ZAT* RANK
(2,000 *Zāt*)

Source	*Page or Folio Reference*	*Class I*	*Class II*	*Class III*
Ain-i Akbari Vol. 1	p. 127	Rs. 12,000 (Per month) 5,760,000 *dams* (annual)	Rs. 11,900 (Per month) 5,712,000 *dams* (annual)	Rs. 11,800 (Per month) 5,664,000 *dams* (annual)
Farhang-i Kardani	ff. 43-49	4,000,000 *dams* (annual)	3,700,000 *dams* (annual)	3,400,000 *dams* (annual)
Selected Documents of Shahjahan's Reign	p. 81	4,000,000 *dams* (annual)	3,700,000 *dams* (annual) 3,800,000[1] (According to the former Dastur-ul-Amal).	3,400,000 *dams* (annual) 3,600,000[1] (According to the former Dastur-ul-Amal)
Dastur-ul Amal-i Alamgiri	ff. 125a-125b	4,000,000 *dams* (annual)	3,700,000 *dams* (annual)	3,400,000 *dams* (annual)
Zawabit-i Alamgiri	ff. 42b-45b	4,000,000 *dams* (annual)	3,700,000 *dams* (annual)	3,400,000 *dams* (annual)
Mumalik Mahrusa i Alamgiri	f. 150a	4,000,000 *dams* (annual)	3,700,000 *dams* (annual)	3,400,000 *dams* (annual)
Khulasat-us siyaq	ff. 48b-49a.	4,000,000 *dams* (annual)	3,700,000 *dams* (annual)	3,400,000 *dams* (annual)
Malumat-ul Afaq	pp. 195-96	4,000,000 *dams* (annual)	5,700,000[2] *dams* (annual)	5,400,000[2] *dams* (annual)

[1] "According to the previous scales in force."

[2] The figures seem to be an error of transcription.

TABLE SHOWING THE PAY FOR *ZAT* RANK
(1,000 *Zāt*)

Source	*Page or Folio Reference*	*Class I*	*Class II*	*Class III*
Ain-i Akbari Vol. 1	p. 128	Rs. 8,200 (Per month) 3,936,000 *dams* (annual)	Rs. 8,100 (Per month) 3,888,000 *dams* (annual)	Rs. 8,000 (Per month) 3,840,000 *dams* (annual)
Farhang-i Kardani	ff. 43-49	2,000,000 *dams* (annual)	1,900,000 *dams* (annual)	1,700,000 *dams* (annual)
Selected Documents of Shahjahan's Reign	pp. 81-82	2,000,000 *dams* (annual)	1,900,000 *dams* (annual)	1,700,000 *dams* (annual)
Dastur-ul Amal-i Alamgiri	ff. 125a-126a.	2,000,000 *dams* (annual)	1,900,000 *dams* (annual)	1,700,000 *dams* (annual)
Zawabit-i Almgiri	ff. 42b-45b	2,000,000 *dams* (annual)	1,900,000 *dams* (annual)	1,700,000 *dams* (annual)
Mumalik-i Mahrusa i Alamgiri	f. 150a	2,000,000 *dams* (annual)	1,900,000 *dams* (annual)	1,700,000 *dams* (annual)
Khulasat-us Siyaq	ff. 48b-49a.	2,000,000 *dams* (annual)	1,900,000 *dams* (annual)	1,700,000 *dams* (annual)
Malumat-ul Afaq	pp. 195-96	2,000,000 *dams* (annual)	1,900,000 *dams* (annual)	1,700,000 *dams* (annual)

CHAPTER III

THE JAGIRDARI SYSTEM AND THE NOBILITY

THE *mansabdars* of the Mughal Empire received their pay either in cash (*naqd*) or in the form of assignments of areas of land from which they were entitled to collect the land revenue and all other taxes imposed or sanctioned by the Emperor. These assignments were known as *jagirs* and *tuyuls*, though sometimes the term *iqta*, used in the time of Delhi Sultans, was also employed. The officers, when paid in cash were known as *naqdi*, and, when holding assignments, as *jagirdars* and *tuyuldars*. The author of *Mirat-al Istilah* suggests that the term *tuyul* was originally used for the assignment held by princes of royal blood but, at least in the time of Aurangzeb, the term was indifferently used for all assignments.[1] Land which was reserved for the income of the crown was called *khalisa* or *khalisa-i sharifa*;[2] and such areas, which were to be assigned, but were for the time being managed by imperial officers, were known as *paibaqi*.[3]

By far the larger part of the Empire was assigned in *jagirs*. In the 10th year of Aurangzeb, for example, out of a total estimated revenue (*jamadami*) of 924 crores of *dams* for the whole Empire, 725 crores were assigned to *jagirdars* or placed in *paibaqi*.[4] Nothing like the *karori* experiment of Akbar, when practically the whole Empire had been placed in the *khalisa*, was repeated in the 17th century. Indeed in the last years of Jahangir's reign, the *khalisa* shrank to 28 crores of *dams*[5] or less than 1/20th of the total *jama*. But since then, especially in the reign of Shahjahan, an expansion of the *khalisa* had taken place. Its *jama* stood at 120 crores out of a total *jama* of 880 crores i.e. it was over 1/7th of the whole empire in Shahjahan's 20th year.[6] In Aurangzeb's 10th year, it amounted to almost one-fifth of the total *jama*.[7] No later information about the precise extent of the *khalisa* is available.

These data show that the *khalisa* covered a very large portion of the Empire, but the Emperor was also in command of a considerable income collected directly by his treasury. Out of this he paid his own troops, artillery men, attendants, etc., and the *naqdi mansabdars*. Still the fact

[1] The *jagirs* of the princes are usually indicated by such phrases as *jagir-i* or *Tuyul-i Wukla-i Sarkar-i Daulat Madar*.

[2] *Mirat-al Istilah*, f. 15a.

[3] *Khulasat-us Siyaq*, f. 24b; *Waqa-i Ajmer*, pp. 74, 375-6; Mamuri, ff. 156b-157a.

[4] *Mirat-al Alam*: f. 214b. The same figures appear in *Malumat-al Afaq*, p. 194.

[5] Qazwini, p. 423. For the *jama* of the Empire, see '*Majalis-as Salatin*'. ff. 115a-b.

[6] Lahori, *Badshah Nama*, II, pp. 710-13.

[7] *Mirat-al Alam*, Op.cit.

remains that no less than 4/5th of the revenue of the Empire had been alienated to the *jagirdars*.

The importance of this fact for the administrative system of the Mughal Empire does not seem to have been grasped fully. Writers of text-books, and even of standard works,[1] in their discussions of revenue and other branches of the administration assume that the machinery of the *khalisa* was identical with the administrative aparatus as a whole. They, therefore, fail to analyse the way in which the *jagirdari* system was integrated with the administration and how the prevalence of this institution created problems for which various devices had to be adopted from time to time. In the present chapter, an attempt will be made to correct this distortion by analysing the *jagirdari* system, the nature of the problems posed by it during the second half of the seventeenth century, and their impact on the Mughal administrative structure.

Assignment of Jagirs

Generally speaking, *jagirs* were assigned in lieu of the salary due to a *mansabdar*, for his *zat* and *sawar* ranks. Such *jagirs* were known as *jagir-i tankhwah* or *tankhwah-i jagir*.[2]

When a *jagir* was allotted to a person conditional upon his appointment to a particular post, the *jagir* was known as *mashrut* or conditional.[3] Thus, in 1672 when Muhammad Amin Khan was appointed *subedar* of Gujarat, the *jagir* of *sarkar* Patan and Beram Gam, which was attached to the post, was granted to him as *mashrut*.[4] *Jagirs*, which involved no obligation of service, being independent of rank, were known as *inam*.[5] It was for the Emperor to decide whether any *mansabdar* would receive his pay in cash or in *jagir*.[6]

Since a *jagir* was given in lieu of cash salary, it was essential that it should yield at least as much as the salary to which the holder was entitled. If it yielded less, he would be a loser, and would not be able to fulfil his obligations. Moreland has quoted a set of terms representing what was regarded as the average or normal revenue yield of each *mahal*[7] or revenue unit, on the basis of which all *jagir* assignments were

[1] In P. Saran's *Provincial Government of the Mughals*, even the *jagirdar's* agents for collecting revenue in the *jagirs* are not mentioned. [2] *Dilkusha*, f. 139a; Allahabad Documents, 789.

[3] *Mirat-i Ahmadi*, Vol. I, p. 303. [4] *Mirat-i Ahmadi*, Vol. I, p. 289.

[5] Lahori, Vol. II, p. 397. Surat was assigned to Jahan Ara Begam as *inam*. Raja Jai Singh was honoured by *inam* assignments; by that time Mirza Raja Jai Singh had been granted the maximum rank permitted to any noble and there was no way of honouring him further except by granting *inam* assignments, *Alamgir Nama*, p. 618.

[6] *Akhbarat*, 45th R.Y. p. 46. In 1701 Aurangzeb issued an order that if the soldiers of the *risalas* of Ruhullah Khan, Muhammad Amin Khan and Siyadat Khan, etc. were not prepared to accept *jagirs* in lieu of their salary, they were to be dismissed.

[7] A *mahal* often corresponded to a *pargana* which was the smallest administrative unit. But it could be a smaller unit, or would cut across the administrative units.

made. In Akbar's time such figures were comprehended under the term *jama*, which has been rendered a little inaccurately as 'valuation'.[1] In the 17th century, the term *jamadami* came into use for the same category of figures. This was so probably because the figures were stated in *dams*, which was calculated at a fixed ratio of 40 *dams* to the rupee. The salaries too were expressed in terms of this unit, although the money in use was the rupee and the original copper *dam* had appreciated much above its former value of 1/40 of a rupee.[2] The value of this new term *jamadami* is that we are now able to distinguish the assessment figures on the basis of which *jagirs* were assigned, from the ordinary *jama* or seasonal assessment of revenue upon the individual peasant of the village.

Whenever a person was assigned a *jagir*, the *pargana* or villages assigned to him were such as bore a *jamadami* in the imperial register exactly equal to his pay. This is shown best by the actual assignment orders which have survived. These state first the rank of the assignee. Then follows the statement of pay which he should get against his rank according to the sanctioned schedules. This is termed *muqarrara talab* or sanctioned claim. To meet this claim, *parganas* with their *jamadami* figures are then specified, the total of the *jamadami* figures being equal to the amount of the pay-claim.[3] In case the sanctioned amount of the pay-claim could only be met by assigning not the total *jama* of a *pargana* but a fraction of it, this fraction was stated. In that case, the *diwani* or Imperial Finance office had to order a division (*qismat*) of the villages of the *pargana* among the assignees, who had obtained claims on its *jama*.[4] However, the assignment of a whole *pargana* (*darobast*) in one *jagir* was always preferred by the administration to dividing it among two or more *jagirdars*.[5]

How the *jamadami* figures were actually worked out in the 17th century is an obscure subject. Whether the system of deriving it from the average of the revenue collection (*hal-i hasil*) of the past ten years (*dah-sala*), as under Akbar,[6] continued under his successors is never directly discussed by any contemporary authority. However, we certainly find that the central government was interested in collecting information about the "papers of *hal-i hasil* of *parganas* and the comparative revenue state-

[1] Cf. Moreland, *Agrarian System of Moslem India*, pp. 56, 209, 212, 240.

[2] Cf. Manucci, II, pp. 374-75. For the appreciation of the *dam* see Moreland, *Akbar to Aurangzeb*, pp. 183-85, and Irfan Habib 'Currency System of the Mughal Empire', *Medieval India Quarterly*, Vol. IV. The *dam* in which the salaries were stated thus became a money of account, having no relation to the actual copper coin of that name.

[3] See the assignment orders published in *Selected Documents of Shah Jahan's Reign*, the sanctioned pay-schedule is given on pp. 79-84 of the volume. See also *Vir Vinod*, II, pp. 428-31 and Moreland's description of assignment orders in *JRAS*, 1936, pp. 641-62.

[4] See *Waqa-i Ajmer*, 470, 637; also Allahabad, No. 880.

[5] *Ruq 'at-i Alamgir*, pp. 26-27; Fraser, 86, ff. 6a-7a.

[6] Moreland, *Agrarian System of Moslem India*, pp. 96-98.

ment of ten years (*muwazana-i dah sala*) of the provinces".[1]

Nevertheless, the problem which had existed in the early years of Akbar's reign, namely that the *jama* was 'a long way' from *hasil*,[2] continued and, if anything, became more acute during the 17th century. During his second Viceroyalty of the Deccan, Aurangzeb represented to Shahjahan that 'the *jamadami* of these provinces (of the Deccan) after the reduction (sanctioned) is 1,449,000,000 *dams*. The actual revenue (*mahsul*) thereof, including the deduction of 1,200,000 rupees which the *diwans* had not written off but put as due to natural calamity (*afat*), comes to 10,000,000 rupees (i.e. 400,000,000 *dams*), which does not come on average to three-monthly (or one-fourth) of the *jamadami*'.[3] This statement cannot be taken to mean that the same state of affairs existed in the other parts of the Empire. Still, the *hasil* seldom amounted anywhere to the full amount of the *jama*. In a document setting out the lease of two *jagirs* in Awadh, we come across the statement that one was an 'eight-monthly' and the other 'of seven months and seven days', because in the former case, the *jama* was 440,000 *dams* and the yield of the lease Rs. 7,333 and annas four, and in the latter the respective figures were 210,000 *dams* and Rs. 3,162.[4] The nature and effect of this difference systematised under the 'rule of months', in so far as it affected the pay and obligations of the *mansabdar* have already been discussed.

An adjustment was sometimes made, if the collection happened to be far below expectations. This reduction was known as *takhfif-i dami*. In such cases, the *jagirdar* was entitled to the amount of the reduction, so as to keep the *jamadami* equal to his pay., This was adjusted either by a cash payment from the treasury or the assignment of additional *jagir* of an equivalent amount.[5] At the same time if the actual collection by the *jagirdar* exceeded the *jamadami* or the 'month ratio' sanctioned for the *jagirdars*, the difference could be recovered from the assignee.[6] Sometimes an honest *jagirdar* himself would report that he had collected revenue in excess of the amount fixed by the 'month ratio'. In such cases, the *sawar* rank of the *jagirdar* might be increased and the surplus revenue adjusted.[7] A periodical correction of the revenue papers concerning

[1] *Mirat-i Ahmadi*, I, 326-7. The statement refers to Gujarat, A.D. 1692. See also *Siyaq Nama*' pp. 100-101, where it is stated that *mauwazana-i dahsala* and other *hasil* papers were to be regularly deposited in the office of the central *diwan*. This manual was written in the time of Aurangzeb; *Selected Documents of Shahjahan's Reign*, pp. 89-90, 194-5; *Ruq'at-i Alamgir*, pp. 88, 107, 164.

[2] *Ain*, II, p. 2; *Akbar Nama*, II, 270, III, p. 117.

[3] *Adab-i Alamgiri*, 27a-27b; *Ruq'at-i Alamgir*, 121-123. [4] Allahabad Documents, 885, 884.

[5] *Selected Documents of Shahjahan's Reign*, p. 177; *Adab-i Alamgiri*, ff. 18b-19a, 24b, 25b, 29b-30a, 39a, 40a-40b, 43a, *Ruqat*, pp. 88, 95-96, 98.

[6] *Adab-i Alamgiri*, ff. 40a-40b; *Ruq'at-i Alamgir*, pp. 130-31; *Ma'asir-i Alamgiri*, p. 170; *Fathiya-i Ibriya*, ff. 117a-b.

[7] Thus, according to the *Akhbarat* (12th R.Y. of Aurangzeb, p. 223), Asad Khan reported to the Emperor that Mukarram Khan had informed him that the actual yield of his *jagir* in the Deccan exceeded the 'month ratio' sanctioned for him. It was ordered that an increase of 100

assignments was also made; the paper value of the *jagir* was often compared with the actual collection, and according to it changes were made in respect of the 'month ratio' in which the *jagir* was classed.[1]

Transfer of Jagirs

The *jagirs* were by their very nature transferable. That no person should have the same *jagir* for a long period was an established principle of the Mughal Empire. Abul Fazl linked it to the way a gardener transplants plants.[2] That all *jagirs*, except for *watan-jagirs*, were subject to *taghaiyur* or transfer after every three or four years was noticed by European travellers of the 17th century from Hawkins to Bernier.[3] The real basis for our statement is, however, the actual evidence of such transfer in chronicles, letters, documents—a whole mass of material that is too voluminous to be cited. It is enough to say that any collection of administrative letters like the *Adab-i Alamgiri* or *Nigar Nama-i Munshi* will provide cases of numerous transfers. No period seems to have been fixed for such assignments. As Bhim Sen says, "the agents of the *jagirdars*" never had "any hope of the confirmation (*bahali*) of the *jagirs* for the following year".[4]

From the view-point of the *jagirdars*, the transfer system had certain complications. For purposes of transfer it was assumed that *Kharif* and *Rabi* crops were of equal value everywhere, except in Bengal and Orissa.[5] But since in fact the *Rabi* and *Kharif* harvests were hardly of equal value anywhere, the *jagirdar* had to suffer heavily as a result of transfers made in mid-year. Sometimes the assignee was required to collect the previous arrears (*baqaya*) and send them to the treasury.[6]

A *jagir* was not only transferred because of a principle. It was often transferred because a *mansabdar*, when sent to serve in a province, had to be assigned a *jagir* there; and similarly, those recalled from there would require *jagirs* elsewhere. When Aurangzeb was Viceroy of the Deccan under Shahjahan, he protested on numerous occasions, though usually unsuccessfully, against the transfer from northern India of the *jagirs* of those who were posted (*tainat*) with him.[7] In 1694 as Emperor he ordered that only those persons who served in the Deccan were to be assigned *jagirs* there.[8] The *Mirat-i Ahmadi* contains instances of persons

---

sawar be made in the rank of Mukarram Khan to offset the excess of his income. Also see *Akbar Nama*, III, 459.

[1] *Akhbarat*, 40th R.Y., P. 9; *Ruq'at-i Alamgir*, p. 10. [2] *Akbar Nama*, II, 332-3.

[3] *Early Travels*, 114; De Laet, tr. Hoyland, 94-95; Bernier, p. 227.

[4] *Dilkusha*, f. 139a.

[5] *Selected Documents of Shahjahan's Reign*, pp. 76-77; Fraser, 86, f. 60b.

[6] *Mirat-i Ahmadi*, Vol. I, p. 305; *Fathiya-i Ibriya*, f. 130b.

[7] *Adab-i Alamgiri*, ff. 18b-19a, 25b, 40a-40b, 43a.

[8] *Akhbarat*, 38th S. Y., p. 46.

appointed *faujdars* and *jagirdars* of the same place in Gujarat.[1] Another consideration which had to be kept in view when transferring and assigning *jagirs* was that the *jagirdars* should be competent to manage such areas as were assigned to them. Thus, an administrative manual written in the time of Farrukh Siyar recommends that the *jagirs* should be assigned on the following principle : The Governor was to have one-fourth of his *jagirs* in seditious (*zor-talab*) areas and the rest in areas classed as medium (*ausat*); the *diwans*, *bakhshis* and other high *mansabdars* should have half of their *jagirs* in 'medium areas' and the other half in revenue-paying (*raiyati*) areas; the *jagirs* of small *mansabdars* were to be placed entirely in *raiyati* areas.[2]

The system of *jagir* transfers was necessary for the unity and cohesion of the Empire. Only by these transfers could the nobles or military commandants be prevented from developing local relations and growing into local potentates. Under this system they could never call any part of the country their own and remained entirely dependent on the will of the Emperor.

Watan-Jagirs

The *watan-jagirs* were the only exception to the general system of *jagir* transfers. The *watan-jagirs* originated from the admission of *zamindars* or territorial chiefs into the Mughal service. The chiefs obtained *mansabs* or ranks, the pay for which was equal to the *jama* of their dominions, but since their dominions had been autonomous, this calculation was arbitrary.[3] Their old dominions were known as their *watans* and they remained with their family. As Raja Indar Singh stated in a representation to Aurangzeb, the established practice was that 'after the death of the holders of *watans*, *mansabs* are given (to thier heirs) according to the assessed revenue (*damha*) of their *watans*'.[4]

Theoretically, the king was entitled to determine the succession to a *watan-jagir*. But, as a rule, the Emperor neither took away, nor resumed any part of the *watan-jagir* from a ruling dynasty.[5] Thus, Aurangzeb's annexation of Jodhpur to the *Khalisa* in 1679 caused the greatest resent-

[1] *Mirat-i Ahmadi*, I, 341, 343.

[2] *Hidayat-al Qawaid*, Aligarh MS. f. 8a.

[3] Cf. The arrangement made with Pratab, the *zamindar* of Palamau (Lahori, *Badshah Nama*, II, pp. 360-61).

[4] *Selected Documents of Aurangzeb's Reign*, p. 121. The *jamadami* of Raja Indar Singh's *watan-jagir* exceeded the pay due on his rank. He, therefore, prayed that either his rank be increased to make its pay equal to the *jamadami;* or that the *jamadami* be reduced to equal the pay for his existing rank. In either case, no one else would be assigned a share in his *watan-jagir*. His *mansab* was increased. *Ruq'at-i Alamgir*, p. 167; Lahori, *Badshah Nama*, I, p. 161.

[5] Except as a temporary measure. Cf. Satish Chandra, *Parties and Politics at the Mughal Court, 1707-40*, p. 31-32.

ment among the Rathors, who thought it was a violation of an established custom.[1] In some other cases in the same reign, neither lack of a direct descendant, nor rebellion, was considered a sufficient reason for resuming a *watan-jagir*. In 1659 Jaswant Singh of Marwar was pardoned despite his various acts of hostility towards Aurangzeb and his *watan* was left untouched.[2] Jagat Singh, son of Mukand Singh Hara, who had a *mansab* of 2,000/1,000, died (A.D. 1681) and left no male issue. His *watan* was conferred on Kishore, son of Ratan Singh, a near relation of the deceased.[3] In the 43rd R.Y. of Aurangzeb, Raja Karan of Bikaner rebelled against the Emperor, and when he submitted through the mediation of Amir Khan, he was pardoned and granted a *mansab* and his *watan-jagir* was not touched.[4]

If the holders of *watan-jagirs* obtained any increase in their ranks—or if from the very beginning they had held a rank the pay for which was not fully met from the *jamadami* of their *watan-jagirs*—they were given ordinary *tankhwa jagirs* in addition to their *watan-jagirs*.[5] Thus, Maharaja Jaswant Singh, though holding the whole of Marwar as his *watan-jagir*, held *jagirs* in Hisar (Delhi province) which, on his appointment as governor of Gujarat for the second time, were transferred to Gujarat.[6]

It was not necessary that a *watan-jagir* should always be held against a rank. In one case, at least, we know it to have been given against *inam* or pay granted without any obligation.[7]

As we have implied above, the *watan-jagir* originated in settlements made with *zamindars* who were already in possession of their *watans* (homelands) before the expansion of the Mughal Empire. Non-*zamindars* did not normally hold any place as *watan-jagirs*. As a concession to these *mansabdars*, Jahangir decided to institute *altun tamgha* (or *al-tamgha*) *jagirs* to be held permanently.[8] But these *jagirs* were confined to the place of birth, or perhaps, the family seat, of the noble concerned and could not compare with the great ancestral dominions of the Rajput chiefs. Very few references to *al-tamgha jagirs* survive from Aurangzeb's reign. But that these were still granted is shown by the request of a high officer that he be assisted in bringing his family from Persia through the assignment of a jagir of "ten lacs of *dams* in the province of Lahore in *al-tamgha*".[9]

[1] *Waqa-i Ajmer*, pp. 82, 83, 245-6, and passim.

[2] Mamuri, f. 107b. [3] *Dilkusha*, f. 83a. [4] Mamuri, f. 116b.

[5] See, for example, Jahangir's *farman* granting *mansab* and *jagir* to Rao Karan of Mewar in *Vir Vinod*, II, p. 239,

[6] *Mirat-i Ahmadi*, I, p. 277.

[7] *Akhbarat*, 25th R.Y., p. 270. To Bhan Prohit, 30 lacs of *dams* in *Pargana* Khor Jogi Garh by way of *watan* in *inam* in addition to a rank.

[8] *Tuzuk*, p. 10.

[9] *Matin-al Insha*, Letters of Ali Quli Khan, *faujdar* of Kuch Bihar (c. 1700), Bodl. Ms., ff. 99b-100a.

Fiscal Rights of the Jagirdars

The assignment orders described in almost set terms the rights which the Emperor granted to the *jagirdars*. The local officials and "the head-men and peasants and cultivators" are informed that "they must answer to the agents (*gumashtas*) of the person named (i.e. the *jagirdar*) for the authorized revenue (*mal-i wajibi*) and all claims of the state (*huquq-i diwani*), properly and honestly".[1] No other right except that of collecting the land revenue and authorized taxes was delegated to the *jagirdar* as *jagirdar*. And this right too he was expected to exercise in conformity with imperial regulations. Moreland has pointed out that Abul Fazl's language leaves no doubt that the *jagirs* were bound by the orders setting forth the procedure according to which the land revenue was to be assessed and collected.[2] Similar language is used in Aurangzeb's comprehensive *farman* on revenue administration to Rasikdas Karori issued in his 8th R.Y. "All revenue-collectors (*amils*) of the *mahals* (*parganas*) of the *jagirdars* are required to follow the regulations contained in it".[3] The order that not more than one-half of the produce was to be taken as land revenue, which was given in Aurangzeb's *farmans* to Rasikdas and Muhammad Hashim, was also to be enforced in the *jagirs*. A curious case, where the *jagirdars* sought to evade this, but were found out, is brought up in an order quoted in the *Mirat-i Ahmadi*. "Because of the high price of grain, the (*jama*) revenue assessed (on the peasants) reached the maximum amount. Then grain became cheap. The *jagirdars* and revenue officials (*mutasaddis*) keeping in view the former *jama*, made the current assessment (*jamabandi*) under threats. If they had decided to take half the share of the harvest, they estimated the harvest at 250 maunds, while the actual harvest was only 100 maunds. (By demanding the revenue as half of 250 maunds i.e. 125 maunds), they made his (the peasant's) life a torture for a year and took all his earnings and compelled him to till the soil by blows. (It is ordered, therefore, that) they should only take half the actual harvest and are not to demand anything in excess of this."[4]

Simple statements requiring the *jagirdars* to take not more than half of the produce also occur elsewhere in the revenue records and other literature of the reign.[5]

The *jagirdars* could also collect, in theory, only such cesses and taxes, besides the land revenue, as were permitted by the government. In the 2nd year of his reign, Aurangzeb abolished the road cess (*rahdari*),

[1] *Selected Documents of Shahjahan's Reign*, pp. 5ff.

[2] *Agrarian System of Moslem India*, pp. 91-92.

[3] Text published by Sarkar in *JASB*. N. S. II (1906), pp. 223-55.

[4] *Mirat-i Ahmadi*, I, p. 263. The order was issued in the 8th R.Y., of Aurangzeb.

[5] *Nigarnama-i Munshi*, pp. 80, 92, 98, 144-5; *Raqaim-i Karaim*, ff. 24a-b; *Durr-al Ulum*; f. 140b.

the *toll* levied on grain and vegetables,[1] and the cesses on eatables and drinks. Previously these cesses were collected by the *jagirdars* and the revenue so derived went to the coffers of the *jagirdars* and the *jama* of the *jagirs* included the income from this source. By the abolition of these cesses the imperial exchequer suffered an annual loss of Rs. 25 lakhs in the *khalisa* lands.[2] It seems that in spite of the repeated orders of the Emperor many officers continued to realise at least some of these cesses, if not all. Khafi Khan tells us that this was partly due to the Emperor's reluctance to punish those who were guilty of violating his prohibitions, and partly to the fact that the *diwans* continued to include the income from the forbidden dues in the *jamadami* of the *jagirs*, and so left the *jagirdars* no option but to collect them in order to get the full amount of their pay.[3] The leniency of the Emperor is certainly seen from the following incident recorded in the *Mirat*. In A.D. 1668 it was reported to the Emperor that Kamal Jalauri, *faujdar* of Palan Pur, used to realise *gau charai* and *khurak-i aspan*. It was ordered that, after an enquiry, he should be asked not to collect them.[4] The fact that upon the complaint of the *mutasaddis* against Kamal Jalauri, the Emperor merely ordered him to desist from the practice and no punishment was meted out shows that such disobedience of orders was only too common. In A.D. 1659 Aurangzeb had appointed Mulla Iwaz Wajih, the *muhtasib*, to see to it that the cesses which had been abolished were not realised and certain *mansabdars* and *ahadis* were also directed to assist Mulla 'Iwaz in case of need. Orders for the abolition of cesses etc. were also sent to all provinces of the Empire.[5] But apparently the *muhtasib* achieved only limited success in his object.

Administration of Jagirs

The *jagirdars* had to employ their own agents to collect the revenue and taxes within their *jagirs*. The arrangements made by the big *jagirdars* were naturally on a more systematic basis than those of the smaller assignees. Thus the administrative structure of the *jagirs* of the princes was usually modelled on that of the *khalisa*. The *amils* in the *parganas* of the *jagirs* of the princes were called *karoris* (revenue collectors), a name otherwise reserved for the revenue collectors in the *khalisa*.[6] They also had an *amin* (revenue assessor), a *fotadar* (treasurer), and a *karkun* (accountant) as independent colleagues.[7] However, some of these

[1] *Alamgir Nama*, I, pp. 437-38. A number of orders of Aurangzeb spread all over his reign, detailing forbidden imposts, are set out in *Mirat-i Ahmadi*, Vol. I, pp. 259, 264, 286, 288.

[2] *Mirat-i Ahmadi*, I, p. 249.

[3] Khafi Khan, II, pp. 88-89; *Mirat-i Ahmadi*, I, pp. 263-64; *Durr-al Ulum*, ff. 255b-56a.

[4] *Mirat-i Ahmadi*, I, p. 275. [6]. *Alamgir Nama*, p. 392.

[5] *Selected Documents of Shahjahan's Reign*, p. 121; *Nigarnama-i Munshi*, p. 8 and passim.

[7] *Nigarnama-i Munshi*, pp. 136-37; *Durr-al Ulum*, ff. 138b-139a.

offices could be occasionally assigned to one person. Thus, Muhammad Muazzam ordered the offices of the *amin* and *karoris* to be combined and held by one person only in the *parganas* of his *jagir.*[1]

The chief agent (*gumashta*) of the ordinary *jagirdar* was the *amil*, also known as *shiqdar*. Sometimes, the duties of the *amin* and of the treasurer were also entrusted to him. Usually the *jagirdars* compelled the *amils* to execute a bond in respect of future collections, as was the case in *khalisa*. The *jagirdars* also generally realised a certain amount, known as *qabz*, from the *amils* and the general practice was to appoint as *amils* persons who offered the highest *qabz* to the *jagirdar.*[2] As a rule, the *jagirdar* appointed only those persons as his agents and officers in his *jagir* who had no vested interest in the locality, for his officers, and in particular the *amils*, who had local connections were likely to work in collusion with the *zamindars* and others to the detriment of the interest of the *jagirdar.*[3] The *jagirdar* sometimes found himself in great difficulty concerning the management of his agents, especially if he was far away. Izad Bakhsh Rasa a high officer of Aurangzeb, complained rhetorically that "the boat of his *jagir* was floundering in the flood of misappropriation raised by his tempestuous *amils* in Northern India, while he was serving in the Deccan".[4]

Some *jagirdars* tried to pass on a part of their burden to the shoulders of their troops by parcelling out their *jagirs* among them and asking them to get their pay by collecting the revenue from the villages assigned to them out of their masters' *jagirs.*[5] A practice which appealed especially to the smaller *jagirdars*, who did not possess enough resources to arrange for the collection of revenue from a distance, was that of *ijara* or revenue-farming.[6] Among the Awadh documents preserved at Allahabad almost all the *ijara* arrangements, which are recorded, were made by the smaller *jagirdars*,[7] while the big *jagirdars* usually had their full force of *amils* and other officers. However, even the grandees sometimes farmed out their *jagirs*. Thus, it was reported in 1696 from Kashmir that the high grandees who had been assigned *jagirs* there had farmed them out to merchants, who were collecting the revenue with the greatest oppression.[8]

The *ijara* was regarded as a scourge for the peasantry. The farmers (*ijaradars*), after having obtained their job by offering the highest bids,

[1] *Nigarnama-i Munshi*, p. 77. [2] *Dilkusha*, f. 139a.

[3] These remarks are based on a study of the 17th century documents in the Allahabad Record Office, concerned with the arrangements made by the *jagirdars* for collecting revenue.

[4] *Riyazul-Wadad*, f. 5b.

[5] Allahabad Documents, 789; *Waqa-i Ajmer*, p. 359.

[6] Cf. Shah Waliullah, *Siyasi Maktubat*, p. 42, where it is recommended that small *mansabdars* should be paid in cash and not through *jagirs*, because such people could not themselves collect revenue from their *jagirs* and could be compelled to farm them out.

[7] Allahabad Documents, 884-87, 889-90.

[8] *Akhbarat*, 39th R.Y. p. 144.

stopped at nothing in order to fulfil their pledges to the *jagirdār* and to make a profit for themselves. Sadiq Khan, the historian of Shahjahan, declares that this practice had become very common during Shahjahan's reign and that it was one of the causes of the ruin of the peasantry.[1] Morally *ijaras* were strongly disapproved of at the Court, and this is proved by the fact that in the case of revenue-farming in Kashmir as mentioned above Aurangzeb took the extreme step of bringing all *jagirs* into the *khalisa* in order to suppress this practice there.[2] But there is no reason to believe that *ijaras* were legally forbidden, for in that case the regular *ijara*-documents preserved at Allahabad would not have been drawn up and written.

Jagirdars and Zamindars

The author of *Mirat-al Istilah*, an 18th century text, defines the term zamindar as "literally meaning master of the land (*sahib-i zamin*) but now (actually) the *malik* (proprietor) of the land of a village or township, who (also) carries on cultivation".[3] A *zamindar*, therefore, was not a person who merely owned the land he cultivated. Many petty *zamindars* corresponded in economic status to better-off peasants, who leased the land they cultivated. On the other extreme stood the various tributary chiefs and autonomous Rajas, who were also called *zamindars* by the Mughal Chancery.

It is a remarkable fact that general revenue regulations issued in the time of Akbar and Aurangzeb exclude the *zamindars* from the framework of the standard revenue machinery prescribed under them. Aurangzeb's *farman* to Rasikdas, for example, insists on the assessment being made directly on the peasants by the officials of the *khalisa* as well as of the *jagirdars*. It mentions the *zamindars* only once and that in connection with illegal exactions.[4] On the other hand, there is considerable evidence that the *zamindars* paid the revenue on behalf of whole villages. The *Waqa-i Ajmer* (1679-80)[5], and the letters of Ra'ad Andaz Khan (c. 1700), relating to Baiswara and Awadh,[6] provide us with numerous examples of *zamindars* paying, or being compelled to pay, the land-revenue (*mal*) in areas which, according to the *Ain's* tables of rates, were under *zabt* or the standard administration.

A possible explanation seems to be that every locality had some land

[1] Sadiq Khan, *Shahjahan Nama*, Or. 174, ff. 10a-b.

[2] *Akhbarat*, op. cit.

[3] *Mirat-al Istilah*, f. 122 b; Moreland, however identified *zamindar* with the chief. For a criticism of his theory on the basis of the evidence of the *Ain-i Akbari*, see Irfan Habib in *Proceedings of the Indian History Congress*, Trivandrum Session, (1958) pp. 320-322.

[4] *JASB*, No. II, 1906 ed. Sarkar, pp. 223-55.

[5] *Waqa-i Ajmer*, pp. 55, 398.

[6] *Insha-i Roshan Kalam*, ff. 2a, 3a, ff.

under *zamindars*, while the rest was held by peasants (*raiyati*) and had no *zamindars* as intermediaries. It is interesting to see that this broad classification occurs in the *Siyaq Nama*, a manual compiled in the reign of Aurangzeb where the land is divided into two classes : *raiyati* (peasant-held) and *ta'alluqa*. The term *ta'alluqa* was now slowly becoming a synonym for *zamindari*.[1]

If the above hypothesis be accepted, then a *jagirdar* had normally to deal with both peasants and *zamindars* in his *jagir*. It is possible that the tendency was to summarily assess the land in the possession of a *zamindar* and to collect the revenue from him without any reference to the peasants. This is suggested by two pairs of documents from Awadh appertaining to Aurangzeb's reign, in both of which the assessee is the *zamindar* (*malik*) or *ta'alluqdar* of the villages for which he paid the revenue. The assessors are in both cases agents of a *jagirdar*. But while in the first pair of documents the land revenue is shown as varying from year to year, in the other it is fixed at the same amount (*bi-l muqta*) for every year.[2] In the second, then, the *jagirdar's* demand was independent of what the peasants actually harvested.

Summary assessment of land revenue and collection through *zamindars* must generally have considerably simplified the task of the *jagirdars* and their agents. And it might be expected that they would welcome the institution of *zamindari*. Yet, it was precisely from the *zamindars* that they met with the greatest opposition and hostility. A heavy assessment would deprive the *zamindars* of their income and in that case they might use their armed retainers, backed in some cases by the peasants, to defy the *jagirdar*. The *Hidayat-al Qawaid* classified the *zamindars* into those who were submissive and revenue paying (*raiyati*) and those who were rebellious (*zor-talab*). It adds that a *jagirdar* holding a small *mansab* would usually have the greatest difficulty in subduing the rebellious *zamindars*.[3] In a semi-humorous petition to God, ascribed to *Izad Bakhsh Rasa*, the first task of a *jagirdar* reaching his assignment is represented to be the suppression of defiant *zamindars*.[4]

By such acts of defiance a *zamindar* might forfeit his *zamindari* rights. But the letters of Rad Andaz Khan make it clear that a *zamindar* could not be dispossessed or appointed by anyone except the Emperor. An official or *jagirdar* could only send his *tajviz* or recommendation to the Court.[5] Sometimes a member of the same old family might be appointed to replace a recalcitrant *zamindar*. In Aurangzeb's time, there are also

[1] *Siyaq Nama*, pp. 35, 36. For the synonymity of *zamindar* and *ta'alluqdar*, see the sale-deeds of Calcutta 1703 cited in Moreland, *Agrarian System*, pp. 191-92. Also see Irfan Habib, *The Agrarian System of Mughal India*, pp. 139, 171, for the terms *ta'alluqa* and *ta'alluqdar*.

[2] Allahabad Documents, 897, 1206, 1220, 1223.

[3] *Hidayat-al Qawaid*, ff. 65a-b.

[4] *Bayaz-i Izad Bakhsh Rasa*, I.O. 4014, f. 2a-2b. I owe this reference to Dr Irfan Habib.

[5] *Insha-i Roshan Kalam*, ff. 3b-4a, 7a.

cases where outsiders were appointed, who were often Muslims.[1] The chief condition prescribed was that the nominee should have an *ulus* or body of armed retainers.[2] In exceptional cases, a *jagirdar* himself might be appointed *zamindar* of an area under his charge. An example of this occurs in a *sanad* of *zamindari* from the court to a *jagirdar* near Mathura. The *sanad* reads : "Whereas it has been submitted to His Majesty that Nawab Bahadur Hasan Ali Khan, *faujdar* of the *chakla* of Islamabad (Mathura) has recommended the grant of the *zamindari* of 25 villages (specified hereunder) in the *pargana* of Sahar in the province of Akbarabad, which was inhabited by rebels and lay in the *jagir* of Nawab Qasim, son of Daulat, to the said Qasim, and he has petitioned that a *farman* be issued from the Court to order the grant of the *zamindari* of the said villages to the said Qasim, therefore, the imperial order has been issued that we have granted the *zamindari* of the said villages to Qasim, so that he might expel the ill-mannered rebels and settle revenue paying peasants there.... So long as these villages are held in his *jagir*, he can keep the land revenue and other taxes (*mal-i wajib wa huquq-i diwani*). And when the said villages are assigned in *jagir* to someone else, he will be answerable for the revenue-collections (*hasil*) to the *amil* (revenue collector) of that place."[3]

The order shows that though a *jagirdar* might be made the *zamindar* of an area, this did not make that locality his *watan-jagir*. The *jagir* remained transferable, while the *zamindari* was a permanent hereditary possession.

It has been suggested that Aurangzeb's reign saw a great increase in the pressure of the administration and of the *jagirdars* upon the *zamindars* as a class.[4] Manucci declared that "usually the viceroys and governors (of the Mughal Empire) are in a constant state of quarrel with the Hindu princes and *zamindars*—with some because they wish to seize their lands; with others to force them to pay more revenue than is customary".[5] The conflict of the state and the *zamindars* over the payment of land revenue was a constant feature of medieval society. That such conflicts were a new phenomenon in the reign of Aurangzeb may be doubted. Detailed evidence on this point from the earlier reigns is not forthcoming, but that may be because we generally lack for the early period the type of material, e.g. the *Akhbarat* and the numerous collections of letters and documents etc. that have survived from Aurangzeb's reign. But even if the pressure upon *zamindars* as a system had been fully inherited, its continuance under Aurangzeb's reign must have some fresh causes as well.

[1] *Insha-i Roshan Kalam*, contains a number of cases of appointment of Muslims (ff. 3b-4a, 7a); see the numerous instances of appointments of *zamindars* in the *Akhbarat*.

[2] *Insha-i Roshan Kalam;* f. 34b.

[3] *Nigarnama-i Munshi*, p. 152.

[4] Irfan Habib, *The Agrarian System of Mughal India*, pp. 334-38.

[5] Manucci, II, pp. 431-432.

As we will see, there was a scarcity of *jagirs*; and even when *jagirs* were actually obtained the revenue collected was less than the *jama*: hence, the 'month-scales'. Under such conditions it should not be surprising that the *jagirdars* began to squeeze the *zamindars* harder during the latter part of Aurangzeb's reign. Under this squeeze, as Manucci tells us, there was usually "some rebellion of the *rajahs* and *zamindars* going on in the Mogul Kingdom".[1] But further investigation is necessary before we can reach any positive conclusion on this point.

Imperial Control Over the Jagirdars

We have said earlier that the *jagirdari* system was an essential aspect of Mughal administration. It does not mean, however, that the *jagirdar* possessed within his *jagir* an absolute power over its inhabitants. On the contrary, his authority was checked by an almost parallel system of administration under the direct control of the king and his ministers.

In the field of revenue collection, the king's intersts were represented in every *pargana* by two officials known as the *qanungo* and the *chaudhari* (*deshmukh* in the Deccan). The former was usually an accountant, the latter a *zamindar*.[2] Their offices were generally hereditary, but they invariably held their appointment on the basis of a *sanad* or imperial order. They could also be removed from their posts by the Emperor. But their appointment was, as a rule, for life and so while *jagirdars* came and went, they stayed on. Every *jagirdar*, or rather the agent of every *jagirdar*, had to rely very heavily on the assistance of these two officials in assessing and collecting the revenue. It was the duty of these officials to assist them, but they also had to check the accounts of collections and to see that no irregular exactions were taken from the peasantry.[3]

The *faujdars* or military commandants appointed by the Emperor had the task of maintaining law and order. And in discharging this duty, they could also operate in the *jagirs*. Some *jagirdars* did, however, obtain the office of *faujdar* for themselves in their *jagirs*. This practice might have been found in the earlier reigns also. In Aurangzeb's reign there are certainly numerous instances of the grants of *faujdari* rights to *jagirdars* by the Emperor.[4]

The *jagirdar* had no judicial powers; every *pargana* had a *qazi* appointed

[1] Manucci, II, p. 462.

[2] This point was made, first, by Charles Elliot after a detailed study of old Mughal records of *Unao* district (quoted by Moreland, in *JRAS*, 1938, pp. 516, ff.).

[3] On the *Qanungo* and his duties, see *Nigarnama-i Munshi*, pp. 91, 140; *Hidayat-al Qawaid*, Aligarh Ms. f. 64a-b; and documents of Farrukh Siyar's reign translated in *Proceedings of Indian Historical Records Commission*, XXXI, part ii, 1945, pp. 142-47. For *chaudharai* or *deshmukhi*, see documents translated by Moreland in *JRAS*, 1938, pp. 516 ff. ; *Mirat-i Ahmadi*, I, p. 216, and *Nigarnama-i Munshi*, p. 80; *Mazhar-i Shahjahani*, p. 189.

[4] *Akhbarat*, 38th R.Y. p. 480, and passim; *Insha-i Roshan Kalam*, ff. 6b, 11b, 24b.

under an imperial *farman*, who heard and settled criminal as well as revenue cases. He was completely independent of the *jagirdar*, and drew his income from the *madad-i ma'ash* granted by the emperor.[1]

Finally, there were the news-reporters, known as *waqa-i navis* and *sewanih navis*. They were expected to report on every matter of importance which occurred in their jurisdiction and to send criticisms and complaints without any respect for persons. The conduct of *jagirdars* or their agents was also one of the subjects on which they sent their reports.[2]

The peasants or inhabitants of a *jagir* could also make complaints direct to the Court;[3] and thus the king reserved the right to intervene and rectify any oppressive act that a *jagirdar* may be guilty of.

The Emperor often ordered enquiries into the administration of various *jagirdars*. Aurangzeb was reprimanded by Shahjahan for not administrating his *jagir* on the lines indicated by the Emperor, and had to explain his conduct.[4] It was, perhaps, natural that the *jagirdars* should sometimes obstruct attempts to collect information about their collections and administrative practices. In 1692 it was reported that the *jagirdars* in Gujarat were preventing *desais* and *muqaddams* from providing information about *hasil* or revenue collections to the officers sent from the Court to collect such information. The Governor of Gujarat thereupon sent *sazavals* or special officials to compel the *jagirdars* to obey orders and allow the imperial officers to collect information freely.[5]

On occasions the Emperor could also order the *jagirdars* to reform their administration. Aurangzeb directed Nasiri Khan to put the administration of his *jagir* on a sound basis and uproot all the seditious elements from there.[6] On Prince Azam's appointment of Muhammad Baqar as port comptroller, Aurangzeb reprimanded the Prince declaring that a thief should not be appointed "guardian of the people".[7] Aurangzeb criticised Prince Muazzam for leaving the administration of his *jagir* in the hands of the Iranis.[8]

At the same time, the imperial administration also undertook some obligations towards the *jagirdars*, particularly of protecting them in the management of their *jagirs* and securing them in the enjoyment of their revenues. The *wakil* of Muhammad Jan Beg, the *qiladar* of Siri Mast Garh, complained to the emperor that Sher Khan, the *faujdar* of Kadak, had realised the revenue of two years from the *jagir* of his client (Muhammad Jan Beg). The emperor ordered the amount to be refunded.[9]

[1] *Siyaq Nama*, p. 36; Allahabad Documents, 782, 1203.

[2] *Nigarnama-i Munshi*, pp. 87-88; See also The English Factoris, 1678-84, Vol. III, (New Series), p. 310.

[3] *Ruq'at-i Alamgir*, ed. Nadvi, p. 119; *Waqa-'i Ajmer*, pp. 217-19; *Ruq'at-i Alamgir*, Kanpur, ed., pp. 40-41; *Mazhar-i Shahjahani*, p. 174.

[4] *Adab-i Alamgiri*, ff. 18a, 19b-20a, 40a-40b.

[5] *Mirat-i Ahmadi*, I, pp. 326-27.

[6] *Adab-i Alamgiri*, f. 168b.

[7] *Raqaim-i Karaim*, f. 1b.

[8] *Raqaim-i Karaim*, f. 8b.

[9] *Akhbarat*, 36th R.Y., p. 8.

The deputy of Alif Khan, the *faujdar* and *qiladar* of Gulbarga, arrested the *amil* of the *jagir* of Sidi Miftah. When this incident was reported to the emperor, he ordered that *gurzbardars* (mace-bearers) be appointed to get the *amil* released and the amount refunded.[1] Saf Shikan Khan, the *jagirdar* of *pargana* Kahni, complained that Bahadur Khan, the *faujdar* of the aforesaid *pargana*, had oppressed the ryots of the locality and that the royts had fled. Saf Shikan Khan also requested that he be appointed the *faujdar* of the aforesaid *pargana*. The emperor ordered Inayat Khan, the *haris* (commandant) of Aurangabad, that he should see to it that the peasants were not oppressed by anyone.[2] It was reported to the emperor by Muhammad Munim that Muhammad Husain Kambo had realised the revenue from the *jagir* of the complainant (Muhammad Munim). The Emperor ordered Aqil Khan to send the culprit to the Court.[3]. The *wakil* of Jamshed Khan complained that Izzat Beg, son of Jahangir Quli Khan, had plundered the *jagir* of his client and had appropriated the goods. The complainant also prayed that *gurzbardars* be appointed. The Emperor ordered Bahramand Khan to direct Jahangir Quli Khan to ask his son to refund the whole amount and warned him that in future such incidents must not be repeated.[4]

The evidence that we have presented above shows that so far as the reign of Aurangzeb is concerned, the *jagirdars* had not yet begun to display any open tendency towards autonomy or independence. On the contrary, in many essential respects, they were not only checked and controlled by the imperial government, but were also quite dependent on it for carrying on the management of their *jagirs*.

Jagirdars and the Peasants

The French traveller, Bernier, has presented us with a closely argued analysis of the causes of the failure of the Mughal Empire, which he prophesied in the early years of Aurangzeb's reign, when outwardly the empire had reached the height of its power. The basic argument of Bernier was that the system of the transfer of *jagirs* led inevitably to oppression and the devastation of the country. "The Timariots (Bernier's term for *jagirdars*), Governors and Revenue contractors," he says, "on their part, reason in this manner. Why should the neglected state of this land create uneasiness in our minds ? And why should we expend our money and time to render it fruitful ? We may be deprived of it in a single moment, and our exertions would benefit neither ourselves nor our children. Let us draw from the soil all the money we can, though the peasant should starve or abscond and we should leave it, when commanded to quit, a dreary wilderness".[5]

[1] *Akhbarat*, 38th R. Y., p. 525.
[2] *Akhbarat*, 38th R. Y., p. 480.
[3] *Akhbarat*, 36th R. Y., p. 18.
[4] *Akhbarat*, 38th R. Y., pp. 480-82.
[5] Bernier, p. 227. He was, rather unjustifiably, trying to equate the *jagirdars* with the French

It would appear that Bernier was excessively influenced by the idea of the sanctity of private property : the transfer of *jagirs* seemed to him a violation of this right and thus provoked his strongest condemnation. However, this is not a sufficient reason for dismissing his statements. Indeed he is supported by an Indian observer, writing in or about 1700, who had no similar preconceptions. "The agents of the *jagirdar*", says Bhim Sen, "having apprehensions concerning the niggardly behaviour of the clerks of the Court, who on every excuse effect a transfer, do not have any hope of the confirmation of the *jagir* for the following year and, therefore, give up the habit of protecting the peasants with firmness. The *jagirdar*, who sends a revenue-collector, first owing to his own difficult circumstances, takes something from him in advance (*qabz*) and the latter, on reaching the *jagir*, keeps thinking that, perhaps, another collector is coming behind him, who has paid a larger *qabz*, and so proceeding tyrannically, is unrelenting in his exactions (*tahsil*). Some peasants are not remiss in paying the authorised revenues, but are made desperate by the evil of this excruciating spoliation."[1]

While there is substance in these remarks of Bernier and Bhim Sen, it should also be borne in mind that a *jagirdar*, who had no permanent interest in his *jagir*, had, as an individual, a great temptation to kill the goose that laid golden eggs for the whole of his class. There is, therefore, no doubt that among the *jagirdars* there existed a natural tendency towards the oppression of the peasantry created by the very basis on which the system was founded—namely, *jagir*-transfers.

Before we accept this generalisation, it is pertinent to raise two questions. First, whether the *jagirdars* were able to put their wishes into effect without any check from the Emperor and the administration ? Secondly, whether the Emperor himself, even if he had the inclination, was in practice able to devise suitable measures to check oppression by the *jagirdars* ?

The last section has been wholly devoted to answering the first question. We have, perhaps, evidence enough to show that the imperial control was not nominal, but real during the larger period of Aurangzeb's reign. We may, therefore, pass on to the second question.

Now, just as it is logical to expect that an individual *jagirdar* would be irresistably driven to denude the land of everything worth taking, the Emperor would be inclined to take more farsighted view. He was concerned not only with immediate and personal acquisitions of his officers but also with the long-term prosperity of the Empire. If the

---

aristocracy of his day, forgetful of the fact that while the French aristocracy enjoyed its feudal privileges, the government of France was coming into the hands of middle class men.

For the oppression of the peasantry in Bengal, see *Fathiya-'Ibriya*, ff. 117b-119a, 125a-126a, 127a-b, 131a-b; see also *The Travels of Peter Mundy*, 1608-1667, Vol. II, p. 73.

[1] *Dilkusha*, ff. 138b-139a.

peasants were starved to death in large numbers, and if cultivation fell off, the revenue resources of the Empire would decline and its foundations would be shaken. That Aurangzeb, for one, realised this, is clear from two *farmans* he issued in his 8th and 13th regnal years. In the first, issued to Rasikdas *karori*, it is specially laid down that its provisions were to be applied in the *jagirs* and the *khalisa* alike. Its main object was to reform and regulate the assessment and collection of land-revenue from the peasants, and to prevent the oppression of the peasants or imposition of excessive burdens upon them. The second *farman*, issued to Muhammad Hashim, takes great care to protect the rights of the peasants to their land; even if the peasants abandoned the land, their right to it was to be respected.[1] We have already quoted the order issued by Aurangzeb, specifically condemning the action of the *jagirdars* in Gujarat, who attempted to extort from the peasants through fraudulent means a far larger amount than they were entitled to.[2] It is extremely difficult to judge how far the *jagirdars* were able to evade the imperial regulations, and oppress the population placed in their charge. Moreland's view that the revenue demand increased very sharply in the 17th century and that the increase in the *jamadami* figures is due to increased oppression has been questioned on the ground that Moreland erroneously assumes that prices remained constant during this period; indeed, prices appear to have doubled. In other words, the *jamadami* really shows only a nominal, not a real, increase,[3] apart from the fact that the *jamadami* might vary considerably from the *hasil*, the actual revenue paid. On the other hand, the fact that *jamadami* figures did not increase in real terms does not necessarily prove that there was no growth in oppression. The total revenue might have remained constant simply because the fall in revenue through decline in cultivation was made up by a heavier revenue demand on the cultivated land.

It is beyond the scope of the present work to attempt a detailed investigation of these questions. From the general remarks quoted above, it would appear that the condition of the peasantry had deteriorated towards the end of Aurangzeb's reign, particularly in such areas as the Deccan. In his last years Aurangzeb was involved in a war in the Deccan which demanded all his resources, energy and attention. The old control over the *jagirdars* must have considerably slackened. It is in this context that we must examine the statements of Manucci and others to the effect that Aurangzeb gave up any serious attempt to check

[1] The texts of these two *farmans* have been published by Sarkar in *JASB*, N.S. II, 1906, pp. 223-255. I have collated the text of the *farman* to Muhammad Hashim with the text in *Durr-al Ulum*, ff. 139b-149b, and *Mirat-i Ahmadi*, I, pp. 268-72.

[2] *Mirat-i Ahmadi*, Vol. I, p. 263; order issued in the 8th R.Y.

[3] Cf. Irfan Habib, *The Agrarian System of Mughal India*, pp. 326-28.

his officers, and that on the complaints of most heinous acts of oppression, he only issued the mildest of reprimands.[1]

But whether this oppression of the peasantry was basically a result of the wars of Aurangzeb, which led to the slackening of imperial control, or whether it was itself the cause of the rebellions, since it drove into the arms of the rebels, the starving peasants who had no other hope left, must be left an open question. The latter alternative has been recently advanced as a theory for explaining the fall of the Mughal Empire.[2] While many cogent arguments have been advanced in support of this view, it should not be allowed to become a premature dogma. Our evidence at present is too limited to allow us to come to any conclusion with assurance. And until the available evidence regarding conditions prevailing in various regions has been carefully analysed, all suggestions on the subject must be treated as strictly tentative.

Crisis in the Jagirdari System

The *Jagirdari* system in its standard Mughal form had worked with tolerable efficiency down to the middle of Aurangzeb's reign. But during the last twenty-six years of Aurangzeb's reign, owing to the increasing strain of the Deccan wars on the financial resources of the Empire and the dislocation of the administration owing to the absence of the emperor and the Court from Northern India, the complicated machinery under which *jagirs* were assigned began to lose its efficiency. Aurangzeb's last years, it is true, only saw the first stage of the disorganisation; but it was the beginning of the end.

In this first stage, the crisis which shook the *jagir* system appeared in the garb of what a contemporary writer called, *be-jagiri*. "A world became *jagirless*", says Mamuri, "and there was no *paibaqi* left. The Emperor repeatedly wrote on the register of salary-claimants: 'There is only one pomegranate to serve a hundred sick men.' At the time of despatching armies and assignments of (military) duties to high officers deserving favour, it became necessary that in view of the scarcity of *paibaqi*, the *jagirs* of some of the nobles be resumed and given to others, on the basis of the registers. The Emperor called for the revenue-register of the *parganas* and cancelled the assignments of a very large number of men; and this became a further cause for the ruin and lamentation of the helpless and penniless ones."[3] This was the direct result, according to the author, of the influx of the large number of Deccani nobles, whom Aurangzeb granted *mansabs* on an increasingly generous scale, in order to entice them from the side of his enemies or to prevent them from becoming rebels.[4]

[1] Manucci, II, p. 382; *Dilkusha*, f. 159a; Khafi Khan, II, p, 550.
[2] By Irfan Habib, *The Agrarian System of Mughal India*, pp. 317-51.
[3] Mamuri, f. 157a. [4] Mamuri, ff. 156b-157a; Khafi Khan, II, p. 396.

The statement that there was no *paibaqi* left—i.e. there were no areas left for assignment in *jagirs*—is one which often occurs in our authorities with reference to Aurangzeb's last years; it is frequently put into the mouth of the Emperor himself or of one of his officers. Aurangzeb wrote to Azam, stating frankly that "there is shortage of *paibaqi* and surfeit of claimants for pay".[1] He is reputed to have said repeatedly that the available area of *paibaqi* was like one pomegranate required to serve a hundred sick men.[2] In 1691 he accordingly forbade the *bakhshis* from recommending new men for *mansabs*.[3] Inayatullah Khan is said to have remonstrated once with the Emperor, submitting that "the list of officers who are daily paraded before your Majesty is unlimited, while the land for granting *jagirs* is limited. How can an unlimited quantity be equal to a limited quantity?"[4]

The scarcity of *paibaqi* land made the routine working of the *jagirdari* system impossible. People appointed to *mansabs* found it very difficult to get *jagirs*. Many officers failed to get their *jagir* for four or five years.[5] And a wit said at the Court that a boy *mansabdar*, newly appointed, would have grown a white beard before he could obtain his *jagir*.[6] Even when a *jagir* was once obtained, there was no certainty that it would not be transferred to some one else without the incumbent getting any other. Thus, several people remained without *jagirs*, though they had been long in service.[7]

Inevitably, influence and money began to count most in all *jagir* allotments. To get a *jagir* one apparently needed a patron (*murabbi*), very hard working and earnest agent (*wakil-i dil soz*), and the wherewithal for getting things done by payment of enormous bribes (*sakht-i rishwat*).[8] The small *mansabdars* could not manage all this and were, therefore, in desperate circumstances. This is admitted by Aurangzeb himself.[9]

The situation also provided a breeding ground for factionalism in its most intense form. Mamuri launches a tirade against the Deccani nobles who deprived the old nobility (*khanazads*) of their *jagirs*.[10] This problem became so serious that, according to Bhim Sen, Aurangzeb's

[1] *Dastur-al Amal-i Agahi*, f. 36; *Raqaim-i Karaim*, f. 28b.

[2] *Yak anar sad bimar* (Mamuri, f. 157b); Khafi Khan, II, pp. 602-03.

[3] Khafi Khan, II, pp. 411-12.

[4] Quoted in Sarkar, *Anecdotes of Aurangzeb*, p. 110. The Emperor retorted : "To believe in the scantiness and limit of God's court (of which he, Aurangzeb, was the mere representative) is the essence of infidelity and sin". This reply, while it shows the optimism of Aurangzeb, provided no solution to the concrete problem facing his *bakhshi*.

[5] Mamuri, ff. 179b, 182b; Khafi Khan, II, p. 396.

[6] Khafi Khan, II, p. 379; Mamuri, f. 179b.

[7] Mamuri, f. 157a; Khafi Khan, II, p. 396.

[8] Mamuri, ff. 156b-157a, 182b; Khafi Khan, II, pp. 396-97.

[9] *Dastur-al Amal-i Agahi*, ff. 64, 65.

[10] Mamuri, ff. 156b-157a.

successor, Bahadur Shah, was persuaded to attack the Rajput states in order to distribute their lands in *jagir* to his officers.[1]

A struggle for *jagir* inevitably developed among the *mansabdars* of the Mughal Empire. But it must be borne in mind that this struggle had not yet become an armed struggle, it was fought out in the form of factional rivalries, bribing of the officials, etc., at the Court. There are hardly any instances where transfer orders were forcibly resisted by the *jagirdars*. Yet the conditions prevailing in the last years of Aurangzeb were bound to result in a situation where transfer orders would no longer be honoured. The *jagirdar* himself might have no rebellious intentions, but he knew that if he relinquished his *jagir*, another *jagir* would not be assigned to him. When precisely this stage arrived is uncertain. But Anand Ram Mukhlis suggests that during the reign of Farrukh Siyar (1713-19) *jagir* assignments by the Court became mere paper orders, so that a large number of persons who were granted *mansabs*, never got *jagirs*.[2] Once this happened, all was over not only with the *jagirdari* system, but with the Mughal Empire.

[1] *Dilkusha*, f. 169b. For a different view see Satish Chandra's *Parties and Politics at the Mughal Court*, pp. 29-34.

[2] *Mirat-al Istilah*, f. 64b.

CHAPTER IV

NOBLES AND POLITICS

AURANGZEB AND THE NOBILITY—FIRST PHASE (1658-66)

THE Emperor in theory enjoyed absolute powers; but he could govern only through his nobles or officers—his *umara* and his *mansabdars*. His policies could only be implemented through them, and therefore, directly or indirectly the opinions and interests of the nobles played their part in their formulation. These opinions could not always have been unanimous, nor could the interests of all nobles have been the same. On important matters of policy the nobles often differed among themselves into groups and factions. Since the Mughal nobility consisted of diverse ethnical and religious elements, there always existed fertile breeding-ground for factions. The immense centralisation of government, the *mansabdari* system (placing all officers on *mansab* in a single hierarchy), the routine of *jagir* transfers, etc., were all designed to suppress such factionalism or to keep it in check. It must, of course, be remembered that factionalism is something more than petty jealousy between individuals. Unless we can find evidence of more or less stable groupings, we cannot assume the existence of factions merely from the fact that a particular officer had certain personal enemies who intrigued against him in tho Court or outside. Moreover, the personal interests of any significant section of nobles, especially of great nobles, were bound to have bearing on, and to become involved with, the larger issues facing the Empire. In the present chapter, therefore, we propose to study the extent of cohesion in the nobility along with the attitude of different groups of nobles towards various imperial policies.

The reign of Shahjahan seems to have been free, broadly speaking, from overt factionalism within the nobility. When a crisis began to develop towards the close of his reign, and each of his sons began to create his own following in the anticipated struggle for the throne, groupings undoubtedly arose. But these groupings generally cut across racial and religious lines, and the promises made by each Prince to individual nobles, or the personal associations of nobles with individual princes, were the chief factors determining their formation. This can best be illustrated by the following tabular analysis of the supporters of the princely contestants (in the case of Aurangzeb and Dara Shukoh, up to the battle of Samugarh) :

SUPPORTERS OF THE CONTENDING PRINCES IN THE WAR OF SUCCESSION, 1958-59

Mansabdars	*Dara Shukoh*				*Aurangzeb*				*Shah Shuja*				*Murad Bakhsh*			
	Mansabdars of 5,000 and above	*Mansabdars of 3,000 to 4,500*	*Mansabdars of 1,000 to 2,500*	*Total*	*Mansabdars of 5,000 and above*	*Mansabdars of 3,000 to 4,500*	*Mansabdars of 1,000 to 2,500*	*Total*	*Mansabdars of 5,000 and above*	*Mansabdars of 3,000 to 4,500*	*Mansabdars of 1,000 to 2,500*	*Total*	*Mansabdars of 5,000 and above*	*Mansabdars of 3,000 to 4,500*	*Mansabdars of 1,000 to 2,500*	*Total*
Muslims																
Iranis ...	3	4	16	23	4	7	16	27	—	1	—	1	—	1	—	1
Turanis ...	1	2	13	16	1	3	16	20	1	1	1	3	—	—	—	—
Afghans ...	—	—	1	1	—	4	19	23	—	—	1	1	—	1	—	1
Other Muslims	—	4	19	23	1	4	28	33	—	1	4	5	1	—	6	7
Total ...	4	10	49	63	6	18	79	103	1	3	6	10	1	2	6	9
Hindus																
Rajputs ...	2	6	14	22	2	2	5	9	—	—	—	—	—	—	2	2
Marathas ...	1	1	—	2	—	2	8	10	—	—	—	—	—	—	—	—
Other Hindus	—	—	—	—	—	—	2	2	—	—	—	—	—	—	—	—
Total ...	3	7	14	24	2	4	15	21	—	—	—	—	—	—	2	2
Grand Total	7	17	63	87	8	22	94	124	1	3	6	10	1	2	8	11

It will be seen that out of 124 *mansabdars* of 1,000 *zat* and above who supported Aurangzeb, 20 were Turanis, 27 Iranis, 23 Afghans, 33 other Muslims, 9 Rajputs, 10 Marathas and 2 other Hindus. Out of 87 supporters of Dara Shukoh, holding *mansabs* of 1,000 *zat* and above, 16 were Turanis, 23 Iranis, one Afghan, 23 other Muslims, 22 Rajputs and 2 Marathas. Shah Shuja was supported by ten *mansabdars* of 1,000 and above — 3 Turanis, 1 Irani, 1 Afghan and 5 other Muslims. Eleven *mansabdars* of 1,000 and above are known to have supported Murad Bakhsh — 1 Irani, 1 Afghan, 7 other Muslims and 2 Rajputs.[1]

Thus, the support Aurangzeb received from the nobility was quite broad-based. In Chapter I we have shown that there was no question of Aurangzeb raising an outcry against the Hindu nobles at this stage. On the contrary, he made great efforts to win over the Rajput Rajas — Rana Raj Singh, Mirza Raja Jai Singh, and even Jaswant Singh — and succeeded to a very great extent. Similarly, there is not the slightest proof that he attempted to rally the Sunni nobles against the Shias.

Aurangzeb's policy after his accession was the same as during his struggle for the throne. He had come to the throne after killing his eldest brother and then his youngest. He had also imprisoned his own father. More than any other Mughal king, he had to justify his seizure of the throne. A legal opinion by which he used to support his action in deposing his father was that he was more competent than his father.[2] This had now to be proved in practice by the achievement of conspicuous success and nothing would be more conspicuous than military conquests. So a vigorous military policy was undertaken. In 1660 Shaista Khan opened a great campaign in Maharashtra. In 1661 Palamau in Bihar was annexed and Mir Jumla occupied Kuch Bihar. In 1662-63 came Mir Jumla's famous invasion of Assam. In 1663 the state of Navanagar in Gujarat was annexed. In 1665 Mirza Raja Jai Singh concluded a successful campaign against Shivaji by the treaty of Purandhar. In 1665-66, the Mughals launched a big attack on Bijapur. In 1666 Shaista Khan occupied Chatgaon (Chittagong). Few decades in the 17th century had seen such hectic military activity.

Such an aggressive policy required the fullest co-operation of the nobility. All dissensions had to be avoided. Moreover, Shahjahan was alive till 1666, and it could not be overlooked that any serious change in imperial policy, adversely affecting the interests of a large section of the nobility, might lead to an attempt at Shahjahan's restoration.

[1] These figures are based on the Appendix at the end of the chapter. Also cf. my paper, "The Religious Issue in the War of Succession, 1658-59", read before Indian History Congress, Aligarh Session, 1960; *Medieval India Quarterly*, Vol. V, pp. 80-87.

[2] See Aurangzeb's letters to Shahjahan, *Adab-i Alamgiri*, ff. 289a-93b; *Ruq'at-i Alamgir* 211-12, 216-18, 223-26; also Qazi Wahab's opinion, *Mirat-i Ahmadi*, I, p. 248.

AURANGZEB AND THE NOBILITY—SECOND PHASE (1666-1679)

It appears that it was about 1666 that Aurangzeb began to adopt a policy which, if not directly opposed to, was at least different in spirit from that of his predecessors. We have seen in Chapter I, that the Emperor began to curtail the recruitment and promotion of Rajputs during this period. Before investigating how this change came about, it is necessary to examine briefly the political situation after 1666.

First, in 1666 after Shahjahan's death, there was no one to replace Aurangzeb and his fears of any future opposition within the nobility probably vanished.

Second, it was clear that the reckless policy of expansion begun in 1659 had proved a complete failure. Mir Jumla's invasion of Assam ended in a hopeless retreat, while the annexation of Kuch Bihar had to be abandoned. Shaista Khan's campaign in Maharashtra ended with the plunder of his own camp and Shivaji's sack of Surat in 1664. If Jai Singh was successful against Shivaji, the fruits of his military victory were snatched away to a great extent by Shivaji's flight from Agra in 1666. Lastly, Jai Singh's invasion of Bijapur ended in a miserable failure and he died broken-hearted in 1667.

With these successive failures, the emperor's attempt at expansion was brought to a halt at least for the time being and a peroid of rebellion began. The Jat rebellion under Gokula broke out in the Braj country in the mid-sixties. The Satnamis rebelled in 1672 and their early successes were surprising. In 1667 the Yusufzais revolted near Peshawar; in 1672 the Afridis also rebelled and Aurangzeb had to go to Hasan Abdal in 1674. In 1670, Shivaji again opened war against the Mughals and sacked Surat for the second time.

A ruler, who had sought to justify the imprisonment of his father and the executions of his brothers by successes in military sphere, found himself a failure despite all his personal exertions. A new *post facto* justification had to be found for his coup of 1658-59. Consistent with the orthodox temperament, which he had been developing, this justification was provided by an emphasis on the Islamic character of the Empire, and a new religious policy was inaugurated to create a religious halo around the imperial crown. The discriminatory policy against the Hindus[1] was coupled with an attempt to associate the Muslim orthod-

[1] In 1665 the duty on goods carried by Hindu merchants was increased to 5 per cent *ad valorem* as against 2½ per cent imposed on Muslims; in 1667 the duty on Muslims was entirely withdrawn though it was reimposed in 1682. The duty on goods carried by English merchants was reduced from 3 per cent to 2 per cent. (Bodl. MS : Fraser 228, ff. 18a-19b). In 1669 came the order for temple-destruction (*Ma'asir-i Alamgiri*, p. 81). That this order was widely enforced is shown by a number of documents (*Waqa-i Ajmer* including *Waqa-i of Ranthambor, Akhbarat, etc.*). At the same time, it is obvious that exceptions were made and grants to Hindu and Jain temples and divines given by Aurangzeb survive, Jnan Chandra of Bombay in *Pakistan*

oxy as closely as possible with the Empire. In the seventies the Emperor's attempt to appeal to Muslim religious divines for support in respect of every political action went so far as to provoke a protest from some of the nobles.

In a letter written to the Emperor in late '70s Mahabat Khan expressed his surprise at the Emperor's policy that had made "fowlers into captives and sparrows into huntsmen. The experienced and able officers of the state are deprived of all trust and confidence while full reliance is placed on hypocritical mystics (*Mashaikhan - i riyā Kosh*) and empty-headed scholars (*ulamayan-i tahī hosh*). Since these men are selling their knowledge and manners for the company of kings, to rely upon them was neither in accordance with the divinely prescribed path, nor suited to the ways of the world. Thus these men are robbers in every way. The country is being laid waste; the army disheartened; the peasantry ravaged; the lowly crying of distress; the higher ones seeking to raise disturbances. (As the saying is,) the finances are given over to the *Qāzī* and the *Qāzī* is satisfied only with bribes."[1] Some times after this letter was written, Aurangzeb went even further and imposed the *jizya* in 1679. This aroused considerable anxiety in the ranks of the nobility, and we are told that "all the high-placed and important men at the court opposed themselves to this measure. They besought the king most humbly to refrain..."[2]

But it was perhaps not only a desire to resurrect his prestige on a new basis that led Aurangzeb to a new religious and Rajput Policy. So long as the Empire was expanding, the nobility as a whole could satisfy its ambitions by looking forward. Once, however, it became clear, as it did by 1667, that any rapid expansion was not to be expected, while disorder broke out within the empire itself, the urge for promotions among the *mansabdars* could not be easily satisfied. In such a situation it must have been highly tempting for the Emperor to enlarge the avenues of income for the majority of the nobility by progressively shutting out a minority. The Rajputs were, owing to their different religion, a section that could be most easily isolated. Their eclipse would also accord with the Emperor's new posture of militant orthodoxy. The Rajputs,

---

Historical Society, Oct. 1957, pp. 247-54, July 1958, pp. 208-13, Oct. 1958, pp. 269-72, January 1958, pp. 55-56, January 1959, pp. 36-39, & April, 1959, pp. 99-100. See also grants to Hindus, particularly Brahmans, calendard by K.K. Datta, *Some Firmans, Sanads and Parwanas* (1578-1802), Patna, 1962, Part II, Nos. 36,45,51,58,60,64,113,117,130,154,219,220,221,262, 263, 278, 279, 280, 300, 308, 325, 326, 330, 364, 374, etc. Note may also be made of the temple of Gopinath with its fine tank built by Naunidha Rai in 1699 at Gopamau in Hardoi District, (A Fuhrer, *Archaeological Survey of India*, p. 279.). In 1679 the *jizya* or poll-tax was imposed on non-Muslims.

[1]R.A.S. Pers. Cat. 173, ff. 8a-11a. The letter was written after Asad Khan's appointment as *wazir* in 1676, since it contains a critical reference to his elevation to this high office.

[2]Manucci, III, 288.

as we have seen, continued to be confirmed in their ancestral domains or *watan-jagirs*, but if the total *mansabs* awarded to them were reduced with the passage of years, their share of imperial *jagirs* outside their homelands, would fall correspondingly. These *jagirs* were the loaves and fishes which Aurangzeb offered to his Muslim nobility in order to rally it more firmly behind his throne. The causes that led to the Rajput rebellion of 1679-80 have been obscured by discrepancies in contemporary accounts and modern controversies. Fortunately, we have now in the *Waqa-i Ajmer* a series of reports by the news-writer of Ajmer covering precisely this period. This sheds valuable light on the events of this conflict and the issues involved in it. On the whole it shows that while there were intrinsic difficulties involved in Jaswant Singh's having died without any male issue, Aurangzeb's policy was not calculated to reconcile the Rajputs; and he obviously made an attempt to use the dispute between Jaswant Singh's officers and Raja Indar Singh, the approved claimant to the throne, to subvert the kingdom of Marwar.[1]

When Raja Jaswant Singh died, he left no son. Pending the decision about the successor, Aurangzeb declared that the whole of Marwar, including the capital, Jodhpur, and with the exception of two *parganas* only, was to be brought into the *khalisa*, and royal officers were despatched to take charge of the territory. This aroused the indignation of the Rathor clansmen, who declared that if Jodhpur, the seat of their clan and the place where the mourning for the dead king was taking place, was taken into the *khalisa*, the prestige of the Rathors would be affected: "During the rule of the Imperial Dynasty, no *bumi* or *zamindar* has been turned out of his native place (*watan*) even for specific faults. The Rathors, who have always been loyal and faithful, ask simply that they be not subjected to exile." They were prepared to give over the whole of Marwar, but not the ill-fortified town of Jodhpur.[2] Aurangzeb refused to withdraw his earlier order, but issued another order that all officers of Jaswant Singh would be left with the *pattas* or assignments corresponding to the *jagirs* granted to them by the late Raja, and they would receive corresponding *mansabs* against these *jagirs*.[3] This was an obvious bribe, and might well have meant the end of the Jodhpur state. At any rate, it would have considerably augmented the control of the Emperor over the internal affairs of Marwar. Jaswant Singh's officers, to their credit, refused to be a party to this deal.[4]

In the meantime it became known that two of the Raja's queens were pregnant and ultimately two sons were born; one of whom was Ajit Singh.

[1] For a detailed discussion see my article 'The Causes of the Rathor Rebellion of 1679-80,' Proceedings of Indian History Congress, Delhi Session, 1961,pp. 135-41.

[2] *Waqa-i Ajmer*, pp. 80-83. [3] Ibid. p. 114.

[4] Despite the Governor's persuasions, they declared that though they knew they could not resist the imperial army, they had decided to die rather than be bought over (*Waqa-i Ajmer*, 116).

This made a change in imperial decision necessary, because it could no longer be assumed that Raja Jaswant Singh had left no successor. The Rathors went to extremes in their attempt to get one of the children recognised as their Raja. Jaswant's chief queen, Rani Hadi, even said that the Rajputs would be prepared to destroy all the temples of Jodhpur and erect mosques instead, if only Jodhpur was conferred upon the Raja's son.[1] They were prepared to give a bigger offering (*peshkash*) than Indar Singh, the rival claimant of the collateral line.[2] They even appealed to the *shariat* in support of their plea.[3] Yet Aurangzeb overruled the claims of Jaswant Singh's children in favour of Indar Singh, who was intensely unpopular in Marwar.[4]

The rebellion of the Rathors and Sisodias was not really a "Rajput Rebellion", if by that is implied that the majority of the Rajputs were involved in it. The Kachwahas, the Haras, the Bhatis, the Rathors of Bikaner, all remained loyal to the Mughals. The *Waqa-i Ajmer* contains report after report of Rajput contingents joining the Mughal army to fight the Rathors.

Yet while most of the Rajputs had not been sufficiently alienated by Aurangzeb's policy so as to rebel against him, the Rajput rebels too were not completely friendless within the rest of the Mughal nobility. The very fact that Prince Akbar should have staked his fortune and placed himself at the head of the rebels shows that he expected some support from the Muslim nobility. Tahawur Khan, his main supporter, enjoyed no mean status. Bahadur Khan Kokaltash, the leading noble of Aurangzeb at the time, had in fact advised Aurangzeb to recognise Ajit Singh.[5] When Prince Akbar fled to the Deccan, Bahadur Khan Kokaltash, then Viceroy of the Deccan, was widely suspected of having closed his eyes and allowed the Prince to proceed unchallenged to the court of Shambhaji.[6]

On the whole, however, the indifference of the rest of the Rajputs to the fate of the Rathors and the complete fiasco of Akbar's rebellion showed that Aurangzeb had greatly consolidated his position, and however harmful his religious and Rajput policies might have been for the Empire in the long run, for the moment they seemed to have been crowned with success. The Rajputs were cowed, the proud Sisodias compelled to seek terms, and the Muslim nobility apparently rallied unanimously behind the Emperor.

[1] *Waqa-i Ajmer*, pp. 167, 244-46.

[2] Ibid., p. 244.

[3] Ibid., pp. 245-46.

[4] Ibid., pp. 241, 270, 277-78.

[5] *Futuhat-i Alamgiri*, f. 75a-b; *Ma'asir-i Alamgiri*, p. 168. Bahadur Khan Kokaltash did not try to keep control over the territory of the Rana, when given command of an army sent into Mewar. (Mamuri, f. 51a).

[6] Khafi Khan, II, pp. 276-77; *Dilkusha*, f. 78b.

The Deccan Problem and The Nobility (1658-89)

Since 1590 the Mughal Empire had been almost continuously involved in operations against the Deccan states. Except for an interruption of twenty years after the settlement of 1636, all peace treaties had been in the nature of cease-fire arrangements, which both sides were prepared to break whenever an opportunity presented itself. In all this the Deccan presented a sharp contrast to Northern India, where Mughal conquests had been as quickly consolidated as they were made. There were, of course, geographical reasons—as the hills there made transport difficult and enabled great fortresses to be built—which may be held partly responsible for the slowness of the Mughal progress in the Deccan.

But there were also additional reasons and one of them was the peculiar attitude which the Mughal nobles had towards the questions of the annexation of the Deccan. Explaining why the Mughals had failed to annex Bijapur, Bernier declares that this was because the generals sent against it "conduct every operation...with langour, and avail themselves of any pretext for the prolongation of war which is alike the source of their emolument and dignity. It is become a proverbial saying that the Deccan is the bread and support of the soldiers of Hindustan."[1] Fryer repeats the same statement calling "Deccan, the Bread of the military men."[2]

Support is lent to these general statements by individual incidents. During the reign of Jahangir, Abdul Rahim Khan-i Khanan is said to have been taxed by Raja Man Singh Kachwaha for his dilatory way in conducting operations. The Khan-i Khanan retorted that the result of Man Singh's own success in Bengal was that he had been deprived of his command there; if he (Khan-i Khanan) also succeeded in the Deccan, he too would have to go.[3] Similarly, in the times of Aurangzeb, when Namdar Khan urged Shaista Khan to make a direct attack on Shivaji, the shrewd noble replied that if the Deccan campaign was so quickly concluded, an attack on Qandhar would be ordered; and if that too succeeded, the contingents would be disbanded.[4]

It was not, however, the deliberate design of the Mughal officers that prolonged the war in the Deccan. The problem of supporting the war through the resources of occupied Deccan only was always there. Owing to the ravages of war, the Deccan had suffered heavily and its resources were diminishing, as is emphasized again and again in the letters written by Aurangzeb himself when he was the Viceroy of the Deccan for the second time. Mughal nobles who were posted in the

[1] Bernier, pp. 196-97.

[2] Fryer, II, p. 51. See also Manucci, III, p. 271.

[3] *Dilkusha*, f. 123a.

[4] Ibid., f. 123a; *English Factories*, 1665-1667, p. 152.

Deccan, therefore, found it very difficult to maintain their requisite contingents and were, therefore, not militarily superior to their Deccan opponents.[1]

In such circumstances, it was inevitable that cases of collusion between Mughal commanders and the Deccanis should be frequently reported. Under Jahangir, the Khan-i Khanan, and later on Khan-i Jahan Lodi, had been suspected of accepting bribes from Ahmadnagar for the favour of ceding some territory. During the earlier part of Aurangzeb's reign a large number of officers from Prince Shah Alam downwards were believed to have been opposed to a forward policy in the Deccan. In 1663 Aurangzeb charged Shah Alam with culpable negligence in crushing the Marathas, and he was replaced by Jai Singh as Viceroy of the Deccan. In 1667 on the recommendation of Prince Shah Alam and Jaswant Singh, Shivaji was pardoned and his son Shambhaji was given the rank of 5,000/5,000; Shivaji was also permitted to conquer as much of Bijapur territory as his resources permitted, or else, he was to confine himself to his own territory and act according to the advice of the *subedar* of the Deccan.[2] There were differences between Dilir Khan, on the one hand, and Prince Shah Alam and Jaswant Singh on the other, when Shah Alam was *subedar* of the Deccan in 1668, because the prince and the Raja were slack in punishing the Marathas.[3] In A.H. 1095 (1682-83) it was alleged that Shah Alam, Saiyid Abdullah Khan, Maumin Khan Najm Sani, and Sadiq Khan were in secret alliance with the king of Bijapur. Aurangzeb severely reprimanded the Prince, arrested Saiyid Abdullah and dismissed the others.[4] Later on Aurangzeb again had to reprimand Shah Alam, along with Bahadur Khan Kokaltash, for adopting a mild attitude towards Abul Hasan, the ruler of Golkunda. Shah Alam informed Ibrahim Khan, the commander of the army of Golkunda, that owing to the mild attitude adopted by Shah Alam towards Abul Hasan he had been sharply censured by the Emperor.[5] In 1685 Shah Alam was arrested on the charge of being in secret alliance with Qutb Shah and of being friendly with Shambhaji.[6]

Bahadur Khan (or Khan-i Jahan Bahadur Zafar Jang Kokaltash), who had for a time been the premier noble of Aurangzeb, was repeatedly suspected of being friendly with the Deccan powers. He was appointed Viceroy of the Deccan in 1672. Dilir Khan, a Mughal noble and Abdul

[1] *Adab-i Alamgiri*, ff. 25b, 27a-b.

[2] *Dilkusha*, f. 35a-35b.

[3] *Dilkusha*, ff. 34b-35a; Shah Alam was opposed to the forward policy of Dilir Khan in the Deccan directed against Bijapur (*Futuhat-i Alamgiri*, f. 59a).

[4] Mamuri, 168b-169a; Khafi Khan, II, pp. 320-21; *Futuhat-i Alamgiri*, f. 100b; *Ma'asir-i Alamgiri*, pp. 293-94.

[5] Mamuri, f. 165a-b; Khafi Khan, II, pp. 300-301.

[6] Mamuri, f. 171a-b; Khafi Khan, II, pp. 330-34; *Dilkusha*, 93b-94a; *Futuhat-i Alamgiri*, ff. 113a-115b; *Ma'asir-i Alamgiri*, pp. 294-95; Manucci, II, pp. 302-4.

Karim, the leader of the Afghan nobles at the Bijapur Court, accused him of sympathy with Shivaji.[1] In 1681 when Shambhaji sacked the towns in the environs of Burhanpur, it was widely believed that Bahadur Khan had accepted a bribe from Shambhaji and marched in the opposite direction while the Maratha ruler escaped with his booty.[2] Aurangzeb himself suspected Bahadur Khan of being in the pay of Adil Shah.[3] There was negligence on Bahadur Khan's part in occupying certain forts and districts of Haiderabad and Aurangzeb had to send *sazawals* and mace-bearers to expedite the work.[4] Subsequently, it was widely believed that Bahadur Khan was wholly opposed to Aurangzeb's forward policy in the Deccan and might well have made a secret alliance with the Marathas.[5] In 1688 when the Jats rebelled near Akbarabad, Bahadur Khan was transferred from the Deccan, ostensibly in order to crush the Jat uprising, but really to rid the Deccan of his presence.[6]

Jaswant Singh, though posted twice to the Deccan, was believed to be at heart an opponent of the expansionist policy. He was suspected of having had a hand in Shivaji's night attack on Shaista Khan's camp in 1663.[7] And we have seen that Dilir Khan alleged during Jaswant Singh's second posting to the Deccan, that he was always slow in pursuing the Marathas.

Mahabat Khan too seems to have enjoyed the same reputation. His cynicism about the imperial efforts in the Deccan is revealed by an anecdote recorded by Khafi Khan. The Emperor once said to Jafar Khan and Mahabat Khan that it was necessary to crush Shivaji. Mahabat Khan retorted that there was no need for an army being sent against Shivaji, as a judgment (*fatwa*) of the Qazi would suffice.[8] In 1671 it was reported to the Emperor that Mahabat Khan had a secret alliance with Shivaji and was not exerting himself against the Marathas. He was, therefore, replaced by Bahadur Khan Kokaltash.[9]

Different sections of the nobles had contacts with, or sympathy for,

[1] *Dilkusha*, 69b. Shivaji proposed to Bahadur Khan Kokaltash that peace should be concluded between the Marathas and the Mughals. Bahadur Khan sent Ganga Ram Gujrati, his servant, to Shivaji in response to his proposal. But Shivaji sarcastically asked Ganga Ram as to what pressure the Mughals had exercised over him to make him conclude peace with them (*Dilkusha*, f. 63a-b); *The English factories*, 1670-77. Vol. 1 (New Series), p. 124.

[2] Mamuri, f. 153b; Khafi Khan, II, pp. 274-75.

[3] *Ruq'at-i Alamgir*, p. 127.

[4] Mamuri, f. 163a.

[5] Mamuri, ff. 167b-168a; *Dilkusha*, ff. 118b-19a; Khafi Khan, II, pp. 313-14; Bahadur Khan Kokaltash pleaded the case of the Marathas before Aurangzeb (*Dilkusha*, ff. 99b-100a).

[6] Mamuri, f. 173b; Khafi Khan, II, p. 316.

[7] *Dilkusha*, f. 24a-b; Mamuri, f. 131a; Khafi Khan, II, p. 175. Aurangzeb was dissatisfied with Jaswant Singh's conduct in the Deccan and so had him recalled and replaced by Jai Singh. Jaswant Singh was also reputed to have accepted 9,000 *pagodas* from Bijapur and to have entered into a secret understanding with that state (*Mirat-al Alam* ff. 190b-91a).

[8] Khafi Khan, II, pp. 216-17. [9] *Dilkusha*, f. 51b.

particular Deccan states. Naturally some of the Rajput *mansabdars* sympathised with the Marathas.[1]

Daud Khan Qureshi was openly opposed to Jai Singh's campaign against Adil Shah and sought to discourage the Muslim soldiery by saying that it was against the dictates of the Quran.[2] The Afghan *mansabdars* in the Deccan seem to have developed a soft corner for Bijapur owing to the presence of a number of their compatriots at the Bijapur court. In 1677 when Bahadur Khan Kokaltash made active preparations for invading Bijapur, the Afghan officers of the imperial army advised Abdul Karim, the leader of the Afghan nobles at Bijapur, to offer peace terms to Bahadur Khan, because if the entire Mughal army under Bahadur Khan were to invade Bijapur, it would be very difficult for the Bijapuris to withstand its onslaught. Aurangzeb was influenced by this and other incidents, and not being satisfied with the conduct of the Afghans in the Deccan, appointed Asad Khan Viceroy of the Deccan in 1678.[3]

In the case of Golkunda, the Persian nobles were suspected of sympathising with Qutb Shah on account of their Shi'ite beliefs. It was alleged that the Irani nobles at the Mughal court were not pressing the siege of Golkunda vigorously.[4] But opposition to the destruction of Golkunda was not confined to the Iranis alone. Aurangzeb asked his chief Qazi, Shaikhul Islam, for his opinion about the war against Golkunda and Bijapur. The Qazi refused to attribute to it the character of a *jihad*; he was consequently asked to go to Haj.[5] Qazi Abdullah, who was appointed in place of Shaikhul Islam, remarked one day that it would be better to conclude a treaty with Golkunda as it would avoid the unnecessary bloodshed of Muslims; Aurangzeb got annoyed and Qazi Abdullah was ordered not to come to the Court and to confine himself to his judicial duties.[6]

But not all the nobles shared this hesitation in extending the Empire in the Deccan. One of the leading protagonists of a forward policy in the Deccan was Mirza Raja Jai Singh, who was sent to retrieve the situation in the Deccan after the discomfiture of Shaista Khan. Jai Singh first concentrated his fire against Shivaji, driving him to seek terms at Purandhar. His plan then was to take the Marathas into a subordinate partnership and make an attempt with their aid upon the kingdom

[1] Khafi Khan, II, p. 229.

[2] *Haft Anjuman*, f. 190b (cited by Sarkar, IV, p. 149).

[3] *Dilkusha*, ff. 67b-68a. Dilir Khan wanted peace with Bijapur because the Afghans were the ruling party in Bijapur (*Dilkusha*, f. 68b).

[4] Mamuri, f. 175b; Bernier, p. 211. Ni'mat Khan Ali through his satirical account of the siege of Golkunda leaves us in no doubt where his sympathies lay.

[5] Mamuri, f. 162a.

[6] Ibid., f. 173a. Peace terms offered by Abul Hasan were rejected by Aurangzeb (Mamuri, f. 174; *Ma'asir-i Alamgiri*, pp. 287-88).

of Bijapur. It appears that Aurangzeb was not prepared to commit such large forces to the Deccan as Jai Singh demanded; nor did he approve of the recruitment and promotions of the Deccanis which Jai Singh recommended for sowing dissensions among the Adil Shahis.[1]

There were naturally objections to Jai Singh's plan from many, who did not believe in an aggressive policy. It is true that the Mughals had started giving *mansabs* to the Marathas since the time of Jahangir. But to ask for co-operation from Shivaji, who maintained for all practical purposes a separate centre for his political power, was another matter. Jai Singh's predecessor in the Deccan, Shaista Khan, had been so hostile to the Marathas that he never employed them either as cavalrymen or foot-troopers.[2] The test came when Shivaji appeared at Agra for the grant of a suitable *mansab*. A number of nobles led by Jaswant Singh (who dismissed Shivaji as a "petty bumia"), Jafar Ḵhan and R'ad Andaz Khan were opposed to any concessions to Shivaji, while Jai Singh's policy was backed up by Amin Khan, Saiyid Murtaza Khan and Aqil Khan.[3] The Emperor seems to have remained undecided, with the unfortunate result that Shivaji was neither crushed nor conciliated.

Ultimately, neither the policy of Jai Singh nor that of his critics prevailed. Whether by design or by force of circumstances, Aurangzeb waged a simultaneous struggle against all the three Deccan Powers, the Marathas, Bijapur and Golkunda. This was a forward policy with almost no qualifications. But it required a tremendous military effort, which exhausted the Mughal Empire, and once it had been undertaken, neither the Deccan nor the Mughal Empire could have been the same again.

The Deccan Problem and The Nobility (1689-1707)

From 1682 to his death in 1707, for over 25 years, Aurangzeb remained in the Deccan. During the first phase of this period, he seemed to have succeeded in smashing all the three centres of political power in the Deccan. Bijapur fell in 1686, Golkunda in 1687, and in 1689, Shambhaji, the Maratha ruler, was captured and executed. It soon became clear, however, that the Marathas would continue the struggle despite their lack of an effective centre. While Mughal armies marched into the Carnatik in pursuit of Rajaram, the Maratha chiefs organised raids all over the Deccan from their innumerable hill-fortresses. Aurangzeb

[1] For a definite account of Jai Singh's plan, see Sarkar, IV, 120-21, which is based largely on *Haft Anjuman.* See also *Alamgir Nama*, p. 913; *Dilkusha*, f. 28b; Khafi Khan, II, p. 184. For Aurangzeb's disapproval of the recruitment of the Deccanis see *Dilkusha*, f. 31b. On 29th Ziqada, 8th R.Y. Aurangzeb told Jai Singh that the Deccanis could not be trusted for their word and deed. (*Jaipur Documents*, No. 98, p. 184); *Nigar Nama-i Munshi*, p. 121.

[2] Mamuri, f. 130a.

[3] Sarkar, *House of Shivaji*, pp. 158-60.

stuck to his resolve of wiping out all political opposition in the Deccan with a will that never slackened. Committing a very large part of his military resources to the task, he declared the war against the Marathas to be a *jihad* (1699). He hoped that this, together with his own presence in the Deccan, would deter any open opposition among his officers to the Deccan war.[1] But the commitment of the immense Mughal military resources in the Deccan on the one hand and the prospects of a long drawn-out war, the outcome of which remained uncertain on the other, created a profound political crisis to which the nobles did not remain indifferent. Doubtless different nobles viewed the Deccan involvement in different ways. To the nobles of the old families—the *khanazads*—the influx of the Deccanis into the Mughal nobility was anathema and they longed for the restoration of their previous dominating position.[2] To others, who were actually fighting in the Deccan, the never-ending war against the elusive Marathas appeared to be futile, many of them desired an agreement with the Marathas so that both parties may live peacefully in the Deccan or in the alternative, they wanted the Emperor to return to North India with his chief officers while leaving his subordinates to carry on a desultory warfare. The historian Bhimsen, an officer of Dalpat Rao Bundela, is a good representative of the opinion favouring a settlement. He was deeply impressed by the desolation which the war had caused in the Deccan, the way in which the Marathas lived on plunder and the extent to which the Mughal military organisation had deteriorated.[3] He was extremely critical of Aurangzeb's strategy. The whole country was being lost and the people were being plundered by the enemy, but the Emperor was concerned only with capturing the Maratha forts (*qila-giri*).[4] Even Asad Khan, the Emperor's *wazir*, believing that no settlement with the Marathas was possible as long as the personal prestige of the Emperor was involved, once ventured to suggest that the Emperor should leave the Deccan since all the objects for which he had come had been achieved, but he only got a severe reproof from the Emperor.[5]

Some nobles were personally anxious to leave the Deccan and return to North India. Bahramand Khan offered a lakh of rupees to the Emperor for permission to go to Delhi for one year.[6] The majority, however, sought safety in half-hearted obedience to the imperial command or in secret understanding with the Marathas. Aurangzeb, it has been said, declared that he had to remain in the Deccan personally, for otherwise his nobles would not carry out his orders.[7] His complaint that his officers

[1] Mamuri, f. 196a; Khafi Khan, II, pp. 478-80.

[2] See Chapter I.

[3] *Dilkusha*, ff. 138b-140a. For the miserable condition of the imperial army in the Deccan; see *Waqa-i Niamat Khan Ali*, pp. 15, 117.

[4] Ibid., f. 146a.

[5] Inayatullah Khan, *Ahkam-i Alamgiri*, ff. 25b-26a.

[6] *Ma'asir-al Umara*, I, p. 457.

[7] Manucci, IV, p. 115.

needed reminders to act according to his orders is preserved in the *Akhbarat*.[1] Bhimsen says that Mughal officers often found private deals with the Marathas more profitable than resisting them.[2] Manucci also makes the same statement and cites the example of Daud Khan Panni, who had a secret agreement with the Marathas.[3] The Deccani nobles, indeed, were most unstable in their loyalties. In 1689 the Haiderabadi nobles, who had recently been taken into Mughal service, caused great damage to the imperial cause by breaking into an open rebellion.[4] In 1691 when Zulfiqar Khan was besieging Jinji, the Deccani nobles accompanying him deserted to Rajaram.[5] Writing under A.D. 1700 Bhimsen says that large numbers of the *mansabdars* of the country (Deccan) were deserting to the Marathas.[6]

In such a situation suspicions and intrigues at the Court and mutual jealousies among the nobles naturally found free play. Aurangzeb himself told Muhammad Murad Khan that he was aware of the exceptional courage in battle shown by him, but some of the nobles did not wish it to be brought to the notice of the Emperor.[7] Tarbiyat Khan was jealous of Muhammad Murad Khan, while a number of leading nobles were jealous of Fathullah Khan.[8] Aurangzeb could not give due promotion to Muqarrab Khan, the captor of Shambhaji, owing to the jealousy of other nobles.[9] There was keen rivalry between Saiyid Lashkar Khan, son of Saiyid Khan-i Jahan Barha, on the one hand, and Zulfiqar Khan Nusrat Jang on the other.[10]

In 1686 when Aurangzeb was besieging Golkunda, some nobles out of jealousy alleged that Saf Shikan Khan son of Qiwamuddin Khan was not pressing the siege vigorously; Aurangzeb thereupon dismissed him and confiscated his property. But when it was established that the allegations were false, Aurangzeb restored Saf Shikan Khan to his former post and *mansab*.[11] In 1699 when Iradat Khan was transferred to the contingent of Tarbiyat Khan, he petitioned to the Emperor that he was prepared to undertake any assignment given by the Emperor but was not prepared to work with Tarbiyat Khan.[12]

[1] *Akhbarat*, 28 Shaban, 43 R.Y. For the indolence, dilatory tactics and cowardice of the Mughal nobles in the Deccan, see *Waqa-i Niamat Khan Ali*, p. 142.

[2] *Dilkusha*, f. 140a-b. [3] Manucci, IV, pp. 98, 228-9. [4] Sarkar, V, p. 68.

[5] *Dilkusha*, f. 99b.

[6] Ibid., f. 140a. An interesting study of one of such deserters, Rahim Dad Khan, has been made by Prof. S. R. Phadke, Proceedings of Indian History Congress, Aligarh Session, 1960, pp. 259-60.

[7] Mamuri, f. 145a-b. There was rivalry between Muhammad Murad and Shuja'at Khan (Ibid., ff. 197b-198b).

[8] Khafi Khan, II, pp. 488-89.

[9] Ibid., pp. 391-92; Mamuri, f. 181a.

[10] *Ma'asir-i Alamgiri*, p. 356.

[11] Khafi Khan, II, p. 359; Mamuri, f. 175b.

[12] *Akhbarat*, 14 Shawwal, 43rd R. Y.

Such instances of rivalry and jealousy among the nobles during the Deccan Wars could be multiplied,[1] but those given above should suffice to reveal their nature.

In this atmosphere the formation of cliques and factions pulling in different directions was inevitable. Since there was a growing doubt about the success of the Mughal cause as a whole, the nobles naturally started looking to their own personal interests. "Nothing", observed Manucci in 1700, "can be more surprising than the way things go in the Mughal Empire. The king, the princes, the governors and the generals have each their own lines of policy, calculated for securing success to their designs."[2]

Two important groups among the greatest nobles arose, which typified the new factionalism. They may be loosely designated as Irani and Turani. Between the nobles of these two races there had been an ancient rivalry, as we have seen in Chapter I. In Aurangzeb's last years the leading Irani nobles were Asad Khan and his son, Zulfiqar Khan, and the leading Turani nobles, Ghaziuddin Khan Feroz Jang and his son, Chin Qilich Khan.

The character of the two groups, and the careers of the leading figures of each, have been carefully analysed by Satish Chandra in his *Parties and Politics at the Mughal Court, 1707–40.* As pointed out by him, the first group was "essentially a family-cum-personal group and was held together by family loyalties, and the personal relations of its adherents with Zulfiqar Khan".[3] Besides Asad Khan and Zulfiqar Khan, Daud Khan Panni, Dalpat Rao Bundela and Ram Singh Hara could be considered members of this group. Their combined *mansabs* at Aurangzeb's death amounted to 25,000 *zat* and 23, 500 *sawar* :

Asad Khan	7,000/7,000
Zulfiqar Khan	6,000/6,000
Daud Khan Panni	6,000/6,000
Dalpat Bundela	3,000/3,000
Ram Singh Hara	3,000/1,500
	25,000/23,500

Ghaziuddin Khan Firoz Jang's group was a "racial-cum-family group" in as much as all its important adherents were Turanis.[4] The combined *mansabs* came to 20,000 *zat*/15,600 *sawars*.

[1] Rivalry between Saf Shikan Khan and Feroz Jang (*Ma'asir-i Alamgiri*, p. 290); Jealousy between Ali Mardan Khan and Zulfiqar Khan (Manucci, III, p. 273); Khudabanda Khan refused to cooperate with Zulfiqar in 1702 in crushing the Marathas because he was jealous of Zulfiqar (*Dilkusha*, f. 137a). For the jealousy between the *Khanazads* on the one hand, and the Deccani nobles who were new entrants in the *Mughal* service on the other, see Mamuri, f. 181a; Khafi Khan, II, pp. 391-92.

[2] Manucci, II, p. 270.

[3] *Parties and Politics*, p. 6.

[4] *Parties and Politics*, p. 9.

Ghaziuddin Khan Firoz Jang	7,000/7,000
Chin Qilich Khan	5,000/5,000
Muhammad Amin Khan	4,000/1,500
Hamid Khan	2,500/1,500
Rahimuddin Khan	1,500/600
	20,000/15,600

An important element common to both groups in the time of Aurangzeb was their deep involvement in the Deccan. Both Zulfiqar Khan and Ghaziuddin Khan had a long record of military service in the Deccan and were certainly his leading generals. Their interest in the Deccan was revealed by their extreme reluctance to accompany Prince Azam to the North after Aurangzeb's death.[1]

But it appears that within the Deccan the two groups were protagonists of different policies. Asad Khan and Zulfiqar Khan believed—or gradually came to believe—in the necessity of placating the Marathas and saving Mughal authority in the Deccan through a settlement with them. In 1698 Zulfiqar Khan captured Jinji, but Rajaram escaped—or was allowed to escape.[2] Only a year earlier Zulfiqar had forwarded a proposal from Rajaram for a settlement to Aurangzeb, but Aurangzeb was not prepared to entertain it.[3] In 1705 when Aurangzeb was hard pressed at Wakinkera, Zulfiqar was summoned along with his officers. The arrival of Zulfiqar Khan changed the situation and the fort fell after a short time. Aurangzeb, however, suspected that it was due to Zulfiqar Khan and Rao Dalpat's intrigues that the Maratha forces escaped unhurt.[4] Later on when Aurangzeb wanted to sow dissension among the Marathas, he handed over Shahu to Zulfiqar Khan to enable him to negotiate with the Maratha *sardars*.[5] Shahu was also given the rank of 7,000/7,000 and the title of Raja.[6] Zulfiqar Khan wrote conciliatory letters to the Maratha *sardars* and asked them to join Shahu, but there was no positive response on their part.[7] Zulfiqar Khan's attempt at placating the Marathas was also noted by a French observer, Francois Martin, who thought that he was seeking to strengthen himself by this alliance.[8]

Daud Khan Panni, a bosom friend of Zulfiqar Khan, had a secret agreement with the Marathas and did not try to crush them when he was governor of Carnatik in 1705.[9]

[1] *Dilkusha*, ff. 162a, 172b; *Azam al Harb*, pp. 188-92; Khafi Khan, II, p. 572.
[2] This aroused Aurangzeb's displeasure (*Ma'asir-i Alamgiri*, pp. 391-2).
[3] *Dilkusha*, f. 122a-b. [4] Ibid., f. 153a.
[5] *Dilkusha*, ff. 154-55b; *Ma'asir-i Alamgiri*, p. 511; Manucci, III, pp. 498-99.
[6] *Raqaim-i Karaim*, f. 23b; *Dilkusha*, f. 98a. [7] *Dilkusha*, ff. 154b-55b.
[8] Quoted by Sarkar, *History of Aurangzeb*, V, p. 101.
[9] Manucci, IV, pp. 98, 228-29; *Mirat-i Ahmadi*, I, p. 403.

In contrast with the attempt at a negotiated settlement with the Marathas repeatedly made by Zulfiqar Khan, Ghaziuddin Khan Firoz Jang adopted a firm and uncompromising attitude towards them. Yet he was reputed to be harbouring ambitions, which were not entirely in conformity with the spirit of loyalty. Isar Das relates an incident which shows that Ghaziuddin Khan was thinking of becoming independent after Aurangzeb, and he might have hoped to carve out a kingdom in the Deccan for himself on the basis of his military successes. It was believed that Aurangzeb had begun to suspect him, and Isar Das goes so far as to allege that Ghaziuddin Khan's blindness had been brought about by a physician sent by Aurangzeb.[1]

The jealousies, rivalries and factionalism within the nobility, which these two groups reveal, give an indication of the serious political crisis that the Mughal Empire would have to face in the future. Aurangzeb's policy might have succeeded—though even this is doubtful—if the majority of his officers had brought loyalty and a singleness of aim and purpose to their task. But their factionalism, while it deprived Aurangzeb precisely of this support, also reflected in a great measure a grievous lack of confidence in the Emperor and the Imperial policy on the part of the great nobles. It is significant that the group led by Ghaziuddin Khan, while it ostensibly supported the Deccan policy of Aurangzeb, also visualised its eventual failure, and thus led to the creation of an independent principality in the Deccan under his son.

[1] *Futuhat-i Alamgiri*, f. 145a-b.

SUPPORTERS OF DARA SHUKOH IN THE WAR OF SUCCESSION 1658-59.

Mansabdars of 5,000 and above.

S. No.	Name and Title	Rank	Racial Group	Sources
1.	Maharaja Jaswant Singh	6,000/6,000 (5,000 ×2-3h)	Rajput	*Tuhfa-i-Shah Jahani*, 29b; *Dilkusha*, 14a; *Alamgir Nama*, 32,41,49,56,59; *Aurang Nama*, 13; *Amal-i-Salih*, III, 284, 449; Hatim Khan, 10a; M. U., III, 599-604.
2.	Rustam Khan Feroz Jang Deccani	6,000/6,000 (5,000 ×2-3h)	Circassian (Turani)	M. U., II, 270-76; *Amal-i-Salih*, III, 298, 449; Mamuri, 98b; Isar Das, 26a; *Aurang Nama*, 20, 25; *Alamgir Nama*, 96, 99; *Dilkusha*, 16a; *Tuhfai Shah Jahani*, 29b; Aqil Khan, 62.
3.	Shah Nawaz Khan Safvi	6,000/6,000 (5,000 ×2-3h)	Irani	*Hatim Khan*, 69a, 72a; M. U., II, 670-76; Mamuri, 107a, 108a; Isar Das, 43a; *Alamgir Nama*, 296, 313, 322; *Amal-i-Salih*, III, 331; Aqil Khan, 110, 111, 118.
4.	Qasim Khan	5,000/5,000(2-3h)	Irani	Isar Das, 20b, 23a; Hatim Khan, 10a, 17a, 18a-b 21a, 29a; *Aurang Nama*, 7; *Tuhfa-i-Shah Jahani*, 29b; *Alamgir Nama*, 33, 41, 65, 72, 96; Mamuri, 97a-b; *Amal-i Salih*, III, 285-87, 450; M. U., III, 95-97; Aqil Khan, 39, 42.
5.	Khalilullah Khan (Controversial figure)	5,000/5,000	Irani	*Aurang Nama*, 20; *Amal-i-Salih*, 111, 451; *Alamgir Nama*, 85, 99; Hatim Khan, 26a, 29a; M.U., I, 775-82; Aqil Khan, 59.

S. No.	Name and Title	Rank	Racial Group	Sources
6.	Raja Rai Singh Sisodia	5,000/2,500	Rajput	*Alamgir Nama*, 65; Hatim Khan, 21a; *Amal-i-Salih*, III, 451; M.U., II, 297-301; Aqil Khan, 39.
7.	Maluji	5,000/5,000	Maratha	*Alamgir Nama*, 66, 71, 96; Mamuri, 97b; Hatim Khan, 21a, 29b; *Amal-i-Salih*, III, 451; Aqil Khan, 39.
		Mansabdars of 3,000 to 4,500		
8.	Rao Satar Sal Hara	4,000/4,000	Rajput	*Dilkusha*, 16a; *Tuhfa-i-Shah Jahani*, 29b; *Aurang Nama*, 20; *Amal-i-Salih*, III, 452; *Alamgir Nama*, 95; M.U., II, 260-63; Isar Das, 26a. Aqil Khan, 60.
9.	Ibrahim Khan	4,000/3,000	Irani	*Alamgir Nama*, 95; Manucci, I, 271; Hatim Khan, 29a; M. U., I, 295-301.
10.	Daud Khan Qureshi	4,000/3,000	Other Muslim	*Dilkusha*, 19a; *Alamgir Nama*, 85, 95, 143, 182, 188, 230; Mamuri, 102a; Isar Das, 23a; M.U., II, 32-37; Aqil Khan, 60.
11.	Baqi Beg Bahadur Khan	4,000/3,000	Other Muslim	*Amal-i-Salih*, III, 277; Isar Das, 9b; Mamuri, 102b; M.U., I, 444-47; *Alamgir Nama*, 125, 170.
12.	Raja Roop Singh Rathor	4,000/3,000	Rajput	*Amal-i-Salih*, III, 300, 453; Hatim Khan, 29a; *Alamgir Nama*, 95, 102; M. U., II, 268-70; Aqil Khan, 60.
13.	Khawaja Abdul Baqa, Iftikhar Khan	3,000/3,000(2-3h)	Turani	*Amal-i-Salih*, III, 453; *Alamgir Nama*, 65; *Aurang Nama*, 8, 13; M.U., I, 200-203; Hatim Khan, 10a, 17a, 21a.
14.	Syed Ibrahim Murtaza Khan	3,000/3,000	Other Muslim	Isar Das, 36a; *Amal-i-Salih*, III, 454.

S. No.	Name and Title	Rank	Racial Group	Sources
15.	Persuji	3,000/2,000	Maratha	*Alamgir Nama*, 66, 71, 140; *Amal-i-Salih*, III, 455; Hatim Khan, 21a, 29b.
16.	Mughal Khan	3,000/2,000	Irani	Isar Das, 36a; *Amal-i-Salih*, III, 455, M. U., III, 490-92.
17.	Mukand Singh Hara	3,000/2,000	Rajput	*Amal-i-Salih*, III, 287, 455; *Dilkusha*, 14b; Isar Das, 20b; *Aurang Nama*, 8; Hatim Khan, 21a; *Alamgir Nama*, 65, 70; Aqil Khan, 41.
18.	Tahir Shaikh Tahir Khan	3,000/1,500	Turani	*Amal-i-Salih*, III, 455; *Aurang Nama*, 20; *Alamgir Nama*, 95; M.U., II, 751-54; Hatim Khan 29a; Aqil Khan, 60.
19.	Syed Qasim Barha[1]	3,000/1,000	Other Muslim	*Alamgir Nama*, 126, 171, 225; Mamuri, 100b; M.U., II, 681-83; Aqil Khan, 101; Hatim Khan, 54b, 66b.
20.	Ram Singh Rathor	3,000/1,500	Rajput	Mamuri, 99a; *Aurang Nama*, 20; *Alamgir Nama*, 85, 95; Hatim Khan, 26a; 29a; *Amal-i-Salih*, III, 455.
21.	Zafar Khan Ahsan	3,000/1,500	Irani	*Alamgir Nama*, 96; Hatim Khan, 29b; *Amal-i-Salih*, III, 455.
22.	Kr. Ram Singh	3,000/2,000	Rajput	Hatim Khan, 29b; *Alamgir Nama*, 96; *Amal-i-Salih*, III, 455; Aqil Khan, 60.
23.	Bairam Deo Sisodia	3,000/1,000	Rajput	*Alamgir Nama*, 95; *Amal-i-Salih*, III, 456.
24.	Abdullah Beg Ganj Ali Khan	3,000/1,000	Irani	M.U., III, 155; *Alamgir Nama*, 427.

[1] After the defeat of Dara Shukoh at Samugarh, Syed Qasim Barha under orders from Dara Shukoh handed over the fort of Allahabad to Shah Shuja and fought on his side at Khajwah.

Mansabdars of 1,000 to 2,500

S. No.	*Name and Title*	*Rank*	*Racial Group*	*Sources*
25.	Syed Sher Khan Barha	2,500/1,200	Other Muslim	*Alamgir Nama*, 65, 95; Hatim Khan, 21a, 29a; M.U., II, 667-68.
26.	Girdhar Das Gaur	2,000/2,000	Rajput	*Alamgir Nama*, 95; Hatim Khan, 29a; *Amal-i-Salih*, III, 458.
27.	Muhammad Salih Tarkhan	2,000/2,000	Turani	Isar Das, 26a; *Amal-i-Salih*, III, 458.
28.	Raja Sujan Singh Bundela	2,000/2,000 (500 ×2-3h)	Rajput	Mamuri, 97b; *Alamgir Nama*, 65, 70; *Aurang Nama*, 8; Hatim Khan, 21a; *Amal-i-Salih*, III, 457.
29.	Iradat Khan	2,000/2,000	Irani	Isar Das, 36a; *Amal-i-Salih*, III, 458; M.U., I, 203-206.
30.	Syed Salabat Khan Barha	2,000/1,500	Other Muslim	Hatim Khan, 47a; *Alamgir Nama*, 170 198; *Amal-i-Salih*, III, 459.
31.	Qabad Khan	2,500/1,500	Turani	*Aurang Nama*, 20; Hatim Khan, 26a, 29a; *Alamgir Nama*, 85, 95; *Amal-i-Salih*, III, 456; Aqil Khan, 60.
32.	Abdullah Khan Saeed Khan	2,000/1,500	Turani	Isar Das, 36a; *Amal-i-Salih*, III, 458; M.U., II, 807.
33.	Sheo Ram Gaur	2,000/1,500	Rajput	*Alamgir Nama*, 57, 95, 102; *Amal-i-Salih*, III, 300, 458; Mamuri, 99a; Hatim Khan, 29a.
34.	Ratan Rathor	2,000/2,000	Rajput	Mamuri, 97a; *Alamgir Nama*, 65, 70; Hatim Khan, 21a; *Amal-i-Salih*, III, 458.

S No.	*Name and Title*	*Rank*	*Racial Group*	*Sources*
35.	Arjun Gaur	2,000/1,500	Rajput	Mamuri, 99b; *Alamgir Nama*, 65, 70; *Amal-i-Salih*, III, 287, 300, 458; *Aurang Nama*, 14; Hatim Khan 21a.
36.	Amar Singh Chandrawat	2,000/1,000	Rajput	*Alamgir Nama*, 65, 71; Hatim Khan, 21a; *Amal-i-Salih*, III, 460.
37.	Faizullah Khan	2,000/1,000	Irani	*Alamgir Nama*, 96; *Amal-i-Salih*, III, 459; M. U., III, 28-30.
38.	Mukhlis Khan	2,000/800	Turani	Hatim Khan, 21a; *Alamgir Nama*, 65; *Amal-i-Salih*, III, 460.
39.	Khushhal Beg Kashghari	2,000/800	Turani	*Alamgir Nama*, 65, 96; Hatim Khan, 21a; *Amal-i-Salih*, III, 460.
40.	Sujan Singh Sisodia	2,000/800	Rajput	Mamuri, 97b; *Amal-i-Salih*, III, 460.
41.	Abdullah Beg Askar Khan Najm Sani	Above 1,000	Irani	Mamuri, 108b; *Alamgir Nama*, 95, 313, 465; Hatim Khan, 26a, 29a, 68b; M. U., II, 809.
42.	Khanjar Khan	1,500/1,500	Turani	*Amal-i-Salih*, III, 321, 461; *Alamgir Nama*, 179, 198-99.
43.	Feroz Khan Mewati	1,500/1,000	Other Muslim	Mamuri, 108a; Hatim Khan, 29b, 68b; *Alamgir Nama*, 96, 205, 313, 440.
44.	Husain Beg Khan Zig	1,500/1,000	Irani	Hatim Khan, 29a; *Alamgir Nama*, 95; M.U., I, 591-93.
45.	Muhammad Beg	1,000/600	Turani	*Alamgir Nama*, 65; *Amal-i-Salih*, III, 466.
46.	Mir Miran	1,500/500	Irani	*Amal-i-Salih*, III, 463; *Alamgir Nama*, 95 ; Hatim Khan, 29a.

S. No.	Name and Title	Rank	Racial Group	Sources
47.	Mir Rustam Khawafi	1,500/500	Irani	*Alamgir Nama*, 232, 274, 399.
48.	Rahmat Khan	1,500/400	Other Muslim	*Alamgir Nama*, 297; *Amal-i-Salih*, III, 463.
49.	Syed Masud Barha	1,500/300	Other Muslim	*Alamgir Nama*, 207, 268.
50.	Syed Feroz Rustam Khan	1,500/200	Other Muslim	Isar Das, 9b; *Alamgir Nama*, 161, 213.
51.	Syed Salar Barha	1,000/1,000	Other Muslim	Hatim Khan, 21a; *Alamgir Nama*, 65; *Amal-i-Salih*, III, 464.
52.	Ghazanfar Khan	1,000/900	Irani	*Alamgir Nama*, 95; Hatim Khan, 29a; M.U., II, 866-67; *Amal-i-Salih* III, 465.
53.	Imam Quli	1,000/800	Irani	*Amal-i-Salih*, III, 465; *Alamgir Nama*, 85.
54.	Muhammad Salih Wazir Khan	1,000/800	Irani	*Alamgir Nama*, 104; Hatim Khan, 31b; *Amal-i-Salih*, III, 465.
55.	Maha Singh Bhadoriya	1,000/800	Rajput	Hatim Khan, 29b; *Alamgir Nama*, 96, 240; *Amal-i-Salih*, III, 465.
56.	Shaikh Muazzam	1,000/800	Other Muslim	*Alamgir Nama*, 96, 106; *Amal-i-Salih*, III, 465.
57.	Asfandiyar Beg	1,000/1,000	Irani	*Alamgir Nama*, 106; *Amal-i-Salih*, III, 464.
58.	Kerat Singh	1,000/900	Rajput	Hatim Khan, 29b; *Alamgir Nama*, 96; *Amal-i-Salih*, III, 465.
59.	Maghol Khan Khawafi	1,000/700	Irani	*Amal-i-Salih*, III, 465; *Alamgir Nama*, 314.

S. No.	*Name and Title*	*Rank*	*Racial Group*	*Sources*
60.	Sultan Husain	1,000/500	Irani	Hatim Khan, 21a, 29a; *Alamgir Nama*, 65, 95; M.U., I, 252.
61.	Fakhir Khan Najm Sani	2,500/1,000	Irani	Hatim Khan, 29b; M.U., III, 26-28; *Alamgir Nama*, 96; Aqil Khan, 60; *Amal-i-Salih*, III, 457.
62.	Yadgar Beg	1,000/500	Turani	*Alamgir Nama*, 65; *Amal-i-Salih*, III, 467.
63.	Muhamad Muqim Mughal Khan S/o Shah Beg Khan	1,000/700	Turani	Hatim Khan, 21a; *Amal-i-Salih*, III, 465; *Alamgir Nama*, 65.
64.	Mahesh Das	1,000/500	Rajput	*Alamgir Nama*, 65; Isar Das, 20b; Hatim Khan, 21a; *Amal-i-Salih*, III, 467.
65.	Gurdhan Das Rathor	1,000/500	Rajput	Hatim Khan, 21a; *Alamgir Nama*, 65; *Amal-i-Salih*, III, 467.
66.	Kishan Singh Taunur	1,000/500	Rajput	Hatim Khan, 29a; *Alamgir Nama*, 95; *Amal-i-Salih*, III, 467.
67.	Khwaja Rahmat-ullah Sarbuland Khan	1,000/500	Turani	Hatim Khan, 29a; *Alamgir Nama*, 96, 113; M.U., II, 477; *Amal-i-Salih*, III 467.
68.	Syed Bahadur Bahkari	1,000/500	Other Muslim	*Alamgir Nama*, 96; Hatim Khan, 29b; *Amal-i-Salih*, III, 467.
69.	Syed Ahmad	1,000/500	Other Muslim	*Alamgir Nama*, 176; *Amal-i-Salih*, III, 467.
70.	Abdul Nabi Khan	1,000/500	Other Muslim	*Alamgir Nama*, 96; Hatim Khan, 29b; *Amal-i-Salih*, III, 467.

S. No.	*Name and Title*	*Rank*	*Racial Group*	*Sources*
71.	Syed Najabat Barha	1,000/500	Other Muslim	*Alamgir Nama*, 96; Hatim Khan, 29b, *Amal-i-Salih* III, 467.
72.	Syed Ghairat Khan Barha or Izzat Khan	1,000/500	Other Muslim	Mamuri, 103b; *Amal-i-Salih*, III, 467; *Alamgir Nama*, 178, 180.
73.	Bheem S/o Bethal Das Gaur	1,000/400	Rajput	*Alamgir Nama*, 65, 95; Mamuri, 99b; *Amal-i-Salih*, III, 468.
74.	Pirthi Raj Thani	1,000/400	Rajput	*Alamgir Nama*, 95, 237; Hatim Khan, 29a.
75.	Syed Munawwar Barha	1,000/400	Other Muslim	Hatim Khan, 29b; *Alamgir Nama*, 96; *Amal-i-Salih*, III, 468.
76.	Syed Maqbool Alam Barha	1,000/400	Other Muslim	*Alamgir Nama*, 96; Hatim Khan, 29b; *Amal-i-Salih*, III, 468.
77.	Syed Ibrahim Dara Shukohi later Mustafa Khan	1,000/400	Other Muslim	Mamuri, 108a; Hatim Khan, 68b; *Alamgir Nama*, 313, 347.
78.	Abbas Afghan	1,000/400	Afghan	*Alamgir Nama*, 213, 215.
79.	Syed Nurul Ayen Barha	1,000/300	Other Muslim	*Amal-i-Salih*, III, 469; *Alamgir Nama*, 96; Hatim Khan, 29b.
80.	Khawaja Muhammad Sadiq Badakhshi	1,000/300	Turani	*Alamgir Nama*, 188, 206.
81.	Ismail Beg	1,000/300	Irani	*Alamgir Nama*, 95, 106; Hatim Khan, 29a; *Amal-i-Salih*, III, 469.

S. No.	Name and Title	Rank	Racial Group	Sources
82.	Ishaq Beg	1,000/300	Irani	Hatim Khan, 29a; *Amal-i-Salih*, III, 469; *Alamgir Nama*, 95, 106.
83.	Muhammad Sharif Qulij Khan S/o Islam Khan Mashhadi	1,000/200	Irani	*Alamgir Nama* 314, 324; *Amal-i-Salih*, III, 469; Hatim Khan, 69a; M.U., I, 166; Aqil Khan, 118.
84.	Muhammad Husain Sildoz	1,000/200	Turani	*Alamgir Nama*, 200, 210, 213.
85.	Shaikh Nizam	1,000/50	Other Muslim	M. U., I, 222; *Alamgir Nama*, 274, 399.
86.	Syed Nahar Khan Barha	Amir	Other Muslim	Mamuri, 99a; Hatim Khan, 32a; *Alamgir Nama*, 104.
87.	Syed Ahmad Bukhari	Amir	Turani	Mamuri, 110a-b.

SUPPORTERS OF AURANGZEB IN THE WAR OF SUCCESSION
1658-59.

Mansabdars of 5,000 and above

S. No.	*Name and Title*	*Rank*	*Racial Group*	*Sources*
1.	Mirza Shuja Najabat Khan Khan-i-Khanan	7,000/7,000	Turani	*Alamgir Nama*, 42, 54, 61, 88, 117; *Dilkusha*, 13b, M.U., III, 821-28; Hatim Khan, 12b, 16a.
2.	Mir Muhammad Saeed Mir Jumla Muazzam Khan.	6,000/6,000(2-3h)	Irani	*Dilkusha*, 18a; *Tuhfa-i-Shah Jahani*, 30b; *Aurang Nama*, 37; Mamuri, 103b; M. U., III, 530-55; *Alamgir Nama*, 84, 190, 267; Hatim Khan, 25b; Manucci, I, 262.
3.	Rana Raj Singh	5,000/5,000	Rajput	*Alamgir Nama*, 129, 194; *Vir Vinod*, II, 419-20,421-27; M. U., II, 206-208, *Amal-i-Salih*, III, 451.
4.	Abu Talib Shaista Khan	6,000/6,000(2-3h)	Irani	*Dilkusha*, 12a, 19a; *Alamgir Nama*, 111, 114, 130, 321; M. U., II, 690-707; Hatim Khan, 26b; Manucci, I, 255.
5.	Shaikh Mir Khawafi	5,000/5,000	Irani	Isar Das, 20b; Mamuri, 97a, 98b; *Aurang Nama*, 41; *Amal-i-Salih*, III, 332; *Alamgir Nama*, 68, 92, 98, 156-57; *Tuhfa-i-Shahjahani*, 30a; Hatim Khan,. 28b; M. U., II, 668-70.
6.	Muhammad Tahir Mashhadi Wazir Khan	5,000/5,000	Irani	*Dilkusha*, 14b; *Alamgir Nama*, 50; Mamuri, 96b; Hatim Khan, 15a; M. U., III, 936-40.
7.	Sarfraz Khan Deccani	5,000/4,000	Other Muslim	*Alamgir Nama*, 47; M. U., II, 469-73.
8.	Champat Bundela	5,000/	Rajput	*Dilkusha*, 15b; *Alamgir Nama*, 78, 92, 163, 207, 217; Hatim Khan, 24b, 28a; Manucci, I, 269-70.

Mansabdars of 3,000 to 4,500

S. No.	*Name and Title*	*Rank*	*Racial Group*	*Sources*
9.	Kartalab Khan (Yaswant Rao)	4,000/4,000 (1,000 ×2-3h)	Other Muslim	Hatim Khan, 20a, 24a, 28a; *Alamgir Nama*, 55, 63, 76, 92; M. U., III, 153.
10.	Ghazi Bijapuri Randola Khan	4,000/4,000	Afghan	*Alamgir Nama*, 76, 93; Hatim Khan, 13a, 24a, 28b; M. U., II, 309.
11.	Jadu Rao	4,000/2,500	Maratha	*Alamgir Nama*, 47, 55; Hatim Khan, 14a, 20a.
12.	Muhammad Beg Zulfiqar Khan	4,000/2,000	Irani	Mamuri, 97a; *Alamgir Nama*, 51, 62, 76, 92, 157; M. U., II, 89-93; Hatim Khan, 21b; Aqil Khan, 39, 59.
13.	Mir Ziauddin Husain Himmat Khan Islam Khan	4,000/2,000	Turani	Mamuri, 97b; *Tuhfa-i Shah Jahani*, 30b; *Alamgir Nama*, 43, 76, 92, 157; M. U., I, 217-20; Hatim Khan, 12b, 24a, 28a; Aqil Khan, 39.
14.	Multafat Khan Azam Khan	4,000/2,500	Irani	*Dilkusha*, 14b; *Aurang Nama*, 26; *Alamgir Nama*, 51, 75, 92; Mamuri, 98b; M. U., III, 500-503; Hatim Khan, 28a.
15.	Mirza Muhammad Mashhadi Asalat Khan	4,000/2,000	Irani	*Alamgir Nama*, 51, 53, 63; Mamuri, 96b; M. U., I, 222-25; Hatim Khan, 15b, 20b. 28b.
16.	Mirza Sultan Safvi	4,000/2,000	Irani	*Alamgir Nama*, 46, 218; M. U., III, 581-83.
17.	Damaji Deccani	4,000/1,300	Maratha	Hatim Khan, 14a; *Alamgir Nama*, 47, 63.
18.	Khawaja Abid Khan	4,000/700	Turani	M. U., III, 120-23; *Alamgir Nama*, 44, 51, 55, 76; Hatim Khan, 13a, 24a.

S. No.	Name and Title	Rank	Racial Group	Sources
19.	Syed Mahmud Nasiri Khan	3,000/2,500	Other Muslim	*Alamgir Nama*, 79,93,126; M.U., I, 782-84; *Amal-i-Salih*, III, 454; Mamuri, 98a; Hatim Khan, 25a.
20.	Fateh Rohela Fateh Jang Khan	3,000/2,500	Afghan	Hatim Khan, 14a,24a,28b; *Alamgir Nama*, 47,51,76,93, 290; M.U., III, 22-26.
21.	Raja Inder Man Dhandera	3,000/2,000	Rajput	*Alamgir Nama*, 43,62,76,92,247; Hatim Khan, 20a, 28a; M.U., II, 265-66.
22.	Mir Malik Husain Bahadur Khan	3,000/1,500	Irani	*Dilkusha*, 14b, 19a; *Alamgir Nama*, 44,51,54,62,92; M. U.,I, 791-813; Hatim Khan, 13a, 16a, 28b; Aqil Khan, 39, 59.
23.	Murshid Quli Khan	3,000/1,500	Irani	*Aurang Nama*, 15; Mamuri, 97b; *Alamgir Nama*, 44,54, 62,67; M.U., III, 493-500; Hatim Khan, 13a, 16a, 18b; Aqil Khan, 39,41.
24.	Hasan Khan Deccani	3,000/2,500	Other Muslim	*Alamgir Nama*, 45; T.U. "H"; Hatim Khan, 13b.
25.	Muzaffar Lodi (Lodi Khan)	3,000/2,000	Afghan	Hatim Khan, 15a, 19b, 28a; *Alamgir Nama*, 51,76,291.
26.	Shamsuddin Kheshgi	3,000/2,000	Afghan	M.U.,II, 676-77; *Alamgir Nama*, 45; Hatim Khan, 13b.
27.	Muftakhar Khan Sipahdar Khan Khan-i-Azam	3,000/2,000	Irani	*Alamgir Nama*, 47,51,62,75,92; Hatim Khan, 14a, 20a, 24a.
28.	Abdur Rehman Bijapuri Sharza Khan	3,000/1,500	Other Muslim	*Alamgir Nama*, 76,92,208-209; T.U. "Sh"; Hatim Khan, 24a.
29.	Abdullah Beg Mukhlis Khan Yakataz Khan	3,000/1,500	Turani	*Alamgir Nama*, 63,78,93; M.U., III, 968-70; Hatim Khan, 20b, 24b, 28b.

S. No.	Name and Title	Rank	Racial Group	Sources
30.	Raja Rajroop Kohistani	3,000/3,000	Rajput	*Alamgir Nama*, 181,187,190, 320.
		Mansabdars of, 1,000 to 2,500		
31.	Hadi Dad Khan	2,500/2,500	Other Muslim	*Alamgir Nama*, 62,108; Hatim Khan, 20a, 28b; *Amal-i-Salih*, III, 456.
32.	Bhel Afghan Purdil Khan	2,500/2,000	Afghan	Hatim Khan, 15a,19b,28a; *Alamgir Nama*, 52. 334.
33.	Muhammad Ibrahim Shujaa't Khan	2,000/1,000	Turani	Hatim Khan, 13b, 16a, 19b, 24a; *Alamgir Nama*, 45,-51,54,61,92.
34.	Dadaji	2,500/1,000	Maratha	*Alamgir Nama*, 48; Hatim Khan, 14b.
35.	Manaji Bhonsle	2,500/1,500	Maratha	*Alamgir Nama*, 128; Hatim Khan, 16a. S. D. A. 7.
36.	Rustam Rao	2,500/1,200	Maratha	Hatim Khan, 14a, 20a; *Alamgir Nama*, 47.55.
37.	Babaji Bhonsle (Habaji)	2,500/1,500	Maratha	*Alamgir Nama*, 54, 63. *Amal-i-Salih*. III. 460.
38.	Sadat Khan	2,000/1,500	Irani	Hatim Khan, 28b; *Alamgir Nama*, 62; *Amal-i-Salih*, III, 458.
39.	Biyas Rao	2,000/1,200	Maratha	*Alamgir Nama*, 48; Hatim Khan, 14b.
40.	Syed Hasan, later on Ikram Khan	2,000/1,000	Other Muslim	*Alamgir Nama*, 92, 346-47; M.U.I, 215-16; *Amal-i-Salih*, III, 459.
41.	Betuji Deccani	2,000/1,000	Maratha	Hatim Khan, 14a, 20a; *Alamgir Nama*, 47,63.
42.	Abdullah Khan Sarai	2,000/1,000	Turani	*Alamgir Nama*, 47, 63.

S. No.	Name and Title	Rank	Racial Group	Sources
43.	Syed Sherzaman Barha Muzaffar Khan	2,000/600	Other Muslim	M.U., II, 465; *Alamgir Nama*, 47,54,61,92; Hatim Khan, 14a, 19b, 28a.
44.	Wali Mihaldar	2,000/1,000	Other Muslim	*Alamgir Nama*, 45; Hatim Khan, 13b, 15b; *Amal-i-Salih*, III, 463.
45.	Mir Shamsuddin Mukhtar Khan S/o Mukhtar Khan	2,000/1,000	Irani	Mamuri, 96b; *Alamgir Nama*, 47, 51, 62, 92; Hatim Khan, 14a, 20a, 28a; M.U., III, 620-23.
46.	Bakhtiyar Khan Khawas Khan	2,000/1,500	Afghan	*Alamgir Nama*, 52, 53, 92, 132; Hatim Khan, 15a-b, 28a.
47.	Muhammad Tahir Saf Shikan Khan	2,000/1,000	Irani	Mamuri, 97a; *Dilkusha*, 14b; *Alamgir Nama*, 53, 68; Hatim Khan, 15b, 20a; M.U., II, 738-40.
48.	Muhammad Aqil Birlas Tahawur Khan	2,000/400	Turani	*Alamgir Nama*, 53,55; Hatim Khan, 16a, 20b, 28a.
49.	Mir Murad Mazandani Ghairat Khan	2,000/400	Irani	*Alamgir Nama*, 54-55, 92; Hatim Khan, 16a, 20b.
50.	Kamal Lodi Harbuz Khan	2,000/500	Afghan	*Alamgir Nama*, 55,63,76,77; Hatim Khan, 19b, 24a, 28b.
51.	Syed Shah Muhammad Murtaza Khan of Bukhara	2,000/500	Turani	Hatim Khan, 15a, 20a, 24a, 28b; *Alamgir Nama*, 51, 68, 77, 101.
52.	Mir Masum Khan	1,500/1,000	Irani	*Alamgir Nama*, 51,210; M.U..II, 676; Hatim Khan, 15a.
53.	Khushhal Beg Qaqshal Qulij Khan	High Rank	Turani	Hatim Khan, 15b,20b,28b; *Alamgir Nama*, 53,63,471,914.
54.	Ahmad Beg Kheshgi Ikhlas Khan	2,000/500	Afghan	Hatim Khan, 19b, 24a, 28b; *Alamgir Nama*, 77.

S. No.	*Name and Title*	*Rank*	*Racial Group*	*Sources*
55.	Beg Muhammad Kheshgi Dindar Khan	2,000/500	Afghan	Hatim Khan, 24a; *Alamgir Nama*, 63, 77, 93, 108.
56.	Ismail Kheshgi Jan Baz Khan	2,000/600	Afghan	*Alamgir Nama*, 62, 76; Hatim Khan, 20a, 24a; M.U., III, 777-78.
57.	Mir Isa Himmat Khan	2,000/200	Turani	M.U., III, 946-49; Hatim Khan, 20a, 24a, 28a; *Alamgir Nama*, 77, 92.
58.	Ilhamullah	1,500/1,500 (500 × 2-3h)	Other Muslim	*Amal-i-Salih*, III, 460; Hatim Khan, 19b, 24a; *Alamgir Nama*, 62; M.U., II, 303-305.
59.	Syed Yusuf	1,000/500	Other Muslim	*Alamgir Nama*, 62; *Amal-i-Salih*, III, 467.
60.	Rad Andaz Beg	1,000/400	Irani	M.U., II, 679-81; *Alamgir Nama*, 63,237; Hatim Khan, 20b.
61.	Alahyar Beg Bukhari	1,000/1,000	Turani	*Alamgir Nama*, 63,94,831; Hatim Khan, 20b; M.U., I, 216.
62.	Sikandar Rohela	1,000/500	Afghan	*Alamgir Nama*, 63,291; Hatim Khan, 20a; *Amal-i-Salih*, III, 468.
63.	Tarmakji Bhonsle	1,500/1,000	Maratha	Hatim Khan, 14a; *Alamgir Nama*, 48.
64.	Man Singh of Gular	1,500/1,000	Rajput	*Alamgir Nama*, 199-200; *Badshah Nama*, II, 738.
65.	Dakuji	1,500/1,000	Maratha	*Alamgir Nama*, 48; Hatim Khan, 14b.
66.	Amar Singh zamindar of Narwar	1,500/1,000	Rajput	*Alamgir Nama*, 77, 215; Hatim Khan, 24b; *Amal-i-Salih*, III, 462.
67.	Muhammad Shah Mughal Qaladar Khan	1,500/1,000	Turani	*Alamgir Nama*, 48; Hatim Khan, 14a.

S. No.	Name and Title	Rank	Racial Group	Sources
68.	Muhammad Sharif Polakji	1,500/1,000	Other Muslim	*Alamgir Nama*, 54; Hatim Khan, 16a, 20b.
69.	Syed Mansur Khan	1,000/400	Other Muslim	Hatim Khan, 28b; *Alamgir Nama*, 63; *Amal-i-Salih*, III, 468; M.U., II, 449-52.
70.	Daulatmand Khan Deccani	1,500/1,000	Afghan	Hatim Khan, 20a, 28b; *Alamgir Nama*, 63, 93; *Amal-i-Salih*, III, 462.
71.	Hayat Afghan Zabardast Khan	1,000/800	Afghan	*Alamgir Nama*, 54, 92; Hatim Khan, 20a, 28a.
72.	Karan Kachhi zamindar of Malwa	1,500/500	Hindu	*Alamgir Nama*, 52, 92; Hatim Khan, 15a, 20a, 28b.
73.	Mir Ahmad	1,500/800	Irani	Hatim Khan, 13b; *Alamgir Nama*, 45,53; M.U., III, 516-18.
74.	Muhammad Munim Khan	1,500/600	Turani	*Alamgir Nama*, 45, 51, 55; M.U., III, 589; Hatim Khan, 13b, 20a, 28b.
75.	Mir Salih	1,500/500	Other Muslim	Hatim Khan, 13b; *Alamgir Nama*, 45.
76.	Ahmad Beg Zulqadar Khan	1,000/500	Turani	*Alamgir Nama*, 63, 77, 448; Hatim Khan, 20b, 28b.
77.	Ismail Khan Niyazi	1,500/300	Afghan	*Alamgir Nama*, 45, 62, 92; Hatim Khan, 24a.
78.	Qazi Nizam Karsarodi	1,500/200	Other Muslim	*Alamgir Nama*, 48, 53; M.U., III, 566-68; Mamuri, 98b; Hatim Khan, 14a, 16a.
79.	Misri Afghan	1,500/500	Afghan	*Alamgir Nama*, 53, 305; Hatim Khan, 15b.
80.	Mir Abul Fazl Mamuri Mamur Khan	1,500/500	Irani	Hatim Khan, 15b, 19b; *Alamgir Nama*, 53, 62, 77.

S.No.	*Name and Title*	*Rank*	*Racial Group*	*Sources*
81.	Shaikh Abdul Aziz	1,000/500	Other Muslim	Mamuri, 97b; *Alamgir Nama*, 62,74, 77; M.U., II, 686; Hatim Khan, 20b; S.D.A. 74.
82.	Saifuddin Mahmud Faqirullah Saif Khan	1,500/700	Turani	Mamuri, 98b; *Alamgir Nama*, 78, 92; M.U.,II, 479-85; Hatim Khan, 24b.
83.	Mir Hoshdar (Hoshdar Khan)	1,500/700	Irani	*Alamgir Nama*, 51, 62, 92; M.U.III, 943-46; Hatim Khan, 14a, 20a, 28a.
84.	Isa Beg Sazawar Khan	1,500/200	Other Muslim	Mamuri, 96b; *Alamgir Nama*, 46, 53, 63, 108; Hatim Khan, 20b, 28b.
85.	Hameeduddin Khan Khanazad Khan	1,500/200	Irani	*Alamgir Nama*, 55, 77, 94, 270, 594.
86.	Shaikh Abdul Qawi	1,500/100	Other Muslim	*Alamgir Nama*, 54, 94, 231; M.U.,I, 225-29.
87.	Mir Bahadur Dil Jan Sipar Khan	1,000/400	Irani	Hatim Khan, 20a; *Alamgir Nama*, 62,127; *Amal-i-Salih*, III, 468; M.U.,I, 535; S.D.A. 29.
88.	Qazalbash Khan	1,500/700	Irani	*Alamgir Nama*, 63, 291; Hatim Khan, 20b.
89.	Mir Askari Aqil Khan	1,500/500	Irani	*Alamgir Nama*, 44, 193-94; M.U., II, 821.
90.	Khawaja Obedullah	1,500/400	Other Muslim	Hatim Khan, 20b, 28b, 65b; *Alamgir Nama*, 63, 301.
91.	Masud Yadgar Ahmad Beg Khan	1,500/600	Turani	*Alamgir Nama*, 78,158, 193, 196; *Arkan-i-Ma'asir-i-Taimuriya*, 126b.
92.	Syed Abdur Rahman Dilawar Khan	1,000/1,000	Other Muslim	Mamuri, 96b; Hatim Khan, 14a, 16a, 28b; *Alamgir Nama*, 48, 55, 62, 93.

S. No.	*Name and Title*	*Rank*	*Racial Group*	*Sources*
93.	Saun Singh	1,000/500	Rajput	*Alamgir Nama*, 55, 77; Hatim Khan, 24b.
94.	Raja Sarang Dhar of Jammun	1,000/500	Hindu	Hatim Khan, 20a, 28a; *Alamgir Nama*, 62, 92, 196, 219, 286.
95.	Khawaja Kalan Kifayat Khan	1,000/200	Other Muslim	Mamuri, 97b; Hatim Khan, 24b; *Alamgir Nama*, 77.
96.	Syed Nasiruddin Khan Deccani	1,000/800	Other Muslim	*Alamgir Nama*, 45, 61, 92; Hatim Khan, 13b, 19b, 28a.
97.	Saifullah Arab	1,000/800	Other Muslim	*Alamgir Nama*, 45; Hatim Khan, 13b.
98.	Bhagwant Singh Hara	2,500/800	Rajput	*Alamgir Nama*, 63, 92, 192; Hatim Khan, 20b, 20a.
99.	Khudawand Habshi	1,000/400	Other Muslim	Hatim Khan, 13b; *Alamgir Nama*, 45.
100.	Ghulam Muhammad Afghan	1,000/400	Afghan	*Alamgir Nama*, 53, 305; Hatim Khan, 15b.
101.	Muhammad Ismail S/o Najabat Khan	1,000/500	Turani	*Alamgir Nama*, 48; Hatim Khan, 14a, 20a.
102.	Abdul Bari Ansari	1,000/500	Other Muslim	Hatim Khan, 19b; *Alamgir Nama*, 62, 92, 291.
103.	Zainul Abidin Bukhari	1,000/300	Turani	*Alamgir Nama*, 45; Hatim Khan, 13b.
104.	Niamatullah	1,000/200	Irani	Hatim Khan, 15a, 20a, 28b; *Alamgir Nama*, 52, 62, 92; M.U.,I, 584-87.
105.	Husain Beg Khan	1,000/400	Other Muslim	*Alamgir Nama*, 55, 218; Hatim Khan, 16a.
106.	Jamal Khan s/o Dilir Khan	1,000/400	Afghan	*Alamgir Nama*, 147.

S. No.	*Name and Title*	*Rank*	*Racial Group*	*Sources*
107.	Muhammad Sadiq	1,000/300	Turani	*Alamgir Nama*, 55, 92, 206.
108.	Ghairat Beg Shuja Khan	1,000/300	Other Muslim	Hatim Khan, 28a; *Alamgir Nama*, 55, 206, 232.
109.	Jamal Nauhani Bijapuri	1,500/800	Afghan	Hatim Khan, 19b, 28a; *Alamgir Nama*, 61, 92; *Amal-i-Salih*, III, 462.
110.	Hameed Kakar Kakar Khan	1,000/700	Afghan	Hatim Khan, 20a, 24a; *Alamgir Nama*, 62, 77, 218.
111.	Masud Mangli Mangli Khan	1,000/600	Afghan	*Alamgir Nama*, 63, 77, 207; Hatim Khan, 20a, 24a, 28b.
112.	Badil Bakhtiyar	1,000/300	Afghan	Hatim Khan, 20a; *Alamgir Nama*, 63, 93, 207.
113.	Saif Bijapuri	1,000/600	Other Muslim	*Alamgir Nama*, 63, 163; Hatim Khan, 20a.
114.	Ibrahim Qarbegi	1,000/400	Other Muslim	*Alamgir Nama*, 63, 94, 163; Hatim Khan, 20b.
115.	Daulat Afghan	1,000/500	Afghan	*Alamgir Nama*, 78.
116.	Muhammad Muqim	1,000/500	Turani	Hatim Khan, 24b; *Alamgir Nama*, 78.
117.	Bahram	1,000/600	Other Muslim	*Alamgir Nama*, 93, 486; Hatim Khan, 28b.
118.	Inayat Khan	1,000/500	Afghan	*Alamgir Nama*, 92, Hatim Khan, 28a.
119	Abu Muslim	1,000/300	Other Muslim	*Alamgir Nama*, 92, 206; Hatim Khan, 28b.
120.	Subh Karan Bundela	1,000/500	Rajput	*Dilkusha*, 14b, 18b; *Alamgir Nama*, 63, 93, 190, 249; Hatim Khan, 16b, 20b, 28b.

S. No.	Name and Title	Rank	Racial Group	Sources
121.	Itibar Khan Khawajasara	1,000/200	Other Muslim	*Alamgir Nama*, 193.
122.	Hakim Muhammad Amin Shirazi	1,000/	Irani	*Alamgir Nama*, 45; Hatim Khan, 13b.
123.	Mir Muhammad Mahdi Urdistani	1,000/	Irani	*Alamgir Nama*, 45; *Ma'asir-i-Alamgiri*, 70; Hatim Khan, 13b; M. U., I. 599-600.
124.	Iradat Barha	Amir	Other Muslim	Mamuri, 98b.

SUPPORTERS OF SHAH SHUJA IN THE WAR OF SUCCESSION
1658-59.

S. No.	Name and Title	Rank	Racial Group	Sources
		Mansabdars of 5,000 and above		
1.	Abdur Rahman S/o Nazar Muhammad Khan	5,000/2,500	Turani	Mamuri, 104b; *Alamgir Nama*, 250, 257, 267, 341; Hatim Khan, 58a; M. U., II, 809-812.
		Mansabdars of 3,000 to 4,500		
2.	Murad Kam Mukarram Khan Safvi	3,000/3,000	Irani	*Alamgir Nama*, 239, 251, 267; Mamuri, 104b, 106a; Hatim Khan, 54b; M.U., III, 583-86; *Amal-i-Salih*, III, 454; Aqil Khan, 104.
3.	Mir Abul Ma'ali	3,000/2,000	Turani	*Alamgir Nama*, 240-41, 251; Hatim Khan, 58b; M. U., III, 557-60.
4.	Syed Qasim Barha	3,000/1,000	Other Muslim	Mamuri, 104a; Hatim Khan, 54b; *Alamgir Nama*, 250, 257, 303; M. U., II, 681-82; Aqil Khan, 104, 124.
		Mansabdars of 1,000 to 2,500		
5.	Syed Alam Barha	2,000/1,000	Other Muslim	*Amal-i-Salih*, III, 325; Isar Das, 9b; *Alamgir Nama*, 239, 252, 258; Mamuri, 105b; *Badshah Nama*, II, 727; M. U., II, 454-56; Aqil Khan, 103, 129.
6.	Nurul Hasan Barha	1,000/400	Other Muslim	Mamuri, 114b; *Alamgir Nama*, 499, 504; *Badshah Nama*, II, 736; *Amal-i-Salih*, III, 468; Aqil Khan, 124.

S. No.	*Name and Title*	*Rank*	*Racial Group*	*Sources*
7.	Abu Muhammad	1,000/800	Other Muslim	*Alamgir Nama*, 349; *Amal-i-Salih*, III, 465.
8.	Hasan Kheshgi	High Rank	Afghan	Hatim Khan, 54b, 58b; Mamuri, 106a; *Alamgir Nama*, 239, 251, 257; Aqil Khan 103, 106.
9.	Ibn Husain (Darogha-i-top Khana)	Amir	Other Muslim	Mamuri, 114b, 117a; *Alamgir Nama*, 544, 554.
10.	Syed Quli Uzbek	Amir	Turani	Hatim Khan, 58b; Mamuri, 116a, 117b; *Alamgir Nama*, 251, 527, 544, 561.

N. B. : Ilahwardi Khan has not been included among the supporters of Shah Shuja because he created dissension in Shah Shuja's camp and tried to paralyse his military effort. He betrayed him at the battle of Khajwah and was put to death by the prince at Akbarnagar. (*Riyaz-us-Salatin*, 217; M.U., I, 207; Aqil Khan, 127; Khafi Khan, 85; Manucci, I, 330-31).

SUPPORTERS OF MURAD BAKHSH IN THE WAR OF SUCCESSION 1658-59.

S. No.	Name and Title	Rank	Racial Group	Sources
	Mansabdars of 5,000 and above			
1.	Shahbaz	5,000/	Other Muslim	Mamuri, 96a, 101b; Isar Das, 10b, 11a, 32b; Hatim Khan, 9a; Manucci, I, 301; M.U.,I, 298; Aqil Khan, 95.
	Mansabdars of 3,000 to 4,500			
2.	Ibrahim Khan[1]	4,000/3,000	Irani	Mamuri, 101b, 102a; Hatim Khan, 41b; Manucci, I, 301-302; M.U., I, 295-301; *Alamgir Nama*, 139, 158; Aqil Khan, 87.
3.	Qutbuddin Khan Kheshgi	3,000/3,000(2-3h)	Afghan	*Alamgir Nama*, 139, 140; *Dilkusha*, 17a-b; Isar Das, 10a, 32b, 34a; *Mirat-i-Ahmadi*, I, 240; M. U., III, 103.
	Mansabdars of 1,000 to 2,5000			
4.	Debi Singh Bundela	2,000/2,000	Rajput	*Alamgir Nama*, 71, 74, 139, 206, 207; Isar Das, 21a; Mamuri, 97b; Hatim Khan, 23a: M.U., II, 295-97.
5.	Syed Hasan Barha	2,000/2,000	Other Muslim	*Amal-i-Salih*, III, 461; Isar Das, 17a; *Alamgir Nama*, 139, 140.
6.	Rana Gharib Das Sisodia	1,500/700	Rajput	Isar Das, 17a, 24a; *Alamgir Nama*, 107; *Amal-i-Salih*, III, 463; Hatim Khan, 33a.

[1] In the battle of Samugarh Ibrahim Khan fought on the side of Dara Shukoh, but after the battle joined Murad Bakhsh. When Murad Bakhsh was arrested Ibrahim Khan refused to serve Aurangzeb and retired from service.

S. No.	Name and Title	Rank	Racial Group	Sources
7.	Sultan Yar	1,500/1,500	Other Muslim	Hatim Khan, 33a; Isar Das, 17a, 24a; *Alamgir Nama*, 107; *Mirat-i-Ahmadi*, I, 235; *Amal-i-Salih*, III, 461.
8.	Dildoz (Dildost)	1,500/1,000	Other Muslim	*Alamgir Nama*, 139, 140; *Amal-i-Salih*, III, 463; *Mirat-i Ahmadi*, I, 233.
9.	Rahmat Khan[1]	1,500/400	Other Muslim	*Mirat-i Ahmadi*, 237, 240; *Alamgir Nama*, 139-40; Hatim Khan, 41b; *Amal-i-Salih*, III, 463.
10.	Syed Shaikhan Barha	1,000/900	Other Muslim	Isar Das, 17a; *Alamgir Nama*, 107; Hatim Khan, 33a; *Badshah Nama*, II, 733.
11.	Syed Mansur Barha	1,000/400	Other Muslim	*Alamgir Nama*, 139, 140; Isar Das, 17a; Hatim Khan, 41a; *Amal-i Salih*, III, 468; *Mirat-i Ahmadi*, I, 235.

[1] In the battles of Dharmat and Samugarh Rahmat Khan fought on the side of Murad Bakhsh. When Murad Bakhsh was arrested Rahmat Khan along with Shah Nawaz Khan Safvi joined Dara Shukoh before the battle of Deorai.

CHAPTER V

NOBLES AND ADMINISTRATION

NOBLES AT THE COURT

IN a system of despotic monarchy, such as that of the Mughals, the fortunes of all officers depended directly or indirectly upon the approbation of the Emperor. The Court, therefore, was the centre towards which the eyes of the nobles were constantly turned. At the same time the Emperor had to govern the empire through the agency of the *mansabdars*, and had all the time to see that they not only carried out his orders, but also that the power which he vested in them was not abused. A study of the relations between the Mughal Court and the nobility, therefore, is not without interest, and may help us in understanding the ties which bound the nobility to the throne.

From the point of view of the Court, the Mughal nobility at any particular time could be divided into two groups: the *tainat-i rakab*, or those who were stationed at the Court; and the *tainat-i subajat*, or those who were posted in the provinces. This division was based purely on the postings of individual officers, who were frequently transferred from one group to the other.

It was an established practice under the Mughals that when a high noble was transferred from one place to another, he presented himself at the Court before proceeding to his new appointment. But in case the transfer was due to some fault committed by the noble, he was not permitted to come to the Court.[1] An officer, who left his post to come to the Court without imperial permission, was liable to be dismissed.[2]

In placing nobles among the *tainat-i rakab* and *tainat-i subajat*, a number of factors had naturally to be kept in view.[3] Nobles who possessed organising capacity and administrative abilities were posted in different parts of the Empire, and were not recalled to the Court unless their presence was absolutely necessary. The nobles present at Court were considered

[1] In 1663, when Shaista Khan was transferred from the Deccan to Bengal on account of his negligence which resulted in Shivaji's night attack on his camp, he was not permitted to come to the Court. (*Dilkusha*, f. 24a-24b; Mamuri, 131a; Khafi Khan, II, p. 175). In 1672, when Muhammad Amin Khan suffered heavy losses at the hands of the Afghans, he was transferred to Gujarat and was directed to proceed directly to that Province without presenting himself at Court (*Ma'asir-i Alamgiri*, p. 121).

[2] *Akhbarat*, 30 R. Y. f. 275.

[3] "The army stationed in the provinces differs in nothing from that about the King's person" (Bernier. p. 218).

a reserve force and were deputed by the Emperor to serve on all important campaigns. Accordingly, military commanders of high rank and ability were often kept at the Court directly under the eyes of the Emperor to be available for any military enterprise required. It was also a commonsense measure for the Emperor to retain a large army with him in order to prevent any *coup d'etat* by a powerful general. An incident involving Fathullah Khan Bahadur Alamgirshahi, an officer at the court of Aurangzeb, shows the vigilance exercised by the Mughals in this respect. One day Fathullah represented that if 5,000 soldiers were given to him, he would undertake to uproot the Marathas from the Deccan. Aurangzeb retorted that before putting so many soldiers under his command, he would first have to keep 5,000 horses in readiness along with an equally efficient commander for his personal protection.[1]

Court Etiquette

Nobles, when at Court, were in duty bound to appear twice a day, morning and evening, before the Emperor. Sometimes a noble was exempted from this obligation either on the ground of illness or pressing private business. At the imperial audience and on ceremonial occasions, certain rules and regulations were strictly observed for placing the nobles in their proper order of precedence. Different rows were fixed for the nobles of different ranks and status, and every noble had to stand at his appointed place.[2]

During the proceedings of the *darbar* no noble was permitted to sit.[3] When the Emperor had taken his place on the throne, no one was permitted to leave his position without the Emperor's permission.[4] In 1683 it was ordered that the *mansabdars* below the rank of 2,000 should not wait to have the *fatiha* read when taking leave of the Emperor.[5] No one was allowed to present a petition to the Emperor directly.[6]

[1] *Ma'asir-ul Umara*, Vol. III, p. 46: For military exploits of Fathullah, see Khafi Khan, Vol. II, pp. 496-500. Aurangzeb confiscated the artillery of Ghaziuddin Khan Firuz Jang (*Ma'asir-i Alamgiri*, pp. 468-69).

[2] This rule was strictly observed and there could be no exception to it. This is highlighted by the well-known incident at the Court, which ultimately led to Shivaji's flight from Agra in A. D. 1666. Shivaji was made to stand along with other *panj hazari* nobles. In front of him there were other grandees of the Empire who had the rank of 7,000. Shivaji resenting this, gave expression to his dissatisfaction and complained to Kunwar Ram Singh (*Alamgir Nama*, pp. 968-69, Khafi Khan, II, pp. 190-91). Matlab Khan once stood in the enclosure on the right side, it was ordered that he should stand outside the enclosure on the left near Munim Khan and above Nusrat Khan, (*Akhbarat*, 27th Jamada I, 44th R.Y.). At the request of Bahramand Khan, Matlab Khan Qarawal Begi was later permitted to stand in the *Katehara* (*Akhbarat*, 16th Shawwal, 45th R.Y.). Mansur Khan, the *darogha* of the Deccan artillery, was permitted to stand inside the *Katehara* (*Akhbarat*, 9th Ramzan, 45th R.Y.).

[3] Manucci, I, pp. 147-48; *Mirat-al Istilah*, 15b.

[4] *Akhbarat*, 40th R.Y., f. 71. [5] *Ma'asir-i Alamgiri*, p. 224. [6] *Akhbarat*, 40th R.Y., f. 71.

Except with the permission of the Emperor, no one could come armed to the *darbar* or to the Emperor's private audience.[1] It was forbidden to come in a *palki* within the *gulal-bar* or the enclosure of the Emperor's residence.[2] In 1693 Aurangzeb ordered that the colour of the garments of the *umara*, when they came to the *darbar* should not be red and should not be dyed in colours that were illegal according to the *shariat*.[3] The nobles were also prohibited from wearing *nima astin* (half-sleeves) and wrapping a shawl round their shoulders in the presence of the Emperor.[4] The offering of betel-leaves (*pan*) by the nobles to each other in the *darbar* was considered as a breach of etiquette and prohibited.[5]

The most important duty which the *mansabdars* had to perform when at Court was mounting guard (*chauki*) at the Palace.[6] It would appear that the practice established by Akbar continued in the same form down to the time of Aurangzeb. This is clear, for example, from the description offered by Tavernier. "The first court is, as I have elsewhere said, surrounded by porticoes with small rooms connected with them, and here it is that the Omarahs stay while they are on guard. For it should be remarked that one of the Omarahs mounts guard every week. He disposes, both in the Court as also about the Emperor's palace or tent when he is in the field, the cavalry under his command, and many elephants. The best of these Omarahs command 2,000 horses, but, when a prince of the blood royal is on guard, he commands up to 6,000."[7] At another place Tavernier says, "The principal nobles mount guard every Monday, each in his turn, and they are not relieved before the end of a week. Some of these nobles command 5,000 or 6,000 horses and encamp under their tents around the town".[8] The *Zawabit-i Alamgiri* gives detailed rules and regulations in respect of absence from *chauki* in case of illness, marriage and death of near relatives.[9]

When the Emperor went in procession and rode on an elephant, the nobles followed him mounted on horses and when the Emperor was on horse-back, the nobles followed him on foot.[10]

Many ceremonies of the Court were considered an exclusive privilege of the Emperor. Jahangir had once issued an order listing the ceremonies which were reserved exclusively for the imperial Court and the

[1] The Emperor permitted Kalal Khan, the *darogha* of the Kahars, to come armed to the *darbar* (*Akhbarat*, 45th R.Y. f. 120b).

[2] Zulfiqar Khan was permitted to come to *Rahlaka* in a *palki* in the same fashion as the late Bahramand Khan (*Akhbarat*, 47th R.Y. f. 15b); *Farhat-al Nazirin*, f. 178b.

[3] Mamuri, f. 140a. [4] *Mirat-al Istilah*, f. 16b. [5] Manucci, Vol.I, p. 202.

[6] For the detailed account of night guard, *Ain*, I, tr. pp. 267–68.

[7] Tavernier, I, pp. 302-3.

[8] Tavernier, I, p. 126. It is the practice of the Hindu princes and commanders to encamp with their tents for 24 hours every week below the royal fortress (Manucci, I, p. 207). He is also probably referring to the *chauki*.

[9] *Zawabit-i Alamgiri*, f. 38a; see also *Indian Travels of Careri*, p. 248.

[10] Tavernier, I, pp. 308 & 310.; *The Travels of Peter Mundy*, 1608-1667, Vol. II, p. 199.

Emperor.[1] One of these was the holding of elephant fights. This ban continued under Aurangzeb, for Aurangzeb reduced the rank of the *zamindar* of Ratlam by 500 *zat* and ordered his *gumashta* (revenue collector) to be brought to the Court for receiving suitable punishment, because the latter used to organise elephant fights.[2]

The real object of these detailed rules of Court etiquette was to impress upon the nobles the magnitude of the imperial prestige and authority. To a cynical observer of the 20th century all these paraphernalia may seem ridiculous and absurd, but in the medieval ages it was considered an essential instrument of government. It was the policy of the medieval emperors to maintain their pomp and splendour as zealously as possible, so that nobles be made to realise that, however great and powerful they may be, they were nothing when compared with the Emperor, and that their authority, power and greatness depended entirely on his sweet will. At the same time the Emperor also wanted to impress the mass of the people in order that they may realise that even the greatest nobles and *amirs* were merely his servants and that the loyalty of his subjects was commanded by him alone.

Titles and Distinctions

Honorary distinctions have existed in all countries, and they have often served as an incentive to the subjects to put forth their best efforts. The policy of the Mughal Emperors was not an exception to this universal rule, and they certainly did succeed in converting things mostly worthless in themselves into highly coveted and dearly prized objects. Among the marks of honour bestowed by them the most important were titles, robes of honour, standards and Kettle-drums, etc. and presents such as jewelled dagger, betel-leaves, etc.

With regard to the titles, we may note a remark of Manucci : "The King confers these names (by which the nobles were known) either as a mark of distinction and of the esteem he holds them in by reasons of their services, or else from friendship and liking. These lords can acquire more wealth as well as more titles." Manucci adds that the Court had become generous in the award of these honorary distinctions under Aurangzeb: "At present there is a very great number of them; but in Shah Jahan's days, it was not so, and it was very hard to acquire these titles, for it was at once necessary to give a heavy payment and produce enough to maintain a great display. But now-a-days Aurangzeb pays less heed to the matter and gives the title but with less pay."[3]

A title once conferred served officially as the name of the noble concerned. A number of titles were reserved for Muslim nobles and others

[1] *Tuzuk*, p. 100. [2] Isar Das, ff. 144b-45a.
[3] Manucci, II, p. 369.

for Hindus, while some titles were reserved for persons of different professions.[1]

Great care was exercised lest a person, who had not reached the requisite status, be given the title 'Khan'.[2] It should be noted that element of heredity in titles is found at least in the time of Aurangzeb; if one of the sons of a deceased noble attained to eminence, he was generally awarded his father's title.[3] Again, no two nobles could have the same title at the same time,[4] although many titles were given to others after the death of their holders, or after the title-holders had relinquished their old titles for new. Thus the titles of Mahabat Khan, Murshid Quli Khan, and Amir Khan were held by successive nobles after the death of their previous holders; while the title of Khan-i Jahan was granted to Bahadur Khan after it had been relinquished by Shaista Khan, the *Amirul Umara*. Great value was attached to those titles, which had been previously borne by important nobles, so that the nobles were often prepared to buy them by offering gifts and bribes.[5]

Along with titles which served for the names of the nobles, elaborate sets of epithets, appellations and forms of address were prescribed for every important noble and had to be used in all official correspondence.[6] Generally titles were awarded at the time of the accession of the Emperor, on the Persian New Years Day (*Nauroz*), on the birth anniversary of the Emperor and on the day of a victory gained by royal arms.[7]

Robes of honour (*khil'ats*) were presented to the nobles as a mark of Imperial favour. These *khil'ats* consisting of three to seven pieces were of different varieties, those granted as a special honour were called *Malbus-i Khas* (or the personal robes of the Emperor).[8] The *khil'ats* were generally awarded on the same occasion as those on which titles

[1] *Zawabit-i Alamgiri*, f. 15a-15b; Manucci, II, 366-69.

[2] *Akhbarat*, 5th Ramzan, 47th R.Y.

[3] Mir Khan was awarded his father's title of Amir Khan (*Ma'asir-i Alamgiri*, p. 489); Muhammad Ismail Itiqad Khan was granted his ancestral title of Zulfiqar Khan in 1689 (*Ibid.*, pp. 331-32); Mirza Lahrasp was granted his ancestral title of Mahabat Khan (*Ma'asir-ul Umara*, III, p. 590); Saiyid Mahmud was awarded his hereditary title of Khan-i Dauran (*Ma'asir-ul Umara*, I, p. 784).

[4] Khafi Khan, II, pp. 627-28, deprecates a violation of this rule under Bahadur Shah, who gave the same title to different persons.

[5] Mir Khan was given his hereditary title of Amir Khan; Aurangzeb reminded him that when his father Mir Khan became Amir Khan, he presented one *lakh* of rupees to emperor Shahjahan for the addition of the letter 'A' (*Alif*) to his title. (*Ma'asir-i Alamgiri*, p. 489); *Farhat-al Nazirin*, f. 179a.

[6] *Alqab Nama*, ff. 10-77; *Zawabit-i 'Alamgiri*, ff. 107b-09b; Fraser, 86, ff. 31b-36a.

[7] This is clear from the lists of titles conferred on such occasions which appear in Court histories, like the *Alamgir Nama* or Lahori's *Badshah Nama*.

[8] For the detailed description of the *khil'at*, see Tavernier, I, p. 163; cf. Manucci, II, p. 464; Irvine, *The Army of the Indian Mughals*, p. 29. When *khil'at -i khas* was awarded to anyone the recipient had to salute (*taslim*) four times before and four times after putting on the *khil'at*. In case of the ordinary *khil'ats* four salutations were considered sufficient. (*Guldasta*, f. 6b.).

were conferred as also for the different seasons. Hindu nobles were sometimes given *khil'ats* on the occasion of *Dasehra*.[1]

Abul Fazl describes the standards which were conferred by the Emperor upon nobles: the *Alam*, the *Chatrtoq*, the *Tumantoq* and the *Jhanda*.[2] A new standard was introduced in the time of Shahjahan, namely the *mahi-maratib*. Lahori tells us that it was first conferred by Shahjahan upon Nasiri Khan in the 4th R.Y. "The *mahi-maratib*", he says, "used to be conferred in old times by the Sultans of Delhi. The practice was borrowed from them by the rulers of the Deccan and is now common in the Deccan. The rulers there give it to the person whom they regard worthy of the highest honour."[3] The *mahi-maratib* seems to have become the highest honour of the Mughal Empire also, and was not to be awarded to any noble below the rank of 7,000. In case of Zulfiqar Khan Nusrat Jang alone this rule was relaxed at the request of his father, the *Wazirul Mumalik* Asad Khan, for at the time the *mahi-maratib* was conferred upon him, he had the rank of 6,000/6,000.[4]

The *'alam* or standard could be awarded to a noble who had the rank of 1,000 and upwards.[5] The *'alam* was conferred by being placed on the shoulder of the recipient and he had to perform the *kurnish* (or kneeling salutation).[6]

The right to play the *naubat* could be granted to a noble as a special favour. But the recipient had to be a man of the rank of 2,000 or above.[7] It was presumed that the recipient would never play the *naqqarah* (kettle-drum) when the Emperor was present, or within a certain distance from the Emperor's residence.[8] The procedure of the award of the *naqqarah* was identical with that of *'alam*, i.e. the *naqqarah* was placed on the shoulder of the recipient and he had to perform the *kurnish*.[9]

Apart from cash-grants, there were varieties of other gifts given to the

[1] *Alamgir Nama*, passim.

[2] For full details, see *Ain*, Vol. I, pp. 29-30.

[3] Lahori, I, pp. 398-99. For the detailed description of *mahi-maratib*, see Thorn, *Memoir of the war in India*, pp. 355-56; *Mirat-al Istilah*, f. 16a; Irvine, *The Army of the Indian Mughals*, p. 33. *Mahi-maratib* is of Persian origin and is reputed to have been established by Khusro Parwez, the King of Persia in A.D. 591. The Mughals borrowed it from Persia (Sleeman, Vol. I, p. 176, as cited by Shiamal Das in *Vir Vinod*, II, p. 190).

[4] *Raqaim-i Karaim*, f. 12a; According to the *Mirat-al Istilah* (f. 16a), *mahi-maratib* could be awarded to a noble holding the rank of 6,000/6,000.

[5] *Mirat-al Istilah*, f. 16a. This is corroborated by contemporary sources. In 1694 Aurangzeb asked Shah Beg Khan to furnish information concerning those *mansabdars* between the ranks of 1,000 and 7,000 who had got the *'alam* and *naqqarah* and who had not. (*Akhbarat*, 38th R.Y. f. 226).

[6] *Mirat-al Istilah*, f. 16a, *Guldasta*, f. 6b.

[7] *Mirat-al Istilah*, f. 16a.

[8] In 1719, Husain Ali Khan entered Delhi beating his drums and declared that he no longer counted hismelf as the servant of the Emperor. (Khafi Khan, II, p. 804).

[9] *Mirat-at Istilah*, f. 16a.

nobles by the Emperor, such as jewelled ornaments, daggers and swords with jewelled hilts, horses and elephants with gold and silver trappings, and *palkis* with gold fringes, etc.[1] Sometimes *padm-i murassa* (a jewel-studded lotus ornament) was also awarded but this was very rare.[2] *Sarpech-i Yamani* (an ornament in front of the turban) was not normally granted to any noble who held a rank below 3,000.[3] Aurangzeb ordered that no *amir* to whom a *sarpech* of jewellery was awarded should wear it except on Sundays. The nobles were not entitled to get the *sarpech* prepared for themselves and were not to wear an unauthorised *sarpech* on their turbans.[4] The award of the ring of sapphire on the bezel of which the title of the recipient was engraved was also considered a rare honour.[5]

There were other ways still in which the Emperor could show his regards for particular nobles. One was through letters of formal goodwill and congratulations which the king wrote to the highest nobles.[6] Again, when the relation of such a noble died, the Emperor would send some one to express his condolences to the bereaved on his behalf.[7]

The highest among the nobility were connected with the imperial family through marriages. Usually, the Emperor and his sons married into families whose members not only held very high ranks but had the prestige of a long aristocratic lineage. Thus, the great Rajput houses and families like those of Itimaduddaula provided brides to the imperial family for generations. The demand of a bride by the Emperor for himself, or for one of his sons, was another mark of distinction, reserved usually only for the greatest families. The Emperor himself, however,

[1] Chandra Bhan Brahman's *Guldasta* contains an interesting passage on the ceremonials associated with the bestowal of such gifts. According to the rules of the Empire, a person who was awarded *mansab* or a promotion or was granted a *jagir* had to salute (*taslim*) four times. The jewels and jewelled ornaments were placed on the head of the recipient, bracelet (*paunchi*), bow-string (r'ud), and *mala* etc., were placed on the hand, collar, ear and neck and he had to salute four times.

Regarding the weapons the rule was that the sword was suspended from the neck of the recipient, the dagger and *jamdhar* was placed on the head, and the quiver on the shoulder; and after performing four salutations ((*taslim*) the recipient was allowed to gird them. The bows and the musket were placed on the shoulder, and the recipient, having offered four salutations, held them in his hand. The shield was placed on the neck and the armour on the shoulder of the recipient, who then put them on. Similarly, on the occasion of the bestowal of horses and elephants, the horse-bridle and the elephant-drivers baton were placed on the shoulder, for which salutations (*taslimat*)were offered by the recipients. (*Guldasta*, f. 6b-7a).

[2] When Jai Singh was deputed to punish Shivaji, he was awarded *Padm-i Murassa* with *khil'ats* etc. (Mamuri, f. 131b).

[3] *Raqaim-i Karaim*, ff. 14a-14b, for an exception to this rule, expressly made in favour of Amin Khan's son.

[4] *Raqaim-i Karaim*, f. 20b.

[5] *Dastur-al amal Agahi*, f. 61; *Raqaim-i Karaim*, f. 13b.

[6] *Adab-i Alamgiri*, ff. 106a, 144b, 150b, *Raqaim-i Karaim*, ff. 5b-6a, 17a-17b.

[7] *Ma'asir-i Alamgiri*, pp. 103, 223.

out of political considerations, never gave his sisters or daughters in marriage to any one outside the imperial family. They either remained unmarried or husbands were found for them within the imperial family.[1] With the other princesses, such strict regard for imperial dignity was not observed, and such marriages were also not considered significant from the political point of view. Thus, for example, in 1672, Murad's daughter, A'isha Banu was married to Muhammad Salih, a noble belonging to a Persian family.[2]

THE SYSTEM OF PRESENTS

The system of nobles offering presents to the Emperor had become a part of the Court etiquette. In fact, it was a general custom all over Asia that "the great are never approached with empty hands".[3] The offering of these presents to the Emperor was really a public act, and it was expected that the worth and glitter of the offering would enhance the splendour of the imperial Court.

Gifts of substance presented by officers went by the name of *peshkash.* There were certain occasions when the *peshkash* was expected from the nobles present at the Court.[4] Such were the anniversaries of the Emperor's accession, the birth-anniversary of the Emperor, the Nauroz (Persian New Year's Day), the birth of a prince or princess, the celebration of a victory and the Emperor's recovery from an illness. The nobles also offered *peshkash* whenever they wanted some particular favour from the Emperor.[5] The *zamindars* offered *peshkash* at the time of their accession to their *gaddi* (throne) while the tributary princes offered an annual *peshkash.*[6] The *peshkash* offered by the *zamindars* and tributary princes was different in nature from the *peshkash* of the ordinary nobles, it was a token of the recognition of the Emperor's supremacy, and also an assertion of the imperial rights in the appointment of a person to the *gaddi.*

Peshkash was often presented not in cash but in jewels, precious articles, etc. Jafar Khan was prepared to pay a very high price for a diamond

[1] This was true at least for the reigns of Shahjahan and Aurangzeb.

[2] *Ma'asir-i Alamgiri,* p. 120. For the treatment of their husbands by these princesses, see Tavernier, I, p. 313.

[3] Bernier, p. 200.

[4] The occasions set out in the following sentence can be picked out from the official chronicle, *Alamgir Nama,* where the account of each is marked by references to articles or amounts offered as *peshkash* by important nobles.

[5] During his second Viceroyalty of the Deccan, Aurangzeb wrote to Mir Jumla that he should send the agent of Shri Ranga Rayal, the *zamindar* of Carnatik to the Court along with *peshkash* (*Adab-i Alamgiri,* f. 77b). Aurangzeb informed Mir Sultan that goods sent by him as *peshkash* were accepted (*Adab-i Alamgiri,* f. 155b). Rana Raj Singh sent two jewelled swords and one jwelled spear to the Emperor as *peshkash* and it was accepted (*Alamgir Nama,* p. 341).

[6] Tavernier, I, pp. 308, 310; *Alamgir Nama,* p. 837; Manucci, II, pp. 348-49; III, p. 411.

to Tavernier in order to be able to present it to the Emperor.[1] Jewels etc. offered by the nobles to the Emperor as *peshkash* were valued and set off against cash. The nobles were expected to offer *peshkash* according to their status.[2]

Besides *peshkash*, there was *nazr*. In 1700 Aurangzeb ordered all *peshkash* offered in cash to be called *nazr*.[3] Next year he ordered that instead of *nazr* the term *niaz* should be used for gifts offered by princes and instead of *peshkash* the term *nisar* for the gifts of nobles.[4] But, perhaps, in earlier time *nazr* was different from *peshkash* only in being less substantial and was offered in thanks-giving on felicitous occasions of lesser importance. Thus, nobles offered presents to the Emperor on occasions of felicity in their families, such as the birth of a son.[5] A *nazr* could be offered by a noble after recovery from an illness.[6] It could also be offered when a noble came to the Court from his post[7] or *jagir*.[8] In one case, it was offered by a noble on his reinstatement. The amounts given were usually small, amounting to a few *muhrs* (minimum one *muhr*) and some rupees (minimum five), even when offered by the highest nobles.

While it is true that the *nazr* was usually only a nominal amount, the *peshkash* must have imposed a real burden on the nobles. How far Bernier is right in stating that the nobles were ruined partly because of the presents they had to offer to the Emperor it is difficult to say.[9] But apart from the financial aspect, the system is open to criticism from an ethical point of view as well. Often the *peshkash* would only be a veiled form of bribe offered to the Emperor in expectation of certain favours. If the sovereign himself presented such a spectacle, the nobles and other officials would not hesitate to follow his example more vigorously and without any check, as we shall see in the subsequent section.

Mansabdars and the Public Service

The Mughal conception of public service was obviously determined by the nature and sphere of state activity. Unlike modern states, 'national reconstruction' was no part of the real purpose of the state; its moral basis, as stated by Abul Fazl, the chief spokesman of Mughal monarchy, lay in the establishment of justice and of law and order, and in the prevention of crimes and of violent conflicts between various sections of the people.[10] The welfare of the people, in general terms, was regarded as

[1] Tavernier, I, pp. 112, 301; Bernier, p. 271.
[2] *Alamgir Nama*, passim. The value of the jewels presented to the Emperor is always quoted.
[3] *Akhbarat*, 9 Jamada II, 44, R.Y. [4] *Ma'asir-i Alamgiri*, p. 440.
[5] *Akhbarat*, 28 Rabi II, and 1st Jamada II, 8th R.Y.; 25 Rabi I, 38 R.Y.
[6] *Akhbarat*, 28 Rabi II, 1st Jamada I, 1st Jamada II, 8th R.Y.; 3 Zilhij and 4 Ziqada, 9th R.Y.
[7] *Akhbarat*, 20 Rajab, 12 R.Y.; 20 Rajab, 43 R.Y.
[8] *Akhbarat*, 28 Rabi II, 8th R.Y. [9] Bernier, p. 213.
[10] *Ain*, Vol. I, 201-3.

a laudable ideal, but was practically visualised as the establishment of charitable institutions, famine relief, *taqavi* loans to the peasants, land and cash grants to scholars and men of religion, etc. The main interest of the state lay in the organisation of the army, the collection of revenue and the functioning of the judiciary. The judiciary was a separate institution in itself, but all the remaining functions of the government were assigned to the *mansabdars*.

The *mansabdari* organisation included all government services, without any official subdivisions into military, financial and executive branches. Military obligations were invariably imposed on each *mansabdar* in accordance with his *sawar* rank. But since separate departments had to be established in the administrative machinery with posts such as *faujdar* (military and civil affairs), *diwan* (finance), *kotwal* (police) and so on, the office held by a *mansabdar* imposed duties of different types upon him. So, while nominally there was no difference between the civil and military duties of a *mansabdar*, yet in fact civil (revenue) and military duties were often assigned to different persons according to their experience or training. Thus, for example, nobles like Jai Singh,[1] Daud Khan Qureshi,[2] Dilir Khan,[3] Bahadur Khan Zafar Jang Kokaltash,[4] Amir Khan,[5] and Dalpat Bundela,[6] were always assigned military duties and no financial and revenue duty was ever required of them. Such instances may, of course, be multiplied. Likewise, some nobles were always assigned financial and executive duties, such as Raja Raghunath,[7] Inayatullah Khan,[8] Fazil Khan,[9] Bahramand Khan,[10] etc.

However, there are also instances of the same *mansabdars* serving in various departments at different times. Thus Amanat Khan, who held the office of the *diwan* of Bijapur, *daftardari-tan*, *bayutat-i rikab* and, finally of the *mutasaddi* of the Port of Surat, was also twice appointed *haris* (or Commandant) of Aurangabad.[11] Ashraf Khan who at various times had held the office of Superintendent of Branding, Royal Librarian and *bakhshi* of Sulaiman Shukoh, and served as *diwan* of Dara Shukoh and Jahan Ara, was also appointed Governor of Kashmir.[12] Ruhullah

[1] *Alamgir Nama*, pp. 30, 184, 306, 315, 324, 414 & 866; Mamuri, f. 131b.

[2] *Ma'asir-al Umara*, II, pp. 32-37.

[3] *Alamgir Nama*, pp. 160 & 315; Mamuri, 131b; Khafi Khan, II, p. 178; *Dilkusha*, f. 28a-28b; *Ma'asir-al Umara*, II, pp. 42 & 56.

[4] *Dilkusha*, f. 51b; *Ma'asir-i Alamgiri*, pp. 123-24; Mamuri, f. 173b; Khafi Khan, II, p. 316.

[5] *Alamgir Nama*, pp. 1045 & 1057; *Ma'asir-i Alamgiri*, p. 61; *Ma'asir-al Umara*, I, pp. 277-87.

[6] *Dilkusha*, ff. 105b, 114b-15a & 153a; *Ma'asir-i Alamgiri*, pp. 284 & 356; *Ma'asir-al Umara*, II, pp. 317-23.

[7] *Alamgir Nama*, pp. 749, 763, 829; *Ma'asir-al Umara*, II, p. 282.

[8] *Ma'asir-i Alamgiri*, pp. 314, 345 & 393.

[9] *Ma'asir-i Alamgiri*, pp. 393-94; Khafi Khan, II, p. 175.

[10] *Ma'asir-al Umara*, I, pp. 484-85.

[11] *Ma'asir-al Umara*, I, pp. 287-90; *Ma'asir-i Alamgiri*, p. 347.

[12] *Ma'asir-al Umara*, I, pp. 272-74.

Khan not only held successively the offices of *mir bakhshi* of *ahadis*, *akhta begi*, *khan-saman*, *akhtabegi* (again), and second *bakhshi*, first *bakhshi*, but also served as *faujdar* of Dhamau and Saharanpur and *subedar* of Orissa.[1] Muhammad Amin Khan was the *sadr-i kul* of Aurangzeb and thus in charge of judicial administration; but he was also assigned a number of military duties throughout his career.[2]

As noted above, the judiciary was generally treated as a separate institution as it required specialised academic training, and the *qazis* and *sadrs* could expect careers in one branch only. Saiyid Jalal Khan Bukhari,[3] Abdul Wahab,[4] and Shaikh-al Islam,[5] for example, made their careers in the judiciary only, and no other duties were ever assigned to them. Amin Khan seems to have been the only exception. The officers of the judiciary were seldom assigned any executive or financial duties probably in order to avoid the possibility of their having any administrative interests. Unlike the modern judiciary, the judiciary of the Mughals was not an independent institution; but still it was to some extent a check on the tyranny of the executive. The nobles and the administrators also considered the judiciary an entirely separate institution, which had nothing to do with the administration of the country. Interference by the judiciary in the administration was often resented by the nobles.[6] Mahabat Khan in a letter to Aurangzeb protested sharply against the increase in the power of the *qazis* (judges) of the Empire.[7]

Theoretically, once a person accepted a *mansab*, he placed his entire services at the disposal of the Emperor, and his duties by no means ended after he had supplied the contingent or fulfilled the other obligations required from him by the rank he held. He could be assigned any duty or work in any department without receiving a specific salary for the office. His *zat* pay covered everything. Naturally if he failed to perform his duty to the Emperor's satisfaction, he would be punished not by the cancellation of any allowance but by a reduction in his *mansab*.[8]

Certain canons seem to have been gradually developed to establish a correspondence between a post and the rank held by the *mansabdar* assigned to that post. On the executive side, there were three important posts in the provinces, namely, the *nazim* or *subedar* (or Governor), the *faujdar* and the *thanedar*. Nobles holding the ranks from 2,500 to 7,000

[1] *Alamgir Nama*, pp. 830, 1061; *Ma'asir-i Alamgiri*, pp. 127, 144, 150, 156, 195 & 281.

[2] *Ma'asir-al Umara*, I, pp. 346-50.

[3] *Mirat-i Ahmadi*, I, p. 218; Lahori, II, p. 365; *Ma'asir-al Umara*, III, pp. 447-51.

[4] Khafi Khan, II, p. 216; *Ma'asir-al Umara*, I, pp. 235-41.

[5] Mamuri, 162a; *Ma'asir-al Umara*, I, pp. 237-39.

[6] *Biyaz-i Izad Bakhsh Rasa*, ff. 8a-11a; Khafi Khan, II, pp. 215-17.

[7] "The Empire depends now on the *qazis*; and a *qazi* is only satisfied with bribes."

[8] When, for example, it was reported that Neknam Khan, the *bakhshi* of the army, and Ikhlas Khan, the *waqia nigar*, had not joined prince Bedar Bakht, the Emperor reduced the *mansab* of both of them. (*Akhbarat*, 16th Shaban, 43rd R. Y.)

were generally appointed governors. Actually the provincial charges varied considerably in importance. On the one hand, there were the *subedaris* of Kabul,[1] Gujarat[2] and Bengal,[3] etc. to which only *mansabdars* of very high ranks were appointed. On the other hand, there were *subas* like Kashmir[4] and Ajmer,[5] etc. to which *mansabdars* of second rank were appointed.

As far as the appointment to the post of *faujdar* was concerned, generally *mansabdars* from the rank of 500 up to the rank of 5,000 were appointed. Actually, the charges of the *faujdar* varied considerably in importance. The governor of Ajmer province was known as *faujdar-i Ajmer*, the whole province being regarded under his *faujdari* jurisdiction.[6] In Gujarat there was the *faujdari* of Sorath, to which only nobles of very high ranks were appointed.[7] Various other examples could also be given such as Baiswara (whose *faujdar* was independent of the governors of Oudh as well as Allahabad),[8] Jaunpur and Carnatik[9] and Raheri,[10] etc. to which *mansabdars* of first rank were appointed. On the other hand, there were very small *faujdaris* e.g. the environs of the city of Ahmadabad,[11] Rai Sen,[12] and Khaun,[13] etc. to which *mansabdars* of low ranks were generally appointed. Some *faujdaris* were assigned to local *jagirdars*,[14] while a few, perhaps,

[1] Mahabat Khan 6,000/5,000 (3,500 × 2-3h) held the charge of the *Subedari* of Kabul (*Alamgir Nama*, 229). After the transfer of Mahabat Khan, Amir Khan 5,000/5,000 (1,000 × 2-3h) was appointed to that post (*Ibid.*, p. 661).

[2] Shah Nawaz Khan Safvi 6,000/6,000 (5,000 × 2-3h) was appointed as *Subedar* of Gujarat (*Alamgir Nama*, p. 210); afterwards Raja Jaswant Singh 7,000/7,000 (5,000 × 2-3h) held the charge of the *subedari* of Gujarat (*Ibid.*, p. 346).

[3] Muazzam Khan Mir Jumla 7,000/7,000 (2-3h) held the charge of the *Subedari* of Bengal (*Alamgir Nama*, p. 676); his successor was Shaista Khan Amir-ul-Umara, 7,000/7,000 (2-3h). (*Ibid.*, p. 848).

[4] Lashkar Khan 2,,500/2,000 held the charge of the *suba* of Kashmir (*Alamgir Nama*, 195); Iftikhar Khan 2,000/1,000 was appointed *subedar* of Kashmir in 1672 (*Ma'asir-al Umara* I, p. 254).

[5] Tarbiyat Khan 4,000/4,000 was appointed as *hakim* of Ajmer in 1659 (*Alamgir Nama*, 119, 304); Iftikhar Khan 3,000/1,200 was appointed *hakim* of Ajmer in 1679 (*Waqa-i Ajmer*).

[6] *Waqa-i Ajmer.*

[7] *Raqaim-i Karaim*, ff. 3b, 9b; *Dastur-al Amal-i Agahi*, f. 38.

[8] *Insha-i Roshan Kalam.*

[9] Zulfiqar Khan, 5,000/5,000, held the charge of the *faujdari* of Karnatik-Haiderabadi *Ma'asir-al Umara*, II, p. 65 ; Qasim Khan 3,500/3,500 (2,000 × 2-3h) held the charge of the *faujdari* of Karnatik-Bijapuri (*Akhbarat*, 15th Safar, 35th R. Y.)

[10] Abdur Razzaq Lari, 5,000/5,000, appointed *faujdar* of Raheri (Khafi Khan, II, P. 405); Fedai Khan, 4,000/4,000, appointed *faujdar* of Gorakhpur (*Adab-i Alamgiri*, 260a); Tarbiyat Khan, 4,000/3,000, appointed *faujdar* of Orissa (*Mirat-al Alam*, f. 208a).

[11] *Akhbarat*, Azam's Camp, 24 Rajab, 47th R. Y.

[12] Mir Faizullah, 500/200, was appointed *qaledar* and *faujdar* of Raisen (*Akhbarat*, 38th R.Y. f. 378).

[13] Aqa Bahram, 500/400, appointed *faujdar* of Khaun (*Akhbarat*, 9th Rajab, 24th R.Y.); Nusrat Khan, 700/500 (2-3h), held charge of the *faujadari* of Jamin, but was suspended later on (*Akhbarat*, 11th Rabi I, 37th R. Y.).

[14] See Chapter III.

in each *subah* were generally at the disposal of the *subedar*, who might govern them through a deputy or appoint a man of his own choice to its substantive charge.[1]

Next to the *faujdar* was the post of the *thanedar*. The precise nature and duties of the *thanedars*, and the extent of the control exercised over them by local *faujdars* is not quite clear. Some of the *thanedaris* were of such importance that nobles of very high rank were appointed to them. Such, for example, were the *thanedaris* of Kolah Pur,[2] Bahrura,[3] and Lohgarh.[4] It is difficult to imagine that control over these *thanedars* was ever exercised by local *faujdars*. On the other hand, there were small *thanedaris* e.g. Saraha,[5] Khanda,[6] etc. to which only petty *mansabdars* were appointed. In 1671 Jaswant Singh 7,000/7,000(5,000 ×2–3h) was appointed as *thanedar* of Jamrud,[7] but this appointment was of a political nature and not of a routine character. In general it appears that nobles from the rank of 200 upwards were appointed *thanedars*.

On the financial and purely administrative side, the post of the *diwan*, the *mir bakhshi*, the second *bakhshi* and the third *bakhshi* were important. The post of the central *diwan* was considered to carry the highest authority, and nobles of the first rank like Muazzam Khan, Wazir Khan and Jafar Khan, etc. were appointed to it.[8] The post of *mir bakhshi* was also almost as important, and it was assigned to the nobles of the first grade like Bahramand Khan,[9] and Zulfiqar Khan.[10] To the post of second and third *bakhshi*, nobles of the second grade were appointed.[11]

A *mansabdar* might not only be given offices in different departments but also be sent to any province on any assignment that the Emperor decided. Throughout the reign of Aurangzeb, as in earlier reigns, there are innumerable cases of nobles being transferred from one province to another, from one end of the Empire to another. The biography of

[1] *Akhbarat*, 36th R.Y. f. 73; 37th R.Y. ff. 201-02.

[2] Khan-i Alam Ikhlas Khan, 6,000/5,000 was appointed *thanedar* of Kolahpur and, after his transfer, his younger brother, Ikhtisas Khan, 4,000/2,600, was appointed to the same *thanedari*, (*Akhbarat*, 4 Rabi I, 42th R.Y.).

[3] Randula Khan, 4,000/4,000, held charge of the *thanedari* of Bahrura and, after his transfer Nagu Ji Mane, 5,000/4,000, was appointed to the same *thanedari* (*Akhbarat*, 8th Moharram, 44th R.Y.).

[4] Muhammad Sadiq Khan, 3,000/1,200, appointed *thanedar* of Lohgarh (*Ma'asir-al Umara*, III, p. 247).

[5] Mohan Singh, 200/50, appointed *thanedar* of Saraha (*Akhbarat*, 24th R.Y. f. 52).

[6] *Alahdad*, 700/500, held the charge of the *thanedari* of Khanda (*Akhbarat*, 28 Rajab, 24th R.Y.).

[7] *Ma'asir-i Alamgiri*, p. 109.

[8] *Zawabit-i 'Alamgiri*, ff. 82a-82b.

[9] Khafi Khan, II, p. 407.

[10] *Ma'asir-i 'Alamgiri*, p. 461.

[11] In the beginning of Aurangzeb's reign Asad Khan, 4,000/2,000, was 2nd *bakhshi* (*Ma' asir-al Umara*, I, p. 311). In 1694 Mukhlis Khan, 2,500/700, was appointed second *bakhshi* (Ma' asir-i Alamgiri, p. 349). In 1704 Mirza Safvi Khan was appointed third *bakhshi* and at that time he had the rank of 3,000/1,000 (*Ma'asir-i Alamgiri*, 482).

almost any noble would bring out the fact that he had been posted at various times to different provinces in the Empire.[1]

From the foregoing facts, some general conclusions may be arrived at about the relationship between the *mansabdari* organisation and the administrative system of the Empire. The *mansabdari* organisation included the military, civil and financial services, i.e. all public services, except the judiciary. A *mansabdar* had a minimum military obligation indicated by his rank, but in addition he could be assigned to do any work in any department. While the *mansab* held by a noble and the post assigned to him were not directly related, a broad correspondence between the two did exist. The *mansabdars* formed in every sense the governing class of the Empire, and were therefore different from the French aristocracy of the later seventeenth and eighteenth centuries, which had been divorced from administrative machinery. The detailed business of the government could not but be carried on with the help of the subordinate employees, who sometimes wielded considerable influence. Broadly, however, the Mughal nobility retained its hold over the administration and preserved its internal cohesion by the system of constant transfers of individual nobles from one province to another, which made the nobility truly imperial (or all-India) in character and tended to moderate the effects of parochial elements and traditions.

Nobles' Conduct in Administration

Since the Mughal nobility combined the status of an aristocracy and the functions of a bureaucracy in one governing group, it is worth asking how they conducted themselves in the latter role. To some extent their conduct was subject to the control of the Emperor who could promote, demote, depose or otherwise reward and punish his officers. But in its turn the imperial policy in exercising such control was largely governed by the object which the Mughal state set before itself. We have said earlier that a rigorous urge for reconstruction in the modern sense could not be expected; at best the administration concerned itself with maintaining law and order and providing for relief of exceptional distress. Emphasis was placed on the mystic or the religious element, in deference to the principle of *sulh-i kul* under Akbar or to the *shariat* under Aurangzeb, and the imperial government stood forth—on paper, at least, if not in actual fact—as the upholder of piety and morality. These considerations apart, the attention of the state was concentrated almost exclusively upon increasing the income, augmenting the military resources and maintaining the administration in a high state of efficiency. An analysis of the reasons for which various officials were

[1] The only class of nobles for which this will not be wholly true was, perhaps, the Deccanis.

demoted by Aurangzeb would show to what misdemeanours the Emperor, limited as the objects of the government were, took particular exceptions. Thus, disobedience of the orders of the Emperor, not discharging duties to the emperor's satisfaction and not maintaining the required contingents were offences for which punishment were most often meted out. Another set of actions, for which an official might suffer, were infringing upon royal prerogative, having some connection with the enemy, sympathising with the rebels or showing cowardice in action. Immoral activities (drinking, etc.) could also bring about reduction in ranks. Finally, tyranny and maladministration, murder and robbery were similarly punished.[1] However, in his dealings with the nobles in the last mentioned sphere, Aurangzeb showed surprising leniency. Khafi Khan says that although he abolished many illegal taxes on the peasants and merchants, he never punished those who continued to levy them; and, indeed, his own Finance Ministry acted in collusion with the nobles by including the yield of such taxes in the *jama* of the *jagirs.*[2] In an order issued in his 8th R.Y., Aurangzeb himself says that many *jagirdars* in Gujarat were demanding land revenue more than the actual yield harvested by the peasants and oppressing them when they failed to meet this demand. But except for reiterating a ban on such malpractices, he prescribed no punishment for those who had been so flagrantly guilty of violating imperial regulations.[3] Even when he punished, Aurangzeb's hand fell very lightly. Even for enormous crimes, nobles escaped with a mere reduction in rank. Aurangzeb himself acquired a reputation for being exceptionally mild towards his officers. He was prepared to forgive or overlook any disobedience to his orders where his own military interests were not directly involved.[4]

When the imperial control was lax, the only controlling force was the noble's conscience. And this could apparently be persuaded to overlook many things. The prevailing practice of bribery provided the best illustration of this. There were a few officers who disdained to take

[1] See *Akhbarat*, 19th Rabi II, 12 R.Y.; 3rd Shaban, 24 R.Y.; 14th Shaban, 43 R.Y.; 5th Shaban, 43 R.Y.; 8th Jamada I, 44 R.Y.; 9th Zilhij, 45 R.Y.; 20th Ramzan, 40 R.Y.; 24th Shaban, 37 R.Y.; 10th Ziqada, 38 R.Y.; 25 R.Y., f. 388; 6th Ziqada, 13 R.Y.; 27th Moharram, 44 R.Y.; 2nd Rabi I, 43 R.Y.; 10th Shaban, 43 R.Y.; 19th Jamada, 45 R.Y.; 5th Rabi I, 43 R.Y.; 11th Moharram, 46 R.Y., 1st Ziaqada, 43 R.Y.; 11th Rabi I, 43 R.Y.; 24 Rabi I, 43 R.Y.; 15th Jamada II, 44 R.Y.; 24thRamzan, 44 R.Y.; 2nd Jamada, 9R.Y.; 23rd Ziqada, 43 R.Y.; 7th Zilhij, 43 R.Y.; Khafi Khan, II, pp. 275, 478-83; Mamuri, ff. 155a, 178b; *Ma'asir-i Alamgiri*, pp. 88-89.

[2] Khafi Khan, II, pp. 88-89.

[3] *Mirat-i Ahmadi*, I, p. 263; *Mazhar-i Shahjahani*, pp. 177, 180.

[4] Manucci, III, p. 260; IV, p. 98 & 100; Bhim Sen also says that Aurangzeb in his last years devoted little thought to the conditions of his Empire, concentrating his entire attention on seizing forts (*Qila-giri*) (*Dilkusha*, f. 146a). *Mazhar-i Shahjahani*, pp. 173–74.

bribes or presents;[1] but the fact that writers of the period should note the presence of this habit in certain individuals as an exception worthy of record, shows that in general the nobles saw nothing wrong in this practice. Indeed, as we have said earlier, the Emperor's own practice of expecting and taking presents served them as an unimpeachable model.

The nobles expected presents in return for doing everything, even for acts done under imperial orders or in accordance with the specified duties of their posts. Thus, according to Manucci, the governors and *faujdars* turned out from villages, houses and lands, people to whom these had been given by imperial *farmans*, unless they paid them presents.[2] The texts of *madad-i ma'ash farmans* which contain injunctions to officials not to take presents and perquisites from the grantees on various pretexts, suggest that Manucci was not by any means exaggerating.[3] At a higher level, the same story could be heard. William Norris, ambassador of the new English East India Company, was told that Aurangzeb had decided to permit his Company to operate in his dominions, but to obtain the necessary document, he had to present Rs. 200,000 to His Majesty and Rs. 100,000 to his officials.[4]

When this was the case where duty was concerned, the price was still higher where it was within the discretion of the noble to take what action he chose. When the English wanted some concessions from the Mughals on the western coast, they sent presents to Bahadur Khan Kokaltash, governor of the Deccan, but were defrauded by the intermediaries. This was unfortunate because, "nothing was to wrought (on Bahadur Khan) without liberal Piscashes (*peshkashes*), he bearing it as high as the King himself."[5] If the aid of a noble was sought for intercession with the Emperor or for the recommendation of a suit, a price had to be paid. Daud Khan took some very fine presents from the queen of Trichinapalli before undertaking to recommend her appeal for protection to the Emperor;[6] he also took Rs. 25,000 from the English to recommend a petition of theirs to Aurangzeb.[7] Nobles at the court, who had access to the Emperor, sold their good offices to the highest bidder. Qabil Khan, Aurangzeb's *mir munshi*, or Chief Secretary, amassed a fortune of 12 lacs of rupees in cash and

[1] *English Factories*, 1661-64, pp. 203-05; Mamuri, f. 175b-79a; Khafi Khan, II, pp. 261 & 375-81.

[2] Manucci, III, p. 232; *Dilkusha*, f. 84a.

[3] Large numbers of such *farmans* have survived. The U.P. Record office at Allahabad has a specially rich collection of these. Their text was standardised from the last years of Akbar onwards.

[4] Manucci, III, pp. 300-01, Cf. H. H. Das, *The Norris Embassy to Aurangzeb*, pp. 221 2,77.

[5] Fryer, pp. 329-30. See also *The English Factories*, 1670-77, Vol I, (New Series) p. 190.

[6] Manucci, III, p. 411.

[7] *Ibid.*, III, pp. 412-13.

valuables during his two and a half years service with the Emperor.[1] Norris had to offer big presents to the *diwan*, Asad Khan, to win his support for his suit before the Emperor.[2] Subordinate officers similarly sold their good offices for interceding with their superiors. Chatar Bhuj, the *peshkar* (personal assistant) of Rashid Khan, the *diwan-i khalsa*, used to receive Rs. 1,000 every year from Muhammad Muqim, *amin* and *faujdar* of a *pargana* which has been left unnamed. To Bali Ram, Chatar Bhuj's successor, the same official sent a *rath* or chariot worth Rs. 250.[3]

From this the next step was to demand presents from those whom a noble could not help but harm. Thus Bhim Sen had to pay money to numerous persons at the Court simply in order to retain his *mansab*.[4] He probably had not committed any fault to deserve losing his rank. But others who might have deserved punishment escaped by offering presents to those whose duty it was to detect and expose them. Manucci declares that Aurangzeb's younger nobles "in their eagerness to become rich, plunder and act wrongfully. They bribe the *waqia navis* (official reporter) and the *khufiya navis* (secret reporter) so that the king may never hear."[5] From this type of blackmail we may pass on to direct extortion. Shaista Khan, Governor of Bengal, presuming upon his high status, was perhaps, boldest in this respect. Bowrey reports of his compelling Chim Khan, a merchant, to pay him Rs. 50,000.[6]

From methods such as these, nobles of moderate ranks were able to amass enormous fortunes. Abdun Nabi, (2,000/1,500), *faujdar* of Mathura, left 13 lacs of rupees, 9,300 *muhrs*, and valuables worth 4½ lacs.[7] Azam Khan Koka, (4,000/4,000), governor of Bengal, left 22 lacs of rupees and 1,12,000 *muhrs*.[8]

Bribery was thus, for all practical purposes, the chief method by which a subject could secure the aid and assistance of the administration, either for his own protection or for the destruction of others, both in accordance with, and in direct opposition to, all the regulations of the state and imperial orders. There seems to have been no serious attempt to check this practice in the time of Aurangzeb. Only when, as in the case of Munshi Qabil Khan, the bribes taken exceeded all bounds, and perhaps annoyed men of higher ranks, did the Emperor take action. This action too was seldom severe; Qabil Khan was dismissed from his office at the Court and his house was confiscated.[9] A more severe attitude was

[1] *Ma'asiri- Alamgiri*, p. 191. [2] Manucci, III, p. 300.

[3] *Akhbarat*, IIth Rajab, 39 R.Y. [4] *Dilkusha*, f. 84a.

[5] Manucci, II, pp. 451-52; also III, p. 291; See also *The English Factories*, 1670-77, Vol. I, (New Series) p. 267.

[6] Bowery, *The Countries Round the Bay of Bengal*, pp. 153-56. See also *The English Factories*, 1661-64, p. 140; 1668-69, p. 315.

[7] *Ma'asir-i Alamgiri*, 83. [8] *Ma'asir-i Alamgiri*, p. 169.

[9] *Ma'asir-i Alamgiri*, pp. 190-91.

naturally shown towards cases of embezzlement—for the imperial treasury was here directly concerned—but it was considered enough if the embezzled money was returned.[1]

The picture that we get of the Mughal governing class, based on accounts of bribery and corruption, is not a flattering one. It is possible that individual Mughal nobles realised that corrupt practices could not be taken too far without destroying all semblance of government, let alone good government. But even if the picture we have drawn is one-sided or exaggerated—possible faults because of the nature and limitations of our evidence—much would remain, after all qualifications have been made, to suggest that the Mughal nobility formed an extremely short-sighted ruling class. Whatever the reasons for this attitude, their immediate personal gains blinded them to all future dangers to the administration. No central policy could be enforced loyally and steadily by such a class. If the civil administration was the first to suffer from its extortions, the military and diplomatic fortunes of the Mughal Empire were bound to suffer in the end. And by the closing years of Aurangzeb's reign that ultimate stage had already arrived.

[1] In 1702, Chatar Bhuj, *peshkar* of the *diwan-i khalisa*, was imprisoned for misappropriating one lac of rupees. He was ordered to be released on payment of Rs. 25,000 and the promise to pay the rest in instalments (*Akhbarat*, 13th Shaban, 45 R.Y.). But Lutfullah Khan, who sold grain-stores, etc. of the fort of Meraj, and misappropriated the proceeds, suffered only a reduction of 300 *sawars* in his *mansab* (*Akhbarat*, 22nd Shawwal, 38 R.Y.). See also *The English Factories, 1670-77*, Vol. I, (New Series) p. 267.

CHAPTER VI

NOBLES AND ECONOMIC LIFE

ROLE OF NOBLES IN COMMERCE

THE Mughal nobility, unlike contemporary European nobility, was not tied to the land; their *jagirs* (or revenue assignments) were transferred from one place to another as a matter of routine, and many of them were *naqdis*, i.e. they received their pay in cash directly from the treasury. But if the Mughal nobles were not hereditary landlords, it does not follow that they were a commercialised ruling class. Salary, not commercial profit, was their main object in life. Nor did they, or any substantial number of them, rise from a mercantile 'middle class', as was the case with a big section of contemporary English 'oligarchy'. The biographical material available for the Mughal nobility is extensive, but examples of men of mercantile origin are hard to find. Mir Jumla, certainly presents a striking instance of a merchant turning into a statesman. Manucci suggests, in a passage on the Pathans, that they combined the profession of warriors and merchants and treated their admission into the ranks of courtiers (on the basis of equipage and following) as a kind of business investment.[1] Another noble who was originally a merchant was one Nurullah Khan who came into prominence towards the middle of Aurangzeb's reign.[2] But this is about all; and we know of no other nobles under Aurangzeb who might have begun their careers as merchants.

But by their very position as members of the ruling class, the nobles could not isolate themselves from the commercial world. Whether holding *jagirs* or receiving pay from treasury, the income of the *jagirdars* was derived mainly in cash. As we have seen in Chapter III the cash nexus was well established, so that the revenue in *jagirs* was also largely collected in cash. It should, therefore, occasion no surprise when we find nobles of the period accumulating enormous treasures in specie, cash and jewels. It would be natural for nobles, who had a large amount of cash in hand, to desire to increase it still further by investing it in trade, either by engaging in trade directly or by making capital advances to merchants. A big source for capital needed for sea-borne trade came from the Mughal aristocrats. We are informed by Tavernier that, "on arrival for embarkation at Surat, you find plenty of money. For it is the principal trade

[1] Manucci, Vol. II, p. 453.

[2] *Riyaz-us Salatin*, p. 224. He is said to have held the rank of 3,000 *zat*.

of the nobles of India to place their money on vessels on speculation for Harmuz, Bassora and Mocha, and even for Bantam, Achin and Philippenes."[1]

Mir Jumla's activities in the commercial sphere offer the most noteworthy example of such business investments. He had frequent business deals with the English,[2] and sometimes he advanced money to the English factors also.[3] Not only did Mir Jumla advance his money to others; he was in a real sense a 'merchant prince'. His ships carried on trade between Arrakan, Southern India[4] and Persia. His interest in sea-borne trade with Persia is well brought out in the following passage from the *English Factories in India*:

> "You (Chamber and his colleagues) will perceive by the coppy of our generall consultation that we have condescended and agreed, for the preservation of the Nabob's amity, that now the junk cannot be restored, he may take his choice either of the *Anne*, with all her ammunition and stores or of your new built shipp. But this year you must not seem (to know) that we do any way condescend to, so that it may come to his knowledge, for you know the Nabob is five times more indebted to us, by his accompt; besides he doth yearely make use (of us) as this last yeare with twenty five tonns of gumlacke whereof he pays noe freight nor custome in Persia."[5]

The attention of the nobles was, however, not only confined to foreign trade, but extended as well, and perhaps, to a greater extent, to internal trade. Here their lack of professional knowledge was more than amply compensated by the abuse of their influence and authority. Aurangzeb's *farman* to officials in Gujarat contain references to such commercial transactions, which yielded handsome profits, entered into by the nobles.[6]

If Mir Jumla offers the best instance of a Mughal noble taking part in sea-borne trade, Shaista Khan is the best example of a noble dabbling

[1] Tavernier, Vol. I, p. 31.

[2] "The Nabob's money wee positively enorder, without, disputing or pretences, to be paid by Mr Trevisa back, and that accompt cleared; and that for the future none undertake such an unthankful and tresspassing part of service. His ship wee shall endeavour to recover, and hope in March next to give you certain advice of our proceedings therin." (*The English Factories in India*, 1661–64, p. 68).

[3] "In the meanwhile Charnock and Sheldon were peremptorily ordered to give respect and accompt of their actions unto Mr Trevisa. The latter was urged to repay the money lent to him by Mir Jumla and was again reminded of the necessity of a large supply of saltpetre." (*The English Factories in India*, 1661-64, p. 153); 1665—67, pp. 135 and 145.

[4] *Waqa-i Deccan*, ed. by Dr Yusuf Husain, No.2 (Ist Moharrum, 1702 A.H.).

[5] *English Factories*, 1661-64, pp. 148-49; for the commercial activities of Mir Jumla, see also J.N. Sarkar, '*The Life of Mir Jumla*', pp. 216-18.

[6] *Mirat-i-Ahmadi*, Vol. I, pp. 286-88. Gujarat; Centre of Commercial activities, *Raqaim-Karaim*, f. 20b.

in internal trade. His unlimited appetite for money found an outlet is his monopolisation of the internal trade of Bengal.

"Shaista Khan used to import by ship salt, *supari* or betelnuts and other articles, and sold them in Bengal on profitable terms. In addition, he accumulated seventeen crores of rupees by procuring two or three tolas of gold for one gold mohur. He also sold salt and supari to the merchants and traders in the city of Dacca. The latter were thus debarred from making purchases and sales on their on account."[1] We learn from the same source that Shaista Khan had established vast "emporiums of salt worth 152,000 rupees at several places".[2]

The English records are full of similar information about the same noble. "The Nabob's (Shaista Khan's) officers oppress the people, monopolize most commodities, even as low as grass for Beasts, caves, firewood, thatch, etc., nor do they want ways to oppress those people of all sorts who trade, whether natives or strangers."[3] Charnock, writing from Patna (July 3, 1664) stated that "Shaista Khan's intentions were : To get the whole trade of peeter (saltpetre) into his own hands, and so to sell it againe to us and the Dutch at his own rates, he well knowing the ships can not goe from the Bay empty. But he is not likely to get above maunds 4 or 5,000 this year. His darogha hath so abused the merchants that they are allmost all runne away. He pretends that all the peeter he buyes is for the king. It was never known he had occasion of more than maunds 1,000 or 1,500 yearely for all his warrs."[4]

Shaista Khan's inordinate interest in making commercial profit by hook or by crook was by no means an exception. About A.D. 1703, it was reported to the emperor that Prince Azimushshan was forcing the purchase of goods for his private trade and called it *Sauda-i Khas*. Aurangzeb censured the prince sternly and sarcastically called the practice *sauda-i kham* (raw deal) and called the prince a fool and a tyrant for practising such plunder of the people.[5]

The Mughal nobles were naturally interested in the trade in luxury goods, especially jewels. Shaista Khan's purchases from Tavernier are an example of this. The French merchant even went to Europe in 1654 to buy jewels on behalf of this potentate.[6]

[1] S.K. Bhuyan; *Annals of the Delhi Badshahat*, Gauhati, 1947, pp. 167-68.

[2] *Ibid.* pp. 169 & 172. Mirza Raja Jai Singh started manufacturing salt in his *jagir* and as a result of this the imperial salt factory in the Pargana of Sanbhar began to incur the loss of one lakh of rupees annually. Shahjahan directed Jai Singh to stop the manufacture of salt at once, otherwise his *jagir* would be transferred (Jaipur Documents, No. 68, 5th Shawwal, 1053 A.H.).

[3] *Diaries of Streynshan Master*, I, p. 80. For the tendency of the officials in Bengal for monopolising the commodities, see *Fathiya-i 'Ibriya*, f. 127a.

[4] *English Factories*, 1661-64, pp. 395-96. [5] *Riyazus Salatin*, pp. 243-44.

[6] Tavernier Vol. I, pp. 320-22. Tavernier says that in matters of trade the Indians were very precise and paid their debts without delay (Vol.I, p. 326). Shaista Khan purchased

Sometimes the emperor himself purchased jewels through the agency of the nobles. Shaista Khan sent one hundred and nine pearls to Aurangzeb but the price recommended by the Khan was exorbitant according to the estimate of the royal experts, so the emperor did not purchase them and they were returned.[1] On an earlier occasion Shaista Khan had sent a jewel and some pearls to Aurangzeb when he was a prince, and the latter had enquired from him about the prices so that the payment be made to him.[2]

The desire for luxuries and for obtaining articles made according to their own tastes and specifications led the nobility in general to have their own *karkhanas*,[3] or workshops, for manufacturing robes, utensils, arms, furniture, etc. which sometimes employed quite a large number of artisans.[4] The character of these *karkhanas* and the attitude of the nobles towards the artisans employed in them is brought out by Bernier in a well-known passage. He says : "Workshops, occupied by skilful artisans, would be vainly sought for in Delhi, which has very little to boast of in that respect. This is not owing to any inability in the people to cultivate the arts, for there are ingenious men in every part of the Indies. Numerous are the instances of handsome pieces of workmanship made by persons destitute of tools, and who can scarcely be said to have received instructions from a master. The rich will have every article at cheap rate. When an Omrah or Mansabdar requires the services of an artisan, he sends to the bazar for him, employing force, if necessary, to make the poor man work; and after the task is finished the unfeeling lord pays, not according to the value of labour but agreeably to his own standard of fair remuneration; the artisans having reason to congratulate himself if the Korah (whip) has not been given in part payment.... The artists, therefore, who arrive at any eminence in their art are those only who are in the service of the king or some powerful Omrah, and who work exclusively for their patron."[5]

Detailed information about the *karkhanas* maintained by the nobles is not available. But by the side of Bakhtawar Khan's proud claim of having established a number of *karkhanas* in various towns[6] may be set the

---

from Tavernier articles worth Rs. 96,000 in 1652; in 1660 he for the second time purchased some articles from Tavernier; in 1666 he again purchased some articles of luxury (Vol.I, pp. 15-16). Shaista Khan asked Tavernier to supply beautiful jewels and assured him that he would pay for them as liberally as the emperor (Vol. I, p. 245).

[1] *Adab-i Alamgiri*, f. 113a.

[2] *Adab-i Alamgiri*, f. 113a-b.

[3] Usually the scholars of today associate the term *karkhana* with the workshops maintained exclusively by the emperor, princes and the nobles. But it must be added that the *karkhanas* were also maintained by foreign trading companies in the 17th century. (*The English Factories*, 1618-21, p. 198). We may assume that the individual traders also maintained *karkhanas*.

[4] For a reference to Bakhtawer Khan's *karkhanas* established with his houses and palaces in Delhi, Agra, Lahore and Burhanpur, see *Mirat-al 'Alam*, f. 253b.

[5] Bernier, pp. 254-56.

[6] *Mirat-al Alam*, f. 253.

historians praise for Shuja'at Khan's *karkhanas*. The cups, plates, vessels, etc. manufactured in this noble's *karkhanas* were much admired by Aurangzeb, and Shuja'at Khan sent these articles as presents to the Emperor and other nobles.[1]

Apart from the nobles, the emperor and the princes and princesses also maintained *karkhanas* for providing their own needs. For instance, we read in a letter from Aurangzeb to Shahjahan that owing to the scarcity of skilled hands, the output of the imperial *karkhanas* and of the *karkhanas* of Princess Jahan Ara had been meagre. The work of the artisans employed in Aurangzeb's own *karkhana* was not admired by the Emperor.[2] In another letter addressed to Jahan Ara Begam, Aurangzeb assures her that the management of the *karkhana* would not be changed and the articles required by her would continue to be manufactured.[3]

While there is a record of the nobles investing capital in commercial enterprise, it can not be said that their interest was always confined to making commercial profit by honest means. On the other hand, they often put obstructions to the free flow of trade so that they may enhance their income, not from the use of their wealth but the misuse of their power. Bribes were always necessary before they would grant the required privileges to traders and merchants.

In A.D. 1667, when the French traders wanted to obtain a *farman* from the Emperor for trade, they had to pay Rs. 30,000 to the Emperor in foreign rarities while they also undertook to give Jafar Khan Rs. 10,000 and a similar amount to other nobles. When all these payments were made, the *Parwana* for trade was issued to the French traders and they were permitted to hire a house in Surat and to pay 2 per cent duty *ad valorem* on their goods.[4]

In 1659 Mir Jumla stopped the trade of the English at Kasimbazar until some presents were offered to him, and then the requisite permission was given.[5] In 1660 Mir Jumla demanded 20,000 pagodas from the English factors, and also asked them to remit 32,000 pagodas which he owed to the Company.[6] When he was *subedar* of Bengal, Mir Jumla had exempted the English traders from custom duties and in return the English traders had to pay Rs. 3,000 annually.[7] In trade and commerce corruption prevailed everywhere and no assistance was rendered by the authorities unless they were paid for it.

Tavernier says : "So true it is that those who desire to do business at the Court of the princes, in Turkey as well as in Persia and India, should not attempt to commence anything unless they had considerable presents ready prepared and almost always an open purse for diverse officers of

[1] *Ma'asir-i 'Alamgiri*, pp. 405-06.
[2] *Adab-i Alamgiri*, f. 25a.
[3] *Adab-i Alamgiri*, f. 196a.
[4] *The English Factories in India*, 1665-67, p. 281.
[5] *The English Factories in India*, 1655-60, pp. 292-93.
[6] *Ibid.*, pp. 391-92.
[7] *Ibid.*, pp. 393-94.

trust whose service they have need."[1] On the change of monarch and on the change of *subedar* the traders had to pay something in order to get the *farmans* and *parwanas* renewed.[2]

The English factors felt uneasy under Shaista Khan in Bengal, who insisted that presents worth Rs. 3,000 be paid to him whether they had any business transaction for the time being or not. "Though wee have at present little or noe business of our masters to mannage, yet wee are not free from trouble under Nabob's government. 'Tis credibly reported that Ballasore and Piply by the king's order is reduced and brought under the province of Bengall, which wee cannot but lament, especially at this time, it falling under the power of a person most unjust and solely addicted to covetiousness. We must fear the yearely present of this place Rs. 3,000 will be exacted, though wee may have noe shipp arrive, the rent and custome of this towne (i.e. Hugli) being his Jageer."[3]

A *farman* of Aurangzeb preserved in the *Mirat-i Ahmadi* illustrates the variety of ways in which Mughal nobles squeezed trade and commerce through illegal cesses and impositions.

Aurangzeb directed the *jagirdars* of the province of Gujarat not to realise cesses such as *rahdari*, *mahi*, *mallahi*, *tarkari*, *tahbazari*, etc. which had been abolished, from the traders and merchants. They were not to purchase grain, etc. at a low price and sell it at a higher price. They were not to accept any *peshkash* offered on behalf of the grain dealers and other merchants and traders. The Emperor further directed them not to impose other illegal cesses on the business community.[4]

While revenues from land remained by far the chief part of income for the nobility during our period, the advantage of supplementing this income by dabbling in commercial speculations of various types seems to have been realised increasingly by a section of the higher nobility. Even princes and members of the royal family, including the Begums, did not disdain from making profit in commercial speculation.[5] On the other hand, while it is true that nobles often misused their official position for their private profit, instances of this type should not be unduly exaggerated. It should be remembered that the interference of the state in

[1] Tavernier, Vol. I, p. 115.

[2] *The English Factories in India*, 1655-60, pp. 197-98. On the death of Mir Jumla, the English traders had to face a lot of difficulty to get their *parwana* renewed by the new *subedar*, Daud Khan (*English Factories*, 1661-64, p. 288).

[3] *The English Factories in India*, 1665-67, pp. 258-59.

[4] *Mirat-i Ahmadi*, Vol. I, pp. 286-88.

rahdari : Road tolls.

mahi : Tax on fishermen on bringing the fish for sale in the market.

mallahi : Impost on merchants, traders and travellers at the ferries.

tarkari : Tax on vegetables brought in the market by the peasants.

tahbazari : Ground rent levied on shop-keepers.

[5] S. Chandra, *Bengal Past and Present*, July-December, 1959, pp. 92-97.

economic affairs was taken for granted in medieval times, as also the seeking of special favours, including the creation of monopolies by suitable bribes, presents, etc.

In spite of the uncertainty of income from the *jagirs*, a considerable number of nobles in Aurangzeb's time had huge resources, obtained mainly from the land revenue, at their command, which they could either have invested as capital or spent on goods required for consumption by themselves, their house-holds and retainers. The high level of personal consumption was, on the whole, more a hindrance than a help to the development of trade and industry, since it resulted in an undue emphasis on the production and procurement of luxury goods. In such a situation there was little incentive for the growth of new methods and techniques of production. The ideas of the nobles concerning industry never went beyond *karkhanas* or establishments employing artisans at low rates for satisfying their needs for luxuries.

The view may accordingly be hazarded that by and large their 'investments' were not of a nature likely to lead to an improvement in the techniques of mass production, however large the patronage extended by them to skilled artisans.

CHAPTER VII

THE ESTABLISHMENT OF THE NOBLES

THE 'SARKAR' OF THE NOBLES

WE have discussed in an earlier chapter the manner in which the *mansabdars* drew their pay. They constituted the governing class of the Empire, but were at the same time almost entirely dependent upon the state for their income. It was the Emperor who assigned them *jagirs* to provide them with their sanctioned income or pay, or, in case they were *naqdis*, paid them in cash. On their part, they were obliged to maintain military contingents and to incur other expenses in the service of the state. Any audit of the disbursement made by them from their own resources was, however, quite alien to the Mughal administration. The personal expenses of the nobles were not checked or inspected, but only the men, material and services provided by them.[1] Each noble, therefore, had a semi-autonomous '*sarkar*' (administration) of his own, which comprised his military contingent, officials, household staff, harem, servants and hangers on.[2] All such administrations were independent units, because the nobles could spend out of their own income whatever they pleased, as long as the military and other obligations to the state were fulfilled. The central position in a noble's *sarkar* was naturally occupied by the financial department responsible for collecting the revenues from his *jagir* through his agents. This income was often augmented by presents and bribes or profits from commercial enterprises. Every noble had a *diwan*, who was in charge of the financial administration of the noble's establishment, and had a large staff under him. Pelsaert remarks, "As a rule all the possessions of the lords and their transactions are not secret, but perfectly well known, for each has his *diwan*, through whose hands everything passes; he has many subordinates, and for the work that could be done by one man, they have ten here; and each of them has some definite charge, for which he must account."[3] It is not clear if the official whom Manucci describes as 'treasurer' was the same as the *diwan*. We are told by him of how "a man, who supplied his (the noble, Jafar Khan's) household with herbs and vegetables during his journey to Kashmir . . . brought his account at the end of the year to the treasurer

[1] See Chapter II.

[2] For the word '*sarkar*' used in this sense, see *Mirat-al Istilah*, f. 92b; also *Ma'asir-i Rahimi*, III, p. 857; *Nigar Nama-i Munshi*, passim (used for Muazzam's *sarkar*). *The English Factories*, 1618-1621, p. 200.

[3] Pelsaert, p. 55.

of this general's household, wishing to be paid for the supplies he has sent in. Having examined the accounts, his official found the amount so enormous that he decided to strike the sum of eighty thousand rupees."[1]

We owe to the author of a versified panegyric of a saint of the Punjab, a very interesting description of the various officials in a noble's *sarkar*. The author, while describing incidents in which he and his brother, both serving nobles, were concerned in 1639, gives designations of a number of officials of the nobles with some hint of their duties. There appears to have been, to begin with, a *Khazina-dar*, treasurer, who kept cash. The *mushrif-i-Khazana* kept the accounts and kept copies of the *sanads,* i.e. *barats* (orders of payment) and *qabz* (receipts). The author who held this office in one noble's *sarkar*, says he was given *daftar-i-taujih* (or accounts) in another. The *mushrif-i-sarkar* undertook actual purchases, but apparently needed authority from other officials of the nobles for concluding particular transactions. For example, a *mushrif* who purchased grain without the knowledge of the *Khan-i-saman* and *Khawansalar* came in for criticism. These two latter officials respectively managed the household and stores, and supervised the actual work of the kitchen. There was yet another official, the *bakhshi-i-sarkar*, who apparently supervised the maintenance of the noble's contingent. There seems to have been well-established conventions which governed the functioning of the noble's *sarkar*. Each official, for any expenditure within his jurisdiction, drew a *barat* on the treasurer. Thus the author's brother, as *Khan-i-saman*, was pressed by a trooper of the noble, to write a *barat* for some amount due to him: but he asked him to approach the *bakhshi-i-sarkar* for the *barat*.[2]

The noble's officials not only had to keep large accounts on behalf of their master, but also arranged for the transfer of money from one place to another, especially from the *jagirs* to the headquarters. This was usually done through *hundis*, or indigenous bills of exchange,[3] and it is quite possible that the nobles were as great users of this instrument as the merchants.

The Nobles' Contingents

The military contingent of a noble naturally formed a very important, if not the most important, part of his establishment. According to the imperial regulations every *mansabdar* had to maintain a number of *tabinan* or *sawars* mounted on horses of standard breeds, the *sawar* number

[1] Manucci, III, p. 416. Jafar Khan, however, ordered the whole amount to be paid.

[2] Surat Singh, *Tazkira-i-Pir Hassu Taili*, written A.H. 1057, MS. (probably autograph) in Library of the Department of History, Aligarh Muslim University.

[3] See *Akhbarat*, 28th Ramzan, 47 R.Y., for Rs. 12,000 sent from Tarbiyat Khan's *jagir* to Burhanpur by *hundi*. See also *Nigar Nama-i Munshi*, pp. 29, 30, 38.

being determined by the *mansab* held by the nobles. The *tabinan* were expected to be held in constant readiness, they thus formed a part of the standing army of the Empire.[1] Troops which were hired by the nobles for a temporary period were known as *sih-bandis* and were usually employed for such tasks as the collection of land revenue or police-duties.[2] They were not considered eligible for musters and were generally regarded with some contempt when compared to the *tabinan*.[3]

It was generally believed that the *mansabdars* did not keep the full contingents required by their ranks. Thus Manucci tells us that "these gentlemen (*mansabdars*) have generally each in his stable fifty, a hundred and up to two hundred horses for show or service. On the day of the review they equip their servitors and mount them on these horses, and pass them off as soldiers, putting to the account of profits the pay these men draw. In every quarter of the empire there are officials who keep an eye on everything, or, at least, ought to do so, for being at a distance from the Court, they do not acquit themselves of their duty as loyal subjects ought. But they are negligent by reason of the presents given them to that intent by the persons interested. Owing to these considerations they practise concealment, and never dream of enforcing the performance of duties."[4]

Manucci is supported in this general statement by Bhim Sen, who declares that during the last days of Aurangzeb, none of the imperial officers, excepting three Rajput chiefs, maintained their requisite contingents of troops.[5] Specific complaints about officials, high and low, not maintaining their contingents abound in the official records of the reign.[6]

The *tabinan* of the *mansabdars* were usually recruited from the recognised 'martial clans', and each *mansabdar* would usually recruit them either from his own clan or a recognised martial clan. The imperial government itself framed regulations about the clan composition of the troops to be presented for muster by the nobles. These, as set forth in the *Khulasat-us Siyaq*, may be summarized as follows :

I. Mughal nobles of Trans-Oxiana, who had come to the Court after the 24th R.Y. (of Aurangzeb), were to present only Mughals at the muster.

II. Mughals who had come earlier, were to have Mughals as one-third of their troops and other races as two-thirds, but the Afghans were not to exceed one-sixth.

[1] See Chapter II.

[2] Cf. Babur Nama, II, Tr. Beveridge, p. 470, (*sih-bandi* misread as *bid-hindi*); *Nigar Nama-i Munshi*, p. 93.

[3] Cf. Asad Beg Qazwinis Memoirs, f. 4a; *Waqa-i Ajmer*, p. 91.

[4] Manucci, II, p. 378, also III, p. 409.

[5] *Dilkusha*, ff. 140a-141a. The three Rajput chiefs were Rao Dalpat Bundela, Ram Singh Hara and Jai Singh Sawai.

[6] See, *Waqa-i Ajmer*, pp. 355-56; *Akhbarat*, 5 Jamada I, 45 R.Y.

III. Saiyids and Shaikhzadas (Indian Muslims) were to recruit from their own races, but the Rajputs and Afghans not to exceed one-sixth.

IV. Afghan nobles were to have two-thirds of Afghans and one-third of other races.

V. Rajputs : The same regulations as for Saiyids and Shaikhzadas (i.e. they were to recruit from their own race).[1] Manucci also refers to this regulation and attributes its establishment to Akbar.[2] Tahauwur Khan, governor of Ajmer in 1680-81, took especial pride in the fact that he only employed Turanis (Trans-Oxonians).[3]

The salary paid to various troopers was a matter of contract between the noble and his troopers; the imperial government did not interfere. In fact, as Manucci says, "the generals and officers keep no fixed rule in paying their soldiers, for to some they will give twenty or thirty rupees, to others forty, fifty or a hundred."[4] It seems that the troopers had normally to bring their own horses so that a man with two horses (*du-aspa*) was paid much more than a man with one horse (*yak-aspa*).[5] As to actual scales of pay, we may judge them from the fact that in 1680 Tahauwur Khan was reputed for paying high salaries to his Turani troopers. None of them are reported to have received less than Rs. 60 or 50 per month, and most of them were *du aspas*.[6] *Yak-aspas* recruited from Gujarat for imperial service in 1685 were not paid more than Rs. 30 per month.[7] The pay of *sih-bandis*, troopers hired for specific purposes, presumably mounted on horses of sub-standard breeds, was much lower. In 1682 they were hired in Gujarat for local service in Prince Azam's 'sarkar' at the rate of Rs. 15 per month per head.[8]

The mode of payment of the salaries was equally varied. We have seen that a noble sometimes distributed his *jagir*, or a part of it, among his troopers, allowing them to collect and keep the revenue thereof. In some cases, the troopers received a *barat* or draft drawn on the revenue collector of their master's *jagir*, the latter honouring it out of the revenue collections.[9] Even when the troopers were paid directly from the headquarters, they did not receive it fully "in coin", but "are always foisted off

[1] *Khulasat-us Siyaq*, f. 54b; Fraser, 86, f. 14b.

[2] Manucci, II, 375.

[3] *Waqa-i Ajmer*, pp. 355-56; Aghar Khan's contingent consisted of only Afghans and Rajputs (Mamuri, f. 145b).

[4] Manucci, II, pp. 378-79.

[5] When the imperial government recruited *sawars* for military service in Gujarat in 1658, men with two and three horses (*du-aspa sih-aspa*) were sanctioned on an average pay of Rs. 60 per month; the *yak-aspa* received Rs. 30 per month (*Mirat-i Ahmadi*, I, p. 315).

[6] *Waqa-i Ajmer*, p. 355.

[7] *Mirat-i Ahmadi*, I, p. 316. According to Bhim Sen things were so cheap in the Deccan in the early years of Aurangzeb's reign that the pay of a *sawar* did not exceed Rs. 15(fifteen)per month.

[8] *Mirat-i Ahmadi*, I, p. 306. [9] *Nigar Nama-i Munshi*, p. 73.

as respects two months pay with clothes and old raiment from the household."[1]

It was a common complaint that the pay of the troopers was always in arrears. We find big nobles like Khan-i Jahan Barha and Iftikhar Khan admitting that their troopers had pay-claims against them for arrears of five and six months.[2] Fryer describes how at Junnar "the new moon brought the soldiers to their several standards, against the Governor's house, by their Salam to refresh his memory of their pay, being fourteen months behind hand."[3] Manucci declares as if it was the normal rule that "there is always due to them (the troopers) the pay for two or three years service". If the soldiers borrowed from the *sarrafs* on the strength of the pay due to them, the general or officer shared a profit in the interest with the *sarrafs*.[4] And, indeed, the muster-masters hoped that distress might drive the soldiers to compound for half the pay due to them.[5]

The treatment meted out to the troopers by the nobles was naturally not uniform. The following passage about the exceptional favours shown by Tahauwur Khan to his Turani troopers shows, through an exception proving the rule, what was really to be expected.

"The treatment of the said Khan towards this group is brotherly and he suffers many rude things from these persons. He does not insist on their standing guard on his camp (*chauki*), on their presence at his court (*haziri*), and on fines for absence (*waza-i ghair haziri*)."[6]

PUBLIC WELFARE ACTIVITIES AND CHARITIES

The Mughal nobility appropriated a very large portion of the surplus produce of the country and it is of interest to know how much of this they spent for the welfare of the ruled. The exact quantity of such expenditure, however, cannot be ascertained, but something can be said about their conception of works of public welfare.

An illustration of the average noble's idea of the most suitable welfare activities is provided by the numerous buildings of public utility erected by Bakhtawar Khan in the earlier part of Aurangzeb's reign. The first in the list is a *sarai* (traveller's inn) which he built near Shahjahanabad and named Bakhtawar Nagar. It had separate quarters for travellers, who came to stay with their families. Nearby he built a mosque, flanked on either side by a *pucca* well and a bath, both for public use. He also built there a market-place with shops (*katra*). Near the inn he laid out a garden, to the north of which he built a tank with steps. Half a *karoh* from the inn was a spring coming out of the Ridge. He built

[1] Manucci, II, pp. 378-79.
[2] *Arzdasht ha-i Muzaffar Khan*, f. 37a-b; *Waqa-i Ajmer*, 91, 105; cf. *Akhbarat*, 9 Ramzan, 38 R.Y.
[3] Fryer, I, 341. [4] Manucci, II, pp. 378-79. [5] Fryer, op. cit. [6] *Waqa-i Ajmer*, pp. 355-56.

a bund over it in order to make a tank for the thirsty and a waterfall for the aesthetes. From here the water of the stream was led by a canal into the garden-tank. He also built a bridge over a flood-stream between Bakhtawar Nagar and Faridabad. Near Kottah at Bakhtawarpura, he built a mosque with a tank and a house for the residence of the poor. He also built rentable cells and verandahs for the maintenance of these buildings. Near Shahjahanabad, again, he built a bridge over the famous *Shah-nahr*, the old west Jamuna Canal, and erected a mosque there. He also built two public gardens, one at Agharabad and the other at Lahore. Finally, he built a mosque at the tomb of Shaikh Nasiruddin Chiragh.[1] This list shows that to Bakhtawar Khan the best objects of buildings for public welfare were inns, bridges, wells, tanks, gardens and mosques. It is curious that though it was his duty to introduce theologians to Aurangzeb, he did not build any *madrasa* or theological college. Thus apart from what we hear of the efforts of other nobles in the direction of public welfare, it would seem that Bakhtawar Khan had exhausted all the possibilities of public works according to the notions of the time. Shaista Khan was well known for his inns and bridges built all over the country at the cost of lakhs of rupees.[2] Mir Jumla constructed a great tank and a garden at Haiderabad.[3] Mir Khalil built a big tank called Khalil Sagar at Narnol.[4] Irij Khan built an inn or *sarai* near Ilichpur,[5] and so on. The mosques constructed by the nobles were, of course, more numerous. Ghaziuddin Khan is also known to have built a *Khanqah* at Delhi.[6]

Sometimes the nobles also opened large free kitchens. In 1660 when a famine raged over Northern India, Aurangzeb ordered all *mansabdars* of 1,000 and above to open free kitchens.[7] Although the distress alleviated through public works of this type should not be underrated, it is obvious that their objectives were very limited. Relief of exceptional and immediate distress, the comfort and convenience of travellers, provision of drinking water, construction of places of worship—these activities sufficed to satisfy the conscience of the great. Works of irrigation, hospitals and academic institutions lay beyond the normal horizons of the nobility.

The Mughal nobility was by no means indifferent to literature and art. Many nobles patronised fine arts and letters, many being themselves good scholars and poets. What they lacked was the conception that literature and art could best prosper and flourish through public institutions, i.e. schools and institutes of higher learning. The result was that the nobles patronised art and learning not so much by building

[1] *Mirat-al Alam*, ff. 252a-53b.
[2] *Ma'asir-i Alamgiri*, p. 223.
[3] *Ma'asir-al Umara*, III, pp. 530-55.
[4] *Ibid.*, I, pp. 785-92.
[5] *Ibid.*, I, pp. 268-72.
[6] *Ma'asir-al Umara*, II, p. 878.
[7] *Alamgir Nama*, p.611. For the free kitchens opened by Shaista Khan see *Fathiya 'Ibriya*, f.132a.

and maintaining institutions as by supporting and employing individual scholars, physicians, poets and artists. Many nobles earned a reputation as patrons in this field.[1] A few nobles also dabbled in science and alchemy. Thus Danishmand Khan, to cite a well known case, employed Bernier in order to discuss with him new principles of medicine.[2] A number of nobles were themselves good scholars and poets.[3] The Mughal nobility was, therefore, by no means uncultured or divorced from intellectual pursuits. What it lacked was a desire to offer science and learning a sustained encouragement, which could only have come through the establishment of academic institutions.

Harem and Household

The nobles maintained very "large establishments of wives, servants, camels and horses".[4] Indeed, the household, of which the *harem* was the main part, must have absorbed a very large part of the income of the nobles.

[1] Itiqad Khan loved both poor and learned men (*Ma'asir-al Umara*, I, pp. 232-34). Sidi Miftah was very fond of learned men; he helped them and spent money on deserving persons. He collected many valuable books from Arabia (*Ibid.*, pp. 579-83). Amir Khan sent much money to the learned and pious men of Persia (*Ibid.*, III, pp. 946-49). Muhammad Saeed was a great patron of writers (*Ibid.*, I, p. 272). Zulfiqar Khan patronised Nasir Ali, a good poet of his days (*Ma'asir-al Kiram*, II, p. 130). Husain Ali Khan patronised Abdul Jalil, a poet of his times (*Ibid.*, p. 276); cf. also Fryer, Vol. I, pp. 333-34; *Ma'asir-al Kiram*, p. 95.

[2] Bernier, pp. 324-25, 352-53. *The Tuhfat-al Hind* was compiled by the orders of Khan-i Jahan Bahadur Kokaltash, Rieu, British Museum Catalogue I, p. 62.

[3] Among scholars we have Danishmand Khan himself (*Mirat-al Alam*, f. 222b); Izad Bakhsh 'Rasa', who was governor of Agra for sometime, was a well known poet and has left a collection of letters in ornate prose (Rieu, III, pp. 985-86). Shaikh Ghulam Mustafa, a *mansabdar* of Aurangzeb, had an excellent knowledge of medicine, astrology, calligraphy, poetry, etc. (*Ma'asir-al Kiram*, II, pp. 74-75). Zafar Khan, governor of Kashmir, has left a *diwan* (*Ibid.*, II, pp. 95-96). Mirza Muhammad Tahir holding a *mansab* of 1,500—wrote an account of Shahjahan's reign and left a *diwan* (*Ibid.*, II, pp. 96-97, 107-08).

The following information about individual nobles' intellectual attainments is taken from the *Ma'asir-al Umara.*

Himmat Khan was a good poet and a scholar of Hindi (III, pp. 946-49); Islam Khan had a poetic bent of mind (I, pp. 217-20). Muhammad Ashraf 3000/500, was interested in mysticism and made a collection from the Masnavi of Maulana Jalaluddin. He wrote *shikasta, nastaliq,* and *naskh* very well (I, 272-74); Hisamuddin, 2,500/1,500 was acquainted with every science and had a poetic bent of mind (I, pp. 584-87); Multafat Khan had a good knowledge of conventional literature and had a poetic bent of mind (III, pp. 500-03). Aqil Khan Razi, the author of *Waqiat-i Alamgir*, had a high rank and was a good poet (II, pp. 821-23). Dianat Khan was interested in learning (II, 59-63). Alahwardi Khan Alamgir Shahi, 4,000/3,000, was a good poet and had a *diwan* to his credit (I, pp. 229-32). Musavi Khan was a foremost scholar of rational science (III, pp. 633-36). Saif Khan, 2,500/1,500, had a poetical bent of mind; he was interested in music and melody and wrote a book called *Rag Darpan* (II, pp. 479-85). Mir Khalil, 5,000/4,000, was well versed in every science and was famous for his calligraphy. He was also skilful in music (I, pp. 785-92).

[4] Bernier, P. 213.

As a rule, a noble had "three or four wives, the daughters of worthy men". All lived together in the noble's *mahal* or palace, which consisted of an enclosure surrounded by high walls. Each wife had a separate apartment and numerous slaves, of her own —10, 20, or even 100 according to her fortune.[1] The large retinue of slaves—slave-girls and eunuchs—had to be provided primarily on account of exceptional regard for the seclusion of aristocratic ladies from the sight of strangers. Fryer comments on the numerous spies on the wives of the nobles—"toothless old women and beardless eunuchs. They also wait on ladies to hand them necessaries as food, water, meat and the like taking them at the door, as to prevent unlawful intruders".[2]

Inside the palace, luxury reigned. There were gardens and tanks within the palace enclosure.[3] The Mughal gardens are justly famous. Great pains were taken to ensure a supply of running water, feeding tanks and forming waterfalls.[4] The life inside the noble's *harem* is thus described by Manucci, who claims to have had the confidence of Naval Bai, the wife of Asad Khan.

"The ladies love to regale themselves with quantities of delicious stews; to adorn themselves magnificently, either with clothes or jewellery, pearls, etcetera; to perfume their bodies with odours and essences of every kind. To this must be added that they have permission to enjoy the pleasure of the comedy and the dance, to listen to tales and stories of love, to recline upon beds of flowers, to walk about in gardens, to listen to the murmur of the running waters, to hear singing and other similar pastimes."[5] Wine also flowed : "In the cool of the evening they drink a great deal of wine, for the women learn the habit quickly from their husbands". The noble himself retired to the *harem* in the evening to drink and enjoy music and dance till midnight.[6]

Since the gardens and luxurious life of the nobles was hidden behind high walls, one can understand Bernier's complaint that in India you could not see and enjoy the country houses of the great as in France.[7] It did not mean, however, that the Mughal nobles spent any less on their *harem*, gardens and domestic luxuries. Bhim Sen says, for example, that Amanat Khan, although he was a *mansabdar* of 700 only, had built a spacious and magnificent house at Fazilpur (Burhanpur) with a garden attached to it, and a number of tanks in the house were fed by a canal.[8]

[1] Pelsaert, pp. 64-65. Pelsaert wrote in the time of Jahangir but his account could be taken as true for that of Aurangzeb as well.

[2] Fryer, I, p. 328. Even a physician was allowed to enter only after the greatest precautions taken to prevent him from seeing anyone (Manucci, II, p. 352).

[3] Pelsaert, p. 64; Bernier, pp. 243, 246-47.

[4] See, e.g. *Mirat-al Alam*, ff. 252b-53a. See also Villiers-Stuart, *Gardens of the Great Mughals*, a pleasant book largely based on field observation.

[5] Manucci, II, pp. 352-53. [6] Pelsaert, 65; cf. Manucci, II, p. 351. [7] Bernier, p. 233.

[8] *Dilkusha*, f. 27a.

Besides their women, the nobles had their animals. Daud Khan, for example, used to spend annually Rs. 250,000 on his pet animals which included tigers, hawks and falcons.[1]

Outside their houses also the nobles maintained considerable pomp and splendour. Bernier says that they 'are never seen out-of-doors but in the most superb apparel; mounted sometimes on an elephant, sometimes on horseback, and not infrequently on a *palkey* attended by many of their cavalry, and by a large body of servants on foot, who take their station in front and at either side of their lord, not only to clear the way, but to flap the flies and brush off the dust with tails of peacocks; to carry the pioquedant and spittoon, water to allay the Omraha's thirst, and sometimes account book and other papers".[2]

Financial Crisis of the Nobility

The reign of Aurangzeb saw a developing crisis in the *jagirdari* system, which was bound to affect the very foundations of the standing of the nobles. The extravagant mode of life of the Mughal nobility has been frequently discussed. Bernier had discovered that "there are very few wealthy *Omrahs*; on the contrary most of them are in embarassed circumstances and deeply in debt". He thought this was due to their large establishments and to the "costly presents" they had to offer to the king.[3] Bhim Sen in the last years of the reign described the acute financial difficulties of the nobles, but attributed them to other causes. The cultivators had ceased cultivating the soil and so not a copper coin reached the *jagirdars*. Moreover, little could be done to encourage cultivation, since the *jagirs* were so quickly transferred. At the same time on various pretexts and excuses, the clerks of the imperial government put up claims (*mutaliba*) against the nobles under all kinds of items, fines, repayment of loans, etc.[4] There is no doubt that the Deccan wars, by devastating vast areas and increasing military burdens, ruined a number of the nobles. A noble like Inayatullah Khan, for example, reported in a petition to the Court that all his elephants and camels had died so that the money lenders (*sahukars*) had no security on which to advance him loans.[5]

The *Akhbarat* of the last years are full of complaints from nobles that they were impecunious and needed help from the Treasury.[6] There was a large number of nobles desiring to leave the Deccan for the North,[7] while a number of Deccani nobles deserted to the Marathas.[8]

[1] Manucci, IV, p. 255. [2] Bernier, pp. 213-14. [3] Bernier, p. 213. [4] *Dilkusha*, ff. 139a-141a.
[5] *Akhbarat*, 4th Jamada, II, 46 R.Y. [6] See, e.g. *Akhbarat*, 14th Safar 44 R.Y.
[7] *Akhbarat*, 27th Shawwal, 38 R.Y.; 13th Ziqada, 39 R.Y.; 4th Zilhijja, 39 R.Y.
[8] *Dilkusha*, ff. 140a-155a.

This financial strain on the nobility was a natural consequence of the acute and increasing financial crisis of the Mughal Empire, which became noticeable in the later part of the 17th century. The brunt of the crisis perhaps fell on the lower nobility, but even the higher nobility could not fully escape its effects. However, the first item to be affected was not the luxuries of the nobles, but as we have seen, their military contingents. Such short-sightedness, inevitable in a class so much devoted to pomp and splendour, led to the growing military weakness of the Empire. Bhim Sen is not, perhaps, far wrong when he puts, as the first cause of the success of the Marathas, the fact that the Mughal military commanders did not maintain their full contingents.[1] This in turn brought further losses to the Empire and a further decline in the income of the nobles And so the vicious circle went on, enveloping the entire nobility, until the nobles, their *harems* and eunuchs, elephants and tigers, all disappeared.

[1]*Dilkusha*, f. 139a-b.

CONCLUSION

Aurangzeb's reign forms the stage of transition from the climax of Mughal Empire under Shahjahan to its disintegration in the 18th century. Signs of such disintegration had become quite apparent many years before Aurangzeb closed his eyes. The failure in the Deccan, the increasing power of the Marathas, the rebellious and recalcitrant attitude of various elements within the Empire, all bore an ominous message for the future.

The study of the nobility, which has been attempted in the foregoing pages, must be viewed against the background of this crisis of the Empire as well as the tendencies inherent in the nobility itself towards disintegration.

The history of the nobility under Aurangzeb may be studied under two clearly marked divisions—the first from the time of his accession up to 1678, and the second from 1679 up to his death in 1707. Prior to the outbreak of the Rajput war and Aurangzeb's subsequent involvement in the Deccan, there was no significant increase either in the number of the *mansabdars* or in the internal racial and religious composition of the nobility that had been in existence since the days of Akbar. During this period, the 'foreign' nobility, that is nobles who had themselves come to India as well as those who were born in India but belonged to families that had migrated to India, continued to occupy a leading position, with the Persians out-numbering the Turanis. Large promotions were given to the Rajputs initially, but by 1678 they had suffered a slight set-back; their proportion among the nobles holding the rank of 1,000 and above declined from 18.7 per cent under Shahjahan to 14.6 per cent during the period 1658-78. At the same time Aurangzeb gave greater preference to Afghans than had been given to them by his predecessors. The general stability of Aurangzeb's nobility is shown by the large number of *khanazads*, or nobles whose fathers or other close relations had been in the Imperial service. During this period (1658-78) nearly a half of Aurangzeb's nobles are known to have belonged to this category; and if more could be known about certain nobles, their actual proportion would probably be higher. However, it is significant that a large proportion of new-comers were also able to attain to high ranks in the nobility.

A study of the *mansabdari* system suggests that there was no apparent laxity, in comparison with earlier periods, in enforcing the branding regulations, i.e. in compelling the *mansabdars* to maintain contingents required by the *sawar* ranks. Aurangzeb seems to have made no change worth noticing in the system of *mansabdari* regulations or the pay-scales. He tried to follow them rigidly just as they had stood in the time of his father. The reduced military obligations and the reduced scales of pay were both inherited from Shahjahan. Aurangzeb also continued to enforce the escheat system, though with some restraint. He is said to have abolished the previous assertion of the imperial right to dispose of or confiscate the property of deceased nobles; but, in fact, there are cases where he did order seizure of their property. There is, therefore, no reason to believe that prior to his departure for the Deccan, Aurangzeb's authority over the nobles had suffered in any way and that the obligations of the *mansabdars* were no longer strictly imposed.

In the same way the system of *jagir* assignments continued to work tolerably well till Aurangzeb's involvement in the Deccan, and the principle of periodic transfers, which was meant to prevent nobles from forming local ties and becoming autonomous potentates, was rigidly adhered to throughout the reign of Aurangzeb.

Finally, Aurangzeb's policy towards the various sections of the nobility, though varying here and there from that of his predecessors, was not without its own restraints. The Rajput war is said to have been partly the result of his policy of discrimination against the Rajputs, but the majority of the Rajput *mansabdars* were not alienated. Nor did Aurangzeb tolerate any well-marked factions and groupings; and no factions grew up till his very last days, when we find Ghaziuddin Khan and Zulfiqar Khan leading two distinct groups.

It is, therefore, not possible to locate the source of the crisis in the affairs of the Empire in any change in the nature and composition of the nobility prior to Aurangzeb's departure for the Deccan. It is, however, possible to say that as it was constituted, the nobility was bound, with the passage of time, to create an unfavourable situation for the Empire. It has been suggested that the system of *jagir* transfers led to oppression by the *jagirdars*, and this oppression, in turn, to rebellion by the oppressed. We have left this an open question. It is true that as administrators and army-commanders, the Mughal nobles of Aurangzeb, specially of his later years, cannot be given a clear certificate. Whether the lack of functional training and specialisation had anything to do with the administrative incompetence of a number of nobles is not directly obvious. But what we know for certain is that the nobles were, by far and large, corrupt and open bribe-takers, and in this they were but pale imitators of the Emperor himself. They often misused their administrative authority to compel merchants and peasants to pay them illegal dues. Immense as were the resources of the nobility, it is difficult to claim that they were devoted to channels leading to positive economic development. The nobles, no doubt, patronised luxury-goods and services; but only an insignificant part of their resources seems to have been laid out as 'capital', whether in trade or in advances to artisans. On the other hand, their habit of engrossing and monopolising was a serious detriment to trade; and they are not known to have made any attempt to encourage science and new techniques of production. The recipients of their patronage were chiefly religious men and poets, who praised them in the present world and prayed for their welfare in the next. Once a serious military crisis appeared in the Deccan, the Empire did not have an adequate reserve of physical and moral resources to cope with it.

The Rajput War and the prolonged Deccan campaigns had a disastrous effect on the nobility. Aurangzeb's annexations in the Deccan were not the work of a military steam-roller, but of a slow and cumbrous machine, which sought energy and strength by recruiting deserters bribed to come over from the enemy. The long war which followed took a heavy toll of life from the Mughal contingents, increased the weakness of the nobility, and diverted the Emperor's attention more and more towards the Deccan, while the administration of North India suffered. The Deccan involvement led to a great influx of the Deccani nobles into the Mughal aristocracy. There was a very great increase in the numerical strength of the nobility; but while the Deccanis (the Bijapuris, the Haiderabadis and the Marathas) were recruited wholesale and given extraordinarily high ranks, the recruitment and promotion of the other older sections suffered. Mamuri speaks eloquently of the depressed position of the *khanazads*. The Marathas, practically insignificant a generation earlier, now outnumbered the Rajputs. Again and again Aurangzeb and his ministers attempted to stop fresh recruitment, but their military and diplomatic needs led them to continue the grant of *mansabs* to new-comers. But a stage arrived, when though *mansabs* were awarded, *jagirs* could not be given, since owing to increase in the number of claimants and the financial strain on the treasury,[1] little was left to be assigned in *jagirs*. When this came to be the case, and when various *jagirdars* held their *jagirs* in disturbed territory where revenue could not be collected, the nobles could no longer be expected to maintain contingents required by their *mansabs*. This, in turn, as Bhimsen saw, further weakened the military strength of the Empire and encouraged fresh rebellions and disturbances.

Once the competition for good *jagirs* became intense and the confidence in the stability of the Empire was shaken, factionalism within the nobility was bound to grow more intense. The factions of Ghaziuddin Khan Firuz Jang and Zulfiqar Khan were the natural result of this situation. With the growth of such factions and rivalries within the nobility, the cohesion and unity in imperial policy and military enterprise naturally suffered. Moreover, it was suspected, perhaps not without justice,

[1] Which precluded transfer of land from the *Khalisa* to *jagirs*.

that some nobles were thinking of carving out independent or semi-independent principalities for themselves—an ambition which came to be only too openly and widely held after the death of Aurangzeb.

One has to be careful in passing moral judgements in history, but it may be correct to say that even from the view-point of the Mughal nobility itself its chief fault was its failure to change and adapt itself to a new developing situation not only in India, but in the whole world. Nothing can remain static and yet survive. Aurangzeb's attempt to give a new religious basis to the Empire may indicate that he felt that a change was called for; but the complete failure of this policy showed that religious revivalism could be no substitute for a thoroughgoing overhaul of the Mughal administrative system and political outlook.

APPENDIX

LIST OF *MANSABDARS* OF AURANGZEB HOLDING THE RANKS OF 1,000 ZAT AND ABOVE.

A. *Mansabdars* WHO HELD OR REACHED THE RANK OF 1,000 ZAT AND ABOVE DURING THE PERIOD, 1658-1678.

		Mansabdars of 5,000 and above					
S.No.	*Name and Title*	*Rank highest during the period*	*Country of birth*	*Group*	*Sub-groups Rajput, Maratha, Afghan, Zamindar, etc.*	*Father or other blood relation in service*	*Authorities*
1.	Umdat-ul-Mulk, Mirza Raja Jai Singh Kachwaha	7,000/7,000 (2-3h)	India	Indian	Rajput-*Zamindar*	Father	Al. 907; S.D.A. 52; M.U., III 568-77
2.	Mirza Shuja, Najabat Khan, Khan-i-Khanan	7,000/7,000 (2-3h)	India	Turani		Father	Al. 117; M.U., III 821-28
3.	Mirza Abu Talib, Shaista Khan, Amir-ul-Umara.	7,000/7,000 (2-3h)	India	Irani		Father	Al. 130; M.U., II 690-707
4.	Mir Malik Husain, Khan-i-Jahan Bahadur, Zafar Jang Kokaltash	7,000/7,000 (6,000 × 2-3h)	India	Irani		Father	M.A. 142; A. M. T. 121a; M.U., I 791-813
5.	Maharaja Jaswant Singh Rathor	7,000/7,000 (5,000 × 2-3h)	India	Indian	Rajput-*Zamindar*	Father	Al. 331-32; M.U., III 599-604

S.N.	*Name and Title*	*Rank highest during the period*	*Country of birth*	*Group*	*Sub-groups Rajput, Maratha, Afghan, Zamindar, etc.*	*Father or other blood relation in service*	*Authorities*
6.	Mir Muhammad Sa'id, Mir Jumla, Muazzam Khan, Khan-i-Khanan, Sipahsalar	7,000/7,000 (5,000 × 2-3h)	Iran	Irani	Deccani	Father	Al. 563; M. U., III 530-55
7.	Khalilullah Khan	6,000/6,000 (2-3h)	Iran	Irani	—	Brother	Al. 119; M.U., I 775-82
8.	Shah Nawaz Khan Safvi	6,000/6,000 (5,000 × 2-3h)	Iran	Irani	—	Father	Al. 209-10; M.U., II 670-76
9.	Umdat-ul-Mulk, Jafar Khan	6,000/6,000 (4,000 × 2-3h)	India	Irani	—	Father	Al. 162; M.U., I 531-35
10.	Mirza Lahrasp, Mahabat Khan	6,000/5,000 (3,000 × 2-3h)	India	Irani	—	Father	Al. 754; M.U., III 590-95
11.	Rana Raj Singh	6,000/6,000 (1,000 × 2-3h)	India	Indian	Rajput-*Zamindar*	Father	Al. 194; M.U.; II 206-08
12.	Shambhaji	6,000/6,000	India	Indian	Maratha	—	M.A. 142; *Jami-al Insha* f. 76a
13.	Muhammad Amin Khan	6,000/5,000 (1,000 × 2-3h)	India	Irani	Deccani	Father	Al. 813,855; M.A. 121; M.U., III 613-20
14.	Mulla Ahmad Naitha	6,000/6,000	India	Indian	Deccani	—	Al. 919-20; T.M. 1076 A.H.; M.U., III 562-66
15.	Husain *Pasha*, Islam Khan Rumi	6,000/6,000	Turkey	Turani	—	—	M.A. 87-88; T.U. 'A'

16.	Mir Muzaffar Husain, Fedai Khan Koka 'Azam Khan	6,000/4,000	India	Irani	—	Father	Al. 1061; T.M. 1089 A.H.; T.U. 'A'; M.U., I 247-53
17.	Kaj Nayak	6,000/-	India	Indian	Deccani-*Zamindar*	—	*Dilkusha*, 59b
18.	Saiyid Ahmad s/o Saiyid Makhdum, Sharza Khan Bijapuri	6,000/-	India	Turani	Deccani	—	B. S, 691
19.	Shaikh Mir Khawafi	5,000/5,000 (2-3h)	—	Irani	—	—	Al. 156-57; M.U., II 668-70
20.	Muhammad Qasim, Qasim Khan, Mu'tamad Khan	5,000'5,000 (2-3h)	India	Irani	—	Father	Al. 1027; M.U., III 95-99
21.	Raja Ram Singh Kachwaha	5,000/5,000 (2-3h)	India	Indian	Rajput-*Zamindar*	Father	Akh. 19th Rabi II, 12th R.Y.; M.U., II, 301-03
22.	Jalal Khan, Dilir Khan	5,000/5,000 (3,000 × 2-3h)	India	Indian	Afghan	Brother	Al. 1030; M.U., II 42-56
23.	Muhammad Tahir, Wazir Khan	5,000/5,000 (2,000 × 2-3h)	Iran	Irani	—	—	Al. 880; M.U., III 936-40
24.	Saiyid Mahmud, Nasiri Khan Khan-i-Dauran	5,000/5,000 (2,000 × 2-3h)	India	Turani		Father	Al. 126, 179; T.M. 1077 A.H.; M.U., I 782-85
25.	Saiyid Mir Khawafi, Amir Khan	5,000/5,000 (1,000 × 2-3h)	—	Irani	—	Brother	Al. 661; M.U., II 476-77; T.U. "S"
26.	Muhammad Ibrahim, Ghairat Khan, Shuja 'at Khan, Khan-i-Alam	5,000/5,000	India	Turani	—	Father	Al. 117; M.U., II 869-72; T.U. *Sh.*
27.	Saiyid Shah Muhammad, Murtaza Khan	5,000/5,000	Bokhara	Turani	—	—	Al. 870; T.M. 1089 A.H.; M.U., III 597-98

S.No.	Name and Title	Rank highest during the period	Country of birth	Group	Sub-groups Rajput, Maratha, Afghan, *Zamindar*, etc.	Father or other blood relation in service	Authorities
28.	Muhammad Ibrahim, Asad Khan	5,000/5,000	India	Irani	—	Father	Al. 880; M.U., I 310-21
29.	Yadgar Beg, Lashkar Khan, Jan Nisar Khan	5,000/5,000	India	—	—	Father	M.A. 105; T.M. 1081 A.H.; M.U., III 168-71
30.	Ibrahim Khan s/o Ali Mardan Khan	5,000/5,000	Iran	Irani	—	Father	Al. 426; M.U., I 295-301
31.	Maluji Deccani	5,000/5,000	India	Indian	Maratha	—	Al. 427; M.U., III 520-24
32.	Raja Rai Singh Sisodia	5,000/5,000 (500×2-3h)	India	Indian	Rajput-*Zamindar*	Father	Al. 1033; T.M. 1083 A.H.; M.U., II 297-301
33.	Daud Khan Qureshi	5,000/4,000 (3,000×2-3h)	India	Indian	—	—	Al. 1033; M.U., II 32-37
34.	Sarfaraz Khan Deccani	5,000/4,000 (1,000×2-3h)	India	Indian	Deccani	—	S.D.A. 48; M.U., II 469-73
35.	Mir Khalil, Khan-i-Zaman, Muftakhar Khan	5,000/4,000	India	Irani	—	Father	S.D.A. 111; M.A. 144; M.U., I, 785-92
36.	Mirza Muhammad Mashhadi, Asalat Khan	5,000/4,000	Iran	Irani	—	—	Al. 855; M.U., I 222-25
37.	Mukarram Khan Safvi, Murad Kam	5,000/4,000	India	Irani	—	Father	Al. 267; M.U., III 583-86

38.	Ikhlas Khan, Abul Muhammad	5,000/4,000	India	Indian	Afghan-Deccani	—	Al. 990; M.A. 81; M.U.,II,59
39.	Tahir Shaikh, Tahir Khan	5,000/3,000	Balkh	Turani	—	—	Al. 960; M.U., II 751-54
40.	Muhammad Beg, Zulfiqar Khan	5,000/3,000	Iran	Irani	—	—	Al. 157; M.U., II 89-93
41.	Mir Ziauddin Husain,Islam Khan	5,000/3,000	—	Turani	—	—	Al. 823; M.U., I 217-20
42.	Abdur Rahman s/o Nazar Muhammad Khan	5,000/2,500	Balkh	Turani	—	—	Al. 267, 341; M.U., II 809-12
43.	Mulla Shafiq Yazdi, Danishmand Khan	5,000/2,500	Iran	Irani	—	—	Al. 880; T.M. 1081 A.H.
44.	'Alaul Mulk Tuni, Fazil Khan	5,000/2,500	Iran	Irani	—	—	Al. 831; M.U., III 524-30
45.	Bahman Yar I'tiqad Khan Mirza	5,000/1,000	India	Irani	—	Father	Al. 762; T.M. 1082 A.H.; M.U., I 232-34
46.	Bahram	5,000/1,000	Turan	Turani	—	—	M.U., I 431-44; Al. 114
47.	Shaikh Abdul Qawi, Itimad Khan	5,000/400	—	—	—	—	Al. 856; *Farhat*, 197a; T.M. 1077 A.H.; M.U., I, 225
48.	Champat Bundela	5,000/–	India	Indian	Rajput-*Zamindar*	—	*Dilkusha*, 15 b
49.	Ranmast Khan Panni, Bahadur Khan	5,000/–	India	Indian	Afghan	—	*Dilkusha*, 68b; M.U., II 64
50.	Netoji (Mohd. Quli Khan, when embraced Islam).	5,000/–	India	Indian	Maratha	—	Al. 971; M.U., III 577-80; *Mirat-ul-'Alam*, 205a
51.	Hakim Daud, Taqarrub Khan	5,000/–	Iran	Irani	—	—	T.U. "T"; M.U., I 490-93

S.No.	Name and Title	Rank highest during the period	Country of birth	Group	Sub-groups Rajput, Maratha, Afghan, Zamindar, etc.	Father or other blood relation in service	Authorities
			Mansabdars of 3,000 to 4,500				
52.	Ghazi Bijapuri, Randula Khan	4,000/4,000 (1,000 × 2-3h)	India	Indian	Deccani	—	Al. 76; M.U., II 309
53.	Yaswant Rao, Kartalab Khan	4,000/4,000 (1,000 × 2-3h)	India	Indian	—	—	Al. 76; M.U., III 153
54.	Rai Singh Rathor	4,000/4,000	India	Indian	Rajput-*Zamindar*	Father	Al. 288; A.M.T. 124a; M.U., II 235-36
55.	Shah Beg Khan	4,000/4,000	—	Turani	—	—	Al. 439; A.M.T. 124a
56.	Shafiullah, Tarbiyat Khan Birlas	4,000/4,000	Turan	Turani	—	—	Al. 845; M.U., I 493-98
57.	Mir Shams-uddin, Mukhtar Khan	4,000/4,000	India	Irani	—	Father	Al. 598; M.U., III 620-23
58.	Hoshdar Khan s/o Multafat Khan	4,000/4,000	India	Irani	—	Father	Al. 47,833; T.M. 1082 A.H.; M.U., III 943-46
59.	Ghalib Khan Bijapuri	4,000/4,000	India	—	Deccani	—	Al. 596, 598; M.A. 33; M.U., II 685
60.	Mir Miran Amir Khan s/o Khalil Ullah Khan Yazdi	4,000/3,000 (2-3h)	India	Irani	—	Father	M.A. 139; M.U., I 277-78
61.	Mirza Jafar, Alahwardi Khan s/o Alahwardi Khan Turkman	4,000/3,000 (2-3h)	India	Irani	—	Father	Al. 1056; T.U. 'A'; M.U., I 229-32; T.M. 1079 A.H.

62.	Inder Man Dhandera	4,000/3,000 (500 × 2-3h)	India	Indian	Rajput-*Zamindar*	—	Al. 43, 339; M.U., II 265-66
63.	Mirza Sultan Safvi	4,000/3,000	India	Irani	—	Father	Al. 880; M.U., III 581-83
64.	Qabad Khan, Mir Akhur	4,000/3,000	Turan	Turani	—	—	Al. 290, 634; M.U., III 99-102; A.M.T. 124a
65.	Namdar Khan	4,000/3,000	India	Irani	—	Father	Al. 1057; M.U., III 830-33
66.	Shaikh Farid *alias* Ikhlas Khan, Ihtisham Khan	4,000/3,000	India	Indian	—	Father	Al. 215,855; *Mirat-i-Aftāb Numa*, f. 573; T.M. 1075A.H.; M.U., I 220-22; A.M.T. 124b
67.	Pir Muhammad, Aghar Khan	4,000/3,000	India	Turani	—	—	Khafi Khan, II 246; M.U., I 274-77
68.	Mir Khan s/o Khalilullah Khan	4,000/3,000	India	Irani	—	Father	Al. 917;M.A. 82;M.U., 781
69.	Jadaun Rai Deccani	4,000/2,500	India	Indian	Maratha-*Zamindar*	Grand-father	Al. 161
70.	Multafat Khan, Azam Khan	4,000/2,500	India	Irani	—	Father	Al. 75; M.U., III 500-03
71.	Rao Bhao Singh Hara	4,000/2,500	India	Indian	Rajput-*Zamindar*	Father	Al. 267; M.U., II 305-07; A.M.T. 123b
72.	Rad Andaz Beg, Shuja'at Khan	4,000/2,500	India	Irani	—	Father	M.A. 116; Kamwar, 256b; T.M. 1084 A.H; M.U., II 679-81; A.M.T. 124b
73.	Khawaja Rahmat Ullah, Sarbuland Khan	4,000/2,500	India	Turani	—	—	M.A. 139; M.U., II 477-79; Al. 304,976

S.No.	Name and Title	Rank highest during the period	Country of birth	Group	Sub-groups Rajput, Maratha, Afghan, *Zamindar*, etc.	Father or other blood relation in service	Authorities
74.	Faizullah Khan	4,000/2,000	India	Irani	—	Father	Al. 870; M.U., III 28-30
75.	Qawamuddin Khan of Asfahan	4,000/2,000	Iran	Irani	—	—	M.A. 130; Mamuri, f. 149b; M.U., III 109-15
76.	Mir Muhammad Ishaq, Mukarram Khan	4,000/1,500 (600×2-3h)	India	Irani	—	Father	M.U.,III 696-701; Akh. 11th Rabi II 37th R.Y.
77.	'Abid Khan, Qulij Khan	4,000/1,500	Turan	Turani	—	—	Al. 1056; M.U., III 120-23
78.	Damaji	4,000/1,300	India	Indian	Maratha	—	Al. 47
79.	Daud Khan panni	4,000/–	India	Indian	Afghan-Deccani	—	M.U., II 63-68; S.D.A. 171
80.	Raziuddin Muhammad Haidera-badi	4,000/–	—	—	Deccani	—	S.D.A. 25
81.	Tahawur Khan, Padshah Quli Khan	4,000/–	India	Irani	—	Father	A.M.T. 123b; M.U., I 447-53; T.M. 1092 A.H.
82.	Qutbuddin Khan Kheshgi	3,500/3,500 (2,000×2-3h)	India	Indian	Afghan	Father	Al. 1033; Akh. 29th Rabi II 8th R.Y.; M.U., III 102-08 *Dastur-al Amal-i Shahjahani*, Add. 6588, f. 25a
83.	Raja Raj Rup of Nurpur	3,500/3,500 (500×2-3h)	India	Indian	Rajput-*Zamindar*	Father	Al. 198,625; T.M. 1072 A.H.; M.U., II 277-81

84.	Raja Anrudh Gaur	3,500/3,000 (2-3h)	India	Indian	Rajput-*Zamindar*	Father	M.U., II 276-77
85.	Raja Sujan Singh Bundela	3,500/3,000 (500×2-3h)	India	Indian	Rajput-*Zamindar*	Father	Al. 342, 486, 908; A.M.T. 124b; M.U., II 291-95
86.	Fateh Rohela, Fateh Jang Khan	3,500/3,000	India	Indian	Afghan	Uncle	Al. 290; M.U., III 22-26
87.	Sa'adat Khan s/o Zafar Khan	3,500/3,000	India	Irani	—	Father	Al. 195; M.U., II 461-63
88.	Mir Ziauddin Ali Mashhadi, Siyadat Khan	3,500/2,500	—	Irani	—	Father	T.M. 1069 A.H.; M.U., II 463-65
89.	Hasan Ali Khan Bahadur	3,500/2,500	India	Irani	—	Father	Al. 452; M.A. 92,93; M.U., I 593-99
90.	Saiyid Sultan, Salabat Khan Barha, Ikhtisas Khan	3,500/2,500	India	Indian	—	Father	Al. 198; T.U. 'A'; M.U., II 457-60
91.	Abdur Rahman Bijapuri, Sharza Khan	3,500/2,000	India	—	Deccani	—	S.D.A. 70; T.U. 'Sh'
92.	Mubariz Khan	3,500/2,000	Badakhshan	Turani	—	—	Al. 957; M.U., III 595-97; A.M.T. 125a
93.	Mir Ahmad Khawafi, Mustafa Khan	3,500/2,000	India	Irani	—	Father	Al. 490, 1049; M.U., III 516-18; A.M.T. 125a; English Factories, 1661-64, p. 103
94.	Rao Karan Bharatiya	3,500/2,000	India	Indian	Rajput-*Zamindar*	Father	Al. 855; A.M.T. 125b; M.U., II 287-91
95.	Abdur Razzaq Gilani, Izzat Khan	3,500/2,000	—	Irani	—	—	M.U., II 475

S.No.	Name and Title	Rank highest during the period	Country of birth	Group	Sub-groups Rajput, Maratha, Afghan, Zamindar, etc.	Father or other blood relation in service	Authorities
96.	Mir Sultan Husain, Iftikhar Khan s/o Asalat Khan	3,500/1,200	India	Irani	—	Father	Al. 158, 880; T.M. 1092 A.H.; M.U., I 252-55
97.	Dildost, Sardar Khan	3,000/3,000 (2,500 × 2-3h)	India	Turani	—	Father	Al. 140,1050; M.U., II 422-23
98.	Mir Muhammad Ishaq, Iradat Khan	3,000/3,000 (1,000 × 2-3h)	India	Irani	—	Father	Al. 127; M.U., I 203-06
99.	Ghazanfar Khan s/o Alahwardi Khan Turkman	3,000/3,000 (1,000 × 2-3h)	India	Irani	—	Father	Al. 864; T. M. 1077 A.H.; M.U., II 866-68
100.	Mir Ahmad, Sa'dat Khan s/o Sa'adat Khan	3,000/3,000 (500 × 2-3h)	India	Irani	—	Father	Al. 1050
101.	Ilhamullah, Rashid Khan	3,000/3,000 (500 × 2-3h)	India	Indian	—	Father	Al. 76,291; M. U., II 303-05
102.	Parsoji Deccani	3,000/3,000	India	Indian	Maratha	Brother	Al. 140, 231, 242; M. U., III 520-24
103.	Muhammad Tahir, Saf Shikan Khan	3,000/3,000	India	Irani	—	Father	Al. 334, 880; Akh. 19th Rajab, 9th R.Y. M.U., II 738-40
104.	Mirza Khan g/s of Abdur Rahim Khan	3,000/3,000	India	Irani	—	Grand-father	Al. 1033; A.M.T. 126a
105.	Mirza Khan Manuchihr	3,000/3,000	India	Irani	—	Father	M.U., III 586-89; T. M. 1083 A.H.

106.	Muhammad Yusuf, Shamsher Khan, Naseer Khan	3,000/2,500 (1,000×2-3h)	—	—	—	—	Al. 196, 1056
107.	Hayat Tarin, Shamsher Khan	3,000/2,500 (500×2-3h)	India	Indian	Afghan	Father	Al. 195, 647; T. M. 1083 A. H.; M. U., II 677-79
108.	Saifuddin Mahmud *alias* Faqirullah Saif Khan	3,000/2,500	India	Turani	—	Father	Akh. 5th Ramzan, 10th R. Y. M. U., II 479-85
109.	Abdullah Khan, Saeed Khan	3,000/2,500	India	Turani	—	Father	Al. 419, 762; M. U., II 807-08
110.	Kirat Singh	3,000/2,500	India	Indian	Rajput	Father	Al. 1061; M.U., III 156-58
111.	Hasan Khan Deccani	3,000/2,500	India	Indian	Afghan-Deccani	—	Al. 45; T. U. "H"
112.	Muzaffar Lodi, Lodi Khan	3,000/2,500	India	Indian	Afghan	—	Al. 291
113.	Bakhtiyar Khan, Khawas Khan	3,000/2,500	India	Indian	Afghan	—	S.D.A. 73; Al. 132
114.	Shamsuddin Kheshgi	3,000/2,000	India	Indian	Afghan	Father	Al. 45; M.U., II 676-77
115.	Abdullah Beg, Yakataz Khan, Mukhlis Khan	3,000/2,000	Turan	Turani	—	Father	Al. 117, 291; T. M. 1070 A. H.; M.U., III 968-71
116.	Abdullah Beg, Ganj Ali Khan	3,000/2,000	Iran	Irani	—	Father	Al. 964; M.U., III 155
117.	Saiyid Izzat Khan, Ghairat Khan	3,000/2,000	India	Indian	—	—	Al. 855-56; M.A. 150
118.	Girdhar Das Gaur	3,000/2,000	India	Indian	Rajput-*Zamindar*	Brother	S. D. A. 28; M.U., II 255-56; A.M.T. 126a

S.No.	Name and Title	Rank highest during the period	Country of birth	Group	Sub-groups Rajput, Maratha, Afghan, Zamindar, etc.	Father or other blood relation in service	Authorities
119.	Mir Abul Ma'ali, Mirza Khan	3,000/2,000	India	Turani	—	Father	Al. 240-41; M.U., III 557-60
120.	Saiyid Qasim Barha, Shahamat Khan	3,000/2,000	India	Indian	—	—	*Adab*.286b; Al. 303, 419; M.U., II 681-83
121.	Jalal Khan Kakar	3,000/2,000	India	Indian	—	Father	Al. 593; Hatim Khan, 103b; M. U., I 530-31
122.	Dataji Deccani	3,000/2,000	India	Indian	Maratha	Father	Al. 625; M.U., I 522
123.	Abu Muhammad g/s of Ibrahim Adil Shah	3,000/2,000	India	Indian	Deccani	—	M. A. 148
124.	Jagjiwan, Udaji Ram	3,000/2,000	India	Indian	Maratha-*Zamindar*	Father	M.U., I 144
125.	Antaji Khandakala	3,000/2,000	India	Indian	Maratha	—	S. D. A. 13
126.	Saiyid Sher Khan Barha *alias* Saiyid Shahab	3,000/1,500	India	Indian	—	Father	S.D.A. 118; Al. 132
127.	Arab Shaikh Mughal Khan	3,000/1,500	India	Turani	—	Father	*Adab*, 279b; M.U., III 623-25
128.	Safi Khan	3,000/1,500	India	Irani	—	Father	Al. 1034; M.U., II 740-42
129.	Saiyid Mansur Barha	3,000/1,500	India	Indian	—	Father	Al. 140, 337; M. U., II 449-52

130.	Abdul Kafi, Nawazish Khan	3,000/1,200	Iran	Irani	—	Father	Al. 474; T. M. 1075 A. H.; M. U., III 828-30
131.	Mir Isa, Himmat Khan s/o Islam Khan Badakhshi	3,000/1,000 (500×2-3h)	India	Turani	—	Father	Al. 880; M. A. 71; M.U., III 946-49
132.	Ahmad Kheshgi, Ikhlas Khan	3,000/1,000	India	Indian	Afghan	—	Al. 77; T.M. 1072 A.H.
133.	Bairam Deo Sisodia	3,000/1,000	India	Indian	Rajput-*Zamindar*	Father	Al. 762; S.D.A. 112; M.U. II 452-54
134.	Muhammad Badi Sultan	3,000/700	Turan	Turani	—	Father	Al. 339; M.U., III 636-37
135	Raghu Nath Rai Rayan	3,000/700	India	Indian	—	—	Al. 763; M.U., II 282
136.	Mir Muhammad Ashraf, Ashraf Khan, Itimad Khan	3,000/500	India	Irani	—	Father	Al. 762,856; M.U.,I 272-74
137.	Saiyid Ali Rizvi Khan	3,000/500	India	Turani	—	Father	Al. 1049; M.U., II 307-09 A. M. T. 124b
138.	Raghu Nath Singh Sisodia-Chandrawat	3,000/300	India	Indian	Rajput	—	Akh. 10th Ramzan, 13th R. Y., Kamwar, 250b
139.	Shaikh Mirak Haravi	3,000/200	Iran	Irani	—	—	Al. 396; M.U., III 518-19
140.	Darab Khan s/o Mukhtar Khan	3,000/–	India	Irani	—	Father	T. U. 'D'; M.U., II 39-42
141.	Mir Taqi	3,000/–	—	Irani	—	Uncle	Al. 755,880; M.A. 97; M.U., III 939
	Mansabdars of 1,000 to 2,700						
142.	Raja Debi Singh Bundela	2,500/2,500 (500×2-3h)	India	Indian	Rajput-*Zamindar*	Father	Al. 206, 758; S. D. A. 117; M. U,; II 295-97

S.No.	*Name and Title*	*Rank highest during the period*	*Country of birth*	*Group*	*Sub-groups Rajput, Maratha, Afghan, Zamindar, etc.*	*Father or other blood relation in service*	*Authorities*
143.	Bheel Afghan, Purdil Khan	2,500/2,000 (2-3h)	India	Indian	Afghan	—	Al. 334,758
144.	Iraj Khan	2,500/2,000	India	Irani	—	Father	Al. 1030; M.U., I 268-72; A.M.T. 126b
145.	Alah Yar Beg, Alah Yar Khan	2,500/2,000	—	Turani	—	—	Hatim Khan, 20b; Al. 141, 831; T.M. 1074 A.H.; M.U.,I 216-17
146.	Masud Yadgar, Ahmad Beg Khan, Masud Khan, grandson of Ahmad Beg Khan	2,500/2,000	India	Turani	—	Grand-father	Al. 78, 158, 196; A. M. T. 126b
147.	Saiyid Mubarak, Murtaza Khan	2,500/2,000	India	Turani	—	—	Al. 832; M. U., III 644-46
148.	Anup Singh	2,500/2,000	India	Indian	Rajput-*Zamindar*	Father	M. U., II 289-91
149.	Sa'adat Khan son-in-law of Khalifa Sultan	2,500/2,000	Iran	Irani	—	—	Al. 212
150.	Subh Karan Bundela	2,500/2,000	India	Indian	Rajput-*Zamindar*	—	Al. 301, 565, 1034; A. M. T. 131a
151.	Abu Talib, Aqidat Khan	2,500/2,000	India	Irani	—	Father	Al. 140, 334
152.	Khwaja Barkhurdar, Ashraf Khan, Barkhurdar Khan	2,500/2,000	India	Indian	—	Father	S. D. A. 74; M. U., I 206-207; T. U. (S.V.)

153.	Nusrat Ullah, Nusrat Khan	2,500/1,500 (700×2-3h)	India	Turani	—	Father	Al. 141, 1061
154.	Baba Ji Bhonsla	2,500/1,500	India	Indian	Maratha	—	Al. 54
155.	Bhagwant Singh s/o Satar Sal Hara	2,500/1,500	India	Indian	Rajput-*Zamindar*	Father	Al. 474-75; A. M. T. 126b
156.	Manku Bilal Deccani	2,500/1,500	India	Indian	Deccani	—	Al. 472
157.	Rao Amar Singh Chandrawat	2,500/1,500	India	Indian	Rajput	Grand-father	Al. 856; Akh. 29th Rabi II, 8th R. Y.; M.U., II 145-47
158.	Afrasiyab Beg, Afrasiyab Khan	2,500/1,500	Turkey	Turani	—	—	M.A. 87, 151-52; M. U., I 244-46
159.	Hisamuddin	2,500/1,500	India	Irani	—	Father	M. U., I 584-87
160.	Mana Ji Bhonsla	2,500/1,500	India	Indian	Maratha	—	S. D. A. 7; Al. 128; Hatim Khan, 16a
161.	Shuja'at Khan *alias* Shad Khan, Mughal Khan	2,500/1,400	India	Turani	—	Father	Al. 193; M. A. 97, 153
162.	Rustam Rao	2,500/1,200	India	Indian	Maratha	—	Al. 47
163.	Saiyid Sher Zaman Barha, Muzaffar Khan	2,500/1,200	India	Indian	—	Father	Al. 54, 291; M. U., II 465
164.	Mir Masum, Masum Khan	2,500/1,200	India	Irani	—	Father	Akh. 13th Ramzan, 13th R. Y.;M. U., II 676; A.M.T. 128a

S.No.	Name and Title	Rank highest during the period	Country of birth	Group	Sub-groups Rajput, Maratha, Afghan, Zamindar, etc.	Father or other blood relation in service	Authorities
165.	Beg Muhammad Kheshgi, Dindar Khan	2,500/1,200	India	Indian	Afghan	—	Al. 965
166.	Qazi Nizam Kardazi, Mukhlis Khan	2,500/1,000	India	Indian	—	—	Al. 48, 195, 294, 860; M.U., III 566-68
167.	Muhammad Munim, Munim Khan	2,500/1,000	India	Irani	—	Father	Al. 45, 454; M.U., III 589.
168.	Mahdi Quli Khan	2,500/1,000	—	—	—	—	Al. 304
169.	Saif Bijapuri	2,500/1,000	India	—	Deccani	—	Al. 440; M. A. 496
170.	Muhammad Kamgar, Kamgar Khan s/o Jafar Khan	2,500/1,000	India	Irani	—	Father	Al. 856; M. A. 140
171.	Sabal Singh Sisodia	2,500/1,000	India	Indian	Rajput	Father	S. D. A. 108; M. U., II 468-69
172.	Trimbakji Bhonsla	2,500/1,000	India	Indian	Maratha	—	Al. 48; *Daftar-i Dewani*, 19th Zilhij 6th R. Y.
173.	Mir Askari, Aqil Khan Razi	2,500/700	India	Irani	—	—	Al. 981; Akh. 15th Shawwal, 10th R. Y.; M.U., II 821; *Riyazush Shura*, 196a
174.	Mir Muhammad Mahdi, Ardistani, Hakim-ul-Mulk	2,500/500	Iran	Irani	—	—	Al. 960; M.A. 70; M. U., I 599-600

175.	Muhammad Aqil Barlas, Tahawur Khan	2,500/500	—	Turani	—	—	Al. 447
176.	Ahmad Beg, Zulqadar Khan	2,500/500	India	Turani	—	—	Al. 448; A.M.T. 126b
177.	Wazir Beg, Iradat Khan	2,500/400	—	—	—	—	Al. 232, 566; A.M.T. 126b
178.	Saiyid Hidayatullah	2,500/200	India	Indian	—	Father	Al. 473; M.U., II 456-57
179.	Raja Bikram Singh of Guler (Punjab)	2,500/–	India	Indian	Rajput-*Zamindar*	Father	M. Akbar, *The Punjab under the Mughals*, 223
180.	Muhammad Quli Mutaqad Khan	2,000/2,000 (1,800×2-3h)	India	Turni	—	Father	M. A. 80; Al. 964; M.U., II 870-71
181.	Mubarak Khan Niyazi	2,000/2,000 (1,000×2-3h)	India	Indian	Afghan	Grand-father	Al. 454, 475; M.U., III 511-13
182.	Sultan Beg, Shah Quli Khan	2,000/2,000 (1,000×2-3h)	—	—	—	—	Al. 860; T. U. (S.V.)
183.	Husain Beg Khan	2,000/2,000 (500×2-3h)	—	—	—	—	Al. 218
184.	Saiyid Hasan Barha, Ikram Khan	2,000/2,000 (500×2-3h)	India	Indian	—	Father	Al. 347, 634; M.U., I 215-16; A.M.T. 128b
185.	Mir Muhammad Hadi, Hadi Khan s/o Rafiuddin Sadr-i-Iran	2,000/2,400	Iran	Irani	—	—	Akh. 13th Ramzan, 13th R. Y.
186.	Mujahid Bijapuri	2,000/2,000	India	Indian	Deccani	—	Al. 140
187.	Abdullah Beg Sarai, Abdullah Khan	2,000/2,000	India	Turani	—	—	Al. 47,874

S.No.	Name and Title	Rank highest during the period	Country of birth	Group	Sub-groups Rajput, Maratha, Afghan, Zamindar, etc.	Father or other blood relation in service	Authorities
188.	Raja Nar Singh Gaur	2,000/2,000	India	Indian	Rajput-*Zamindar*	Father	Al. 268, 865
189.	Muhammad Salih, Makarmat Khan	2,000/2,000	—	—	—	—	Al. 294,960; Akh. 13th Ziqada, 9th R.Y.
190.	Raja Todar Mal	2,000/2,000	India	Indian	—	—	Al. 874, 885; M.U., II 286-87
191.	Muhammad Ali Beg, Ali Quli Khan s/o Ali Mardan Khan	2,000/2,000	Iran	Irani	—	Father	Al. 885; M.A. 109,110; Kamwar, 255a;A.M.T. 128a
192.	Saiyid Abdul Nabi	2,000/1,500 (700×2-3h)	India	Indian	—	Father	Al. 960; Kamwar, 249a; M.U., II 448
193.	Baizan Beg, Qaladar Khan	2,000/1,500 (500×2-3h)	—	—	—	—	Al. 194,885
194.	Jagat Singh Hara s/o Mukand Singh Hara	2,000/1,500 (500×2-3h)	India	Indian	Rajput-*Zamindar*	Father	Al. 221,1034; *Dilkusha*, 79b; M.U., III 510
195.	Naruji Deccani	2,000/1,600	India	Indian	Maratha	—	Akh. 13th Ramzan, 13th R.Y.
196.	Arslan Quli, Arslan Khan	2,000/800 (2-3h)	India	Irani	—	Father	Al. 817, 1067; M.U., I 277
197.	Mirza Muhammad, Khanjar Khan	2,000/1,500	India	Turani	—	—	Al. 817, 870; T.U. (S.V.)
198.	Mulla Yahya, Mukhlis Khan	2,000/1,500	India	Indian	Deccani	—	Al. 871; M.U., III 565

199.	Saiyid Ali s/o Afzal Khan	2,000/1,500	India	—	Deccani	—	Al. 834
200.	Poran Mal Bundela	2,000/1,500	India	Indian	Rajput-*Zamindar*	—	Al. 986
201.	Fateh Ullah Khan s/o Sa'id Khan Tarkhan	2,000/1,500	India	Turani	—	Father	Al. 339,400; T.M. 1069 A.H.
202.	Saiyid Hasan Khan Barha s/o Saiyid Dilir Khan	2,000/1,500	India	Indian	—	Father	T.U. (S.V.); M.U., II 414-15
203.	Khwaja Obedullah Khan	2,000/1,200	—	—	—	—	Al. 473; M.A. 88
204.	Vyas Rao or Biyas Rao	2,000/1,200	India	Indian	Maratha	—	Al. 48
205.	Ali Quli Beg, Ali Quli Khan	2,000/1,000	—	—	—	—	Al. 291; A.M.T. 131a
206.	Wali Mahaldar	2,000/1,000	—	—	—	—	Al. 45
207.	Dadaji	2,000/1,000	India	Indian	Maratha	—	Al. 48
208.	Khushhal Beg Qaqshal, Qulij Khan, Sa'adat Khan	2,000/1,000	—	Turani	—	—	Al. 471,914
209.	Mir Ibrahim Husain, Multafat Khan	2,000/1,000	India	Irani	—	Father	Akh. 25th Rabi II, 19th R.Y; Al. 880; M.U., III 611-13
210.	Saiyid Munawwar Khan Barha	2,000/1,000	India	Indian	—	Father	Al. 1034;M.U., II 465-68
211.	Shaikh Abdul Karim Thanesari	2,000/1,000	India	Indian	—	—	Al. 220
212.	Saiyid Feroz Khan Barha, Ikhtisas Khan	2,500/1,500 (500×2-3h)	India	Indian	—	Uncle	Al. 440,1034; M.U., II 473-75; *Fathiya Ibriya* 158b

S.No.	Name and Title	Rank highest during the period	Country of birth	Group	Sub-groups Rajput, Maratha, Afghan, Zamindar, etc.	Father or other blood relation in service	Authorities
213.	Medni Singh s/o Prithi Singh of Srinagar	2,000/1,000	India	Indian	Rajput-*Zamindar*	—	Al. 604; Kamwar, 236b
214.	Tanuji	2,000/1,000	India	Indian	Maratha	—	Al. 47
215.	Prithi Singh s/o Raja Jaswant Singh Rathor	2,000/1,000	India	Indian	Rajput	Father	Al. 917; T.M. 1077 A.H.
216.	Muhammad Ali Khan	2,000/1,000	India	Irani	—	Father	Al. 964; M.U., III 625-27
217.	Nusrat Khan, Qaladar Khan	2,000/1,000	—	—	—	—	Al. 981; Akh. 19th Rajab 9th R.Y.
218.	Ani Rai Brahman	2,000/1,000	India	Indian	—	—	S. Ahmad, "*Umrai Hunud*" 64
219.	Marahmat Khan	2,000/900	—	—	—	—	Al. 972
220.	Jahangir Quli Khan	2,000/900	—	—	—	—	Akh. 9th Ramzan, 13th R.Y.; A.M.T. 132a
221.	Muhammad Isma'il, Itiqad Khan	2,000/1,000	India	Irani	—	Father	M.A. 156, 158
222.	Isma'il Kheshgi Husainzai, Janbaz Khan	2,000/500 (2-3h)	India	Indian	Afghan	—	Al. 45,464, 635; T.U. (S.V.) M.U., III 777-78
223.	Yaqut Khan	2,000/700 (100×2-3h)	India	Indian	Deccani	—	S.D.A. 10

224.	Qazalbash Khan	2,000/800	—	Irani	—	—	Al. 291
225.	Abdullah Beg, Askar Khan Najm Sani	2,000/750	India	Irani	—	—	Al.465; Akh. 16th Ramzan, 13th R.Y.; M.U., II 809
226.	Itibar Khan	2,000/700	—	—	—	—	Al. 856
227.	Syed Sultan Karbalai	2,000/700	India	Irani	—	—	Al. 880
228.	Diyanat Khan, Hakim Jamalai Kashi	2,000/700	—	Irani	—	—	B.N. II, 728; Al. 594
229.	Yalingtosh Khan Bahadur	2,000/700	India	Turani	—	—	M.A. 156; Manucci II 43; M.U., III 971-72
230.	Kamal Lodi, Harbuz Khan	2,000/600	India	Indian	Afghan	—	Al. 77,875
231.	Mir Imamuddin, Rahmat Khan	2,000/600	Iran	Irani	—	—	Al. 140,855-56; T.M. 1076 A.H.; M.U., III 111-112
232.	Ruh-ullah Khan s/o Khalilullah Khan	2,000/600	India	Irani	—	Father	Al. 870;M.U., II 309-315
233.	Yakataz Khan	2,000/600	—	—	—	—	Al. 1062; M.A. 104
234.	Muhammad Ali s/o Taqarrub Khan	2,000/500	India	Irani	—	Father	Al. 856; M.A. 140
235.	Mir Murad Mazandani, Ghairat Khan	2,000/400	Iran	Irani	—	—	Al. 54
236.	Ziauddin, Rahmat Khan	2,000/300	India	Irani	—	Father	M.U., II 283-86

S.No.	*Name and Title*	*Rank highest during the period*	*Country of birth*	*Group*	*Sub-groups Rajput, Maratha, Afghan, Zamindar, etc.*	*Father or other blood relation in service*	*Authorities*
237.	Saiyid Masud Barha	2,000/300	India	Indian	—	—	Al. 268
238.	Muhammad Beg, Teer Andaz Khan	2,000/300	India	Irani	—	Father	S.D.A. 198; A.M.T. 127a
239.	Saiyid Muzaffar Barha, Shuja'at Khan	2,000/250	India	Indian	—	Father	Al. 129; T.M. 1069 A.H.
240.	Mulla Abdul Salam Lahori, Teacher of Dara Shukoh	2,000/–	India	Indian	—	—	*Farhat*, 197a
241.	Ri'ayat Khan	1,500/1,500 (2-3h)	—	—	—	—	Al. 400
242.	Pahar Singh Gaur of Inderkhi	1,500/1,000 (2-3h)	India	Indian	Rajput-*Zamindar*	—	Isar Das, 94a
243.	Murad Quli Sultan Ghakkar	1,500/1,500 (500×2-3h)	India	Indian	—	—	Al. 219,635
244.	Mir Fateh, Fateh Khan	1,500/1,000 (2-3h)	—	—	—	—	Al. 342,880,917
245.	Dilir Khan s/o Bahadur Rohela	1,500/1,000 (800×2-3h)	India	Indian	Afghan	Father	*Adab*. 279a; Al. 965
246.	Shahbaz Khan Afghan	1,500/1,500	India	Indian	Afghan	—	Al. 197,475,625

247.	Mir Muhammad Murad, Saiyid Muhammad Khan	1,500/1,500	—	—	—	—	S.D.A. 74
248.	Hayat Afghan, Zabardast Khan	1,500/1,500	India	Indian	Afghan	—	Al. 291
249.	Faujdar Khan	1,500/1,500	India	Indian	Afghan	—	Al. 342,625
250.	Khwaja Inayatullah	1,000/700	—	—	—	—	Al. 339,885
251.	Gopal Singh s/o Raja Sarup	1,500/1,500	India	Indian	Rajput-*Zamindar*	Father	Al. 1056
252.	Kamil Khan	1,500/1,500	India	Indian	Afghan	—	Al. 1044; Akh. 20th Rabi II, 12th R.Y.
253.	Baguji Deccani	1,500/1,500	India	Indian	Maratha	—	Akh. 22nd Shaban, 4th R.Y
254.	Saiyid Abdur Rahman, Dilawar Khan	1,500/1,500	India	Indian	—	Father	*Daftar-i Dewani*, No. 2986; Hatim Khan, 14a
255.	Sarang Dhar *Zamindar* of Jammun	1,500/1,500	India	Indian	*Zamindar*	—	Al. 286-87
256.	Hasan s/o Dilawar Khan Deccani	1,500/1,500	India	Indian	—	—	S.D.A. 37
257.	Jagat Singh	1,500/1,400	India	Indian	Rajput	—	*Daftar-i Dewani*, No. 2986
258.	Kesri Singh Bhartiya	1,500/1,400	India	Indian	Rajput-*Zamindar*	—	Al. 1047
259.	Sidi Faulad, Faulad Khan	1,500/1,200	India	Indian	—	—	Kamwar, 250b; M.U., I 503; T.M. 1092 A.H.
260.	Rambhaji Deccani	1,500/1,200	India	Indian	Maratha	—	Al. 293

S.No.	Name and Title	Rank highest during the period	Country of birth	Group	Sub-groups Rajput, Maratha, Afghan, *Zamindar*, etc.	Father or other blood relation in service	Authorities
261.	Sikandar Rohela	1,500/1,200	India	Indian	Afghan	—	Al. 291
262.	Mas'ud Mangli, Mangli Khan	1,500/1,000 (200 × 2-3h)	India	Indian	Afghan	—	Al. 1039
263.	Qalandar Beg, Qalandar Khan	1,500/1,000 (200 × 2-3h)	India	Turani	—	Father	S.D.A. 74; M.U., I 192-94
264.	Rai Makrand	1,500/1,200	India	Indian	*Zamindar*	—	Al. 835
265.	Bhoj Raj Kachwaha	1,500/1,200	India	Indian	Rajput	—	*Selected Waqa'i of the Deccan*, 52; Al. 917
266.	Mitr Seṇ Bundela	1,500/1,200	India	Indian	Rajput-*Zamindar*	—	Al. 302,1062; A.M.T. 132b
267.	Dildar Beg, Dildar Khan	1,500/1,000	India	Turani	—	Father	Al. 140
268.	Kamgar Khan s/o Kamyab Khan	1,500/1,000	India	Irani	—	Father	Al. 141,457,1061
269.	Muhammad Ismail, Ismail Khan s/o Najabat Khan	1,500/1,000	India	Turani	—	Father	Al. 755; M.U., II 781
270.	Daku Ji	1,500/1,000	India	Indian	Maratha	—	Al. 48
271.	Muhammad Sharif Polakji	1,500/1,000	India	Indian	—	—	Al. 54
272.	Misri Afghan	1,500/1,000	India	Indian	Afghan	—	Al. 454-55

273.	Hameed Kakur, Kakur Khan	1,500/1,000	India	Indian	Afghan	—	Akh. 19th Rajab, 9th R.Y. Al. 77, 218; Hatim Khan, 20a, 24a
274.	Raja Man Singh of Guler (Punjab)	1,500/1,000	India	Indian	Rajput-*Zamindar*	—	Al. 199,287
275.	Harjis Gaur	1,500/1,000	India	Indian	Rajput-*Zamindar*	Father	Al. 270, 982; T.U. (S.V.)
276.	Chatar Bhuj Chauhan, *Zamindar* of Ajaun	1,500/1,000	India	Indian	Rajput-*Zamindar*	—	Al. 270; T.M. 1079A.H.
277.	Aqa Yusuf	1,500/1,000	—	—	—	—	Al. 270, 448
278.	Mir Rustam Khawafi	1,500/1,000	Iran	Irani	—	Father	Al. 399
279.	Mir Ibrahim, Mir Tuzuk	1,500/1,000	—	—	—	—	Al. 448; Kamwar, 260a
280.	Abul Baqa	1,500/1,000	—	—	—	—	Al. 197
281.	Raja Amar Singh Narori	1,500/1,000	India	Indian	Rajput-*Zamindar*	Father	Al. 447,1056; A.M.T. 131b; M.U.,II 227-28
282.	Yazdani, Cousin of Hasan Ali Khan Alamgir Shahi	1,500/1,000	India	Turani	—	Uncle	Hatim Khan, 54b; Al. 240
283.	Raja Kishan Singh Taunur	1,500/1,000	India	Indian	Rajput-*Zamindar*	—	Al. 304, 428
284.	Mir Ibrahim, Mohtasham Khan s/o Shaikh Mir	1,500/1,000	India	Irani	—	Father	Al. 856; M.A. 130; M.U., III 646-50
285.	Udai Bhan Rathor	1,500/1,000	India	Indian	Rajput-*Zamindar*	—	Al. 334

S.No.	Name and Title	Rank highest during the period	Country of birth	Group	Sub-groups Rajput, Maratha, Afghan, Zamindar, etc.	Father or other blood relation in service	Authorities
286.	Saiyid Ibrahim Dara Shukohi, Mustafa Khan	1,500/1,000	—	—	—	—	Al. 964
287.	Muhammad Salih Tarkhan	1,500/1,000	India	Turani	—	Father	Al. 447;M.U.,III 560-62
288.	Ali Quli, Tashrif Khan, Muftakhar Khan	1,500/1,000	—	Irani	—	Father	Al. 565
289.	Firuz Mewati, Firuz Khan	1,500/1,000	India	Indian	—	—	Al. 440; T.M. 1075 A.H
290.	Man Singh s/o Rup Singh Rathor	1,500/700	India	Indian	Rajput-*Zamindar*	Father	*Adab.* 315b; Al. 158,447; M.U.,II 270
291.	Jag Ram Kachwaha	1,500/1,000	India	Indian	Rajput	—	Al. 1056
292.	Asadullah, Ikram Khan s/o Mulla Ahmad Naitha	1,500/1,000	India	Indian	—	Father	Al. 957; T.U. (S.V.); M.U., III 564-65
293.	Farhad Chela	1,500/1,000	—	—	—	—	Akh. 24th Shaban, 11th R.Y.
294.	Raghu Ji s/o Manaji Bhonsla	1,500/1,000	India	Indian	Maratha-*Zamindar*	Father	S.D.A. 7
295.	Mir Ghiyasuddin	1,500/900	—	—	—	—	*Daftar-i Dewani*, No. 2986
296.	Sharza Rao Kawa	1,500/900	India	Indian	Maratha	—	S.D.A. 7
297.	Mustafa Khan Kashi	1,500/900	Iran	Irani	—	—	Akh. 30th Zilhij, 13th R.Y.; M.U.; III, 637-41

298.	Mirza Niamatullah, Sohrab Khan	1,500/900	India	Irani	—	Father	Al. 885; S.D.A. 74; M.U.,I 586-87
299.	Jalal Afghan	1,500/800	India	Indian	Afghan-Deccani	—	Al. 972
300.	Raghu Nath Singh Bhartiya	1,500/900	India	Indian	Rajput-*Zamindar*	—	Al. 1061-62
301.	Buzurg Umeed Khan	1,500/900	India	Irani	—	Father	Al. 140,856,956; M.U.,I 453-54
302.	Mir Raziuddin	1,500/800	—	—	—	—	Al. 862
303.	Salabat Deccani	1,500/700 (100×2-3h)	—	—	Deccani	—	S.D.A. 5
304.	Raghu Nath Singh Meerath	1,500/800	India	Indian	Rajput-*Zamindar*	—	Akh. 29th Rabi II, 8th R.Y.; A.M.T.132a; 20th Ziqada, 10th R.Y.
305.	Yahya Pasha	1,500/700	Turkey	Turani	—	—	M.A. 110; Kamwar, 255a
306.	Raji s/o Afzal Khan	1,500/700	India	—	Deccani	—	Al. 834; A.M.T. 131b
307.	Sardar Qiyam Khan, Alaf Khan	1,500/700	India	Indian	Afghan	—	Al. 290
308.	Masud Khan	1,500/700	—	—	—	—	S.D.A. 74
9.	Hizbar Khan s/o Alahwardi Khan	1,500/700	India	Irani	—	Father	M.A. 145; M.U.,III 496
310.	Mir Muhammad Muazzam, Siyadat Khan, Muazzam Khan	1,500/700	India	Irani	—	Father	Al. 210,334; M.U.,II 676; A.M.T. 127b

S.N.	Name and Title	Rank highest during the period	Country of birth	Group	Sub-groups Rajput, Maratha, Afghan, *Zamindar*, etc.	Father or other blood relation in service	Authorities
311.	Abul Fateh s/o Shaista Khan	1,500/700	India	Irani	—	Father	Al. 140
312.	Saifuddin Safvi, Kamyab Khan	1,500/700	India	Irani	—	Father	Al. 870; M.U., III 479
313.	Shaikh Abdul Aziz, Abdul Aziz Khan, Dilawar Khan	1,500/700	India	Indian	—	—	S.D.A. 74; Al. 141; M.A. 132; M.U., II 686-88
314.	Khwaja Nur, Mutamad Khan (eunuch)	1,500/600	—	—	—	—	Al. 294,448, 960
315.	Mahesh Das Rathor	1,500/600	India	Indian	Rajput		Al. 163
316.	Mir Fazlullah, Fazlullah Khan	1,500/600	India	Irani	—	Father	Al. 158,1061
317.	Raghu Nath Singh Rathor, s/o Sunder Das Rathor	1,500/600	India	Indian	Rajput	Father	Al. 635
318.	Yusuf Bijapuri, Yusuf Khan	1,500/600	India	Indian	Deccani	—	Al. 742,880
319.	Shafqatullah, Sazawar Khan	1,500/600	India	Irani	—	Father	Al. 127, 880; M.U., II 440-41
320.	Muhammad Beg	1,500/600	—	—	—	—	Al. 908
321.	Muhammad Darab Khan	1,500/600	India	Irani	—	Father	Al. 917
322.	Munawwar Khan *Zamindar*	1,500/600	India	Indian	Afghan-*Zamindar*	—	*Daftar-i Dewani*, No. 2986; Al. 956

323.	Mir Saleh son-in-law of Shah Nawaz Khan Safvi	1,500/500	—	Irani	—	—	Al. 45, 334; T.M. 1074 A.H.
324.	Karan Kachi	1,500/500	India	Indian	Rajput-*Zamindar*	—	Al. 52
325.	Daulatmand Khan	1,500/500	India	Indian	—	Father	Al. 93, 989
326.	Mir Abul Fazl Mamuri, Mamur Khan	1,500/500	—	Irani	—	—	Al. 53, 77
327.	Farhad Beg, Ali Mardan Khani, Farhad Khan	1,500/500	Iran	Irani	—	Father	Al. 268, 287, 880
328.	Qabad Beg	1,500/500	—	Turani	—	—	Al. 163, 290
329.	Ishaq Beg	1,500/500	—	—	—	—	Al. 195
330.	Raja Prithi Chand	1,500/500	India	Indian	Rajput-*Zamindar*	—	Al. 237
331.	Lutfullah Khan	1,500/500	India	Indian	—	Father	Al. 918; M. A. 71; M.U., III 171-77
332.	Muhammad Mansur, Makarmat Khan	1,500/500	Iran	Irani	—	Grand-father	Al. 448, 755
333.	Ali Beg Khan	1,500/500	Turkey	Turani	—	—	M. A. 87; M. U., I 244
334.	Abdullah s/o Randula Khan	1,500/500	India	Indian	—	Father	*Daftar-i Dewani*, No. 2986
335.	Husain Beg Khan Zig	1,500/400	Iran	Irani	—	—	Al. 55; M.U., I 591-93
336.	Hameeduddin, Khanazad Khan	1,500/400	India	Irani	—	Father	Al. 270, 594

S.N.	Name and Title	Rank highest during the period	Country of birth	Group	Sub-groups Rajput, Maratha, Afghan, Zamindar, etc.	Father or other blood relation in service	Authorities
337.	Mir Niamatullah s/o Khalilullah Khan Yazdi	1,500/400	India	Irani	—	Father	Al. 270; M. U., III 342
338.	Alah Dad s/o Ikhlas Khan	1,500/400	India	Indian	Afghan	Father	Al. 291, 573-74
339.	Abdul Qadir, Diyanat Khan	1,500/350	India	Irani	—	Father	Al. 917. M.U., II 59
340.	Mu'in Khan	1,500/300	—	—	—	—	Al. 832
341.	Abdur Rahim Khan s/o Islam Khan	1,500/300	India	Irani	—	Father	Al. 960; M. U., II 812-13
342.	Muhammad 'Abid, Nawazish Khan s/o Zahid Khan	1,500/300	India	—	—	Father	M. A. 97; Kamwar, 252b; M. U., II 371-72
343.	Muhamad Sadiq, Dilawar Khan	1,500/200	—	Turani	—	—	Al. 232, 206, 287
344.	Murad Khan, Iltifat Khan	1,500/250	India	Irani	—	Father	Al. 870; M. U., II 733
345.	Hakim Salih Shirazi, Salih Khan	1,500/250	Iran	Irani	—	—	Al. 1061-62
346.	Shah Beg Khan Kashghari, Shahi Khan	1,500/500	Turan	Turani	—	—	Al. 401; M.A. 158; Kamwar 263b, 265b
347.	Saiyid Feroz Rustam Khani	1,500/200	India	Indian	—	—	Al. 161

348.	Shaikh Nizam Qureshi	1,500/100	India	Indian	—	—	Al. 1034
349.	Hakim Muhammad Amin Shirazi	1,500/50	Iran	Irani	—	—	Al. 399
350.	Sardar Beg, Ihtimam Khan	1,500/–	India	Turani	—	Father	A.M.T. 131a
351.	Mirza Muhammad Tahir, Inayat Khan	1,500/–	India	Irani	—	Father	M. U., II 762
352.	Shaikh Ali Bijapuri	1,500/–	India	Indian	Afghan-Deccani	—	*Dilkusha*, 26b
353.	Ahmad Khan s/o Sidi Miftah	1,500/–	India	Indian	Deccani-*Zamindar*	Father	M. U., I 582
354.	Muhammad Beg Turkman, Kartalab Khan	1,500/–	Iran	Irani	—	—	M. U., II 706-8; T. U. (S.V.) Al. 326,343
355.	Sher Singh Rathor	1,000/1,000 (2-3h)	India	Indian	Rajput	Father	Al. 441
356.	Mahrawal Jaswant Singh of Dungarpur	1,000/1,000 (800×2-3h)	India	Indian	Rajput-*Zamindar*	Father	Akh. 16th Zilhij, 38th R. Y.; Ojha, Vol. III, Part I, 115
357.	Inder Singh s/o Rao Rai Singh	1,000/1,000 (700×2-3h)	India	Indian	Rajput-*Zamindar*	Father	S.D.A. 121; M.U., II 236
358.	Bahram s/o Qazalbash Khan	1,000/1,700	India	Irani	—	Father	Al. 486, 1039
359.	Raja Maha Singh Bahdoriya	1,000/1,000 (500×2-3h)	India	Indian	Rajput-*Zamindar*	Father	Al. 1044; M.U., II 229-30
360.	Shaikh Abdul Hamid s/o Shaikh Mansur Bijapuri	1,000/1,000 (100×2-3h)	India	Indian	Deccani	Father	S. D. A. 47

S.N.	Name and Title	Rank highest during the period	Country of birth	Group	Sub-groups Rajput, Maratha, Afghan, Zamindar, etc.	Father or other blood relation in service	Authorities
361.	Ram Singh s/o Ratan Rathor	1,000/1,000	India	Indian	Rajput-*Zamindar*	Father	Al. 486
362.	Sarbaz Khan	1,000/800 (600×2-3h)	India	Indian	Afghan	—	Akh. 5th Jamada, II, 12th R. Y.
363.	Qadir Dad Khan	1,000/800 (400×2-3h)	India	Turani	—	Father	Hatim Khan, 164a; Al. 1030; A.M.T. 132a
364.	Umar Tarin	1,000/1,000	India	Indian	Afghan	—	Al. 270, 287-88
365.	Abdul Hameed Bijapuri	1,000/1,000	India	Indian	Deccani	—	Al. 163, 291
366.	Chatru Ji Deccani	1,000/1,000	India	Indian	Maratha	—	Al. 206
367.	Mir Baqar Khan	1,000/1,000	India	Irani	—	Father	Al. 206, 573; A.M.T. 131b
368.	Mahmud Dilzaq	1,000/1,000	—	Turani	—	—	Al. 487; *Mirat-ul-'Alam*, 160a-b
369.	Imam Abardi	1,000/1,000	—	—	—	—	Al. 635
370.	Man Dhata	1,000/1,000	India	Indian	Rajput-*Zamindar*	Father	Al. 647-48
371.	Murad Khan, *Zamindar* of Tibet	1,000/1,000	India	Indian	*Zamindar*	—	Al. 860
372.	Raja Jai Singh	1,000/1,000	India	Indian	Rajput-*Zamindar*	—	Al. 964
373.	Raja Bahruj	1,000/1,000	India	Indian	Rajput-*Zamindar*	Father	Al. 340; T.M. 1076 A. H.; M. U., II 219

374.	Rustam Khan s/o Qazalbash Khan	1,000/900	India	Irani	—	Father	S. D. A. 74; Akh. 17th Rabi II 12th R. Y.
375.	Ghairat Beg, Shuja'Khan	1,000/900	—	—	—	—	Al. 232, 856
376.	Saiyid Anwar	1,000/900	—	—	—	—	Al. 862-63
377.	Sarfaraz Khan Beg	1,000/900	—	—	—	—	Al. 290; T. U. (S.V.)
378.	Qalandar Daudzai, Qalandar Khan	1,000/900	India	Indian	Afghan	—	Al. 308, 960
379.	Kunda Ji Deccani (Embraced Islam)	1,000/800	India	Indian	Deccani	—	Al. 1062; M. U., III 580
380.	Saiyid Bahadur Barha	1,000/800	India	Indian	—	—	Al. 293
381.	Imam Quli Qarawal, Aghar Khan	1,000/800	—	Irani	—	—	Al. 216; T. U. (S.V.); Ruq. No 5/10 p. 11; *Fathiya Ibriya* 158 b
382.	Saiyid Nasiruddin Khan Deccani	1,000/800	India	Indian	Deccani	—	Al. 45
383.	Mirza Ruhullah s/o Yusuf Khan Tashqandi	1,000/800	India	Turani	—	Father	M.U., III 966-67
384.	Mir Burhani	1,000/800	—	—	—	—	Al. 1050
385.	Saifullah Arab	1,000/800	—	—	—	—	Al. 45
386.	Suraj Mal Gaur	1,000/800	India	Indian	Rajput-*Zamindar*	Father	Al. 192

S.N.	Name and Title	Rank highest during the period	Country of birth	Group	Sub-groups Rajput, Maratha, Afghan, *Zamindar*, etc.	Father or other blood relation in service	Authorities
387.	Inderman Bundela	1,000/700	India	Indian	Rajput	Father	*Daftar-i Dewani*, 2983; S.D.A. 112; Al. 989
388.	Khwaja Shah, Sharif Khan	1,000/700	—	—	—	—	M. A. 140
389.	Ghulam Muhammad Afghan	1,000/700	India	Indian	Afghan	—	Al. 475
390.	Hasan Beg	1,000/700	—	—	—	—	Al. 163
391.	Darwesh Beg Qaqshal	1,000/700	—	Turani	—	—	Al. 303
392.	Mana Ji s/o Wanerath Ji	1,000/700	India	Indian	Maratha	—	*Daftar-i Dewani*, No. 2986
393.	Tama Ji *Zamindar* of Kachh	1,000/700	India	Indian	Rajput-*Zamindar*	—	Al. 625
394.	Haji Ahmad Sa'id s/o Maulana Muhammad Sa'id	1,000/700	India	Indian	—	—	*Farhat*; 198b-99a; Al. 885
395.	Kamaluddin s/o Dilir Khan	1,000/700	India	Indian	Afghan	Father	M. A. 140
396.	Saiyid Muqtadar	1,000/600	—	—	—	—	Al. 217
397.	Abul Makarim s/o Iftikhar Khan	1,000/600	India	Irani	—	Father	Al. 334
398.	Saiyid Hamid Bukhari Mujahid Khan	1,000/600	—	Turani	—	Father	Al. 249, 918; M. U., III 598
399.	Mirza Ali Arab, Qaladar Khan	1,000/600	India	Irani	—	Father	S.D.A. 74; Al. 565; M.U., III 115-20

400.	Daran Khan	1,000/600	—	—	—	—	Al. 856
401.	Muhammad Abid, brother of Faizullah Khan	1,000/600	India	Irani	—	Brother	Al. 140, 843
402.	Bhim Singh of Srinagar	1,000/600	India	Indian	Rajput-*Zamindar*	Father	Al. 960
403.	Saiyid Ahmad Khan Khattab	1,000/600	—	—	—	—	Al. 964; M.A. 105
404.	Garkhu Ji s/o Wankar Rao	1,000/600	India	Indian	Maratha	—	*Daftar-i Dewani*, 2986
405.	Nuri Beg, Turktaz Khan	1,000/600	—	Turani	—	—	M.A. 149; Al. 216, 908
406.	Saun Singh of Kali Bhet	1,000/500	India	Indian	Rajput-*Zamindar*	—	Al. 55; Hatim Khan, 16b
407.	Daulat Afghan	1,000/500	India	Indian	Afghan	—	Al. 78
408.	Muhammad Muqim, Muqim Khan	1,000/500	India	Turani	—	Father	Al. 78, 487
409.	Inayat Afghan	1,000/500	India	Indian	Afghan	—	Al. 268
410.	Mir Arab Bakhazri	1,000/500	—	Irani	—	—	Al. 271
411.	Abbas Afghan	1,000/500	India	Indian	Afghan	—	Al. 270
412.	Kalyan Singh of Bandhu	1,000/500	India	Indian	Rajput-*Zamindar*	—	Al. 215
413.	Darwesh Muhammad	1,000/500	—	—	—	—	Al. 221
414.	Abdul Bari Ansari	1,000/500	India	Indian	—	—	Al. 291
415.	Qadir Dad Ansari	1,000/500	India	Indian	—	—	Al. 635

S.No.	Name and Title	Rank highest during the period	Country of birth	Group	Sub-groups Rajput, Maratha, Afghan, *Zamindar*, etc.	Father or other blood relation in service	Authorities
416.	Asad Kashi, Asad Khan	1,000/500	India	Irani	—	—	*Daftar-i Dewani*, No. 2986; Al. 404,565
417.	Daud	1,000/500	India	Indian	—	—	Al. 291
418.	Mir Ali Akbar	1,000/500	—	—	—	—	*Daftar-i Dewani*, No. 2986
419.	Mir Baqi, Baqi Khan	1,000/500	Iran	Irani	—	Father	Al. 966
420.	Tatar Beg, Uzbek Khan	1,000/500	—	Turani	—	—	Al. 52, 53; Hatim Khan, 15a, 28b, 565
421.	Bhao Singh, Murid Khan	1,000/500	India	Indian	*Zamindar*	Father	Al. 981; M.U., II 281
422.	Hamid Khan, s/o Shaikh Mir	1,000/500	India	Irani	—	Father	Al. 856
423.	Sidi Ibrahim	1,000/500	India	Indian	Deccani-*Zamindar*	—	Al. 626
424.	Saiyid Shuja'at Khan, Bahadur Bhakkari	1,000/500	India	Indian	—	Father	M.U., II 460-61
425.	Mir Bahadur Dil, Jan Sipar Khan	1,000/500	India	Irani	—	Father	S.D.A. 29; M.U., I 535-37
426.	Raghu Ji Ghoparay	1,000/500	India	Indian	Maratha	—	S.D.A. 107
427.	Nurul Hasan	1,000/500	—	—	—	—	Al. 565
428.	Prem Singh, *Zamindar* of Srinagar	1,000/500	India	Indian	Rajput-*Zamindar*	—	Al. 872

429.	Iftikhar, Mufakhir Khan s/o Fakhir Khan	1,000/450	India	Irani	—	Father	Al. 401,635,832; M.U., III 27-28
430.	Mukhtar Beg, Nawazish Khan	1,000/400	Turkey	Turani	—	Father	M.A. 152; M.U., I 247
431.	Mir Mahmud, Aqidat Khan	1,000/400	Iran	Irani	—	Brother	M.A. 109,113; Kamwar, 255b; M.U., I 224-25
432.	Jamal Khan	1,000/400	India	Indian	Afghan	Father	Al. 147
433.	Manohar Das Sisodia	1,000/400	India	Indian	Rajput	Father	Al. 140
434.	Khudawand Habshi, Habsh Khan	1,000/400	India	Indian	—	—	Al. 45
435.	Wali Beg Kalali	1,000/400	India	—	—	—	*Akh.* 9th Ramzan, 13th R.Y. Al. 876
436.	Muhammad Salim	1,000/400	India	Indian	—	—	Al. 196 Akh. 8th R. Y.
437.	Shaikh Nizam s/o Shaikh Farid	1,000/400	India	Indian	—	Father	Al. 399; Hatim Khan 38b; M.U., I 222
438.	Malik Jewan, Bakhtiyar Khan	1,000/400	India	Indian	Afghan-*Zamindar*	—	Al. 742; T.M. 1076 A.H.
439.	Ahmad Beg Najm Sani	1,000/400	India	Irani	—	Brother	Al. 885
440.	Ali Beg, Ihtimam Khan	1,000/400	India	Irani	—	Father	Al. 215; M.U., III 498
441.	Gada Beg	1,000/400	—	—	—	—	Al. 870
442.	Raja Sher Singh, *Zamindar* of Chamba	1,000/400	India	Indian	Rajput-*Zamindar*	—	Al. 843

S.No.	Name and Title	Rank highest during the period	Country of birth	Group	Sub-groups Rajput, Maratha, Afghan, Zamindar, etc.	Father or other blood relation in service	Authorities
443.	Khwaja Sadiq Badakhshi	1,000/400	Turan	Turani	—	—	Al. 977
444.	Saiyid Yadgar Husain Barha	1,500/600	India	Indian	—	—	Al. 1062; Hatim Khan, 56b. *Akh.* 17th Zilhij, 20th R.Y.
445.	Banwali Das Bhartiya	1,000/400	India	Indian	Rajput	Father	Al. 1047; A.M.T. 132a
446.	Badal Bakhtiyar	1,000/350	India	Indian	Afghan	—	Al. 1034
447.	Saiyid Zainul Abidin Bukhari	1,000/300	—	Turani		—	Hatim Khan, 13b; Al. 45
448.	Abu Muslim	1,000/300	—	—	—	—	Al. 206
449.	Saiyid Mirza Sabzwari	1,000/300	Iran	Irani	—	—	Al. 346
450.	Saiyid Ali	1,000/300	—	—	—	—	Al. 918
451.	Darbar Khan Khwajasara	1,000/300	—	—	—	—	Al. 960
452.	Pahla Wijai	1,000/300	India	Indian	Maratha	—	*Akh.* 13th Ramzan, 13th R.Y.
453.	Haji Muhammad Shafi, Shafi Khan	1,000/300	—	—	—	—	*Akh.* 22nd Safar, 20th R.Y.; Al. 870
454.	Muhammad Shuja, Shuja'at Khan s/o Qiwamuddin Khan	1,000/300	Iran	Irani	—	Father	M.A. 153; Kamwar, 263a; M.U., III 114-115
455.	Bakhtawar Khan	1,000/250	—	—	—	—	Al. 960; M.A. 140; T.U. (S.V.)

456.	Nazir Khan Khwajasara	1,000/250	—	—	—	—	Al. 742
457.	Mansur, Nasir Khan brother of Abdullah, King of Kashghar	1,000/250	Turan	Turani	—	—	Al. 762
458.	Muhammad Qasim Ali Mardan Khani	1,000/250	Iran	Irani	—	Father	Al.268
459.	Mir Mahdi Yazdi	1,000/200	—	Irani	—	—	Al. 163
460.	Niamatullah s/o Hisamuddin Khan	1,000/200	India	Irani	—	Father	Al. 52
461.	Khwaja Kalan, Kifayat Khan	1,000/200	—	—	—	—	Al. 77
462.	Isa Khan	1,000/200	—	—	—	—	*Akh.* 13th Ramzan, 13th R.Y.
463.	Qutab Kashi	1,000/200	—	Irani	—	—	Al. 268
464.	Mir Abul Hasan Shah Shuja'i	1,000/200	—	—	—	—	Al. 161
465.	Amanullah	1,000/200	India	Irani	—	Father	Al. 197; M.U., I 232
466.	Muhammad Husain Sildoz	1,000/200	—	Turani	—	—	Al. 210
467.	Sher Afghan	1,000/200	India	Indian	Afghan	—	Al. 287
468.	Barq AndazKhan	1,000/200	—	—	—	—	Al. 861
469.	Mulla Iwaz Wajih	1,000/200	Balkh	Turani	—	—	Al. 392;M.A. 150, 156
470.	Mir Aziz	1,000/200	—	—	—	—	Al. 861

S.No.	Name and Title	Rank highest during the period	Country of birth	Group	Sub-groups Rajput, Maratha, Afghan, Zamindar, etc.	Father or other blood relation in service	Authorities
471.	Amanat Khan Mirak Muinuddin	1,000/200	India	Irani	—	Father	M.A. 110; M.U., I 258-68
472.	Mir Yaqub, Shamsher Khan	1,000/150	India	Irani	—	Father	Al. 195; M.U., II 670; T.M. 1086 A.H.
473.	Khwaja Ismail Beg Kirmani	1,000/150	—	Irani	—	—	Al. 218, 487
474.	Islam Quli	1,000/100	Turan	Turani	—	—	M.A. 76; Kamwar, 249a
475.	Mahdi, Cousin of Abdullah King of Kashghar	1,000/100	Turan	Turani	—	—	Al. 565-66
476.	Inayat Khan	2,000/2,000	Iran	Irani	—	—	M.U., II 813-18. *The English, Factories*, 1661-64, 203, 205
477.	Mir Abdul Mabud (Bhakkari)	1,000/—	India	Indian	—	—	*Selected Waqai of the Deccan*, 68
478.	Chand Khan s/o Mir Murtaza	1,000/—	India	Turani	—	Father	Mamuri, 149a; A.M.T.132a
479.	Bhagwant	1,000/—	India	Indian	Rajput	—	S.D.A. 104
480.	Ikram Khan Sadr	1,000/—	—	—	—	—	A.M.T. 131b
481.	Raja Jaswant Singh Bundela	1,000/—	India	Indian	Rajput-*Zamindar*	Father	M.A. 169; M.U., II 293-94
482.	Mani Ram	1,000/—	India	Indian	—	—	S.D.A. 40
483.	Raja Chatar Singh of Chamba (Punjab).	1,000/—	India	Indian	Rajput-*Zamindar*	Father	M. Akbar, "*Punjab under the Mughals*", 226

484.	Shaikh Abul Fateh, Qabil Khan	1,000/—	India	Indian	—	—	A.M.T. 132a.M.A. 190, *Adab*, 1b
485.	Rao Muhkam Singh s/o Amar Singh Chandrawat.	High Rank[1]	India	Indian	Rajput-*Zamindar*	Father	M.U. II, 147-48
486.	Ahmad Beg Kamil s/o Mirza Fazil	Amir	Iran	Irani	—	—	*Mirāt-ul-'Alam*, 281b

[1] The rank of Muhkam Singh is not given—but when his father Amar Singh was given the title of Rao, he was promoted to the hereditary rank of 1,000/900; subsequently Amar Singh was promoted to the rank of 1,500/900. After the death of Amar Singh, Muhkam Singh was awarded the *Tika* and the hereditary title of Rao. (M.U., II 147-48).

B. MANSABDARS WHO HELD OR REACHED THE RANK OF 1,000 *ZAT* AND ABOVE DURING THE PERIOD, 1679-1707

Mansabdars of 5,000 and above

S. No.	*Name and Title*	*Rank highest during the period*	*Country of birth*	*Group*	*Sub-groups Rajput, Maratha, Afghan, Zamindar, etc.*	*Father or other blood relation in service*	*Authorities*
1.	Mirza Abu Talib, Shaista Khan, Amir-ul-Umara	7,000/7,000 (2-3h)	India	Irani	—	Father	T.M. 5; A.M.T. 121a; M.U., II 690-706
2.	Mir Malik Husain, Khan-i-Jahan Bahadur, Zafar Jang Kokaltash	7,000/7,000 (6,000×2-3h)	India	Irani	—	Father	M.A. 142; T.M. 9; A.M.T. 121a; M.U., I 798-813
3.	Mir Shahabuddin, Ghaziuddin Khan Bahadur Firoz Jang	7,000/7,000 (3,000×2-3h)	Turan	Turani	—	Father	*Akh.* 6th Jamada II, 46th R.Y.; Z.A. 165a; M.A. 302, 481; T.M. 27; M.U., II 872-79
4.	Sidi Masud, Masud Khan	7,000/7,000 (2,000×2-3h)	India	Indian	Deccani-*Zamindar*	—	Isar Das, 126a, 144a; S.D.A. 222; Kamwar, 281b; B.S.767; M.A. 315-16
5.	Jamshed Khan Bijapuri	7,000/7,000 (1,200×2-3h)	India	Indian	Deccani	—	*Akh.* 20th Shaban, 37th R.Y.; Z.A.164b; Kamwar, 301a; T.M. 17
6.	Abdur Rauf Miyana, Dilir Khan	7,000/7,000	India	Indian	Afghan-Deccani	—	Z.A. 164a; M.A. 280; B.S. 756: M.U., II 56-59; T.U., S.V.

7.	Raja Shahu	7,000/7,000	India	Indian	Maratha	—	S.D.A. 215; M.A. 332; *Raqaim-i-Karaim*, 23b; A.M.T. 121b; Kamwar, 281b; M.U., II 342-58.
8.	Shaikh Nizam Junaidi Haiderabadi, Muqarrab Khan, Khan-i-Zaman, Fateh Jang	7,000/7,000	India	Indian	Deccani	—	Z.A. 131b; T.M.8; M.A.324; M.U., I 794–98
9.	Saiyid Makhdoom, Sharza Khan, Rustam Khan	7,000/7,000	India	Indian	Deccani	—	S.D.A. 199; Z.A. 164a; M.A. 176, 280, 480; M. U., II 502–504; Chandr Bhan Brahman, *Guldasta*, 4b–5a
10.	Saiyid Abdul Qadir Khan	7,000/7,000	—	—	Deccani	—	*Akh.* 23rd Rajab, 39th R.Y.; S.D.A. 222
11.	Muhammad Ibrahim, Asad Khan	7,000/7,000	India	Irani	—	Father	S.D.A. 169; Z.A. 164b; M. A. 392; M.U.,*I* 310-321
12.	Azizuddin, Bahramand Khan	7,000/7,000	India	Irani	—	Father	*Daftar-i-Dewani*, (Haiderabad), 25th Jamada II, 23rd R.Y.; T.M. 16; M.A. 369, 374; M.U.,I 454-57
13.	Alauddin Nayak (Former *bakhshi* of Pidia Nayak)	7,000/7,000	India	Indian	Deccani	—	Kamwar, 301b, 309b
14.	Habsh Khan[1]	7,000/7,000	—	—	Deccani	—	*Daftar-i-Dewani*, 18th Jamada II, 33rd R.Y.; No. 784

[1] Dr. Yusuf Husain Khan has misread this name as Hasan Khan (S.D.A. 222).

S.N.	Name and Title	Rank highest during the period	Country of birth	Group	Sub-groups Rajput, Maratha, Afghan, Zamindar, etc.	Father or other blood relation in service	Authorities
15.	Muhammad Ibrahim Khalilullah Khan, Mahabat Khan	7,000/6,000 (1,000×2-3h)	Iran	Irani	Deccani	—	S.D.A. 170; Z. A. 165a. M.A. 269; M.U.,III 627-32
16.	Chaghta Khan Bahadur, Fateh Jang Kashghari	7,000/—	Turan	Turani	—	—	T.U., S.V.
17.	Saiyid Muzaffar Haiderabadi	7,000/—	—	—	Deccani	—	T.M. 1097 A. H.; Kamwar, 272b; M. A. 227
18.	Ikhlas Khan, Khan-i-Alam	6,000/5,000 (2–3h)	India	Indian	Deccani	—	Z. A. 131b–132a; M. A. 324, 384; M.U.,I 816-17; A.M.T. 121b
19.	Mir Miran, Amir Khan	6,000/5,000 (3,000×2-3h)	India	Irani	—	Father	*Akh.* 25th Shawwal, 25th R.Y. M.U.,I 277-87
20.	Ibrahim Khan s/o Ali Mardan Khan	6,000/6,000 (2,000×2-3h)	Iran	Irani	—	Father	M.A. 236, 497; Kamwar, 299b; T.M.27; M.U.,I 295-301
21.	Rana Raj Singh	6,000/6,000 (1,000×2-3h)	India	Indian	Rajput-*Zamindar*	Father	T. M. 1092 A.H.; M.U.,II 206-8; A.M.T. 122b
22.	Saiyid Latif, Sarfaraz Khan Deccani	6,000/6,000 (1,000×2-3h)	India	—	Deccani	—	*Akh.* 14th Shaban, 43rd R.Y.; Z.A. 162b; M.A. 480, 513; M.U., II 499-500

23.	Daud Khan Panni	6,000/6,000	India	Indian	Afghan Deccani	Uncle	S. D. A. 171; Z.A. 161a; M.A. 483; M.U.,II 63-68
24.	Muhammad Ismail, Itiqad Khan, Zulfiqar Khan Bahadur Nusrat Jang	6,000/6,000	India	Irani	—	Father	*Raqaim-i-Karaim,* 12a; *Akh.* 16th Shawwal, 45th R.Y.; M.A. 332, 374, 392; M.U.,II 93-106
25.	Muhammad Amin Khan	6,000/5,000 (1,000 × 2-3h)	India	Irani	Deccani	Father	A.M.T. 122a; M.U., III 613-620; Al. 855
26.	Kanhuji Shirke	6,000/5,000	India	Indian	Maratha	—	*Daftar-i-Dewani,* No. 2980; M. A. 220, 495; Kamwar, 271 a; A.M.T. 122 a
27.	Mir Husaini Beg, Ali Mardan Khan Haiderabadi	6,000/5,000	India	—	Deccani	—	Z. A. 125; M. A. 364; T.M. 20; M. U., II 824-25; A.M.T. 123a; *Dilkusha,* 95b
28.	Ismail Khan Mokha	6,000/5,000	India	Indian	Afghan-*Zamindar*	Deccani	M. A. 369; M.U.,I 291-92; T. U., S.V.; A. M. T. 121b
29.	Satvad Dafalya	6,000/5,000	India	Indian	Maratha-*Zamindar*	—	M.A. 395
30.	Hasan Khan Rohela	6,000/5,000	India	Indian	Afghan Deccani	—	Z.A. 163b; T.U., S.V.
31.	Husain Khan, Fateh Jang Khan Miyana	6,000/5,000	India	Indian	Afghan Deccani	—	*Akh.* 19th Jamada II, 45th R. Y.; S. D. A. 204; Z.A. 162a; M. A. 225; M.U.,III 30-32
32.	Abid Khan, Qulij Khan	6,000/1,500	Turan	Turani	—	—	M. A. 185; T. M. 1098 A.H. M. U., III 120-23

S.N.	*Name and Title*	*Rank highest during the period*	*Country of birth*	*Group*	*Sub-groups Rajput, Maratha, Afghan, Zamindar, etc.*	*Father or other blood relation in service*	*Authorities*
33.	Man Singh s/o Sanbhaji	6,000/1,000	India	Indian	Maratha	—	Kamwar, 281b; S. D. A. 216
34.	Rai Bhan	6,000 —	India	Indian	Maratha-*Zamindar*	—	*Dilkusha*, 145b
35.	Achpat Nayar	6,000 —	India	Indian	Deccani	—	*Dilkusha*, 112b
36.	Raja Ram Sing Kachwaha	5,000/5,000 (2-3h)	India	Indian	Rajput-*Zamindar*	Father	*Vir Vinod*, II 1296; A.M.T. 122b; T. M. 1099 A.H.; M. U., II 301-303
37.	Jalal Khan, Dilir Khan	5,000/5,000 (3,000×2-3h)	India	Indian	Afghan	Brother	Al. 1030; T. M. 1093 A.H.; M.U., II 42-56
38.	Muhammad Beg, Kartalab Khan, Shuja ʿat Khan	5,000/5,000	Iran	Irani	—	—	M. A. 383; Kamwar, 294b; T.M. 14; M. U., II 706-8; A.M.T.124a
39.	Rana Jai Singh	5,000/5,000	India	Indian	Rajput-*Zamindar*	Father	M. A. 212; A. M. T. 122b; M. U., II 208
40.	Shuja ʿat Khan Haiderabadi	5,000/5,000	India	—	Deccani	—	M. A. 234; T. U., SV; T. M. 1095 A. H; A.M.T. 123a
41.	Achla Ji Nimbalkar Deccani	5,000/5,000	India	Indian	Maratha	—	*Akh.* 26th Rajab, 37th R.Y.; M.A. 271; Kamwar, 276b A. M. T. 122b
42	Ruhullah Khan	5,000/5,000	India	Irani	—	Father	S. D. A. 169; Z. A. 165a; T. M. 3; M.U., II 309-315

43.	Rana Amar Singh II	5,000/5,000	India	Indian	Rajput-*Zamindar*	Father	*Vir Vinod*, Vol., III 745, 749, 751; M. A. 404
44.	Abdul Muhammad, Ikhlas Khan Miyana	5,000/5,000	India	Indian	Afghan	—	S. D. A. 183; T. M. 17
45.	Mir Qamruddin, Chin Qulij Khan Bahadur	5,000/5,000	India	Turani	—	Father	M. A. 506; M. U., III 875, 927; Kamwar, 301a; *Mirat-i-Aftab Numa*, 578
46.	Ran Mast Ali Khan Panni, Bahadur Khan, alias Rustam Khan	5,000/5,000	India	Indian	Afghan Deccani	—	S. D. A. 171; Z.A. 160b; M. U. II, 64-65
47.	Muhammad Ibrahim, Ghairat Khan, Shuja 'at Khan, Khan-i-Alam	5,000/5,000	India	Turani	—	Father	*Akh.* 17th Zilhij, 44th R.Y.; T. M. 20; M.U.,II 869-72
48.	Nek Nihad Khan	5,000/5,000	India	Indian	—	Father	*Akh.* 13th Shawwal. 38thR.Y.
49.	Ahsan Khan	5,000/5,000	—	—	Deccani	—	Z.A. 164b
50.	Parya Nayak or Pidia Nayak	5,000/5,000	India	Indian	Deccani *Zamindar*	—	*Dilkusha*, 95b; M. A. 513; Khafi Khan II, 370
51.	Malu Ji	5,000/5,000	India	Indian	Maratha	—	S. D. A. 187, 206
52.	Moinullah	5,000/5,000	—	—	—	—	S. D. A. 203
53.	Jagna Nayak	5,000/5,000	India	Indian	Deccani *Zamindar*	—	S. D. A. 205; Mamuri, 205b

S.N.	Name and Title	Rank highest during the period	Country of birth	Group	Sub-groups Rajput, Maratha, Afghan, *Zamindar*, etc.	Father or other blood relation in service	Authorities
54.	Padshah Quli Khan	5,000/5,000	—	—	Deccani	—	S.D.A. 222
55.	Khwaja Rahmatullah, Sarbuland Khan	5,000/4,000	India	Turani	—	—	T.M. 1090 A. H.; M. U., II 477-79; Al. 976; A.M.T.124b
56.	Bhaku Banjara	5,000/4,000	India	Indian	—	—	M. A. 393; A. M. T. 122b
57.	Mir Muhammad Khalil Sipahdar Khan, Khan-i-Zaman, Muftakhar Khan	5,000/4,000	India	Irani	—	Father	M. A. 209; T. M. 1095 A. H.; M. U., I 785-92; A.M.T. 122b
58.	Nagu Ji Mane or Naku Ji	5,000/4,000	India	Indian	Maratha	—	*Akh.* 8th Muharram, 44th R.Y.; *Dilkusha*, 122a
59.	Sidi Salim Khan	5,000/4,000	India	Indian	*Zamindar*-Deccani	—	S. D. A. 207; Z.A. 164b
60.	Mahram Khan	5,000/4,000	—	—	—	—	S. D. A. 219
61.	Saiyid Muhammad Qaladar of Bangalore	5,000/4,000	—	—	Deccani	—	Isar Das, 131a-b
62.	Muhammad Husain, Sipahdar Khan, Nasiri Khan	5,000/3,500 (500 × 2-3h)	India	Irani	—	Father	M. A. 481, 496; Kamwar 286b; M. U., II 949-51; *Mirat-i-Aftab Numa*, 583
63.	Bahraji Pandhre	5,000/3,000 (500 × 2-3h)	India	Indian	Maratha	—	*Akh.* Ist Jamada II, 38th R.Y.

64.	Sa'adatmand Khan	5,000/3,000 (500×2-3h)	—	—	—	—	S.D.A. 207
65.	Sher Baz Khan	5,000/3,000	India	Indian	Afghan	—	*Akh.* 8th Jamada, I, 44th R.Y.
66.	Sume Shankar	5,000/3,000	India	Indian	Maratha-*Zamindar*	—	Isar Das, 165b; Mamuri, 206a; Khafi Khan II, 532
67.	Pars Ram	5,000/3,000	India	Indian	Maratha	—	Mamuri, 156b
68.	Sidi Khan Muhammad s/o Sidi Masud	5,000/3,000	India	Indian	Deccani-*Zamindar*	Father	Isár Das, 126a
69.	Khevji	5,000/2,500	India	Indian	Maratha	—	Waqai Papers Jaipur, 17th Ziqada, 47th R.Y.
70.	Hasan Ali Khan Bahadur Alamgir Shahi	5,000/2,500	India	Irani		Father	M. A. 189; T.M. 1097 A. H.; M.U.,I 593-99
71.	Shaikh Miran, Munawwar Khan or Mannu Khan	5,000/2,500	India	Indian	Deccani	—	M. A. 324, 364, 384; T.M. 22; M. U., III 654-55; Kamwar, 279A
72.	Sujan Rao or Shiv Bhan Rao	5,000/2,000	India	Indian	Maratha	—	M. A. 421; Kamwar, 291a; A. M. T. 123a
73.	Raja Bhim Singh	5,000/2,000	India	Indian	Rajput-*Zamindar*	Father	T. M. 6; S. D. A. 170; Z.A. 166a; M. A. 212, 369
74.	Saiyid Shah	5,000/2,000	—	—	Deccani	—	*Akh.* 24th Shawwal, 45th R. Y.
75.	Rana Ji Janardan	5,000/2,000	India	Indian	Maratha	—	*Daftar-i-Dewani*, No. 2978

S.N.	Name and Title	Rank highest during the period	Country of birth	Group	Sub-groups Rajput, Maratha, Afghan, Zamindar, etc.	Father or other blood relation in service	Authorities
76.	Janku Ji	5,000/1,200	India	Indian	Maratha	—	*Akh.* 26th Rajab, 37th R.Y.
77.	Jang Ju Khan Deccani	5,000/—	India	Indian	Afghan-Deccani	—	T. U., S. V.
78.	Nathu Ji Deccani	5,000/—	India	Indian	Maratha	—	A. M. T. 123a
79.	Pam Nayak Uncle of Pidia Nayak	5,000/—	India	Indian	*Zamindar*	—	*Dilkusha*, 95b; B.S. 750; T. M. 1099 A.H.
	Mansabdars of 3,000 to 4,500						
80.	Qasim Khan Kirmani	4,500/2,500 (1,000 × 2-3h)	Iran	Irani	—	—	*Akh.* 15th Safar, 36th R.Y.; Khafi Khan II, 284; T.M.7; M.U., III 123-26
81.	Mir Shamsuddin, Mukhtar Khan	4,000/2,500 (2-3h)	India	Irani	—	Father	*Akh.* 26th Rajab, 45 R. Y.; T. M. 1095 A. H; M. A. 460; M. U., III 620-23
82.	Ghazi Bijapuri, Randula Khan	4,000/4,000 (1,000 × 2-3h)	India	Indian	Deccani	—	M. U., II 309; A.M.T. 124a
83.	Muhammad Amir, Shah Quli Khan	4,000/4,000	—	—	Deccani	—	S.D.A. 222; M. A. 194

84.	Yaswant Rao or Baswant Rao Deccani	4,000/4,000	India	Indian	Maratha	—	M. A. 219; Kamwar, 271a; A. M. T. 123b
85.	Shaikh Abdullah, Ikhtisar Khan	4,000/4,000	India	Turani	—	—	*Akh.* 4th Rabi I, 42nd R.Y.; 15th Jamada II, 44th R.Y.; M. A. 324
86.	Abdullah Khan adopted son of Abul Hasan of Haiderabad	4,000/4,000	India	Indian	Deccani	—	M. A. 303; A.M.T. 124a
87.	Tarbiyat Khan Barlas, Shafiullah	4,000/4,000	Turan	Turani	—	—	T.M. 1096 A. H.; M.U..I 493-98
88.	Abdul Hameed	4,000/4,000	—	—	—	—	S.D.A. 124
89.	Mahda Ji Naik	4,000/4,000	India	Indian	—	Father	S.D.A. 134
90.	Miran b/o Nek Niyat Khan	4,000/4,000	India	Indian	—	Brother	*Akh.* 25th Jamada II, 44th R.Y.; S.D.A. 203
91.	Ghalib Khan	4,000/3,500	India	Turani	--	—	M. A. 473; A.M.T. 124a
92.	Muhammad Khalil, Zabardast Khan	4,000/3,000	India	Irani	—	Father	*Akh.* 22nd Ramzan, 40th R.Y.; 28th Muharram, 43rd R.Y.; M. A. 497; M. U., I 300; Kamwar 299a
93.	Ibrahim Ghori	4,000/3,000	India	Indian	Afghan	—	S.D.A. 219
94.	Muhammad Murad Khan, Saulat Jang Bahadur	4,000/3,000	India	Turani	—	Father	Mamuri, 200a; Kamwar, 292b

S.No.	Name and Title	Rank highest during the period	Country of birth	Group	Sub-groups Rajput, Maratha, Afghan, *Zamindar*, etc.	Father or other blood relation in service	Authorities
95.	Mir Sadruddin, Saf Shikan Khan	4,000/3,000	Iran	Irani	—	Father	Z.A. 160 b; Kamwar, 273A; M.U.,II 746-47
96.	Izzat Khan, Saf Shikan Khan	4,000/3,000	India	Indian	—	—	Mamuri, 174a; M. A. 150; Kamwar, 265a; Al. 855
97.	Sikandar Be Khan, Askandar Khan	4,000/3,000	Turan	Turani	—	—	M.A. 262,280; A.M.T. 124a
98.	Pir Muhammad, Aghar Khan	4,000/3,000	India	Turani	—	—	Khafi Khan, II, 246; Kamwar 268b; Isar Das, 164b;M.U.,I 274-77
99.	Abdur Razzaq Lari	4,000/3,000	Iran	Irani	Deccani	—	S.D.A.195; M.A.347;M.U.,II 818-21
100.	Muhammad Ramzani, Abu Nasar, Shaista Khan II	4,000/2,500	India	Irani	—	Father	M.A.442,516; Kamwar, 294b; M.U.,I 292-93; A.M.T. 124a
101.	Rao Bhao Singh Hara	4,000/2,500	India	Indian	Rajput-*Zamindar*	Father	Al.267; A.M.T.123b; Gahlot, *Rajputane Ka Itihas*, 74; Kamwar, 272b
102.	Faizullah Khan	4,000/2,000	India	Irani	—	Father	M.A.210; M.U.,III 26-30; T.M. 1092A.H.; A.M.T. 124a
103.	Namdar Khan	4,000/2,000	India	Irani	—	Father	M.U.,III 830-33

104.	Mir Muhammad Ishaq, Mukarram Khan	4,000/1,500 (600 × 2-3h)	India	Irani	—	Father	*Akh.* 11th Rabi II, 37th R.Y.; M.U., III 695-701; T.M.36
105.	Mir Muhammad Ibrahim, Muhtasham Khan	4,000/1,500 (500 × 2-3h)	India	Irani	—	Father	*Akh.* 19th Ramzan,25th R.Y.; *Akh.* 18th Shaban, 24th R.Y.
106.	Mir Muhammad Khalil, Tarbiyat Khan, son of Darab Khan	4,000/2,200	India	Irani	—	Father	M.A.381, 485,505; T.M.22; A.M.T.123b;M.U., I 498-503
107.	Muhammad Amin Khan, Chin Bahadur	4,000/1,500	Turan	Turani	—	Uncle	Kamwar, 279b; M.A.481, 506, 518; M.U.,I 346-50
108.	Mir Muhammad Askari, Aqil Khan Razi	4,000/1,000	India	Irani	—	—	T.M.8; M.U.,II 821-23; A.M. T.174b. *Riyaz-us-Shura*, 196; *Mirat-ul-Khiyal*, 360-62
109.	Ashraf Khan, Itimad Khan	4,000/500	India	Irani	—	Father	A.M.T.124b; M.U.,I 272-74; T.U.,S.V.
110.	Mir Muhammad Hadi, Hakim-ul-Mulk	4,000/500	Iran	Irani	—	—	Z.A.161a; M.A.362; Kamwar, 284b, 286a; M.U.,I 599-600
111.	Shaikh Ladu	4,000/—	India	Turani	Deccani	—	M.A. 297; Kamwar, 279a
112.	Raja Chhatar Sal Bundela	4,000/—	India	Indian	Rajput-*Zamindar*	Father	Kamwar, 291; *Dilkusha*, 157b-158a; M.U.,II 510-12
113.	Baji Chavan Dafle s/o Satva Ji Dafle	4,000/—	India	Indian	Maratha-*Zamindar*	Father	*Akhbarat*, Cited by Sarkar *History of Aurangzeb*, V, 209
114.	Siya Ji	4,000/—	India	Indian	Maratha	—	S.D.A.128; Sharma, *The Religious Policy of the Mughal Emperors*, 178

S.No.	Name and Title	Rank highest during the period	Country of birth	Group	Sub-groups Rajput, Maratha, Afghan, Zamindar, etc.	Father or other blood relation in service	Authorities
115.	Tahawur Khan, Padshah Quli Khan	4,000/—	India	Irani	—	Father	M.A.188; A.M.T.123b; M.U. I 447-53; T.M.1092 A.H.
116.	Mohibb-i-Ali, Askar Khan Haiderabadi	4,000/—	India	—	Deccani	—	*Dilkusha*, 95a; Kamwar, 286b M.A.369; *Proceedings of the Deccan History Conference*, 1945, p. 30, Document No.20; A.M.T. 126a
117.	Mir Shamsuddin alias Mukhlis Khan	3,500/3,000	Iran	Irani	—	Father	M.A.374.405; T.M.13; Z.A. 165b; Kamwar, 289a; M.U., III 641-44
118.	Jan Sipar Khan b/o Darab Khan Bani Mukhtar	3,500/2,500 (1,000×2-3h)	India	Irani	—	Father	*Akh.*6th Zilhij, 39th R.Y.; 11th Ramzan 43rd R.Y.; A.M.T. 127a
119.	Ilhamullah, Rashid Khan	3,500/3,000 (500×2-3h)	India	Indian	—	Father	S.D.A.181; M.U., II 303-305; Kamwar. 274b; A.M.T. 124b
120.	Mir Qamruddin, Mukhtar Khan	3,500/3,000 (1,000×2-3h)	India	Irani	—	Father	*Akh.*5th Jamada I, 38th R.Y.; M.A.220,370; Kamwar, 275a; M.U., III 655-60
121.	Mughal Khan, Arab Shaikh	3,500/3,000	Turan	Turani	—	Father	S.D.A. 170; M.A.246; M.U., III 623-25.
122.	Muhammad Yar Khan	3,500/3,000	India	Irani	—	Father	*Akh.*8th Rabi II, 39th R.Y.; M.A.384,462; Kamwar, 296a; M.U., III 706-711; *Mirat-i-Aftab Numa*, 592
123.	Muhammad Saeed, Feroz Khan	3,500/3,000	—	—	—	—	Isar Das, 164a

124.	Mian Hazin, Haibat Khan	3,500/3,000	—	—	—	—	Isar Das, 164a
125.	Anrudh Hara of Bundi	3,500/3,000	India	Indian	Rajput-*Zamindar*	Father	Isar Das, 95a; Kamwar, 273a; A.M.T. 127a
126.	Hameeduddin Khan Bahadur s/o Sardar *Khan*	3,500/2,800	India	Turani	—	Father	*Akh.* 26 Ramzan, 45th R.Y.; M.A. 485, 505; M. U., I 605-11
127.	Mirza Sadruddin Muhammad Khan Safvi, Shah Nawaz Khan	3,500/2,500	India	Irani	—	Father	M. A. 433, 439, 505; Kamwar, 292a; A. M. T. 124b; T.M. 30; M.U., III 692-94
128.	Safi Khan	3,500/2,000	India	Irani	—	Father	*Akh.* 28th Shawwal, 38th R. Y; T. M. 5
129.	Anup Singh s/o Rao Karan Bhuratiya.	3,500/2,000	India	Indian	Rajput-*Zamindar*	Father	Kamwar, 277b; M. U., II 289-91; A.M.T. 124b
130.	Jakia Deshmukh	3,500/2,000	India	Indian	Maratha-*Zamindar*	—	Mamuri, 200a; M.A. 513; Kamwar, 302a
131.	Muhammad Hasan, Himmat Khan	3,500/2,000	India	Irani	—	Father	M. A. 282; T. M. 7; M.U., III 949-51
132.	Indar Singh s/o Rai Singh	3,500/2,000 (300 × 2-3h)	India	Indian	Rajput-*Zamindar*	Father	*Dilkusha*, 76a; M. A. 175; M. U., II 236 T. U. (Habib Ganj Collection) 206a
133.	Raja Udat Singh Bundela of Orcha	3,500/1,600	India	Indian	Rajput-*Zamindar*	—	*Akh.* 25th Rabi I, 38th R.Y.; M. A. 350; Kamwar, 282a, 297b; A. M. T. 124b

S.No.	Name and Title	Rank highest during the period	Country of birth	Group	Sub-groups Rajput, Maratha, Afghan Zamindar etc.	Father or other blood relation in service	Authorities
134.	Qawamuddin Khan of Asfahan	3,500/1,500[1]	Iran	Irani	—	—	M. A. 139; M. U., III 109-115; T. M. 1091 A. H.
135.	Udai Singh Bundela	3,500/1,500	India	Indian	Rajput *zamindar*	—	M. U. II, 294; M.A. 473
136.	Mir Muhammad Hasan, Khanazad Khan Ruhullah *Khan* II	3,500/1,200	India	Irani	—	Father	M. A. 340, 349, 386, 404; T. M. 16; M. U., II 315-317; A. M. T. 126b
137.	Saiyid Ayub	3,500/700	—	—	—	—	*Akh.* 19th *Shawwal*, 45th R.Y.
138.	Saiyid Aughlan Siyadat Khan	3,500/500	Turan	Turani	—	—	Kamwar, 272a, 275a; M.U., II 494-96
139.	Tarsu Ji or Parsu Ji	3,500/—	India	Indian	Maratha	—	A. M. T. 125b
140.	Raja Bharat Singh of Shahpur	3,500/—	India	Indian	Rajput-*Zamindar*	Father	J. S. Gahlot, *Rajputanae Ka Itihas*, 558
141.	Buzurg Umeed Khan	3,500/—	India	Irani	—	Father	T. M. 6; M. U., I 453-54; A. T.M. 127a
142.	Imam Quli, Aghar Khan	3,500/—	India	Turani	—	—	T. M. 3; T. U. "A"
143.	Muhammad Ishaq, Tarbiyat Khan	3,500/—	India	Irani	—	Father	M. U., I 503; Kamwar, 296a; A. M. T. 124b

144.	Sultan Hussain alias Iftikhar Khan s/o Abdul Hadi, Asalat Khan	3,500/—	India	Irani		Father	T. M. 1092 A. H; M.U., I 252-55
145.	Dildost, Sardar Khan s/o Sarfaraz Khan Chaghta	3,000/3,000 (2,500 × 2-3h)	India	Turani	—	Father	Kamwar, 268b; T. M. 1098 A. H. , M.U.,II pp. 422-23
146.	Mir Ahmad, Sa 'adat Khan S/o Sa'adat Khan	3,000/3,000 (500 × 2-3h)	India	Irani		Father	Al. 1050; Kamwar, 277b
147.	Taku Ji	3,000/3,000	India	Indian	Maratha	—	*Akh.* 10th Ziqada, 38th R.Y. (Left the Mughal service in 1694)
148.	Dalpat Rao Bundela	3,000/3,000	India	Indian	Rajput-*Zamindar*	Father	*Dilkusha*, 157a; T. M. 23; M.A. 392; M.U.,II317-323
149.	Basdev, *Zamindar* of Chatlan Kara	3,000/3,000	India	Indian	*Zamindar*	—	M.A. 495; A.M.T.125b
150.	Abul Khair	3,000/3,000	India	Indian	—	Father	M.A. 515; M.U., II 687; Mamuri, 181b; Khafi Khan II, 392
151.	Neta Ji s/o Jan Rao	3,000/3,000	India	Indian	Maratha	—	S.D.A. 175
152.	Dholu Ji s/o Sambha Ji	3,000/3,000	India	Indian	Maratha	—	S.D.A. 176
153.	Anand Rao	3,000/3,000	India	Indian	Maratha	—	*Akh.* 10th Ziqada, 38th R.Y.
154.	Saifuddin Mahmud, alias Faqir Ullah, Saif Khan	3,000/2,500	India	Turani	—	Father	Kamwar, 265a; *Akh.* 5th Ramzan, 10th R.Y. Al.966; M.U.,II 479-85; A.M.T. 125b

[1]Mamuri, (149b,) says that Qawamuddin Khan had the rank of 5,000/3,000 but the other sources do not confirm the statement of Mamuri.

S.No.	Name and Title	Rank highest during the period	Country of birth	Group	Sub-groups Rajput, Maratha, Afghan, Zamindar, etc.	Father or other blood relation in service	Authorities
155.	Shaikh Mir, Tahawur Khan, Fedai Khan	3,000/2,500	India	Irani	—	Father	M.A.432, 493; M.U.,II 745-46
156.	Abu Muhammad Khan Bijapuri	3,000/2,500	India	Indian	Deccani	—	M.A. 351; A.M.T. 125a
157.	Saleh Khan, Fedai Khan	3,000/2,500	India	Irani		Father	*Akh.* 5th Jamada I, 38th R.Y; M.A. 368; M.U.,III 33-34
158.	Durga Das Rathor	3,000/2,500	India	Indian	Rajput	—	M.A. 395; Kamwar, 286b, 299b; Isar Das, 168a-b; A.M.T. 125b
159.	Bhan Purohit	3,000/2,500	India	Indian	Maratha-*Zamindar*	—	S.D.A. 187; (Name misread editor as Mian Parbat in S.D.A. 187.)
160.	Lutfullah Khan	3,000/2,500	India	Indian	—	Father	*Akh.* 3rd Safar, 36th R.Y; 27 Zilihij, 43rd R.Y;M.A. 412, 441; M.U.,III171-77
161.	Hafizullah Khan s/o Sa'adatullah Khan	3,000/2,000	India	Indian	—	Father	M.A. 407, 432; T.M.13; M.U.,II 520
162.	Indar Singh s/o Rana Raj Singh	3,000/2,000	India	Indian	Rajput	Father	M.A. 405, 481; Kamwar, 286a, 289a

163.	Kishna Ji	3,000/2,000	India	Indian	Maratha	—	Isar Das, 117a-b
164.	Saiyid Qasim Barha, Shahamat Khan	3,000/2,000	India	Indian	—	—	Kamwar, 268b; M.U.,II 681-83
165.	Irij Khan Qazalbash	3,000/2,000	India	Irani	—	Father	*Dilkusha*, 77b; A.M.T. 126b; M.U.,I 268-72
166.	Shariful Mulk, nephew of Abul Hasan of Haiderabad	3,000/2,000	India	—	Deccani	—	Kamwar, 276b; M.A.269; A.M.T. 125b; M.U.,II 688-907
167.	Lashkar Khan, Munawwar Khan Barha	3,000/2,000	India	Indian	—	Father	S.D.A. 171; Z.A. 165b; M.U.,II 465-68; M.A.314
168.	Muhammad Pairagi	3,000/2,000	India	Indian	—	—	S.D.A. 187
169.	Mir s/o Miran	3,000/2,000	India	Indian	—	Father	S.D.A. 203
170.	Muhammad Ali	3,000/2,000	India	—	—	—	S.D.A. 208
171.	Raja Udat Singh Bhaduriya	3,000/2,000	India	Indian	Rajput-*Zamindar*	Father	Kamwar, 272a, 277b; Saeed Ahmad, *Umrai Hunud*, p. 65; A.M.T. 131b
172.	Sohrab	3,000/2,000	—	—	Deccani	—	*Daftar-i-Dewani*, No.2978
173.	Sume Nayak	3,000/2,000	India	Indian	—	—	Kamwar, 299b; 300b
174.	Patang Rao	3,000/2,000	India	Indian	Maratha	—	Waqai papers Jaipur, 13th Zilhj, 25th R.Y. Reference given by Dr. Satish Chandra

S.No.	Name and Title	Rank highest during the period	Country of birth	Group	Sub-groups Rajput, Maratha, Afghan, *Zamindar*, etc.	Father or other blood relation in service	Authorities
175.	Jadrawat	3,000/2,000	India	Indian	Maratha	—	*Daftar-i-Dewani*, No. 2980, 31st R.Y. of Aurangzeb
176.	Jewa Ji Pandit	3,000/2,000	India	Indian	Maratha	—	Isar Das, 161a-b
177.	Man Singh s/o Rup Singh Rathor	3,000/1,800	India	Indian	Rajput-*Zamindar*	Father	*Akh.* 4th and 24th Shaban, 24th R.Y; M.A. 405; M.U.,II 270; Kamwar, 286b, 289b
178.	Khawaja Hamid, Hamid Khan Bahadur s/o Abad Khan	3,000/1,700	India	Turani	—	Father	M.A. 481; A.M.T. 125b; M.U.,III 765-69
179.	Rao Ram Singh Hara	3,000/1,500 (200 × 2-3h)	India	Indian	Rajput-*Zamindar*	Father	*Akh.* 15th Rabi II, 44th R.Y; M.A. 505; T.M.23; M.U.,II 323-24
180.	Saiyid Sher Khan	3,000/1,500 (200 × 2-3h)	India	Indian	—	Father	*Akh.* 14th Zilhij, 25th R.Y; T.M. 1095 A.H.
181.	Muhammad Taqi, Atibar Khan alias Wafir Haiderabadi	3,000/1,500	India	—	Deccani	—	S.D.A. 170; Z.A.165b; M.A.269; T.U. "A"
182.	Ali Quli Khan	3,000/1,500	India	Irani	—	Father	S.D.A. 188; Kamwar,288a
183.	Abdul Qadir s/o Abdul Razzaq Lari	3,000/1,500	India	Irani	Deccani	—	*Akh.* 27th Shawwal, 38th R.Y; M.A. 271; Kamwar, 276b

184.	Aziz Khan Bahadur Chaghta s/o Bahadur Rohela	3,000/1,500	India	Indian	Afghan	Father	T.M. 48; M.A. 518; *Akh.* 4th Zilhij, 38th R.Y.; Kamwar, 302b
185.	Saiyid Hamid Khan, Mujahid Khan s/o Murtaza Khan	3,000/1,500	—	Turani	—	Father	Kamwar, 268b, 284a; M.U.,III598
186.	Badar Ji or Pada Ji	3,000/1,500	India	Indian	Maratha	—	M.A.480; A.M.T.125b
187.	Qalia Tajammul Zamindar of Tibbat	3,000/1,000 (500×2-3h)	India	Indian	*Zamindar*	Father	*Akh.* 12th Rabi I, 43rd R.Y.
188.	Mir Isa, Himmat Khan	3,000/1,000 (500×2-3h)	India	Turani	—	Father	T.M.1092 A.H.; M.U.,III 946-48
189.	Burhanuddin, Itimad Khan, Fazil Khan	3,000/1,400	Iran	Irani	—	Uncle	T.M.14; *Akh.* 32rd Muharram, 44th R.Y;M. U.,III 34-38; M.A. 317, 369, 424
190.	Muhammad Sadiq, Fateh-Ullah Khan Bahadur Alamgir Shahi	3,000/1,400	Turan	Turani		—	M.A. 384, 443, 472, 496; M.U.,III 40-47; Kamwar, 273a
191.	Muazzam Khan, Siyadat Khan	3,000/1,200	India	Irani	—	Father	T.M.10; S.D.A. 170; M.A. 246; Kamwar, 274a
192.	Khuda Banda Khan	3,000/1,200	India	Irani	—	Father	T.M. 22; M.U.,I 814-16; M.A. 432, 514
193.	Kamgar Khan	3,000/1,000	India	Irani	—	Father	T.M. 27; S.D.A. 170;M.A. 405; M.U., III 159-60; Kamwar, 289a

S.No.	Name and Title	Rank highest during the period	Country of birth	Group	Sub groups Rajput, Maratha, Afghan Zamindar etc.	Father or other blood relation in service	Authorities
194.	Nahar Khan	3,000/1,000	India	Indian	Afghan	—	*Akh.*11th Muharram,46th R.Y.
195.	Saiyid Abul Hasan Haiderabadi	3,000/1,000	India	Indian	Deccani	—	S.D.A.168
196.	Baji Rao	3,000/1,000	India	Indian	Maratha	—	*Akhbarat* 38th R.Y. Sharma, "The Religious Policy, of the Mughal Emperors" p. 179
197.	Iftikhar Khan s/o Shariful Mulk Haiderabadi	3,000/1,000	India	—	Deccani	Father	M.A. 297; M.U.,II689; Kamwar, 279a; A.M.T. 125a
198.	Saiyid Mubarak, Murtaza Khan	3,000/1,000	India	Turani	—	—	*Akh.* 9th Zilhij; 45 R.Y; M.U.,III 644-46;M.A.273
199.	Hakim Shamsa, Shamsuddin Khan	3,000/1,000	—	—	Deccani	—	M.A.190;A.M.T.125b
200.	Mir Ali Naqi Safvi, Mirza Safvi Khan	3,000/1,000	Iran	Irani	—	—	T.M. 23; M. A. 482; Kamwar, 299a; M.U.,III 653-54; A.M.T.126a
201.	Amir Khan Sindhi, Mir Abdul Karim, Multafat Khan, Khanazad Khan	3,000/1,000	India	Irani	—	Father	M.A.330; T.M.41; M.U.,I 303-310

202.	Muhammad Badi Balkhi	3,000/700	Balkh	Turani	—	Father	*Akh.* 5th Zilhij, 38th R.Y.; M.A. 350; Kamwar, 284b; M.U.,III 636-37
203.	Saiyid Ali, Rizvi Khan	3,000/500	India	Turani		Father	M.U.,II 307-309;A.M.T. 124b
204.	Raja Bishan Singh	3,000/400	India	Indian	Rajput-*Zamindar*	Father	M.A.217;T.M.11;M.U.,II 303
205.	Shaikh Makhdom Thattavi, Fazil Khan	3000/—	India	Indian	—	—	M.A.191; M.U.,III 32-33; A.M.T.126a
206.	Shamsher Khan Tarin, Husain Khan	3,000/—	India	Indian	Afghan	—	M.U.,II 683-84; A.M.T.125a
207.	Jadaun Rai Deccani	3,000/—	India	Indian	Maratha-*Zamindar*	—	*Dilkusha,* 79b; A.M.T.125b
208.	Muhammad Ishaq, Najabat Khan	3,000/—	India	Turani	—	Father	T.M. 13
209.	Kair Andesh Khan Kambo Meeruthi.	3,000/—	India	Indian	—		*Dilkusha,* 125a; M.A.441; *Mirat Aftab Numa,* 581
210.	Jagat Rai Deshmukh of Nusrat Abad	3,000/—	India	Indian	Maratha-*Zamindar*	—	A.M.T. 125b
211.	Nurullah Khan	3,000/—	—	—	—	—	*Riyaz-us Salatin,* p. 224, *Akh.* 21st R.Y.
212.	Saiyid Murad Ali, Mubarik Khan.	*Umrai Uzam*	India	Irani	—	Father	*Raquaim-i-Karaim,* 3a-b, 9a

S. No.	Name and Title	Rank highest during the period	Country of birth	Group	Sub-groups Rajput, Maratha, Afghan, *Zamindar*, etc.	Father or other blood relation in service	Autherities
		Mansabdars of 1,000 to 2,700					
213.	Yalingtosh Bahadur	2,700/700	India	Turani	—	—	Kamwar,268a, 276b; M.U., III 971-72.Manucci,II,43
214.	Alah Yar Khan	2,500/2,500 (1,000×2-3h)	India	Turani	—	Father	*Akh.* 9th Shawwal, 25th R.Y; T.M. 47
215.	Raja Debi Singh Bundela	2,500/2,500 (500×2-3h)	India	Indian	Rajput-*Zamindar*	Father	Mamuri, 154a; S.D.A.117; Al. 758
216.	Mukhtar Beg, Nawazish Khan	2,500/2,500 (500×2-3h)	Turkey	Turani	—	Father	*Akh.* 23rd Safar, 36th R.Y; M.A.195; M.U.,I 246-47; Kamwar, 268, 277b
217.	Kishore Singh Hara of Kota	2,500/3,000	India	Indian	Rajput-*Zamindar*	Father	*Akh.* 28th Jamada, II, 39th R.Y; *Dilkusha*, 117b; M.U.,II 323-24
218.	Khawaja Muhammad Arif, Mujahid Khan.	2,500/2,800	India	Turani	—	Father	*Akh.*16th Rabi II, 39th R.Y; Kamwar, 273a; M.A.199,241; M.U.,III 123
219.	Rustam Dil Khan	2,500/2,500	India	Irani	—	Father	*Hadiqai Alam*, 2b-3b; *Akh.*11th Ramzan, 43rd R.Y; M.A.493-94; Kamwar, 299b; M.U.,II 324-28; T.M. 25

220.	Bahruz Khan	2,500/1,500 (1,000 × 2-3h)	—	—	—	—	*Akh.* 26th Rajab, 45th R.Y.
221.	Ibadullah	2,500/2,400	—	—	—	—	*Akh.* 24th Rajab, 24th R.Y.
222.	Subh Karan Bundela	2,500/2,200	India	Indian	Rajput-*Zamindar*	—	A.M.T. 131a
223.	Raja Ram Singh Sisodia	2,500/2,000	India	Indian	Rajput-*Zamindar*	Father	A.M.T. 123a
224.	Mir Muhammad Fazil, Qamruddin Khan	2,500/2,000	India	Turani	—	Father	S.D.A.171; M.A. 332
225.	Manku Ji Deccani s/o Tanka Ji	2,500/2,000	India	Indian	Maratha	—	S.D.A.179; M.A. 297
226.	Mahan Ji s/o Manku Ji	2,500/2,000	India	Indian	Maratha	Father	S.D.A. 134
227.	Sambha Ji Bandhara s/o La Ji Bandhara.	2,500/2,000	India	Indian	Maratha	—	S.D.A. 179
228.	Sadhu Ji S/o Nagu Ji	2,500/2,000	India	Indian	Maratha	Father	S.D.A. 179
229.	Bhali Rao s/o Karlu Ji Bandhara.	2,500/2,000	India	Indian	Maratha	—	S.D.A. 179
230.	Naro Ji Raghav	2,500/2,000	India	Indian	Maratha	—	*Daftar-i-Dewani*, No. 2981
231.	Rao Budh Singh of Bundi	2,500/1,000 (2-3h)	India	Indian	Rajput-*zamindar*	—	*Akh.*2nd Rabi I, 43rd R.Y; A.M.T.126b; *Akh.* Ramzan, 45th R.Y.
232.	Muhammad Rashid, Arslan Khan, Khanazad Khan, Saeed Khan.	2,500/1,800	India	Turani	—	Father	M.A.440; T.M. 17

S.No.	*Name and Title*	*Rank highest during the period*	*Country of birth*	*Group*	*Sub-groups Rajput, Maratha, Afghan, Zamindar etc.*	*Father or other blood relation in service*	*Authorities*
233.	Arslan Quli, Arslan Khan s/o Ilahwardi Khan	2,500/800 (2-3h)	India	Irani	—	Father	M.U.,I 277; A.M.T. 128b
234.	Tahir Shaikh, Tahir Khan	2,500/1,500	Turan	Turani	—	—	M.U.,II 751-54
235.	Najabat Khan s/o Saiyid Muzaffar Haiderabadi	2,500/1,500	India	—	Deccani	Father	Kamwar, 272b, 297a
236.	Abdul Qadir, Dianat Khan	2,500/1,500	India	Irani	—	Father	*Akh.*13 Rabi II, 39th R.Y; M U.,II 59-63; A.M.T. 127b
237.	Bharawar Khan, Najabat Khan s/o Mirza Shuja Najabat Khan	2,500/1,500	India	Turani	—	Grand father	S.D.A.170; M.A.470; M.U., II 870-72
238.	Mahad Ji Mane	2,500/1,500	India	Indian	Maratha	—	*Akh.* 11th Rajab, 39th R.Y.
239.	Shaikh Abdullah (servant of Shah Alam)	2,500/1,000 (500 × 2-3h)	—	—	—	—	Z.A. 163b
240.	Abdul Qadir, Mutabar Khan	2,500/1,500	India	Indian	—	—	S.D.A.181; Khafi Khan II, 402; M.U.,III 565-66
241.	Fateh brother of Nek Neyat Khan	2,500/1,500	India	Indian	—	Brother	S.D.A. 203
242.	Raghu Ji	2,500/1,500	India	Indian	Maratha	—	*Akh.* 5th Zilhij, 38th R.Y.

243.	Khwaja Mir Khawafi, Salabat Khan	2,500/1,200	India	Irani	—	Father	M.A.177,341; M.U.,II 742-46 A.M.T. 126b
244.	Abdul Nabi b/o Hasan Khan Rohala	2,500/1,200	India	Indian	Afghan	Brother	S.D.A. 188, 208
245.	Saiyid Sherzaman Barha, Muzaffar Khan	2,500/1,200	India	Indian	—	Father	T.M.1097 A.H; M.U.,II 465; Al. 54, 291
246.	Muhammad Ali Khan s/o Hakim Daud	2,500/1,000	India	Irani	—	Father	Kamwar, 272a; T.M. 1098 A.H; M.U.,III 625-27
247.	Kamaluddin Khan	2,500/1,000	India	Indian	Afghan	Father	*Akh.* 9th Zilhij, 38th R.Y;S.D. A.171; M.A.171;A.M.T.128a
248.	Debi Das, Ikhlas Kesh, Ikhlas Khan	2,500/1,000	India	Indian	—	—	M.U.,I 350-52
249.	Mir Sultan Husain, Talai Muhammad Yar Khan	2,500/1,000	India	Irani	—	Brother	*Akh.*15th Jamada I, 44th R.Y.; M.A.350; A.M.T. 127b
250.	Saifullah Khan alias Muftakhar Khan	2,500/1,000	India	Irani	—	Father	Z.A.161b; T.M.4; Kamwar, 271b
251.	Kondaji	2,500/1.000	India	Indian	Maratha-*Zamindar*	—	*Akh.* 4th Jamada I, 43rd R.Y. M.U.,III 580
252.	Munim Khan	2,500/1,000	India	Turani	—	Father	M.A.459,497; Kamwar, 299b; A.M.T.127a;M.U.,III667-77
253.	Siyadat Khan s/o Saiyid Aughlan	2,500/700	India	Turani	—	Father	Kamwar,289b; M.A.407, 473; M.U.,II 495

S.No.	Name and Title	Rank highest during the period	Country of birth	Group	Sub-groups Rajput, Maratha, Afghan, Zamindar etc.	Father or other blood relation in service	Authorities
254.	Hayat Beg Khan, Baqi Khan	2,500/600	India	Turani	—	Father	Kamwar, 30lb,302a; M.A.497 515; M.U.I, 458-61
255.	Ahmadullah	2,500/400	—	—	—	—	*Akh.*20th Ramzan, 40th R.Y.
256.	Muhammad Ibrahim, Multafat Khan, Khanazad Khan	2,500/400	India	Irani	—	Father	M.A.351,407,440,459; T.M. 1092 A.H; M.U.,III 611-13
257.	Muhammad Masih, Murid Khan, Khanazad Khan	2,500/400	India	Turani	—	Father	*Akh.* 18th Shaban, 24th R.Y.; M.U.,III 949
258.	Dindar Khan alias Marahmat Khan	2,500/250	Iran	Irani	—	Father	Kamwar, 270b; M.U.,III833; A.M.T. 126b
259.	Inayatullah Khan	2,500/250	India	Irani	—	—	M.A.441;505; Kamwar, 288b; M.U.,II 828-32
260.	Kishan Singh	2,500/—	India	Indina	Rajput-*Zamindar*	Father	*Akh.* 24th Rajab, 24th R.Y.
261.	Ghazanfar Khan S/o Qabad Khan	2,500/—	India	Turani	—	Father	*Dilkusha,* 124a-b; Kamwar, 286b,270b
262.	Ram Chand *Zamindar* and *Thanedar* of Kahtanun	2,000/3,000	India	Indian	Maratha-*Zamindar*	—	M.A.423; A.M.T. 127b
263.	Rao Ram Chand s/o Dalpat Bundela.	2,000/2,000 (1,000×2-3h)	India	Indian	Rajput-*Zamindar*	Father	*Akh.* 27th Muharram, 44th R.Y.; A.M.T. 127b

264.	Muhammad Quli, Mutaqad Khan.	2,000/2,000 (1,000×2-3h)	India	Turani	—	Father	*Akh.* 43rd R.Y.; M.A.80; M.U. II, 870-71; Al. 964
265.	Muhammad Hadi Haiderabadi, Hadi Khan	2,000/2,400	India	—	Deccani	—	*Akh.* 13th Ramzan, 43rd R.Y.
266.	Mahman Ji	2,000/2,000 (500×2-3h)	India	Indian	Maratha	—	S.D.A. 209
267.	Mana Ji (Maya Ji) s/o Anku Ji	2,000/2,000	India	Indian	Maratha	—	*Akh.* Jamada, I, 44 R.Y.
268.	Jai Singh Sawai	2,000/2,000	India	Indian	Rajput-*Zamindar*	Father	*Akh.*9th Ramzan, 44th R.Y.; M.A.424,456; Mamuri, 201b M.U.,II 81-83
269.	Abdullah s/o Rustam Zaman Bijapuri	2,000/2,000	India	Indian	Deccani	Father	S.D.A.124; M.A.190
270.	Rao Dena Ji (Vena Ji) Salvi	2,000/2,000	India	Indian	Maratha	—	*Daftar-i-Dewani*, No. 2980
271.	Alah Dad Khan Kheshgi	2,000/1,000 (2-3h)	India	Indian	Afghan	Father	*Akh.* 16th Rajab, 24th R.Y.; A.M.T.127a; M.A.473-74; M U.,III 778-81; *Dastur-al Amal-i-Shah Jahani*, Add. 6588, 25a
272.	Muhammad Ibrahim Qureshi, Shamsher Khan	2,000/1,000 (600×2-3h)	India	Indian	—	Uncle	*Akh.* 26th Safar, 45 R.Y.; T.U. "*Sh*"; Kamwar, 297a
273.	Muhammad Taqi, s/o Darab Khan Bani Mukhtar	2,000/1,500	India	Irani	—	Father	M.A.221; Kamwar, 271b
274.	Ijtima Khan	2,000/1,500	—	—	—	—	T.U. "A"

S.No.	Name and Title	Rank highest during the period	Country of birth	Group	Sub-groups Rajput, Maratha, Afghan, *Zamindar*, etc.	Father or other blood relation in service	Authorities
275.	Lodi Khan	2,000/1,500	India	Indian	Afghan	—	*Akh.* 13th Rajab, 24th R.Y.
276.	Abdur Rasul Khan Bilgrami	2,000/1,500	India	Indian	—	—	S.D.A.191; *Akh.* 16th Ziqada, 40th R.Y.; M.U.,II 836-37
277.	Yasin Khan	2,000/1,500	—	—	—	—	*Akh.* Jamada I, 44th R.Y.
278.	Ram Singh s/o Ratan Rathor	2,000/1,400	India	Indian	Rajput-*Zamindar*	Father	Mamuri, 163b-164a; Al. 486
279.	Hasan Ali Khan, Abdullah Khan Barha(Later Qutb-ul-Mulk)	2,000/1,000	India	Indian	—	Father	*Akh.* 26th Rajab, 45th R.Y; M.U.,III 130-140
280.	Shiv Singh	2,000/1,300	India	Indian	Rajput	—	S.D.A. 171
281.	Asadullah, Ikram Khan Deccani	2,000/1,200	India	Indian	Deccani	Father	S.D.A.172;M.U.,III564-65
282.	Muhammad Ibrahim, Salabat Khan	2,000/1,200	—	—	—	—	S.D.A. 170
283.	Jafar Khan, Murshid Quli Khan, Kartalab Khan	2,000/1,100	India	Indian	—	—	M.A. 483; M.U.,III 751-55
284.	Teema Ji	2,000/1,000 (100×2-3h)	India	Indian	Maratha	—	S.D.A. 209
285.	Afrasiyab Khan	2,000/1,000	Turkey	Turani	—	Father	Kamwar,270a; M.U.,I 244-46; A.M.T. 131a

286.	Isu Ji Deccani	2,000/1,000	India	Indian	Maratha	—	Kamwar, 279a; Saeed Ahmad, "*Umrai Hunud*", 373
287.	Arju Ji s/o Shambha Ji	2,000/1,000	India	Indian	Maratha	—	M.A. 258
288.	Sar Andaz Khan Panni Bijapuri	2,000/1,000	India	Indian	Afghan-Deccani	—	*Akh.* 25th Ramzan, 47th R.Y.; M.A.470; *Farhat-ul-Nazirin*, 173a
289.	Obedullah Khan b/o Khwaja Lutfullah Khan	2,000/1,000	—	—	—	Brother	M.A. 459
290.	Turktaz Khan	2,000/1,000	Turan	Turani	—	—	*Akh.* 5th Rajab, 24th R.Y.; Khafi Khan II, 473
291.	Jagat Singh Hara	2,000/1,000	India	Indian	Rajput-*zamindar*	Father	Mamuri, 164a; *Dilkusha*, 79b; M.U.III, 510; A.M.T. 128b
292.	Mirand s/o Nek Niyat Khan	2,000/1,000	India	Indian	—	Father	S.D.A. 203
293.	Sidi Yaqut	2,000/1,000	India	Indian	Deccani-*Zamindar*	Father	S.D.A. 207
294.	Murtaza s/o Masud Khan	2,000/1,000	India	Indian	—	Father	S.D.A. 225
295.	Khalilullah Khan, Amanullah Khan	2,000/1,000	India	Irani	—	Father	T.M.22; Kamwar,275b; T.U. "A"; A.M.T. 128b
296.	Abu Mansur, Iradat Khan, Itiqad Khan	2,000/1,000	India	Irani	—	Father	S.D.A.170; T.M.14; M.A. 251; 351
297.	Mirza Inayatullah, Saif Khan s/o Faqirullah.	2,000/1,000	India	Turani	—	Father	T.M.25; A.M.T. 127b

S.No.	Name and Title	Rank highest during the period	Country of birth	Group	Sub-groups Rajput, Maratha, Afghan, Zamindar, etc.	Father or other blood relation in service	Authorities
298.	Abdur Rahman Bijapuri, Sharza Khan	2,000/1,000	India	—	Deccani	—	S.D.A.70; T.U. "*Sh*"
299.	Maku Ji	2,000/1,000	India	Indian	Maratha	—	*Akh.* 20th Ramzan, 40th R.Y.
300.	Haji Ali	2,000/1,000	—	—	—	—	*Akh.* 20th Ramzan, 40th R.Y.
301.	Sujan Singh s/o Anup Singh	2,000/1,000	India	Indian	Rajput	Father	*Azam-al Harb*, 168, *Akh.* Ziqada, 44th R.Y.
302.	Ghazi	2,000/1,000	—	—	—	—	S.D.A. 207
303.	Ani Rai Brahman *dewan-i-tan.*	2,000/1,000	India	Indian		—	S.Ahmad, *Umrai Hunud*, 64
304.	Jahangir Quli Khan	2,000/900	—	—	—	—	*Akh.* 9th Ramzan, 13th R.Y.; Kamwzr, 277b; A.M.T.132a
305.	Saiyid Azmatullah Khan	2,000/900	India	—	—	Father	*Akh.* 2nd Rajab, 43rd R.Y.; M.A. 381; A.M.T. 128a
306.	Latif Khan *darogha* of *ghusal Khana*	2,000/700	—	—	—	—	*Halat-i-Mumalik Makrusai Alamgiri* 179a; *Raqaim-i-Karaim*, 6a
307.	Abul Makarim, Jan Nisar Khan	2,000/700	India	Irani	—	Father	M.A.341; M.U., I 537-40; *Dilkusha*, 126a; Kamwar, 283a

308.	Mirza Matlab, Matlab Khan, Murtaza Khan	2,000/700	India	Irani	—	—	M.A.402; 505; T.M. 22; M.U.,III 650-53
309.	Nazar Beg, Aurang Khan	2,000/700	Turan	Turani	—	Father	M.A. 194
310.	Bulbaris Khan	2,000/600	Turan	Turani	—	—	M.A.439; Kamwar, 292a
311.	Ali Alam Haiderabadi	2,000/500	—	—	Deccani	—	*Akh.*8th Ziqada, 39th R.Y.
312.	Rao Ji	2,000/500	India	Indian	Maratha	—	*Akh.*25th Jamada, II 44th R.Y.
313.	Bahar Nabi	2,000/500	India	Idian	—	—	S.D.A. 199
314.	Sher Andaz Khan or Teer Andaz Khan	2,000/500	India	Irani	—	Father	S.D.A.198; T.M.20; Kamwar, 297a
315.	Dau Ji (left the Mughal Service in 1694)	2,000/500	India	Indian	Maratha	—	*Akh.*10th Ziqada, 38th R.Y.
316.	Jau Ji	2,000/500	India	Indian	Maratha	—	*Akh.*20th Ramzan, 40th R.Y.
317.	Mirza Muizz-Fitrat, Mosvi Khan	2,000/400	Iran	Irani	—	—	M.A.312; T.M.2; Kamwar, M.U.,III633-36; *Riyaz-us.-Shura*, f.337. *Mirat-ul-Khiyal*,p358
318.	Muhammad Shuja, Shuja' at Khan, Saf Shikan Khan	2,000/300	Iran	Irani	—	Father	M.A.153; M.U.,III 114-15; Kamwar, 263-b, 273a-b; A.M.T. 128a
319.	Darbar Khan Khawaja Sara.	2,000/300	—	—	—	—	T.M.1096 A.H; Al 960

S.No.	Name and Title	Rank highest during the period	Country of birth	Group	Sub-groups Rajput, Maratha, Afghan Zamindar etc.	Father or other blood relation in service	Authorities
320.	Abdur Rahman Khan s/o Islam Khan Mashhadi	2,000/200	India	Irani	—	Father	T.M.14; M.U.,I167; Kamwar 289b
321.	Mirak Muinuddin, Amanat Khan Khawafi	2,000/200	India	Irani	—	Father	M.U.,I 258-68; A.M.T.127a
322.	Shah Khwaja Husaini, Sharif Khan	2,000/—	—	Turani	—	—	T.M. 1093 A.H.
323.	Hayat Shaikh, Mughal Khan, Tahir Khan	2,000/—	India	Turani	—	Father	Kamwar, 268a; T.M.20; A.M.T. 125a
324.	Sulaiman Khan	2,000/—	India	Indian	Afghan Deccani	Brother	M.A.518; *Farhat-ul-Nazirin*, 182b; A.M.T.128b; M.U.,II 64-68
325.	Mir Jamaluddin Husain, Safdar Khan	2,000/—	India	Irani	—	Father	M.A.335; T.M.2; Kamwar, 282a; M.U.I, 252
326.	Uzbek Khan Naudarti	2,000/—	Turan	Turani	—	—	T.U. "A"
327.	Qazi Haider, Haider Khan, Munshi of Shivaji	2,000/—	—	—	Deccani	—	Kamwar, 274b; M.A.234; T.U. "H"
328.	Itimad Khan alias Mulla Tahir	2,000/—	—	Irani	—	—	Z.A.163a;Khafi Khan,II,380
329.	Madho Ji Narain	2,000/—	India	Indian	Maratha	—	*Akhbarat* as cited by Sarkar, *History of Aurangzeb*,V, 211

330.	Lachman Pati	2,000/—	India	Indian	Hindu	—	S.D.A. 208
331.	Abdul Aziz Miyana	2,000/—	India	Indian	Afghan Deccani	—	*Akh.*20th Ramzan, 40th R.Y.
332.	Rustam Ali alias Inayat Khan	2,000/—	—	—	—	—	T.M. 1093 A.H.
333.	Mirza Askari, Wazir Khan	2,000/—	India	Irani	—	Grand father	*Mirat-i-Aftab Numa*, 594; *Lendisyana*, *Diplomatic Correspondence of Aurangzeb*, folios unmarked
334.	Mir Khan Bahmani, Multafat Khan	1,500/1,500 (1,200×2-3h)	India	Indian	—	—	*Akh.*24th Rajab, 24th R.Y.; S.D.A.173; Kamwar, 289b
335.	Raja Durag Singh	1,500/1,200 (2-3h)	India	Indian	Rajput-*Zamindar*	—	S.D.A. 171
336.	Sidi Qasim, Faulad Khan	1,500/1,200 (1,100×2-3h)	India	Indian	Deccani	—	*Akh.*18th Shaban, 24th R.Y.
337.	Khudadad Khan Kheshgi	1,500/1,000 (2-3h)	India	Indian	Afghan	Father	S.D.A.188; *Akh.*20th Rajab, 24th R.Y.
338.	Inayat Khan	1,500/1,000 (2-3h)	India	Irani	—	Father	*Akh.* 6th Shawwal, 25th R.Y.; Kamwar, 270b, 280a
339.	Muhammad Baqa, Muzaffar Khan s/o Khan-i-Jahan Kokaltash	1,500/1,000 (2-3h)	India	Irani	—	Father	S.D.A.140; Kamwar, 273a
340.	Manohar Das Qaladar of Sholapur	1,500/1,500 (500×2-3h)	India	Indian	Rajput	—	*Akh.*14th Zilhij, 25th R.Y.

S.NO.	Name and Title	Rank highest during the period	Country of birth	Group	Sub-groups Rajput, Maratha, Afghan, Zamindar, etc.	Father or other blood relation in service	Authorities
341.	Raja Jaswant Singh Bundela	1,500/1,000 (2-3h)	India	Indian	Rajput-*Zamindar*	Father	S.D.A.150-51; Mamuri, 165a; M.A.273; M.U.,II 293-94
342.	Pahar Singh Gaur, *Zamindar* of Inderkhi	1,500/1,000 (2-3h)	India	Indian	Rajput-*Zamindar*	—	Isar Das, 94a
343.	Nurul-Dahr Barha, Saiyid Saif Khan	1,500/700	India	Indian	—	Father	M.A.266,341; Kamwar, 283a
344.	Shukrullah Khan Khawafi	1,500/1,000 (500×2-3h)	—	Irani	—	—	*Akh.*20th Shaban, 37th R.Y.; Kamwar, 270a; T.M.8
345.	Gopal Singh s/o Raja Sarup Singh	1,500/1,500	India	Indian	Rajput-*Zamindar*	Father	A.M.T.131b; Al. 1056
346.	Shiv Ji s/o Maru Ji	1,500/1,500	India	Indian	Maratha	—	S.D.A. 177
347.	Nur Singh	1,500/1,400	India	Indian	Rajput	—	*Akh.*12th Shawwal, 40th R.Y.
348.	Abdul Salam s/o Abdur Rahim Miyana.	1,500/1,300	India	Indian	Afghan	Father	S.D.A. 126
349.	Wafadar Khan, Zabardast Khan g/s Saeed Khan	1,500/900 (400×2-3h)	India	Turani	—	Grand-father	Kamwar, 275a; M.A. 255; Hatim Khan, 164a
350.	Yaqub Khan	1,500/1,300	India	Irani	—	Father	Z.A.163b; M.A.495; M.U.I., 300

351.	Qalandar Beg, Qalandar Khan	1,500/1,000 (200×2-3h)	India	Turani	—	Father	S.D.A.74; M.U.II, 192-194
352.	Kakar Khan	1,500/1,200	India	Indian	Afghan	—	*Akh.*8th Ziqada, 39th R.Y.; M.A.350; A.M.T. 131b
353.	Sidi Faulad, Faulad Khan	1,500/1,200	India	Indian	—	—	Kamwar,250b,270b; T.M. 1092 A.H.
354.	Nusrat Khan, Sipahdar Khan s/o Khan-i-Jahan Kokaltash	1,500/1,000 (200×2-3h)	India	Irani	—	Father	S.D.A.140; M.A.241; Kamwar, 273a
355.	Bijai Singh	1,500/1,200	India	Indian	Rajput	Father	*Dilkusha*, 167b; M.A.424; M.U.II,81
356.	Azizullah Khan s/o Khalilullah Khan	1,500/1,000	India	Irani	—	Father	Kamwar,284a; M.A.349,461; M.U.II, 823-24
357.	Muhkam Singh	1,500/1,000	India	Indian	Rajput *zamindar*	Father	M.U.II, 147
358.	Dilir Khan or Dilawar Khan s/o Bahadur Khan Rohela.	1,500/1,000	India	Indian	Afghan	Father	*Akh.*28th Ziqada, 38th R.Y.
359.	Shukrullah Khan Najm Sani, Askar Khan	1,500/1,000	India	Irani	—	Father	M.A.242; Kamwar, 273b
360	Sher Afgan	1,500/1,000	India	Irani	—	Father	A.M.T.131a; M.A. 381
361.	Shaikh Nurullah, Qadir Dad Khan Ansari	1,500/1,000	India	Indian	—	Father	S.D.A.136; T.M.4; M.U.III, 140
362.	Muhammad Mansur, Makarmat Khan	1,500/1,000	Iran	Irani	—	Grand-father	M.A.303; M.U.III, 632 Isar Das, 133b

S.NO.	Name and Title	Rank highest during the period	Country of birth	Group	Sub-groups Rajput, Maratha, Afghan Zamindar etc.	Father or other blood relation in service	Authorities
363.	Daundi Rao or Bonbir Rao	1,500/1,000	India	Indian	Maratha	—	M.U.I,498;M.A.382;A.M.T. 131a
364.	Fredun Khan	1,500/1,000	India	Indian	—	Father	M.A.506; A.M.T. 131b
365.	Kan Rao (or Kishan Rao) s/o Kaku Ji	1,500/1,000	India	Indian	Maratha	—	S.D.A.177; *Akh.* Jamada, II, 44th R.Y.
366.	Rana Ji	1,500/1,000	India	Indian	Maratha	—	*Akh.*5th Ziqada, 38th R.Y.
367.	Saiyid Ibrahim	1,500/1,000	India	Indian	—	—	*Akh.* Ist Shaban, 24th R.Y.
368.	Behari Chand s/o Dalpat Bundela.	1,500/1,000	India	Indian	Rajput	Father	*Azam-al Harb*, 168; *Farhat. ul-Nazirin*, 206b.
369.	Abdul Samad Khan	1,500/1,000	India	Indian	Afghan	—	*Akh.*19th Rajab, 43rd R.Y. *Mirat-i Aftab Numa*, 586
370.	Sadhu Ji s/o Shiv Ji Nelkar	1,500/1,000	India	Indian	Maratha	Father	S.D.A. 177
371.	Shiv Singh s/o Nur Singh	1,500/1,000	India	Indian	Rajput	Father	Kamwar, 297a; *Akh.*12th Shawwal, 40th R.Y.
372.	Rao Ratan Singh, Islam Khan	1,500/1,000	India	Indian	*zamindar*	Father	M.U.II,147; Lendisyana, *Diplomatic Correspondence of Aurangzeb*; T.U. S.V.

373.	Muhammad Jan. Kartalab Khan	1,500/1,000	—	—	—	—	T.M.28; *Akh.* 45th R.Y.
374.	Mir Husain b/o Rahim Khan	1,500/1,000	—	—	—	Brother	*Akh.* 30th Muharram, 43rdR.Y.
375.	Hirday Sah Bundela	1,500/1,000	India	Indian	Rajput *zamindar*	Father	*Akhbar*, Ist Jan. 1707 A. D. cited by B. D. Gupta "Satar Sal Bundela". p. 63
376.	Aman Ullah Khan	1,500/700 (200×2-3h)	India	Irani	—	Father	M.A.488; M.U.I, 293-95; A.M.T.128b
377.	Param Deo s/o Kesri Singh Sisodia	1,500/900	India	Indian	Rajput *zamindar*	Father	S.D.A.125
378.	Mir Muhammad Husain, Amanat Khan II	1,500/900	India	Irani	—	Father	M. A. 347; T.M.11; M.U. I, 287-90
379.	Mustafa Khan Kashi	1,500/900	Iran	Irani	—	—	Kamwar, 286a; M.U.III, 637-41; Khafi Khan, II, 441
380.	Shabbir Panni	1,500/900	India	Indian	Afghan	Brother	Akh. Jamada, II, 45th R.Y.
381.	Satar Sal Rathor	1,500/850	India	Indian	Rajput *zamindar*	—	S.D.A. 171; Farhat-ul Nazirin, 206b; Akh. Rabi I, 45th R.Y.
382.	Hasan	1,500/800	India	Indian	Afghan	Father	S.D.A. 208
383.	Shaikh Raziuddin Khan	1,500/800	—	—	—	—	Al.862; M.A. 187

S.NO.	Name and Title	Rank highest during the period	Country of birth	Group	Sub-groups Rajput, Maratha, Afghan Zamindar etc.	Father or other blood relation in service	Authorities
384.	Raghu Nath Singh Meerath	1,500/800	India	Indian	Rajput	—	Kamwar, 266b; A.M.T.132
385.	Saifuddin Khan Safvi, Kamyab Khan	1,500/700	India	Irani	—	Father	Akh.11th Zilhij, 25th R.Y. M.U.III,479
386.	Asalat Khan s/o Muzaffar Haiderabadi	1,500/700	India	—	—	Father	M.A. 494; Kamwar,272b; A.M.T. 128b
387.	Jafar Ali Yaminul Mulki	1,500/600 (100x2-3h)	India	Irani	—	—	Akh. 29th Muharram,43rd R.Y.
388.	Nand Nayak	1,500/700	India	Indian	—	—	S.D.A.205
389.	Ahlullah Khan	1,500/700	—	—	—	—	S.D.A.170
390.	Tuku Ji s/o Bahr Ji	1,500/700	India	Indian	Maratha	Brother	S.D.A.176
391.	Auchi Auhal Rao s/o Faranku Ji.	1,500/700	India	Indian	Maratha	—	S.D.A.183
392.	Sohrab Beg, Mirza Niamatullah	1,500/600	India	Irani		Father	M. A.251; M·U.I,586,87
393.	Saiyid Yusuf Khan Bukhari	1,500/600	—	Turani		—	MA.517; Kamwar,270b.

394.	Sayid Mujeeb, Bakhsh Khan s/o Muzaffar Haiderabadi.	1.500/600	India	—	Deccani	—	Akh.2nd Rabi I, 36thR.Y.
395.	Sangram Khan Ghori alias Nahar Khan	1,500/600	India	Indian	Afghan	—	Akh-11th Muharram,46th R.Y; Dilkusha,91a.
396.	Saiyid Badan s/o Saiyid Abdul Hasan	1,500/600	India	—	—	Father	S.DA.219
397.	Khawaja Khan son-in-law of Siyadat Khan Aughlan	1,500/600	Turan	Turani	—	Uncle	M.A.518; Akh. Ramzan, 45th R.Y.;M.U.I,503.
398.	Khawaja Nur, Mutamad Khan Khawajasara	1,500/600	—	—	—	—	T.M.1095 A.H; M.A195; Al. 448, 960;Kamwar,268b
399.	Shah Quli Khan Mahram	1,500/500	—	—	—	—	Azam-al Harb,171.
400.	Shaikh Sulaiman Fazil Khan	1,500/500	India	Indian	—	—	Z.A.162b; M.A.189; T.M. 3; Kamwar 268a
401.	Sardar Beg, Ihtimam Khan, Sardar Khan	1,500/500	India	Turani	—	Father	T.M.4; M·U.II,491-94; Kamwar, 287b; M. A. 250 295,-314
402.	Shaikh Abdul Aziz, Abdul Aziz Khan, Khidmat Talab Khan Bahadur.	1,500/500	India	Indian	—	—	M.U.II, 686-88; T M.1096 A.H.
403.	Sarup Singh s/o Raja Udat Singh.	1 500/500	India	Indian	Rajput-*zamindar*	Father	M.A.386; Dilkhusha, 117b.
404.	Ayman Khan	1,500/500	—	—	—	—	Akh 5th Shaban24hR.Y.

S.NO.	Name and Title	Rank highest during the period	Country of birth	Group	Sub-groups Rajput, Maratha, Afghan Zamindar etc.	Father or other blood relation in service	Authorities
405.	Mir Abu Ala Balkhi Arshad Khan	1,500/500	Balkh	Turani	—	—	Akh.10th Rabi I,45thR.Y.; T.M.14
406.	Jalu Ji s/o Saru Ji	1,500/500	India	Indian	Maratha	—	S.D.A.174
407.	Aku Ji s/o Malu Ji	1,500/500	India	Indian	Maratha	Father	S.D·A.206
408.	Padam Singh Bundela	1,500/500	India	Indian	Rnjput *zamindar*	Father	Akh. 1st Jan., 1707 A.D. cited by B.D. Gupta, Satar Sal Bundela, p. 63
409.	Syed Niaz Khan	1,500/500	—	Turani	—	—	M.U.II,832
410.	Talib Khawajasara, Khidmatgar Khan	1,500/350	—	—	—	—	M.A.341, 350;T.M.16
411.	Haider Quli	1,500/400	—	—	—	—	Akh.29th Muharram,43rd. R.Y.
412.	Abdur Rahim Khan brother of Firuz Jang.	1,500/300	Turan	Turani	—	Brother	Akh.23rd Ziqada, 43rdR.Y.; M.A.405
413.	Rahimuddin Khan	1,500/600	Turan	Turani		Father	M.A.481;A.M.T.131a
414.	Kamdar Khan	1,500/300	—	—		—	Mumalik-i-Mahrusai Alamgiri, 201a

415.	Shafqatullah, Ṣazawar Khan	1,500/250	India	—		Father	M.A. 255; M.U.II,440-41; A.M.T.131b
416.	Hakim Salih Shirazi Salih Khan	1,500/250	Iran	Irani		—	Kamwar, 271b; Al.1061-62.
417.	Hakim Sadiq Khan, Hakim-ul-Mulk s/o Mohsin Khan Shirazi	1,500/200	—	Irani	—	Father	Kamwar, 301b
418.	Shahi Khan or Shah Beg Kashghari (Abdullah Khan)	1,500/200	Turan	Turani	—	—	M.A.175; Kamwar, 265b.
419	Rahman Khan	1,500/200	—	—	—	—	Z.A.107a; Mumalik-i Mahrusai Alamgiri,179a
420.	Bakhtawar Khan Khawajasara	1,500/–	—	—	—	—	T.M.1095 A.H.;T.U. "S.V"; AM.T.131b.
421.	Abdur Rahim Khan s/o Islam Khan Mashhadi	1,500/-	India	Irani		Father	T.M. 1093 A.H.; M.U.II, 812-813; A.M.T.131a
422.	Dev Afgan, Mutamad Khan	1,500/–	India	Irani		Father	M.A·196; T.M.1101/A.H; Kamwar, 268b
423.	Badiuzzaman Mahabat Khani, Rashid Khan	1,500/–	India	—		—	M.A.206; T.M.7; Kamwar, 267b
424.	Haji Shafi, Shafi Khan	1,500/–	—	—		—	T.U. "S.V."; Kamwar, 274a
425.	Saiyid Asalat Khan II	1,500/–	India	Irani		Father	T.U. "S.V."

S.No.	Name and Title	Rank highest during the period	Country of birth	Group	Sub-groups Rajput, Maratha, Afghan Zamindar etc.	Father or other blood relation in service	Authorities
426.	Husain Ali Khan Barha	1,500/-	India	Indian	—	Father	Khafi Khan II, 575; M.U.I, 321-38
427.	Arslan Khan	1,500/-	Turan	Turani	—	—	M.A. 381; T.U. "S.V."
428.	Ilyas Khan	1,500/-	—	—	—	—	T.U. "S.V."
429.	Afzal Beg, Afzal Khan	1,500/-	Iran	Irani	—	—	Kamwar, 302a; T.U. "S.V."
430.	Alah Yar Khan, Ihtimam Khan, Ikhlas Khan	1,500/-	—	—	—	—	T.M. 12
431.	Khawaja Muhammad, Amanat Khan	1,500/-	Turan	Turani	—	—	M.U.III, 729-46; T.U. "S.V."
432.	Mir Muhammad alias Kifayat Khan	1,500/-	India	Irani	—	—	T.M.9
433.	Khawaja Abdullah	1,500/-	India	Turani	—	—	T.M.9
434.	Shahsawar Khan	1,500/-	—	—	—	—	A.M.T. 131a
435	Aqa Bahram, Qawamuddin Khan Asfahani	1,400/1,000	Iran	Irani	—	—	Akh. 9th Rajab. 24th R.Y.; T.M. 1091 A.H
436.	Bhali Rao s/o Saru Ji	1,200/1,200	India	Indian	Maratha	Brother	S.D.A. 175

437.	Asfandiyar, foster brother of Prince Akbar.	1,100/1,000	—	—	—	—	Kamwar, 306a; Akh.45th R.Y.
438.	Muhtasham Khan	1,000/1,200 (1,000x2-3h)	—	—	—	—	Akh. 15th Jamada II,46th R.Y; 16th Rajab, 24th R.Y.
439.	Saiyid Muhammad s/o Shujaul Mulk	1,000/2,000	—	—	—	—	Akh. 25th Jamada, II,44th R.Y.; S.D.A. 173
440.	Muhammad Beg Khan	1,000/1,000 (2–3h)	—	Turani	—	—	Akh. Ist Rabi II, 38th R.Y.
441.	Jaswant Singh Rawal of Dungarpur	1,000/900 (800x2–3h)	India	Indian	Rajput—*zamindar*	Father	Akh. 16th Zilhij, 38th R.Y.
442.	Khuman Singh or Guman Singh	1,000/900 (800x2–3h)	India	Indian	Rajput—*zamindar*	Father	Akh. 16th Zilhij, 38th R.Y. Ojha; "*History of Rajputana*" Vol. III, part I, 119
443.	Raja Sarup Singh s/o Anup Singh	1,000/750 (2–3h)	India	Indian	Rajput—*zamindar*	Father	Akh. 22nd Ziqada, 43rdR.Y. M.U.II, 291; Kamwar, 289a
444.	Raja Maha Singh Bhadoriya	1,000/1000 (500x2–3h)	India	Indian	Rajput—*zamindar*	Father	M.U.II, 229-30; A.M.T. 132a
445.	Iftikhar Khan, Mafakhir Khan s/o Fakhir Khan	1,000/1,500	India	Irani		Father	Akh. 24th Rajab, 45th R.Y. M.U.III, 28
446.	Kapur Singh Hara	1,000/1,000 (500x2–3h)	India	Indian	Rajput	—	S.D.A. 171
447.	Rehman Dad Khan	1,000/1,500	India	Indian	—	—	Akh. 15th Jamada,II,46th R.Y.

S.No.	Name and Title	Rank highest during the period	Country of birth	Group	Sub-groups Rajput, Maratha, Afghan Zamindar etc.	Father or other blood relation in service	Authorities
448.	Mamur Khan, Dilir Khan[1]	1,000/1,200	India	Indian	Afghan	Father	Akh. 4th Ziqada, 46th R.Y. Kamwar, 273a; A.M.T. 132.a.
449.	Samandar Beg, Samandar Khan	1,000/1,200	—	—		—	Akh. Ist Muharram,45th R.Y.
450.	Fazil Beg, Tahauwar Khan	1,000/1,000	Iran	Irani		Brother	Kamwar, 276b; M.A.273; M.U. I, 425; A M.T.132a
451.	Malu Ji s/o Saru Ji	1,000/1,000	India	Indian	Maratha	—	S.D.A.175
452.	Raja Man Dhata	1,000/1,000	India	Indian	Rajput *zamindar*	Father	Kamwar, 270a; M.A. 207; M. Akbar, The Punjab under the Mughals, 225
453.	Khawaja Yaqub Naqshbandi Bukhari, Sarbuland Khan	1,000/1,000	—	Turani	—	—	T.M.1096 A.H.; Kamwar, 266a
454.	Raja Bakht Buland, Dindar Khan	1,000/1,000	India	Indian	*zamindar*	—	M.A.340; A.M.T.132a
455.	Saiyid Wajihuddin Barha	1,000/1,000	India	Indian	—	Father	Akh. 10th Rabi I, 45th R.Y.
456.	Iradat Khan s/o Azam Khan Koka.	1,000/1,000	India	Irani	—	G. Father	M.A.472; A.M.T. 131b

457.	Muhammad Khan Bijapuri	1,000/1,000	India	Indian	Afghan Deccani	—	Akh. 15th Jamada II,36th R.Y.
458.	Muhammad Murad Khan	1,000/1,000	India	Irani	—	Father	M.A.242; Kamwar, 273b.
459.	Rawal Ram Singh of Dungarpur s/o Khuman Singh	1,000/1,000	India	Indian	Rajput *zamindar*	Father	Ojha, History of Rajputana, Vol.III, Part I, 122
460.	Ahmad Khan	1,000/1,000	India	Indian	—	Father	S.D.A. 170; M.U.I,274; A.M.T. 128b
461.	Bajey s/o Jan Rao	1,000/1,000	India	Indian	Maratha	—	S.D.A. 175
462.	Siva Ji s/o Saru Ji	1,000/1,000	India	Indian	Maratha	Brother	S.D.A. 175
463.	Yasa Ji s/o Bahar Ji	1,000/1,000	India	Indian	Maratha	—	S.D.A. 175
464.	Dalu Ji s/o Bahar Ji	1,000/1,000	India	Indian	Maratha	—	S.D.A. 175
465.	Anba Ji	1,000/1,000	India	Indian	Maratha	—	S.D.A. 177
466.	Naba Ji s/o Lahu Ji	1,000/1,000	India	Indian	Maratha	—	S.D.A. 178
467.	Saiyid Asadullah s/o Saiyid Ahmad	1,000/1,000	India	—		—	S.D.A. 178
468.	Mana Ji s/o Sambha Ji	1,000/1,000	India	Indian	Maratha	Father	S.D.A. 179
469.	Abdul Majid Khan	1,000/1,000	—	—	—	—	Akh. 45th R.Y.

[1]Presumably identical with Ma'mur Khan mentioned as holding 1000/1000 (2h-3h) in Aurangzeb's *farman* of A.H. 1089, tr. pub. in *Jour. U.P. Hist Soc.*, XVI (1943), p. 148

S.No.	Name and Title	Rank highest during the period	Country of birth	Group	Sub-groups Rajput, Maratha, Afghan Zamindar etc.	Father or other blood relation in service	Authorities
470.	Kalyan Singh	1,000/1,000	India	Indian	Rajput	—	Akh. 20th Zilhij, 38th R.Y.
471.	Waheed Khan s/o Jakiya	1,000/1,000	India	Indian		—	Kamwar, 289b.
472.	Zafar Khan	1,000/600 (300x2-3h)	India	Irani		Father	Akh. 20th Rajab,24th R.Y.
473.	Gopal Singh s/o Muhkam Singh Sisodia (Hereditary Rank).	1,000/900	India	Indian	Rajput *zamindar*	Father	M.U.II, 147
474.	Anba Ji s/o Maka Ji	1,000/500 (300x2-3h)	India	Indian	Maratha	—	S.D.A. 209
475.	Muhammad Rafi	1,000/800	Iran	Irani		Uncle	Akh. 38th R.Y. Vol. IV,p.54. M.U.III,801-806
476.	Saifullah Khan Mir Bahr	1,000/800	—	—		—	M.U.II,486-89; Al. 45
477.	Ram Rao s/o Ganpat Rao	1,000/400 (300x2-3h)	India	Indian	Maratha	—	S.D.A. 204
478.	Mana Ji s/o Nagu Ji	1,000/700	India	Indian	Maratha	Father	S.D.A. 179
479.	Khandu Ji s/o Jao Ji	1,000/700	India	Indian	Maratha	—	S.D.A. 178
480.	Deo Ji s/o Manku Ji	1,000/700	India	Indian	Maratha	Father	S.D.A. 178

481.	Malu Ji	1,000/700	India	Indian	Maratha	—	Kamwar, 277b; S.D.A.176
482.	Siv Ji s/o Sambha Ji	1,000/700	India	Indian	Maratha	Father	S.D.A. 177
483.	Fedai Khan s/o Ibrahim Khan	1,000/700	India	Irani	—	Father	Kamwar, 272b; M.A. 236-37
484.	Hayat Khan	1,000/700	—	—	—	—	Mumalik-i-Mahrusai Alamgiri, 201a; Khafi Khan,II, 332, 505
485.	Inderman s/o Pahar Singh Bundela.	1,000/700	India	Indian	Rajput *zamindar*	Father	Daftar-i-Dewani, No. 2983. S.D.A. 112; Al. 290,302,989
486.	Sultan Singh	1,000/700	India	Indian	Rajput	—	Azam-al Harb, 197;Akh. Jamada I, 44 R.Y.
487.	Raja Udai Singh s/o Maha Singh Bhadoriya.	1,000/600 (300x2-3h)	India	Indian	Rajput *zamindar*	Father	M.U.II, 230; S.D.A. 171
488.	Saiyid Abdullah Khan Barha alias Saiyid Mian.	1,000/600	India	Indian			M.U.II, 489-91; A.M.T. 127b
489.	Ruhullah, Neknam Khan s/o Himmat Khan Mir Isa	1,000/600	India	Turani		Father	Akh. 16th, Shaban, 43rd R.Y. M. A. 495, 949; Kamwar, 289a
490.	Mir Khan s/o Amir Khan	1,000/600	India	Irani		Father	Akh. 25th Rajab, 47th R.Y. M.A. 493; M.U.I, 286; A.M.T. 132a

S.No.	Name and Title	Rank highest during the period	Country of birth	Group	Sub-groups Rajput, Maratha, Afghan Zamindar etc.	Father or other blood relation in service	Authorities
491.	Muhammad Jafar s/o Mahram Khan	1,000/600	India	—	—	—	S.D.A. 219
492.	Raja Kalyan Singh zamindar of Bhadawar	1,000/600	India	Indian	Rajput zamindar	—	M.A.382; Kamwar, 288a
493.	Muhammad Jan, Atish Khan	1,000/600	India	Irani	—	Father	Z.A.161b; T.M.11; M.U.I, 255-58.
494.	Ahmad Saeed Khan	1,000/600	—	—	—	—	Azam-al-Harb, 197
495.	Shakur Khan Bijapuri	1,000/500	India	Indian	Deccani	—	Akh. 5th Zilhij, 47th R.Y.
496.	Barkhurdar Beg, Mir Abdul Salam Khan	1,000/500	India	Irani	—	Father	M.U.II. 741-42
497.	Bahr Ji	1,000/500	India	Indian	Maratha	—	Akh. 20th Ramzan, 40th R.Y.
498.	Rad Andaz Khan	1,000/500	India	Irani	—	Father	Kamwar, 287b
499.	Raja Bhagwant Singh s/o Jaswant Singh Bundela.	1,000/500	India	Indian	Rajput *zamindar*	Father	Dilkusha, 96a; M.U.II,294
500.	Mustafa s/o Masud Khan	1,000/500	India	Indian	—	Father	S.D.A. 225
501.	Mirza Beg Khan	1,000/500	—	—	—	—	S.D.A. 211

502.	Agha Khirad	1,000/500	—	—	—	—	S D.A. 208
503.	Bir Bhan	1,000/500	India	Indian	Maratha	—	S D A. 205
504.	Bayazid s/o Musa	1,000/500	India	—		Father	S.D.A. 205
505.	Badhay s/o Miran	1,000/500	India	Indian		Father	S.D.A. 203
506.	Abul Fateh s/o Dilir Khan Bijapuri.	1,000/400	India	Indian		Father	Akh. 45th R.Y.
507.	Saiyid Muhammad	1,000/400	India	Turani		Father	Akh. Rabi I, 45 R.Y. Jamada, II, 45th R.Y.
508.	Miyana Khan	1,000/500	India	Indian	Afghan	—	Akh. 16th Ziqada, 40th R.Y.
509.	Raja Suraj Mal s/o Raja Bhim.	1,000/500	India	Indian	Rajput *zamindar*	Father	Akh. 15th Muharram,38th R.Y.
510.	Qazi Akram Akram Khan	1,000/500	India	—		—	M.A. 506 Proc. Ind. Hist. Congress, 1950, 219-221.
511.	Mir Bahadur Dil, Jan Sipar Khan	1,000/500	India	Irani		Father	T.M.13; M.U.I, 535-37
512.	Abdul Wahid, Mir Khan	1,000/500	—	—		—	S.D.A. 172; M.A. 192
513.	Sidi Ibrahim	1,000/500	India	Indian	*zamindar*	—	Kamwar, 277b; Al. 626
514.	Bahadur Singh	1,000/500	India	Indian	Rajput	Father	Kamwar, 289a; M.A.405; A.M.T. 132a
515.	Muhammad Sami, Nusrat Khan s/o Khan-i-Jahan Kokaltash	1,000/500	India	Irani	—	Father	Akh. 16th Jamada I, 45th R.Y.; M.A. 241, 246; Kamwar, 273.a

S. No.	Name and Title	Rank highest during the period	Country of birth	Group	Sub-groups Rajput, Maratha, Afghan, Zamindar etc.	Father or other blood relation in service	Authorities
516.	Darab Khan	1,000/500	India	Irani		Father	M.U.II, 39-42; Kamwar, 265b; T.M. 1090 A.H.
517.	Neta Ji s/o Khandu Rao	1,000/450	India	Indian	Maratha	Father	S.D.A. 210
518.	Fateh s/o Hasan Rohela	1,000/450	India	Indian	Afghan	Father	S.D.A 208
519.	Raja Manohar Das	1,000/400	India	Indian	Rajput *zamindar*	Father	Mamuri, 188b: Al. 140
520.	Shaikh Mustafa	1,000/900	—	—	—	—	Akh. 15th Rabi I, 44th R.Y; Jamada I, 44th R.Y.
521.	Baya Ji	1,000/500	India	Indian	Maratha	—	S.D.A. 187; Akh. Jamada I, 44th R.Y.
522.	Abul Fateh s/o Khan-i-Jahan Kokaltash	1,000/400	India	Irani		Father	M.A. 406: A.M.T.131b
523.	Mir Ibrahim' Marahmat Khan s/o Amir Khan	1,000/400	India	Irani		Father	M.A. 481; M.U.III,713
524.	Yakataz Khan	1,000/400	Turan	Turani		—	M.U.I, 503; T.M. 1091 A.H. Kamwar, 267a, 288a
525.	Muhammad Raza	1,000/400	India	—		Father	M.A. 516; A.M.T. 132a; M.U. II, 825

No.	Name	Rank					Source
526.	Marahmat Khan s/o Khawaja Talib, Shah Nawaz Khan	1,000/400	India	Irani		Father	Kamwar, 299a.
527.	Dil Singh	1,000/400	India	Indian	Rajput *zamindar*		Akh. Rabi I, 45th R.Y.
528.	Chet Singh	1,000/500	India	Indian	Rajput		Akh. Shaban, 45th R.Y.
529.	Raja Udai Singh of Chamba s/o Chatar Singh	1,000/600	India	Indian	Rajput *zamindar*	Father	*Dastur-al-Amal-i-Shahjahani*, Add. 6588, 22a; M. Akbar, *The Punjab under the Mughals*, p. 226
530.	Saiyid Karamullah Barha	1,000/500	India	Indian		—	Dilkusha, 77b; Kamwar, 306a; Akh. 17th Zilhij, 20th R. Y.
531.	Chandhuji	1,000/1,000	India	Indian	Maratha	—	Akh. Shaban, 45th R.Y.
532.	Rao Joghat	1,000/500	India	Indian	Maratha		Akh. Shaban, 45th R.Y.
533.	Birmuji	1,000/500	India	Indian	Maratha		Akh. Shaban, 45th R.Y.
534.	Rao Man Singh s/o Jadaun Rai.	1,000/900 (300x2-3h)	India	Indian	Maratha *zamindar*	Father	M.U.I, 522; Akh. Jamada I, 44th R.Y.
535.	Bhao Singh	1,000/500	India	Indian	Rajput *zamindar*		Akh. Rabi I, 45th R.Y.
536.	Abdul Shakur Haiderabadi	1,000/500	India	Indian	Deccani	—	Akh. 45th R.Y.
537.	Murtaza Quli Khan	1,000/300	—	—	—	—	Akh. 10th Jamada I, 36th R.Y. Kamwar, 269b

S. No.	Name and Title	Rank highest during the period	Country of birth	Group	Sub-groups Rajput, Maratha, Afghan, Zamindar etc.	Father or other blood relation in service	Authorities
538.	Saif Khan s/o Saifuddin Mahmud.	1,000/300	India	Turani	—	Father	M.U.II. 484-85
539.	Saiyid Sharaf Khan	1,000/300	—	—	—	—	Z.A. 163b; T.U. "S.V."
540.	Lang Nayak	1,000/300	India	Indian		—	S.D.A. 205
541.	Sharif	1,000/300	—	—	—	—	Z.A. 164a; Kamwar,268b
542.	Qutbuddin Khan ambassador of Turan	1,000/200	Turan	Turani	—	—	M.A. 440; A.M.T. 132a; *Farhat-ul-Nazarin*, 178a
543.	Haqiqat Khan	1,000/200	—	—	—	—	S.D.A. 172
544.	Muhammad Zaman Khan Lohani.	1,000/200	India	Indian	Afghan	Father	S.D.A. 218
545.	Anwar Khan s/o Hakim Aleemuddin.	1,000/150	India	Indian	—	Father	Z.A. 162b; S.D.A. 170.
546.	Shah Mohsin, Hasan Bakhsh Khan.	1,000/100	—	—	—	—	*Mumalik-i-Mahrusai Alamgiri*. 179a; Z.A. 107a.
547.	Inayat Khan Khawafi	1,000/100	Iran	Irani	—	—	M.U.II, 813-818
548.	Muhammad Quli Khan	1,000/100	Turan	Turani	—	—	M.A. 472; A.M.T. 132a
549.	Rustam, Mutamad Khan	1,000/100	India	Turani	—	Father	T.M.18

550.	Qabil Khan Mir Munshi brother of Abul Fateh Qabil Khan.	1,000/70	India	Indian	—	Brother	M. A. 190-91; Kamwar, 268a
551.	Khawaja Yaqut Khan, Mahram Khan.	1,000/-	India	Indian	—	—	T.M.24
552.	Bahram Khan	1,000/-	India	Irani		Father	A.M.T. 131b
553.	Khawaja Musa Sarbuland Khan	1,000/-	—	—	—	—	Kamwar, 302a; *Mirat-i. Aftab Numa*, 583
554.	Parshutam Singh	1,000/-	India	Indian	Rajput	—	A.M.T. 132a
555.	Abdur Rahim s/o Burhanuddin, Fazil Khan	1,000/-	India	Irani	—	Father	T.M. 20
556.	Jalaluddin Khan s/o Mir Miran.	1,000/-	India	Irani	—	Father	T.M. 17
557.	Vyankat	1,000/-	India	Indian	Maratha *zamindar*	—	Sarkar, *History of Aurangzeb*, Vol. V, 208
558.	Padam Singh s/o Rao Karan	1,000/-	India	Indian	Rajput	Father	Dilkusha, 79b
559.	Niamatullah Khan s/o Ruhullah Khan	1,000/-	India	Irani	—	Father	*Mirat-i-Aftab Numa*, 593
560.	Haibatullah Arab	1,000/-	—	—	—	—	M.A. 397
561.	Basharat Khan	1,000/-	—	—	—	—	A.M.T. 131a
562.	Hashim	1,000/-	—	—	—	Deccani	Mamuri, 168a; S.D.A.239

S. No.	*Name and Title*	*Rank highest during the period*	*Country of birth*	*Group*	*Sub-groups Rajput, Maratha, Afghan, Zamindar etc.*	*Father or other blood relation in service*	*Authorities*
563.	Nand Lal	Amir (1,000)[1]	India	Indian		—	*Farhat-ul-Nazirin*, 207a
564.	Jagdeo Rai s/o Dataji	High Rank	India	Indian	Maratha *zamindar*	Father	M.U.I, 522; *Dilkusha* 79b; Isar Das, 138 Sarkar, *History of Aurangzeb*, Vol. V, 212
565.	Muhammad Aslam Khan	High Rank	India	Irani	—	Father	M.U.III, 666-667.
566.	Izad Bakhsh Rasa (Qaladar of Akbarabad).	High Rank	India	Irani		Grand-father	*Dilkusha*, 127a
567.	Devji	High Rank	India	Indian	Maratha	Brother	Waqai Papers Jaipur, 17th Ziqada, 47th R.Y. (Reference given by Dr. Satish Chandra)
568.	Kishore Das, Qaladar of Sholapur	High Rank[2]	India	Indian	Rajput *zamindar*	Father	M.A. 228
569.	Ajit Singh Rathor (For a short period).	High Rank[3]	India	Indian	Rajput *zamindar*	Father	Mirat-i-Ahmadi, I, 341; M.U. III. 755-60

1. In the same authority Satar Sal Rathor is mentioned as amir, but in S.D.A. his rank is given as 1,000/500. So I have also placed Nand Lal in the category of *hazaris*.
2. Sholapur was the fort of considerable strategic importance and nobles of high rank were appointed there (Akh. 14th Zilhij, 25th R.Y.).
3. Ajit Singh's actual *mansab* is nowhere given, it being only stated that he was granted a *mansab* and appointed *faujdar* and *Jagirdar* of *parganas* Jalor and Sanchor. His lieutenant Durga Das was given the rank of 3,000/2500 (See No. 158). His own rank is, therefore, likely to have been quite high.

570.	Madan Singh S/o Sambhaji	High Rank	India	Indian	Maratha	—	Isar Das, 154b-155a; M.A. 473
571.	Kheluji, Commander of Sambhaji	High Rank	India	Indian	Maratha	—	Isar Das, 155a
572.	Ramaji, Commander of Sambhaji.	High Rank[1]	India	Indian	Maratha	—	Isar Das, 155a
573.	Januji, Commander of Sambhaji	High Rank	India	Indian	Maratha	—	Isar Das, 155a
574.	Sultan Husain, Ashan Khan, Mir Malang.	High Rank	India	Irani	—	—	M.U.I, 301-303
575.	Malbar Rao	High Rank	India	Indian	Maratha	—	*Raqaim-i-Karaim*, 29a

1. Isar Das says that the three Commanders of Sambhaji and his son Madan Singh were given *Mansab-i-'Aliya*. Generally the *mansabdars* of 1,000 and above were recorded as having the *Mansab-i-'Aliya*.

BIBLIOGRAPHY

Note : The abbreviation 'Br. M.' represents the British Museum; 'I.O.', the India Office Library; and 'Bodl.', the Bodleian Library, Oxford.

A. CHRONICLES

YUAN-CHAO-PI-SHI, *The Secret History of the Mongol Dynasty*, tr. (with intr. and notes) Wei Kwei Sun, Aligarh, 1957.

BABUR, *Babur Nama*, English translation (from the original Turki text) by A.S. Beveridge, London, 1922.

BAYAZID BIYAT, *Tazkara-i-Humayun wa Akbar*, ed. M. Hidayat Hosain, Bib. Ind. 1941.

ABUL FAZL, *Akbar Nama*, Bib. Ind., Calcutta, 1873-87.

ABDUL QADIR BADAYUNI, *Muntakhab-ut Tawarikh*, ed. Ahmad Ali and Lees, Bib. Ind., Calcutta, 1865-68.

ASAD BEG QAZWINI, Memoirs. MS. Br. M. Or. 1996.

ABDUL BAQI NIHAWANDI, *Ma'asir-i-Rahimi*, ed. Hidayat Husain, Bib. Ind. 1910-31.

JAHANGIR, *Tuzuk-i-Jahangiri*, ed. Saiyid Ahmad Khan, Ghazipur and Aligarh, 1863-64.

MUTAMAD KHAN, *Iqbalnama-i-Jahangiri*, lithographed, Nawal Kishore, 1870.

MUHAMMAD SHARIF NAJAFI, *Majalis-us-Salatin*, MS. Br. M. Or. 1903.

ABDUL HAMID LAHORI, *Badshah Nama*, ed. Maulvi Kabiruddin and Maulvi Abdur Rahim, Bib. Ind. Calcutta, 1867-68.

AMIN QAZWINI, *Badshah Nama*, MS. Br. M. Or. 173; Add. 20,734. I have also used a transcript of Raza Library (Rampur) MS. in the Department of History, Aligarh.

MUHAMMAD SALIH KAMBO, *Amal-i Salih*, ed. G. Yazdani, Bib. Ind. Calcutta, 1923-46.

MUHAMMAD WARIS, *Badshah Nama* (Continuation of Abdul Hamid Lahori's *Badshah Nama*). Br. M. Add. 6556, Or, 1675. Transcript in the Department of History, Aligarh. (This MS. is defective at the end, lacking the list of *mansabdars*).

SIDHARI LAL, *Tuhfa-i-Shah Jahani*, MS. I. O. 337.

MUHAMMAD SADIQ KHAN, *Shahjahan Nama*, MS. Br. M. Or. 174; Or. 1671. The author has suppressed his identity and has given a fictitious name. The autobiographical facts which he has given are palpably false. Yet the author was a contemporary—indeed, probably, a high officer—of Shah Jahan and the work is of considerable importance. It gives us several important pieces of information missing in the official chronicles.

SHIHABUDDIN TALISH, *Fathiya-i-Ibriya*, MS. Bodl. Or. 589. The first part of the book has been printed under the title *Tarikh-i-Muluk-i-Asham*. Calcutta, 1848.

MUHAMMAD KAZIM, *Alamgir Nama*, Bib. Ind., Calcutta, 1865-73.

HATIM KHAN, *Alamgir Nama*, MS. Br. M.Add. 26,233. An abridgement of Muhammad Kazim's *Alamgir Nama*, but giving certain facts omitted by Muhammad Kazim.

AQIL KHAN RAZI, *Waqiat-i-Alamgiri*, ed. Zafar Hasan, Aligarh, 1946. The attribution of the work to Aqil Khan Razi is not free of doubt. While some parts of this small work contain very interesting information, some statements, specially in the earlier portion, are difficult to believe, and suggest that its author was writing on the basis of hearsay.

SHAIKH MUHAMMAD BAQA, *Mirat-al Alam*, MS. Abdus Salam. 84/314, Azad Library, Aligarh Muslim University, Aligarh.

SHAIKH MUHAMMAD BAQA, *Mirat-i-Jahan Numa*, (A version of the preceding) MS. Br. M. 1998.

ABUL FAZL MAMURI, *Tarikh-i-Aurangzeb*, MS. Br. M. Or. 1671. Continuation of Sadiq Khan's *Shahjahan Nama*. Like Sadiq Khan, the autobiographical facts given by Abul Fazl

Mamuri appear also to be, at least in part, fictitious. No such officer is known to us from our other evidence.

ALAH YAR BALKHI, *Ausaf Nama-i-Alamgiri,* MS. Cambridge University Library, Brown Cat. 100, Pers. 477. A eulogy, in prose and verse, of Aurangzeb.

SA'T-I-NUHZAT-I-ALAMGIR PADSHAH, MS. Brochet, i, 703, Supp. Pers. 477.

ISAR DAS NAGAR, *Futuhat-i-Alamgiri,* MS. Br. M. Add. 23,884.

SUJAN RAI BHANDARI, *Khulasat-ut Tawarikh,* ed. Zafar Hasan, Delhi, 1918.

BHIM SEN, *Nuskha-i Dilkusha,* MS. Br. M. Or. 23.

SAQI MUSTA'ID KHAN, *Ma'asir-i Alamgiri,* Bib. Ind. Calcutta, 1871.

NI'MAT KHAN-i 'ALI, *Waqiat-i Ni'mat-Khan-i-Ali,* lithographed, Nawal Kishor, Lucknow, 1928.

Annals of Delhi Padshahat, Assamese Chronicle, tr. by S. K. Bhuyan, Gauhati, 1947.

Alqab Nama, MS. Br. M. Or. 1913; Containing titles of the princes and the nobles of Aurangzeb.

RAI CHATURMAN SAKSENA, *Chahar Gulshan,* Abdus Salam, 292/62, Azad Library, Aligarh. Portion translated and annotated by Sir Jadu Nath Sarkar, *India of Aurangzeb,* 1901.

KAM RAJ, *A'zam-al-Harb,* MS. Br. M.Or. 1899.

MUHAMMAD HASHIM KHAFI KHAN, *Muntakhab-al Lubab,* ed. K.D. Ahmad and Haig, Bib. Ind., Calcutta, 1860-74. Khafi Khan has copied extensively from Sadiq Khan and Abul Fazl Ma'muri; but for the reign of Aurangzeb he adds some new information.

ALI MUHAMMAD KHAN, *Mirat-i Ahmadi,* ed. Syed Nawab Ali, Baroda, 1927-28.

KAMWAR KHAN, *Tazkarat-ut Salatin-i Chaghata,* MS. Lytton, 40/2 Maulana Azad Library, Aligarh.

MIRZA MUHAMMAD BIN RUSTAM alias Mntamad Khan bin Qabad alias Diyanat Khan, *Tarikh-i-Muhammadi,* 2 Vols. MS. I. O. 3890. I have also used the press copy of Part VI of the Vol. II, edited by Mr. Imtiaz Ali Arshi, 1960, being published by the Department of History, Aligarh Muslim University, Aligarh.

GHULAM HUSAIN, *Riyaz-us Salatin,* Bib. Ind. 1890.

B. ADMINISTRATIVE LITERATURE, ACCOUNTANCY MANUALS, ETC.

ABUL FAZL, *Ain-i Akbari,* Nawal Kishor ed., 1882. The translation, where cited, is that of Blochmann (I) and Jarrett (II & III) revised by Phillott, Vol. I, Calcutta, 1927 and 1939; and Sarkar, Vols. II and III, Calcutta, 1949.

YUSUF MIRAK, *Mazhar-i Shahjahani,* A.D. 1634, Vol. II, ed. Pir Hisamuddin Rashidi, Karachi, 1961. Vol. II is devoted to the administrative history of Sind during the Mughal period down to 1634.

Dastur-al Amal-i Shahjahani wa Shuqqajat-i Alamgiri, MS. Br. M. Add. 6,588.

Dastur-al Amal-i Alamgiri, MS. Br. M. Add. 6,599.

Dastur-al Amal-i Ilm-i-Navisindgi, MS. Br. M. Add. 6,599 ff. 134-185.

Zawabit-i Alamgiri, MS. Br. M. Or. 1641.

Khulasat-us Siyaq, MS. Sir Sulaiman Collection, 410/143, Maulana Azad Library, Aligarh.

HIDAYATULLAH BEHARI, *Hidayat-al Qawaid,* MS. Abdus Salam Collection, 379/149, Maulana Azad Library, Aligarh.

JAGAT RAI SHUJAI KAYATH SAKSENA, *Farhang-i Kardani,* MS. Abdus Salam Collection, 315/85, Maulana Azad Library, Aligarh.

Dastur-Al Amal, MS. Bodl. Fraser, 86.

MUNSHI NAND RAM KAYASTH SRIVASTAVA, *Siyaq Nama,* 1694-96, lithographed, Nawal Kishor, Lucknow, 1879.

Dastur-al-Amal-i-Shah Jahani, Late Aurangzeb, MS. Sir Sulaiman Collection, 675/53, Maulana Azad Library, Aligarh.

HAJI KHAIRULLAH, *Dastur-i Jahan Kusha,* MS. Abdus Salam Collection, 328/98, Azad Library, Aligarh.

JAWAHAR MAL BEKAS, *Dastur-al Amal*, MS. Subhanullah Collection, 954/4, Maulana Azad Library, Aligarh.

C. RECORDS AND DOCUMENTS INCLUDING COLLECTANEA

Records preserved at the Central Record Office (U.P.), Allahabad. The Collection consists of farmans, sale deeds, gift deeds, judgments, etc., and other documents concerning grants. A few documents belong to the 16th, but most appertain to the 17th and 18th centuries.

Jaipur Records (Sitamau transcripts) designated *Akhbarat-i Darbar-i-Mualla.* Daily court reports and news letters sent by the agent of the Raja of Amber. The *Akhbarat* report the main transactions publicly contracted at the court, such as appointments, promotions and demotions of the *mansabdars*, postings of officials, news received from provinces and expeditions, the Emperor's instructions on particular problems of administration, etc.

Documents preserved at Jaipur (now, at Bikaner). Transcripts of selected documents in the Department of History, Aligarh.

Selected Documents of Shah Jahan's Reign, Daftar-i-Dewani Haiderabad, 1950.

Selected Waqai of the Deccan (1660-71), ed. Yusuf Husain Khan, Haiderabad, 1953.

Selected Documents of Aurangzeb's Reign, ed. Yusuf Husain Khan, Haiderabad, 1959.

Waqa-i-Ajmer, A.D. 1678-80. Asafiya Library, Haiderabad, Fan-i-Tarikh, 2242; transcript in the Department of History, Aligarh, Nos. 15 and 16. The volumes contain reports of a news-writer who was first posted to Ranthambor, and then to Ajmer and finally accompanied the imperial army under Padshah Quli Khan in the Rajput war. The reports give extremely useful information about the working of the Mughal administration and about the Rathor rebellion of 1679-80.

Ahkam-i-Alamgiri, ed. Sir Jadu Nath Sarkar. This is the Persian text of the *Anecdotes of Aurangzeb*, translated also by J. N. Sarkar.

Collection of *Farmans* of Aurangzeb and Farrukh Siyar, MS. Fraser, 228.

Imperial Farmans (1577-1805 A. D.) *granted to the Ancestors of ... the Tikayat Maharaj,* translations in English, Hindi and Gujarati by K.M. Jhaveri, Bombay, 1928.

Some Firmans, Sanads and Parwanas (1578-1802), preserved in Bihar, calendared by K. K. Datta, Patna, 1962.

D. COLLECTIONS OF LETTERS

KHAN JAHAN SAIYID MUZAFFAR KHAN BARHA, *Arzdasht-ha-i-Muzaffar*, pre-1656. MS. Add. 16,859. This collection also contains a letter written by Aziz Koka to Jahangir.

BALKRISHAN BARHAMAN, Letters of Shaikh Jalal Hisari and Balkrishan Barhaman, written towards the end of Shahjahan's reign and early years of Aurangzeb. MS. Br. M. Add. 16,859.

Insha-i-Zubdat-ul Araiz, MS. in possession of Prof. S. Nurul Hasan, Aligarh. Letters written by Aurangzeb to Shah Jahan relating to the Qandahar Campaign of 1652.

AURANGZEB, *Adab-i Alamgiri*, MS. Abdus Salam Collection, 326/96, Azad Library, Aligarh. A collection of letters written by Qabil Khan on behalf of Aurangzeb before his accession. The letters are addressed to Shahjahan, prince Muhammad Sultan, Muazzam Khan Mir Jumla, Najabat Khan, Khan-i Dauran Nasiri Khan and others. This collection also includes letters written by Muhammad Sadiq on behalf of prince Akbar in 1680 during the Rathor rebellion.

Ruq'at-i Alamgir, ed. Saiyid Najib Ashraf Nadvi, Azamgarh, 1930. Contains the correspondence of Aurangzeb with Shahjahan, Jahan Ara Begam, Dara Shukoh, Shah Shuja, Murad Bakhsh and other princes and nobles; largely extracted by the editor from the *Adab-i Alamgiri.*

MUNSHI BHAGCHAND, *Jami-al Insha,* MS. M. Or. 1702. Letters of Jai Singh and the letters exchanged between Mughal and Persian courts.

IZID BAKHSH 'RASA', *Riyaz-al Wadad,* A.D. 1673-1695. MS. Br. M. Or. 1725. The author's own letters.

BHUPAT RAI, *Insha-i Roshan Kalam,* MS. Abdus Salam Collection, 339/109, Maulana Azad Library, Aligarh. Letters written on behalf of Ra'dandaz Khan, *faujdar* of Baiswara.

SHIVAJI, *Khutut-i Shivaji,* Royal Asiatic Society, London, MS. 173.

AURANGZEB, *Raqaim-i Karaim,* MS., Sir Sulaiman Collection, 412/145, Maulana Azad Library, Aligarh.

AURANGZEB, *Kalimat-i Taiyabat,* letters collected by Inayatullah Khan, MS., Abdus Salam, 322/92, Maulana Azad Library, Aligarh.

AURANGZEB, *Dastur-al 'Amal-i Agahi,* letters collected by Raja Bahar Mal in 1743, MS., Abdus Salam 323/93, Maulana Azad Library, Aligarh.

LEKH RAJ MUNSHI, *Matin-al Insha* or *Mufid-al Insha,* letters written on behalf of Ali Quli Khan, *faujdar* of Kuch Bihar, and collected by Champat Rai in 1700 A.D., MS. Bodl. 679.

Durr-al Ulum, Collection of letters and documents belonging to Munshi Gopal Rai Surdaj, collected and arranged by Sahib Rai Surdaj, A.D. 1688-89. Bodl. MS. Walkar 104.

MALIKZADA, *Nigar-Nama-i Munshi,* lithographed, Nawal Kishor, 1882. A very important collection of letters and administrative documents.

Collection of letters, called in the Lindesiana Catalogue "Reports from the Deccan," but actually correspondence between Mewar and the Mughal Court, etc., John Ryland Library, MSS. 353.

SHAH WALI-ULLAH, *Shah Wali-ullah Ke Siyasi Maktubat,* ed. with Urdu tr. by K. A. Nizami, Aligarh, 1950.

E. BIOGRAPHIES AND TAZKIRAS

SURAT SINGH, *Tazkira-i Pir Hassu Taili,* written A.H. 1057, MS. (probably autograph) in Library of the Department of History, Aligarh.

SHER KHAN LODI, *Mirat-al Khiyal,* litho. Abdus Salam Collection 628/49, Azad Library, Aligarh.

GHULAM ALI AZAD, *Khazana-i Amirah,* Bib Ind.

Ma'asir-al Karam, lithographed : Haiderabad, 1913.

SHAH NAWAZ KHAN, *Ma'asir-al-Umara,* ed. Molvi Abdur Rahim, Bid. Ind. 1888. 3 Vols. The famous biographical dictionary of Mughal nobles.

KEWAL RAM, *Tazkirat-al-Umara,* MS. Br. M.Add. 16,703.

F. MISCELLANEOUS WORKS

AMINUDDIN KHAN, *Malumat-ul Afaq,* Nawal Kishor Edition, 1870. Essentially a work describing wonders of the world, and curious happenings, it also describes the duties and functions of the officials of the Mughal government like the *Dewan-i A'la, Bakhshis, Darogha-i Dagh-i-Tasih, Sadrus 'Sudur* and Qanungo etc. and gives revenue tables. At the end of the book is given a table containing the pay schedules of *mansabdars.*

Tarikh-i Arkan-i Ma'asir-i Taimuriya, MS. Br.M. Or. 1772.

CHANDRA BHAN BARHAMAN, *Guldasta,* MS. Sir Sulaiman Collection, 666/44, Azad Library, Aligarh.

G. DICTIONARIES

ABDUR RASHID TATTAWI, *Farhang-i Rashidi,* A.D. 1653-54. Ed. Abu Tahir Zulfiqar Ali Murshidabadi, Asiatic Society of Bengal, 1875.

MUNSHI TEKCHAND 'BAHAR', *Bahar-i Ajam*, A.D. 1739-40. Nawal Kishor, 1916.

ANAND RAM MUKHLIS, *Mirat-al-Istilah*, a glossary of technical terms, A.D. 1745. MS. in Anjuman Taraqqi Urdu Library, Aligarh.

H. EUROPEAN SOURCES

Early Travels in India (1583-1619), ed. W. Foster, London, 1927.

Jahangir and the Jesuits, tr. C. H. Payne, London, 1930.

Purchas His Pilgrimes, Vols. III and IV, James Maclehose and Sons, Glasgow.

THOMAS ROE, *The Embassy of Sir Thomas Roe*, 1615-19, ed. W. Foster, London, 1926.

The English Factories in India, 1618-69, ed. W. Foster, 13 Vols. Oxford, 1906-27. Since the volumes are not numbered, they have been cited by the years that each volume covers.

PETER MUNDY, *Travels*, Vol. II : Travels in Asia, 1630-34, ed. R. C. Temple, Hakluyt Society, 2nd Series, London, 1914.

DE LAET, *Description of India and Fragment of Indian History*, tr. J. S. Hoyland and annotated by S. N. Banerjee: *The Empire of the Great Mogol*, Kitab Mahal, Bombay, 1928.

JEAN BAPTISTE TAVERNIER, *Travels in India*, 1640-67, tr. V. Ball, London, 1889.

FRANCOIS BERNIER, *Travels in the Mogul Empire* 1656-68, tr. A. Constable, ed. Smith.

JEAN DE THEVENOT, *The Indian Travels of Thevenot and Careri*, older translations, ed. S. N. Sen, New Delhi, 1949.

The English Factories in India, (New Series), ed. Sir Charles Fawcett, Oxford, 1936.

JOHN MARSHALL, *Notes and Observations on East India*, ed. S. A. Khan, *John Marshall in India*, London, 1927.

THOMAS BOWREY, *A Geographical Account of Countries Round the Bay of Bengal*, 1669-79, ed. R. C. Temple, Cambridge, 1905.

JOHN FRYER, *A New Account of East India and Persia being Nine Years Travels*, 1627-81, ed. William Crooke, Hakluyt Society, 2nd Series, London, 1909, 1912 and 1915.

STREYNSHAM MASTER, *The Diaries of Streynsham Master*, 1675-80, ed. R. C. Temple, Indian Records Series, London, 1911.

PELSAERT, *Jahangir's India*, tr. Geyl & Moreland, Cambridge, 1925.

NICCOLAO MANUCCI, *Storia Do Mogor*, 1653-1708, tr. W. Irvine, Indian Texts Series, Government of India, London, 1907-8.

MODERN WORKS

ABDUL AZIZ, *The Mansabdari System and the Mughal Army*, Lahore, 1945.

S. AHMAD, *Umra-i-Hunud*. (Urdu).

MUHAMMAD AKBAR, *The Punjab Under the Mughals*, Lahore, 1948.

SATISH CHANDRA, *The Parties and Politics at the Mughal Court*, (1707-40), Aligarh, 1959.

M. S. COMMISSARIAT, *A History of Gujarat*, Vol. II, (1573 to 1758) Orient Longmans, 1957.

W. CROOKE, *The Tribes and Castes of the North-Western Provinces and Oudh*, Calcutta, 1896.

H. H. DAS, *The Norris Embassy to Aurangzeb*, Calcutta, 1959.

M. FARUKI, *Aurangzeb and His Times*, Bombay, 1935.

A. FUHRAR, *The Monumental Antiquities and Inscriptions in the North-Western Provinces and Oudh*, Allahabad, 1891.

IRFAN HABIB, *The Agrarian System of Mughal India* (1556-1707). Bombay, 1963.

IBN HASAN, *The Central Structure of the Mughal Empire and its Practical Working up to the Year 1657*, Oxford, 1936.

D. IBBETSON, *Punjab Castes*, Lahore, 1916.

WILLIAM IRVINE, *The Army of the Indian Mughals*, London, 1903.

R. P. KHOSLA, *The Mughal Kingship and the Nobility*, Allahabad, 1934.
LEVY, *Social Structure of Islam*, Cambridge, 1957.
W. H. MORELAND, *India at the Death of Akbar*, London, 1920.
—*Agrarian System of Moslem India*, Cambridge, 1929.
—*From Akbar to Aurangzeb*, London, 1923.
MAULANA SHIBLI NAUMANI, *Aurangzeb Alamgir Per Ek Nazar*.
GAURI SHANKAR HERA CHAND OJHA, *Rajputanae Ka Itihas* Vol. III, Ajmer, 1937.
BENI PRASAD, *History of Jahangir;* 2nd ed. Allahabad, 1930.
K. QANUNGO, *Dara Shukoh*, Calcutta, 1952.
BISHESHWAR NATH REU, *Mewar Ka Itihas*, Vo. I, 1940.
P. SARAN, *The Provincial Government of the Mughals* (1526-1658), Allahabad, 1941.
JADU NATH SARKAR, *History of Aurangzeb—Mainly based on Persian Sources*, 5 vols. Calcutta, 1912, 1916 and 1930.
—*House of Shivaji*, 1960.
—*Shivaji and His Times*, 4th ed. 1948.
—*Studies in Aurangzeb's Reign*, Calcutta, 1933.
—*Mughal Administration*, Calcutta, 1920.
JAGDISH NARAIN SARKAR, *The Life of Mir Jumla*, Calcutta, 1951.
B. P. SAXENA, *History of Shah Jahan of Delhi*, Allahabad, 1958.
S R. SHARMA, *The Religious Policy of the Mughal Emperors*, Oxford, 1940; 2nd ed. Bombay, 1962.
KAVIRAJ SHYAMALDAS, *Vir Vinod*, 4 Vols, This history of Mewar in Hindi which is based on an extensive study of Persian and Rajasthani sources, often gives full texts of *farmans* and *nishans* issued by the Mughal Emperors and princes to the Ranas of Udiapur.
S. N. SEN, *The Military System of the Marathas*,, Bombay, 1958.
V. A. SMITH, *Akbar the Great Mogul* (1542-1605). 2nd ed. Oxford, 1919.
VILLIERS STUART, *Gardens of the Indian Mughals*, London, 1913.
THORN, *Memoir of the War in India*.
JAMES TOD, *Annals and Antiquities of Rajasthan*, popular ed., 2 Vols. London, 1914.
R. P. TRIPATHI, *Some Aspects of Muslim Administration*, Allahabad, 1936.
—*Rise and Fall of the Mughal Empire*, Allahabad, 1956.
H. H. WILSON, *A Glossary of Judicial and Revenue Terms, and C., of British India*, London, 1875.

INDEX